Writing Arguments
Concise Edition

Eighth Edition

John D. Ramage
Arizona State University

John C. Bean
Seattle University

June Johnson
Seattle University

 Pearson

330 Hudson Street, NY NY 10013

Director of English: Karon Bowers
Executive Producer and Publisher: Aron Keesbury
Development Editor: Steven Rigolosi
Marketing Manager: Nicholas Bolt
Program Manager: Rachel Harbour
Project Manager: Nathaniel J. Jones, SPi Global
Cover Designer: Pentagram
Cover Illustration: Christopher DeLorenzo
Manufacturing Buyer: Roy L. Pickering, Jr.
Printer/Binder: LSC Communications, Inc.
Cover Printer: Phoenix Color/Hagerstown

Acknowledgments of third-party content appear on page 309, which constitute an extension of this copyright page.

Cataloging-in-Publication Data is on file with the Library of Congress

1   18

Rental Edition ISBN 10:   0-134-75975-3
Rental Edition ISBN 13: 978-0-134-75975-3
A la Carte ISBN 10:   0-134-76152-9
A la Carte ISBN 13: 978-0-134-76152-7
Access Code Card ISBN 10:   0-134-80785-5
Access Code Card ISBN 13: 978-0-134-80785-0
Instructor Review Copy ISBN 10:   0-134-76157-X
Instructor Review Copy ISBN 13: 978-0-134-76157-2

Brief Contents

Detailed Contents

Preface

Through many editions, *Writing Arguments* has sustained its reputation as a leading college textbook in argumentation. By focusing on argument as a collaborative search for the best solutions to problems (as opposed to pro/con debate), *Writing Arguments* treats argument as a process of inquiry as well as a means of persuasion. Users and reviewers have consistently praised the book for teaching the critical thinking skills needed for writing arguments: how to analyze the occasion for an argument; how to analyze arguments rhetorically; how to ground an argument in the values and beliefs of the targeted audience; how to develop and elaborate an argument; and how to respond sensitively to objections and alternative views. We are pleased that in this new edition, we have improved the text in key ways while retaining the text's signature strengths.

What's New in the Eighth Edition?

Based on our continuing research into argumentation theory and pedagogy and on our own experiences as classroom teachers, we have made significant improvements in the eighth edition that will increase students' understanding of the value of argument and help them negotiate the rhetorical divisiveness in today's world. Here are the major changes in the eighth edition:

- **Use of Aristotle's "provisional truths" to address post-truth, post-fact challenges to argument.** This edition directly engages the complexity of conducting reasoned argument in a public sphere that is often dominated by ideological camps, news echo chambers, and charges of fake news. A revised Chapter 1 uses Aristotle's view of probabilistic or provisional truths to carve out a working space for argument between unachievable certainty and nihilistic relativism. Chapter 1's view of argument as both truth-seeking and persuasion is carried consistently throughout the text. This edition directly tackles the challenges to reasoned argument posed by dominant ideological perspectives, siloed echo chambers, and a dependence on social media as a source of news.

- **A reordering, refocusing, and streamlining of chapters to create better pedagogical sequencing and coherence.** The previous edition's Chapter 2, which focused on argument as inquiry combining summary writing and exploratory response, has been refocused and moved to Chapter 8. Previous Chapter 2 material on the genres of argument has now been placed in an expanded Chapter 7 on rhetorical analysis. This new sequencing allows students to focus first on understanding the principles of argument (Chapters 1-6) and then to switch to the critical thinking process of joining an argumentative conversation through reading and strong response. (See "Structure of the Text" later in this preface for further explanation.)

- **A new chapter on collaborative rhetoric as a bridge-building alternative to persuasion.** Chapter 10, new to this edition, blends ideas from Rogerian communication with practices from conflict resolution to help prepare students for their roles in private, public, and professional life amidst clashing values and views. Explanations, guidelines, and exercises emphasize nonjudgmental listening, self-reflection, a search for common ground, and suggestions for encouraging ongoing problem-solving through learning, listening, and respectful use of language.

- **A substantially revised chapter on visual and multimodal arguments**. Chapter 9 on visual and multimodal rhetoric now includes a new example and guidelines for making persuasive videos as well as a new exercise to apply image analysis in the construction of visual arguments.

- **A revised chapter on rhetorical analysis.** Chapter 7, "Analyzing Arguments Rhetorically," has been expanded by consolidating rhetorical instruction from several chapters into one chapter and linking it to the critical thinking skills required for joining an argumentative conversation.

- **Updated or streamlined examples and explanations throughout the text along with many new images.** Instructors familiar with previous editions will find many new examples and explanations ranging from a new dialog in Chapter 1 to illustrate the difference between an argument and a quarrel to a streamlined appendix on logical fallacies at the end. New images, editorial cartoons, and graphics throughout the text highlight current issues such as legalizing marijuana, plastics in the ocean, graffiti in public places, a soda tax, cultural and religious diversity, refugees, travel bans, and cars' carbon footprints.

- **New student essay to illustrate APA style.** A new student researched essay, "Exploring the Causes of Math Anxiety," illustrates APA style.

- **A new professional reading in Chapter 6.** "Oh, How I Will Miss the Plastic Bag," by Alexander Chancellor, adds to the conversation about proposed and legislated bans on plastic grocery bags.

What Hasn't Changed? The Distinguishing Features of *Writing Arguments*

The eighth edition of *Writing Arguments* preserves the text's signature strengths praised by students, instructors, and reviewers:

- **Argument as a collaborative search for "best solutions" rather than as pro-con debate.** Throughout the text, *Writing Arguments* emphasizes both the truth-seeking and persuasive dimensions of argument—a dialectic tension that requires empathic listening to all stakeholders in an argumentative conversation and the seeking of reasons that appeal to shared values and beliefs. For heated arguments with particularly clashing points of view, we show the value of Rogerian listening and, in this eighth edition, point to collaborative rhetoric as a shift from making arguments to seeking deeper understanding and common ground as a way forward amid conflict.

- **Argument as a rhetorical act**.   *Writing Arguments* teaches students to think rhetorically about argument: to understand the real-world occasions and contexts for argument, to analyze the targeted audience's underlying values and assumptions, to understand how evidence is selected and framed by an angle of vision, to appreciate the functions and constraints of genre, and to employ the classical appeals of *logos, pathos,* and *ethos.*

- **Argument as critical thinking.**   When writing an argument, writers are forced to lay bare their thinking processes. Focusing on both reading and writing, *Writing Arguments* emphasizes the critical thinking that underlies reasoned argument: active questioning, empathic reading and listening, believing and doubting, asserting a contestable claim that pushes against alternative views, and supporting the claim with a logical structure of reasons and evidence—all while negotiating uncertainty and ambiguity.

- **Consistent grounding in argumentation theory.**   To engage students in the kinds of critical and rhetorical thinking that argument demands, we draw on four major approaches to argumentation:
  - **The enthymeme as a rhetorical and logical structure.**   This concept, especially useful for beginning writers, helps students "nutshell" an argument as a claim with one or more supporting *because* clauses. It also helps them see how real-world arguments are rooted in assumptions granted by the audience rather than in universal and unchanging principles.
  - **The three classical types of appeal—*logos, ethos,* and *pathos.*** These concepts help students place their arguments in a rhetorical context focusing on audience-based appeals; they also help students create an effective voice and style.
  - **Toulmin's system of analyzing arguments.**   Toulmin's system helps students see the complete, implicit structure that underlies an enthymeme and develop appropriate grounds and backing to support an argument's reasons and warrants, thus helping students tailor arguments to audiences. Toulmin analysis highlights the rhetorical, social, and dialectical nature of argument.
  - **Stasis theory concerning types of claims.**   This approach stresses the heuristic value of learning different patterns of support for different types of claims and often leads students to make surprisingly rich and full arguments.

- **Effective writing pedagogy.**   This text combines explanations of argument with best practices from composition pedagogy, including exploratory writing, sequenced and scaffolded writing assignments, class-tested "For Writing and Discussion" tasks, and guidance through all stages of the writing process. To help students position themselves in an argumentative conversation, the text teaches the skills of "summary/strong response"—the ability to summarize a source author's argument and to respond to it thoughtfully. The moves of summary and strong response teach students to use their own critical and rhetorical thinking to find their own voice in a conversation.

- **Rhetorical approach to the research process.** Appendix 2 of *Writing Arguments* teaches students to think rhetorically about their sources and about the ways they might use these sources in their own arguments. Research coverage includes reading and evaluating sources rhetorically, taking purposeful notes, integrating source material effectively (including rhetorical use of attributive tags), and citing sources using two academic citation systems: MLA (8th edition) and APA. The text's rhetorical treatment of plagiarism helps students understand the conventions of different genres and avoid unintentional plagiarism.

- **Extensive coverage of visual rhetoric.** Chapter 9 is devoted entirely to visual and multimodal rhetoric. Additionally, many chapters include an "Examining Visual Rhetoric" feature that connects visual rhetoric to the chapter's instructional content. The images that introduce each part of the text, as well as images incorporated throughout the text, provide opportunities for visual analysis. Many of the text's assignment options include visual or multimodal components, including advocacy posters or speeches supported with presentation slides.

- **Effective and engaging student and professional arguments.** The professional and student arguments, both written and visual, present voices in current social conversations, illustrate types of argument and argument strategies, and provide fodder to stimulate discussion, analysis, and writing.

Structure of the Text

Writing Arguments provides a coherent sequencing of instruction while giving instructors flexibility to reorder materials to suit their needs.

- Part One focuses on the principles of argument: an overview of argument as truth-seeking rather than pro-con debate (Chapter 1); the *logos* of argument including the enthymeme (Chapter 2); Toulmin's system for analyzing arguments (Chapter 3) and the selection and framing of evidence (Chapter 4); the rhetorical appeals of *ethos* and *pathos* (Chapter 5); and acknowledging and responding to alternative views (Chapter 6).

- Part Two shifts to the process of argument—helping students learn how to enter an argumentative conversation by summarizing what others have said and staking out their own position and claims. Chapter 7 consolidates instruction on rhetorical analysis to help students think rhetorically about an argumentative conversation. Chapter 8 focuses on argument as inquiry, teaching students the groundwork skills of believing and doubting, summarizing a source author's argument and speaking back to it with integrity.

- Part Three expands students' understanding of argument. Chapter 9 focuses on visual and multimodal argument. Chapter 10, new to the eighth edition, teaches the powerful community-building skill of collaborative rhetoric as an alternative to argument. It focuses on mutual understanding rather than persuasion.

- Part Four (Chapters 11-15) introduces students to stasis theory, showing the typical structures and argumentative moves required for different claim types: definition, resemblance, causal, evaluation, and proposal arguments.

- The book concludes with two appendixes. Appendix 1 provides a discussion of informal fallacies. Appendix 2 provides a concise guide to evaluating, using, and documenting sources.

Revel

Revel is an interactive learning environment that deeply engages students and prepares them for class. Media and assessment integrated directly within the authors' narrative lets students read, explore interactive content, and practice in one continuous learning path. Thanks to the dynamic reading experience in Revel, students come to class prepared to discuss, apply, and learn from instructors and from each other.

Learn more about Revel

- http://www.pearson.com/revel

Supplements

Make more time for your students with instructor resources that offer effective learning assessments and classroom engagement. Pearson's partnership with educators does not end with the delivery of course materials; Pearson is there with you on the first day of class and beyond. A dedicated team of local Pearson representatives will work with you not only to choose course materials but also to integrate them into your class and assess their effectiveness. Our goal is your goal—to improve instruction with each semester.

Pearson is pleased to offer the following resources to qualified adopters of *Writing Arguments*. Several of these supplements are available to instantly download from Revel or on the Instructor Resource Center (IRC); please visit the IRC at www.pearsonhighered.com/irc to register for access.

- **INSTRUCTOR'S RESOURCE MANUAL,** by Hannah Tracy (Seattle University). Create a comprehensive roadmap for teaching classroom, online, or hybrid courses. Designed for new and experienced instructors, the Instructor's Resource Manual includes learning objectives, lecture and discussion suggestions, activities for in or out of class, research activities, participation activities, and suggested readings, series, and films as well as a Revel features section. Available within Revel and on the IRC.

- **POWERPOINT PRESENTATION.** Make lectures more enriching for students. The PowerPoint Presentation includes a full lecture outline and photos and figures from the textbook and Revel edition. Available on the IRC.

Acknowledgments

We are happy for this opportunity to give public thanks to the scholars, teachers, and students who have influenced our approach to composition and argument. For this edition, we owe special thanks to our long-time teammate and colleague at Seattle University, Hilary Hawley, who aided us in researching public controversies and finding timely, available readings on these issues. Hilary wrote the framing introductions, the headnotes, and the critical apparatus for many of the anthology units. Her experience teaching argument, especially he public controversies over sustainability, food, immigration, and health, shaped these units. We are also grateful to another of our Seattle University colleagues, Hannah Tracy, for writing the Instructor's Resource Manual, a task to which she brings her knowledge of argumentation and her experience teaching civic and academic argument. We thank Stephen Bean for his research on self-driving cars and on issues related to legalizing marijuana. Finally, we thank Kris Saknussemm and Janie Bube for their design contributions to several of the visual arguments in this edition.

We are particularly grateful to our talented students—Jesse Goncalves (argument on math anxiety), Hadley Reeder (argument on high school dress codes) and Camille Tabari (PSA video "It's a Toilet, Not a Trash Can")—who contributed to this edition their timely arguments built from their intellectual curiosity, ideas, personal experience, and research. Additionally, we are grateful to all our students whom we have been privileged to teach in our writing classes and to our other students who have enabled us to include their arguments in this text. Their insights and growth as writers have inspired our ongoing study of rhetoric and argumentation.

We thank too the many users of our texts who have given us encouragement about our successes and offered helpful suggestions for improvements. Particularly we thank the following scholars and teachers who reviewed the previous edition of *Writing Arguments* and whose valuable suggestions informed this new edition:

Max Hohner, Eastern Washington University

Jeff Kosse, Iowa Western Community College

Jeremy Meyer, Arizona State University

Jennifer Waters, Arizona State University

We wish to express our gratitude to our developmental editor Steven Rigolosi for his skill, patience, diligence, and deep knowledge of all phases of textbook production. Steve's ability to provide timely guidance throughout the production process made this edition possible.

As always, we thank our families, who ultimately make this work possible. John Bean thanks his wife, Kit, also a professional composition teacher, and his children Matthew, Andrew, Stephen, and Sarah, all of whom have grown to adulthood since he first began writing textbooks. Our lively conversations at family dinners, which now include spouses, partners, and grandchildren, have kept him engaged in arguments that matter about how to create a just, humane, and sustainable world. June Johnson thanks her husband, Kenneth Bube, a mathematics professor and researcher, and her daughter, Janie Bube. Ken and Janie have played major roles in the ongoing family analysis of argumentation in the public sphere on wide-ranging subjects. Janie's knowledge of environmental issues and digital design and Kenneth's of mathematical thinking and the public perception of science have broadened June's understanding of argument hotspots. They have also enabled her to meet the demands and challenges of continuing to infuse new ideas and material into this text in each revision.

John C. Bean

June Johnson

PART ONE
Principles of Argument

Factory farming, the mass production of animals for meat on an industrial model, shown in this photo, is a network of controversial issues, including cruelty to animals, healthfulness of meat diets, disconnection of people from their food, strain on environmental resources, and economic effects on small farming.

Chapter 1

Argument: An Introduction

Learning Objectives

In this chapter you will learn to:

1.1 Explain common misconceptions about the meaning of *argument*.

1.2 Describe defining features of argument.

1.3 Understand the relationship of argument to the process of truth-seeking and inquiry.

This book is dedicated to the proposition that reasoned argument is essential for the functioning of democracies. By establishing a separation of powers and protecting individual rights, the U. S. Constitution places argument at the center of civic life. At every layer of democracy, government decisions about laws, regulations, right actions, and judicial outcomes depend on reasoned argument, which involves listening to multiple perspectives. As former Vice President Al Gore once put it, "Faith in the power of reason—the belief that free citizens can govern themselves wisely and fairly by resorting to logical debate on the basis of the best evidence available, instead of raw power—was and remains the central premise of American democracy."[1]

Yet, many public intellectuals, scholars, and journalists have written that we are now entering a *post-truth era*, where the "best evidence available" becomes unmoored from a shared understanding of reality. How citizens access information and how they think about public issues is increasingly complicated by the unregulated freedom of the Internet and the stresses of a globalized and ethnically and religiously diverse society. Many citizens now focus on the entertainment dimension of news or get their news from sources that match their own political leanings. One source's "news" may be another source's "fake news." In fact, the concept of argument is now entangled in post-truth confusions about what an argument is.

What, then, do we mean by *reasoned argument*, and why is it vital for coping with post-truth confusion? The meaning of reasoned argument will become clearer in this opening chapter and throughout this text. We hope your study of reasoned argument will lead you to value it as a student, citizen, and professional.

---

[1] Al Gore, *Assault on Reason*. New York: Penguin, 2007, p. 2.

We begin this chapter by debunking some common misconceptions about argument. We then examine three defining features of argument: It requires writers or speakers to justify their claims; it is both a product and a process; and it combines elements of truth-seeking and persuasion. Finally, we look closely at the tension between truth-seeking and persuasion to encourage you to use both of these processes in your approach to argument.

What Do We Mean by Argument?

1.1 **Explain common misconceptions about the meaning of** *argument.*

Let's begin by examining the inadequacies of two popular images of argument: fight and debate.

Argument Is Not a Fight or a Quarrel

To many, the word *argument* connotes anger and hostility, as when we say, "I just had a huge argument with my roommate," or "My mother and I argue all the time." We picture heated disagreement, rising pulse rates, and an urge to slam doors. Argument imagined as fight conjures images of shouting talk-show guests, flaming bloggers, or fist-banging speakers.

But to our way of thinking, argument doesn't imply anger. In fact, arguing is often pleasurable. It is a creative and productive activity that engages us at high levels of inquiry and critical thinking, often in conversation with people we like and respect. When you think about argument, we invite you to envision not a shouting match on cable news but rather a small group of reasonable people seeking the best solution to a problem. We will return to this image throughout the chapter.

Argument Is Not Pro-Con Debate

Another popular image of argument is debate—a presidential debate, perhaps, or a high school or college debate tournament. According to one popular dictionary, *debate* is "a formal contest of argumentation in which two opposing teams defend and attack a given proposition." Although formal debate can develop critical thinking, it has a key weakness: It can turn argument into a game of winners and losers rather than a process of cooperative inquiry.

For an illustration of this weakness, consider one of our former students, a champion high school debater who spent his senior year debating the issue of prison reform. Throughout the year he argued for and against propositions such as "The United States should build more prisons" and "Innovative alternatives to prison should replace prison sentences for most crimes." We asked him, "What do you personally think is the best way to reform prisons?" He replied, "I don't know. I haven't thought about what I would actually choose."

Here was a bright, articulate student who had studied prisons extensively for a year. Yet nothing in the atmosphere of pro-con debate had engaged him in truth-seeking inquiry. He could argue for and against a proposition, but he hadn't experienced the wrenching process of clarifying his own values and taking a personal stand. As we explain throughout this text, argument entails a desire for truth-seeking; it aims to find the best solutions to complex problems. We don't mean that arguers don't passionately support their own points of view or expose weaknesses in views they find faulty. Instead, we mean that their goal isn't to win a game but to find and promote the best belief or course of action.

Arguments Can Be Explicit or Implicit

Before we examine some of the defining features of argument, we should note also that arguments can be either explicit or implicit. *Explicit* arguments (either written or oral) directly state their contestable claims and support them with reasons and evidence. *Implicit* arguments, in contrast, may not look like arguments at all. They may be bumper stickers, billboards, posters, photographs, cartoons, vanity license plates, slogans on a T-shirt, advertisements, poems, or song lyrics. But like explicit arguments, they persuade their audience toward a certain point of view.

Consider the poster in Figure 1.1—part of one state's recent citizen campaign to legalize marijuana. The poster's comparative data about "annual deaths," its beautiful green marijuana leaves, and its cluster of peanuts make the implicit argument that marijuana is safe—even safer than peanuts.

The poster's intention is to persuade voters to approve the state initiative to legalize pot. But this poster is just one voice in a complex conversation. Does marijuana have dangers that this poster makes invisible? Would children and adolescents

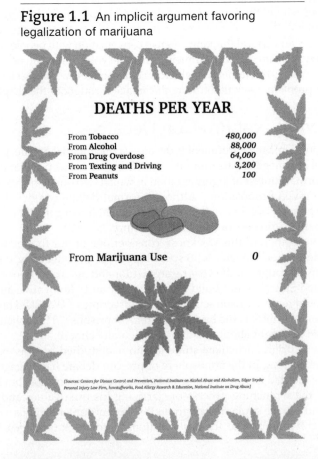

Figure 1.1 An implicit argument favoring legalization of marijuana

DEATHS PER YEAR

From **Tobacco**	480,000
From **Alcohol**	88,000
From **Drug Overdose**	64,000
From **Texting and Driving**	3,200
From **Peanuts**	100
From **Marijuana Use**	0

[Sources: Centers for Disease Control and Prevention, National Institute on Alcohol Abuse and Alcoholism, Edgar Snyder Personal Injury Law Firm, howstuffworks, Food Allergy Research & Education, National Institute on Drug Abuse]

have more access or less access to marijuana if the drug were legalized? Is marijuana a "gateway drug" to heroin and other, harder drugs? How would legalization of marijuana affect crime, drug trafficking, and prison populations? What would be the cultural consequences if marijuana became as socially acceptable as alcohol?

In contrast to the implicit argument made in Figure 1.1, consider the following explicit argument—a letter to the editor submitted by student writer Mike Overton. As an explicit argument, it states its claim directly and supports it with reasons and evidence.

An Explicit Argument Opposing Legalization of Marijuana

LETTER TO THE EDITOR BY STUDENT MIKE OVERTON

Proponents of legalizing marijuana claim that pot is a benign drug because it has a low risk of overdose and causes few deaths. Pot is even safer than peanuts, according to a recent pro-legalization poster. However, pot poses grave psychological risks, particularly to children and adolescents, that are masked if we focus only on death rate.

Several studies have shown adverse effects of marijuana on memory, decision making, and cognition. In one study, Duke University researchers examined IQ scores of individuals taken from childhood through age 38. They found a noticeable decline in the IQ scores of pot smokers compared with nonusers, with greater declines among those who smoked more. Daily pot smokers dropped, on average, eight IQ points.

There is also a clear link between pot usage and schizophrenia. Many studies have shown an increased risk of schizophrenia and psychosis from pot usage, particularly with regular use as an adolescent. Studies find that regular pot smokers who develop schizophrenia begin exhibiting symptoms of the disease earlier than nonusers, with the average diagnosis occurring 2.7 years earlier than for nonusers.

These are devastating mental illnesses that cut to the core of our well-being. We need to be sure our policies on marijuana don't ignore the documented mental health risks of pot, particularly to adolescents in the critical phase of brain development. I urge a "no" vote on legalizing marijuana in our state.

The Defining Features of Argument

1.2   Describe defining features of argument.

We now examine arguments in more detail. (Unless we say otherwise, by *argument* we mean explicit arguments that attempt to supply reasons and evidence to support their claims.) This section examines three defining features of such arguments.

Argument Requires Justification of Its Claims

To begin defining argument, let's turn to a humble but universal area of disagreement: the conflict between new housemates over house rules. In what way and in what circumstances do such conflicts constitute arguments?

AVERY: (*grabbing his backpack by the door*) See you. I'm heading for class.

DANIEL: (*loudly and rapidly*) Wait. What about picking up your garbage all over the living room?—that pizza box, those cans, and all those papers. I think you even spilled Coke on the rug.

AVERY: Hey, get off my case. I'll clean it up tonight.

With this exchange, we have the start of a quarrel, not an argument. If Daniel's anger picks up—suppose he says, "Hey, slobface, no way you're leaving this house without picking up your trash!"—then the quarrel will escalate into a fight.

But let's say that Daniel remains calm. The dialogue then takes this turn.

DANIEL: Come on, Avery. We had an agreement to keep the house clean.

Now we have the beginnings of an argument. Fleshed out, Daniel's reasoning goes like this: You should clean up your mess because we had an agreement to keep the house clean. The unstated assumption behind this argument is that people should live up to their agreements.

Now Avery has an opportunity to respond, either by advancing the argument or by stopping it cold. He could stop it cold by saying, "No, we never agreed to anything." This response pushes Avery's hapless housemates into a post-truth world where there is no agreement about reality. Unless stakeholders have a starting place grounded in mutually accepted evidence, no argument is possible. Their dispute can be decided only by power.

But suppose that Avery is a reasonable person of good will. He could advance the argument by responding this way:

AVERY: Yes, you are right that we had an agreement. But perhaps our agreement needs room for exceptions. I have a super-heavy day today.

Now a process of reasonable argument has emerged. Avery offers a reason for rushing from the house without cleaning up. In his mind his argument would go like this: "It is OK for me to wait until tonight to clean up my mess because I have a super-heavy day." He could provide evidence for his reason by explaining his heavy schedule (a group project for one course, a paper due in another, and his agreement with his boss to work overtime at his barista job throughout the afternoon). This reason makes sense to Avery, who is understandably immersed in his own perspective. However, it might not be persuasive to Daniel, who responds this way:

DANIEL: I appreciate your busy schedule, but I am planning to be at home all day, and I can't study in this mess. It is unfair for me to have to clean up your stuff.

Fleshed out, Daniel's argument goes like this: "It is not OK for you to leave trash in the living room, because your offer to clean your mess tonight doesn't override my right to enjoy a clean living space today." The dialogue now illustrates what is required for reasonable argument: (1) a set of two or more conflicting claims ("it is OK / is not OK to leave this mess until tonight") and (2) the attempt to justify the claims with reasons and evidence.

The first defining feature of argument, then, is the attempt to justify claims with reasons and evidence. Avery and Daniel now need to think further about how they can justify their claims. The disagreement between the housemates is not primarily about facts: Both disputants agree that they had established house rules about cleanliness, that Avery is facing a super-heavy day, and that Avery's mess disturbs Daniel.

The dispute is rather about values and fairness—principles that are articulated in the unstated assumptions that undergird their reasons. Avery's assumption is that "unusual circumstances can temporarily suspend house rules." Daniel's assumption is that "a temporary suspension—to be acceptable—cannot treat other housemates unfairly." To justify his claim, therefore, Avery has to show not only that his day is super-heavy but also that his cleaning his mess at the end of the day isn't unfair to Daniel. To plan his argument, Avery needs to anticipate the questions his argument will raise in Daniel's mind: Will today's mess truly be a rare exception to our house rule, or is Avery a natural slob who will leave the house messy almost every day? What will be the state of the house and the quality of the living situation if each person simply makes his own exceptions to house rules? Will continuing to spill food and drinks on the carpet affect the return of the security deposit on the house rental?

In addition, Daniel needs to anticipate some of Avery's questions: Are temporary periods of messiness really unfair to Daniel? How much does Daniel's neat-freak personality get in the way of house harmony? Would some flexibility in house rules be a good thing? The attempt to justify their assumptions forces both Avery and Daniel to think about the degree of independence each demands when sharing a house.

As Avery and Daniel listen to each other's points of view (and begin realizing why their initial arguments have not persuaded their intended audience), we can appreciate one of the earliest meanings of the term *to argue*, which is "to clarify." As arguers clarify their own positions on an issue, they also begin to clarify their audience's position. Such clarification helps arguers see how they might accommodate their audience's views, perhaps by adjusting their own position or by developing reasons that appeal to their audience's values. Thus Avery might suggest something like this:

AVERY: Hey, Daniel, I can see why it is unfair to leave you with my mess. What if I offered you some kind of trade-off?

Fleshed out, Avery's argument now looks like this: "It is OK for me to wait until the end of the day to clean up my mess because I am willing to offer you a satisfactory trade-off." The offer of a trade-off immediately addresses Daniel's sense of being treated unfairly and might lead to negotiation on what this trade-off might be. Perhaps Avery agrees to do more of the cooking, or perhaps there are other areas of conflict that could become part of a trade-off bargain—noise levels, sleeping times, music preferences. Or perhaps Daniel, happy that Avery has offered a trade-off, says it isn't necessary: Daniel concedes that he can live with occasional messiness.

Whether or not Avery and Daniel can work out a best solution, the preceding scenario illustrates how the need to justify one's claims leads to a clarification of facts and values and to the process of negotiating solutions that might work for all stakeholders.

Argument Is Both a Process and a Product

As the preceding scenario revealed, argument can be viewed as a *process* in which two or more parties seek the best solution to a question or problem. Argument can also be viewed as a *product*, with each product being any person's contribution to the conversation at a given moment. In an informal discussion, the products are usually short pieces of conversation. In more formal settings, an orally delivered product might be a short, impromptu speech (say, during an open-mike discussion of a campus issue) or a longer, carefully prepared formal speech (as in a PowerPoint presentation at a business meeting or an argument at a public hearing for or against a proposed city project).

Similar conversations occur in writing. Roughly analogous to a small-group discussion is an exchange of the kind that occurs regularly online through informal chat groups or more formal blog sites. In an online discussion, participants have more thinking time to shape their messages than they do in a real-time oral discussion. Nevertheless, messages are usually short and informal, making it possible over the course of several days to see participants' ideas shift and evolve as conversants modify their initial views in response to others' views.

Roughly equivalent to a formal speech would be a formal written argument, which may take the form of an academic argument for a college course; a grant proposal; an online posting; a guest column for the op-ed* section of a newspaper; a legal brief; a letter to a member of Congress; or an article for an organizational newsletter, popular magazine, or professional journal. In each of these instances, the written argument (a product) enters a conversation (a process)—in this case, a conversation of readers, many of whom will carry on the conversation by writing their own responses or by discussing the writer's views with others. The goal of the community of writers and readers is to find the best solution to the problem or issue under discussion.

Argument Combines Truth-Seeking and Persuasion

In thinking about argument as a product, writers will find themselves continually moving back and forth between truth-seeking and persuasion—that is, between questions about the subject matter (What is the best solution to this problem?) and about audience (What do my readers already believe or value? What reasons and evidence will most persuade them?). Writers weave back and forth, alternately absorbed in the subject of their argument and in the audience for that argument.

Neither of the two focuses is ever completely out of mind, but their relative importance shifts during different phases of the development of an argument. Moreover, different rhetorical situations place different emphases on truth-seeking versus persuasion. We can thus place arguments on a continuum that measures the degree of attention a writer gives to subject matter versus audience. (See Figure 1.2.) At the full truth-seeking (left) end of the continuum might be an exploratory piece that lays out several alternative approaches to a problem and weighs the strengths and weaknesses of each with no concern for persuasion. At the other (persuasion)

---

* *Op-ed* stands for "opposite-editorial." It is the generic name in journalism for a signed argument that voices the writer's opinion on an issue, as opposed to a news story that is supposed to report events objectively, uncolored by the writer's personal views. Op-ed pieces appear in the editorial-opinion section of newspapers, which generally features editorials by the resident staff, opinion pieces by syndicated columnists, and letters to the editor from readers. The term *op-ed* is often extended to syndicated columns appearing in newsmagazines, advocacy websites, and online news services.

Figure 1.2 Continuum of arguments from truth-seeking to persuasion

Truth Seeking   **Persuasion**

Exploratory essay	Delayed thesis argument	Classical argument	One-sided argument	Outright propaganda
Essay examining all sides of an issue and possibly not arriving at a conclusive answer	Argument as inquiry; asking audience to think out the issue with the writer	Argument, aimed at a neutral or skeptical audience, that shows awareness of different views	Argument aimed at a friendly audience (often for fundraising or calls to action)	Aggressive onesided argument that simply delivers a message

end of the continuum would be outright propaganda, such as a political advertisement that reduces a complex issue to sound bites and distorts an opponent's position through out-of-context quotations or misleading use of data. (At its most blatant, propaganda obliterates truth-seeking; it will use any tool, including bogus evidence, distorted assertions, and outright lies, to win over an audience.) In the middle ranges of the continuum, writers shift their focuses back and forth between inquiry and persuasion but with varying degrees of emphasis.

As an example of a writer focusing primarily on truth-seeking, consider the case of Kathleen, who, in her college argument course, addressed the definitional question "Is American Sign Language (ASL) a 'foreign language' for purposes of meeting the university's foreign language requirement?" Kathleen had taken two years of ASL at a community college. When she transferred to a four-year college, the chair of the foreign languages department would not allow her ASL coursework to count toward Kathleen's foreign language requirement. "ASL isn't a language," the chair said summarily. "It's not equivalent to learning French, German, or Japanese."

Kathleen disagreed, so she immersed herself in developing her argument. While doing research, she focused almost entirely on the subject matter, searching for what linguists, neurologists, cognitive psychologists, and sociologists have said about the language of deaf people. Immersed in her subject matter, she was only tacitly concerned with her audience, whom she thought of primarily as her classmates and the professor of her argument class—people who were friendly to her views and interested in her experiences with the deaf community. She wrote a well-documented paper, citing several scholarly articles, that made a good case to her classmates (and the professor) that ASL is indeed a distinct language.

Proud of the A she received on her paper, Kathleen decided for a subsequent assignment to write a second paper on ASL—but this time aiming it directly at the chair of the foreign languages department and petitioning her to accept ASL proficiency for the foreign language requirement. Now her writing task fell closer to the persuasive end of our continuum. Kathleen once again immersed herself in research, but this time she focused not on subject matter (whether ASL is a distinct language) but on audience. She researched the history of the foreign language requirement at her college and discovered some of the politics behind it (the foreign language requirement had been dropped in the 1970s and reinstituted in the 1990s, partly—a math professor told her—to boost enrollments in foreign language courses). She also interviewed foreign language teachers to find out what they knew and didn't know about ASL. She discovered that many teachers thought ASL was "easy to learn," so that accepting ASL would give students a Mickey Mouse way to avoid the rigors of a "real" foreign language class. Additionally, she learned that foreign language teachers valued immersing students in a foreign culture; in fact, the foreign language requirement was part of her college's effort to create a multicultural curriculum.

This increased understanding of her target audience helped Kathleen reconceptualize her argument. Her claim that ASL is a real language (the subject of her first paper) became only one section of her second paper, much condensed and abridged. She added sections showing the difficulty of learning ASL (to counter her audience's belief that learning ASL is easy), showing how the deaf community forms a distinct culture with its own customs and literature (to show how ASL would meet the goals of multiculturalism), and showing that the number of transfer students with ASL credits would be negligibly small (to allay fears that accepting ASL would threaten enrollments in language classes). She ended her argument with an appeal to her college's public emphasis (declared boldly in its mission statement) on eradicating social injustice and reaching out to the oppressed. She described the isolation of deaf people in a world where almost no hearing people learn ASL, and she argued that the deaf community on her campus could be integrated more fully into campus life if more students could talk with them. Thus the ideas included in her new argument—the reasons selected, the evidence used, the arrangement and tone—all were determined by her primary focus on persuasion.

Our point, then, is that all along the continuum, writers attempt both to seek truth and to persuade, but not necessarily with equal balance. Kathleen could not have written her second paper, aimed specifically at persuading the chair of the foreign languages department, if she hadn't first immersed herself in truth-seeking research that convinced her that ASL is indeed a distinct language. Note that we are not saying that Kathleen's second argument was better than her first. Both arguments fulfilled their purposes and met the needs of their intended audiences. Both involved truth-seeking and persuasion, but the first focused primarily on subject matter whereas the second focused primarily on audience.

Argument and the Problem of Truth in the 21st Century

1.3 **Understand the relationship of argument to the process of truth-seeking and inquiry.**

The tension that we have just examined between truth-seeking and persuasion raises an ancient issue in the field of argument: Is the arguer's first obligation to truth or to winning the argument? And just what is the nature of the truth to which arguers are supposed to be obligated?

Early Greek rhetoricians and philosophers—particularly the Sophists, Socrates, Plato, and Aristotle—all wrestled with this tension. In Plato's *Dialogues*, these questions were at the heart of Socrates' disagreement with the Sophists. The Sophists were professional rhetoricians who specialized in training orators to win arguments. Socrates, who valued truth-seeking over persuasion and believed that truth could be discovered through philosophic inquiry, opposed the Sophists. For Socrates (and Plato), Truth resided in the ideal world of forms, and through philosophic rigor humans could transcend the changing, shadowlike world of everyday reality to perceive the world of universals where Truth, Beauty, and Goodness resided. Through his method of questioning, Socrates would gradually peel away layer after layer of false views until Truth was revealed. The good person's duty, Socrates believed, was not to win an argument but to pursue this higher Truth. Socrates and Plato distrusted professional rhetoricians because these professionals were interested only in the power and wealth that came from persuading audiences to the orator's views. In contrast, Plato's pupil Aristotle maintained Plato's commitment to ethical living but valued rhetoric as a way of reaching conclusions or what he called "probable truth" in the realm of everyday living—the best answers available to people who were willing to think deeply and argue reasonably about a problem. Aristotle taught rhetoric and argument as collective inquiry in search of new understanding—probable truths and best solutions supported persuasively by reasons and evidence that could be shared and agreed upon.

Let's apply these perspectives to a modern example. Suppose your community is divided over the issue of raising environmental standards versus keeping open a job-producing factory that doesn't meet new guidelines for waste discharge. In a dispute between jobs and the environment, which is the best course? The Sophists would train you to argue any side of this issue on behalf of any lobbying group willing to pay for your services. This relativism and willingness to manipulate language led over time to the term *sophistry* being associated with trickery in argument. If, however, you applied Aristotle's practical concern for "probable truth," you would be inspired to listen to all sides of the dispute, peel away unsatisfactory arguments through reasonable inquiry, and commit yourself to a course of action that you have come to believe is the best for as many stakeholders as possible.

In sum, Plato was concerned with absolute truths residing in the spiritual world of forms, while Aristotle valued rhetoric's focus on probable truths in our messy human world. Aristotle's view is thus close to that expressed by Al Gore at the beginning of this chapter. Aristotle and Gore would agree that truth—the search for best solutions—is messy and complicated and needs to be negotiated in an ongoing spirit of argument. Every day we face complex questions with multiple stakeholders. Do sanctuary cities make citizens safer, as many sheriffs and police departments argue, or do they shelter criminals and endanger citizens, as some people contend? Should all controversial speakers be allowed to speak on college campuses, or should universities carefully monitor and restrict these public forums? There are no simple or clear-cut answers to these questions, but one thing is certain: People can't carry on productive argument if they retreat to siloed echo chambers where they encounter only those views with which they already agree. Daniel the neat freak has to encounter Avery the slob; otherwise, no growth is possible. Argument works only if we are willing to question and clarify our own positions and engage in dialogue with those stakeholders with whom we disagree.

This truth-seeking approach to argument helps us combat various traps that we may fall into. A first trap is that we might become intellectually lazy, failing to question easily found or sensationalist information and views. We might succumb to "desirability bias"[2]–the tendency to accept information that "we want to believe." Or we might cling to what political scientist Morgan Marietti calls "sacred values"[3]—religious or secular beliefs that are so central to our worldviews and identities that we accept them as absolute, unquestionable, and inviolable. For example, for some persons a woman's right to control her own body is a sacred value; for others, an unborn fetus's right to life is a sacred value. Because we hesitate to question our sacred values, our emotional adherence to them can create a network of beliefs that interpret the world for us. Emerging from our own siloed echo chambers is the best way to seek a shareable reality in what otherwise might seem a post-truth world. However, as we have seen, truth-seeking takes intellectual work and ethical commitment. To restore the value of argument as truth-seeking, we must accept the world as pluralistic, recognizing that others may not value what we value.

If we accept this pluralistic view of the world, do we then endorse the Sophists' radical relativism, freeing us to argue any side of any issue? Or do we doggedly pursue some modern equivalent of Aristotle's "probable truth"?

If your own sympathies are with argument as truth-seeking, then you must admit to a view of truth that is tentative, cautious, and conflicted, and you must embrace argument as process. In the 21st century, truth-seeking does not mean finding the "right answer" to a disputed question, but neither does it mean a valueless relativism in which all answers are equally good. Seeking truth means taking responsibility for determining the "best answer" or "best solution" to the question; it means considering the good of the entire community when taking into consideration the interests of all stakeholders. It means making hard decisions in the face of uncertainty. Viewed in this way, argument cannot "prove" your claim, but only make a reasonable case for it. Even though argument can't provide certainty, learning to argue effectively has deep value for society and democracy: It helps communities settle conflicts in a rational and humane way by finding, through the exchange of ideas, the best solutions to problems without resorting to violence.

For Writing and Discussion

Role-Playing Arguments

On any given day, the media provide evidence of the complexity of living in a pluralistic culture. Issues that could be readily decided in a completely homogeneous culture raise questions in a society that has fewer shared assumptions. Use the following case as the subject for a "simulation game" in which class members present the points of view of the people involved.

---

[2] Ben Tappin, Leslie van der Leer, and Ryan McKay define "desirability bias" in their op-ed piece, "Your Opinion Is Set in Stone." *The New York Times*, May 28, 2017, SR 8.

[3] Morgan Marietta, "From My Cold, Dead Hands: Democratic Consequences of Sacred Rhetoric." *The Journal of Politics* Vol. 70, No. 3, July 2008.

Case: HPV Vaccines for Sixth Grade Girls (and Boys)

In 2007 the pharmaceutical company Merck developed a vaccine against the sexually transmitted HPV virus (human papillomavirus), some strains of which can cause cervical cancer as well as genital warts. The company launched an extensive television campaign promoting the vaccine (which would bring substantial profits to Merck) and advised that girls should get the vaccine before they reach puberty. Following recommendations from doctors and medical researchers, several states passed laws mandating that the HPV vaccine for girls be included among the other vaccinations required of all children for entry into the sixth or seventh grades (depending on the state). These laws sparked public debate about the benefits versus potential adverse effects of vaccines, and about the state's versus parents' role in determining what vaccines a child should get.

Your task:

Imagine a public hearing addressing what your state's laws should be concerning HPV vaccinations for prepubescent children. Your goal isn't to make your own decision about this case but rather to bring to imaginative life all the viewpoints in the controversy. Hold a mock hearing in which classmates play the following roles: (a) a cancer specialist who supports mandatory HPV vaccination for girls; (b) a public health specialist who supports expanding the requirement to include boys; (c) a skeptical person concerned about the potential adverse effects of vaccines in general; (d) a religiously conservative parent who believes in abstinence and monogamy and opposes the cultural message of the HPV vaccination.

Chapter 2
The Core of an Argument

A Claim with Reasons

Learning Objectives

In this chapter you will learn to:

2.1 Describe the key elements of classical argument.

2.2 Explain the rhetorical appeals of *logos*, *ethos*, and *pathos*.

2.3 Distinguish between issue and information questions and between genuine and pseudo-arguments.

2.4 Describe the basic frame of an argument.

In Chapter 1 we explained that argument is best viewed not as a quarrel or as a pro-con debate, but rather as a conversation of reasonable stakeholders seeking the best solution to a shared problem or issue. As a conversation of stakeholders, argument is both a process and a product. The rest of Part One provides an overview of the parts of an argument along with the general principles that make arguments effective. This chapter focuses on the core of an argument, which is a structure of claim, reasons, and evidence. The remaining chapters of Part One cover the same territory with more elaboration and detail.

The Classical Structure of Argument

2.1 Describe the key elements of classical argument.

The core of an argument can best be understood by connecting it to the ancient pattern of classical argument revealed in the persuasive speeches of ancient Greek and Roman orators. Classical argument has the organizational structure shown in Figure 2.1, and it typically includes these sections:

- *The introduction.* Writers of classical argument typically begin by connecting the audience to the issue by showing how it arises out of a current event or by using an illustrative story, memorable scene, or startling statistic—something that grabs the audience's attention. They continue the introduction by focusing the issue—often by stating it directly as a question or by briefly summarizing opposing views—and providing needed background and context. They conclude the introduction by presenting their claim (thesis statement) and forecasting the argument's structure.

- *The presentation of the writer's position.* The presentation of the writer's own position is usually the longest part of a classical argument. Here writers present the reasons and evidence supporting their claims, typically choosing reasons that tie into their audience's values, beliefs, and assumptions. Usually

Figure 2.1 Organization plan for an argument with classical structure

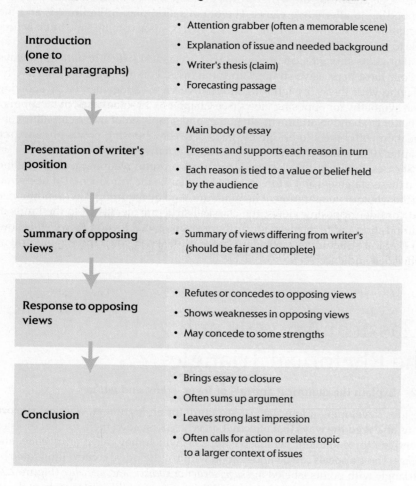

Organization Plan for an Argument with a Classical Structure

Introduction (one to several paragraphs)	• Attention grabber (often a memorable scene) • Explanation of issue and needed background • Writer's thesis (claim) • Forecasting passage
Presentation of writer's position	• Main body of essay • Presents and supports each reason in turn • Each reason is tied to a value or belief held by the audience
Summary of opposing views	• Summary of views differing from writer's (should be fair and complete)
Response to opposing views	• Refutes or concedes to opposing views • Shows weaknesses in opposing views • May concede to some strengths
Conclusion	• Brings essay to closure • Often sums up argument • Leaves strong last impression • Often calls for action or relates topic to a larger context of issues

each reason is developed in its own paragraph or sequence of paragraphs. When a paragraph introduces a new reason, writers state the reason directly and then support it with evidence or a chain of ideas. Along the way, writers guide their readers with appropriate transitions.

- *The summary and critique of alternative views.* When summarizing and responding to opposing views, writers have several options. If there are several opposing arguments, writers may summarize all of them together and then compose a single response, or they may summarize and respond to each argument in turn. As we explain in Chapter 6, writers may respond to opposing views either by refuting them or by conceding to their strengths and shifting to a different field of values.

- *The conclusion.* Finally, in their conclusion, writers sum up their argument, often restating the stakes in the argument and calling for some kind of action, thereby creating a sense of closure and leaving a strong final impression.

In this organization, the body of a classical argument has two major sections—one presenting the writer's own position and the other summarizing and responding to alternative views. The organization plan in Figure 2.1, and the discussion that follows, have the writer's own position coming first, but it is possible to reverse that order.

For all its strengths, an argument with a classical structure may not always be your most persuasive strategy. In some cases, you may be more effective by delaying your thesis, by ignoring alternative views altogether, or by showing great sympathy for opposing views (see Chapter 6). In some cases, in fact, it may be better to abandon argument altogether and simply enter into a empathic conversation with others to bridge the gaps between opposing points of view (see Chapter 10 on collaborative rhetoric as an alternative to classical argument). In most cases, however, the classical structure is a useful planning tool. By calling for a thesis statement and a forecasting statement in the introduction, it helps you see the whole of your argument in miniature. And by requiring you to summarize and consider opposing views, the classical structure alerts you to the limits of your position and to the need for further reasons and evidence. As we will show, the classical structure is particularly persuasive when you address a neutral or undecided audience.

Classical Appeals and the Rhetorical Triangle

2.2   Explain the rhetorical appeals of *logos*, *ethos*, and *pathos*.

Besides developing a template or structure for an argument, classical rhetoricians analyzed the ways that effective speeches persuaded their audiences. They identified three kinds of persuasive appeals, which they called *logos*, *ethos*, and *pathos*. These appeals can be understood within a rhetorical context illustrated by a triangle with points labeled *message*, *writer or speaker*, and *audience* (Figure 2.2). Effective arguments pay attention to all three points on this *rhetorical triangle*.

Figure 2.2 The rhetorical triangle

Message
LOGOS: *How can I make the argument internally consistent and logical? How can I find the best reasons and support them with the best evidence?*

Audience
PATHOS: *How can I make the reader open to my message? How can I best appeal to my reader's values and interests? How can I engage my reader emotionally and imaginatively?*

Writer or Speaker
ETHOS: *How can I present myself effectively? How can I enhance my credibility and trustworthiness?*

As Figure 2.2 shows, each point on the triangle corresponds to one of the three persuasive appeals:

- *Logos* (Greek for "word") focuses attention on the quality of the message—that is, on the internal consistency and clarity of the argument itself and on the logic of its reasons and support. The impact of *logos* on an audience is referred to as its *logical appeal*.

- *Ethos* (Greek for "character") focuses attention on the writer's (or speaker's) character as it is projected in the message. It refers to the writer's credibility. *Ethos* is often conveyed through the writer's investment in his or her claim; through the fairness with which the writer considers alternative views; through the tone and style of the message; and even through the message's professional appearance on paper or screen, including correct grammar, flawless proofreading, and appropriate formats for citations and bibliography. In some cases, *ethos* is also a function of the writer's reputation for honesty and expertise independent of the message. The impact of *ethos* on an audience is referred to as the *ethical appeal* or *appeal from credibility*.

- *Pathos* (Greek for "suffering" or "experience") focuses attention on the values and beliefs of the intended audience. It is often associated with emotional appeal. But *pathos* appeals more specifically to an audience's imaginative sympathies—their capacity to feel and see what the writer feels and sees. Thus, when we turn the abstractions of logical discourse into a tangible and immediate story, we are making a pathetic appeal. Whereas appeals to *logos* and *ethos* can further an audience's intellectual assent to our claim, appeals to *pathos* engage the imagination and feelings, moving the audience to a deeper appreciation of the argument's significance.

A related rhetorical concept, connected to the appeals of *logos*, *ethos*, and *pathos*, is that of *kairos*, from the Greek word for "right time," "season," or "opportunity." This concept suggests that for an argument to be persuasive, its timing must be effectively chosen and its tone and structure in right proportion or measure. You may have had the experience of composing a contentious e-mail and then hesitating before clicking the "send" button. Is this the right moment to send this message? Is my audience ready to hear what I'm saying? Would my views be better received if I waited for a couple of days? If I send this message now, should I change its tone and content? *Kairos* refers to this attentiveness to the unfolding of time. We will return to this concept in Chapter 5, when we consider *ethos* and *pathos* in more depth.

Given this background on the classical appeals, let's turn now to *logos*—the logic and structure of arguments.

Issue Questions as the Origins of Argument

2.3 **Distinguish between issue and information questions and between genuine and pseudo-arguments.**

At the heart of any argument is an *issue*, which we can define as a controversial topic area (such as legalizing marijuana or building a wall between Mexico and the United States) that gives rise to differing points of view and conflicting claims. A writer can usually focus an issue by asking an issue question that invites alternative answers. Thus the topic area "abortion" gives rise to issue questions such as the following: Should abortion be legal? Should the federal government authorize Medicaid payments for abortions? When does a fetus become a human person? What would be the consequences of outlawing abortion? Each of these issue questions opens up one strand in the complex debate about abortion.

Difference between an Issue Question and an Information Question

Of course, not all questions are issue questions that can be answered reasonably in differing ways. Some questions ask for information rather than for arguments. Rhetoricians have traditionally distinguished between *explication*, which is writing that sets out to inform or explain, and *argumentation*, which sets out to change a reader's mind. The following example illustrates the difference between an issue question and an information question:

> *Issue question*: Should health insurance policies be required to cover contraceptives? (Reasonable persons can disagree.)

> *Information question*: How does the teenage pregnancy rate in the United States compare with the rate in Sweden? (Reasonable persons assume that a "right answer" to this question is available.)

Although the difference between the two kinds of questions may seem simple, the distinction can become blurry. Suppose we asked "Why is the teenage pregnancy rate in Sweden lower than in the United States?" Although this might seem to be an informative question with a right answer, we can also imagine disagreement. One writer might emphasize Sweden's practical, secular sex-education courses, leading to more consistent use of contraceptives among Swedish teenagers. Another writer might point to the higher use of birth-control pills among teenage girls in Sweden (partly a result of Sweden's generous national health program) and to less reliance on condoms for preventing unwanted pregnancy. Another might argue that moral decay in the United States or a breakdown of the traditional family is responsible for the higher teenage pregnancy rate in the United States. Thus, what initially looks like a simple information question becomes an issue question.

How to Identify an Issue Question

You can generally tell whether a question is an information question or an issue question by determining whether your purpose is (1) to explain or teach something to your audience or (2) to change their minds about something. Often the same question can be an information question in one context and an issue question in another. Let's look at the following examples:

- *How does a diesel engine work?* (This is an information question because reasonable people who know about diesel engines will agree on how they work. This question would be posed by an audience of new learners asking experts for an explanation.)
- *Why is a diesel engine more fuel efficient than a gasoline engine?* (This also seems to be an information question because experts will probably agree on the answer. Once again, the audience seems to be new learners, perhaps students in an automotive class.)
- *What is the most cost-effective way to produce diesel fuel from crude oil?* (This could be an information question if experts agree and you are addressing new learners. But if you are addressing engineers and one engineer says process X is the most cost-effective and another engineer argues for process Y, then the question is an issue question.)
- *Should the present highway tax on diesel fuel be increased?* (This is certainly an issue question. One person says yes; another says no; another offers a compromise.)

For Writing and Discussion

Information Questions Versus Issue Questions

Working as a class or in small groups, decide which of the following questions are information questions and which are issue questions. Many of them could be either, depending on the rhetorical context. For those questions, create hypothetical contexts to show your reasoning.

1. What percentage of public schools in the United States are failing?
2. What is the effect on children of playing first-person-shooter video games?
3. What effect will the advent of self-driving cars have on truck drivers?
4. Should people get rid of their land lines and have only cell phones?

Difference between a Genuine Argument and a Pseudo-Argument

Although every argument is sparked by an issue question with alternative answers, not every dispute over answers constitutes a rational argument. Rational arguments require three additional factors: (1) reasonable participants who operate within the conventions of reasonable behavior; (2) potentially sharable assumptions that can serve as a starting place or foundation for the argument; (3) confidence that evidence used in an argument is verifiable. Lacking these conditions, disagreements remain stalled at the level of pseudo-arguments. Let's look at each of these conditions in turn.

PSEUDO-ARGUMENTS CAUSED BY UNREASONABLE BEHAVIOR Reasonable behavior in argument assumes the possibility of growth and change; disputants may modify their views as they acknowledge strengths in an alternative view or weaknesses in their own. Such growth becomes impossible—and argument degenerates to pseudo-argument—when disputants are so rigidly committed to their positions that they can't imagine alternative views. Consider the case of the true believer and the fanatical skeptic.

From one perspective, true believers are admirable persons, guided by unwavering values and beliefs. True believers stand on solid rock, unwilling to compromise their principles or bend to the prevailing winds. But from another perspective, true believers can seem rigidly fixed, incapable of growth or change. In Chapter 1, we mentioned that arguers can cling to *sacred values*—either religious or secular principles that they consider absolute, inviolable, indisputable. When true believers from two clashing belief systems—each with its own set of sacred values—try to engage in dialogue with each other, a truth-seeking exchange of views becomes difficult. Once true believers push each other's buttons on global warming, guns, or some other issue, each disputant resorts to an endless replaying of the same prepackaged arguments based on absolute principles. Disagreeing with a true believer is like ordering the surf to quiet down. The only response is another crashing wave.

In contrast to the true believer, the fanatical skeptic dismisses the possibility of ever believing anything. Skeptics often demand proof where no proof is possible. So what if the sun has risen every day of recorded history? That's no proof that it will rise tomorrow. Short of absolute proof, which never exists, fanatical skeptics accept nothing. In a world where the most we can hope for is increased audience adherence to our ideas, the skeptic demands an ironclad, logical demonstration of our claim's rightness.

PSEUDO-ARGUMENTS CAUSED BY LACK OF SHARED ASSUMPTIONS As we have seen, reasonable argument degenerates to pseudo-argument when there is no possibility for listening, learning, growth, or change. In this section, we look more closely at a cause of unreasonableness in argument: lack of shared assumptions.

A lack of shared assumptions necessarily dooms arguments about purely personal opinions—for example, someone's claim that opera is boring or that pizza tastes better than nachos. Of course, a pizza-versus-nachos argument might be possible if the disputants assume a shared criterion about nutrition. For example, a nutritionist could argue that a vegetable-laden pizza is better than nachos because pizza provides more balanced nutrients per calorie than nachos do. But if one of the disputants responds, "Nah, nachos are better than pizza because nachos taste better," then he makes a different assumption—"My sense of taste is better than your sense of taste." This is a wholly personal standard, an assumption that others are unable to share.

Lack of shared assumptions can also doom arguments when the disputants have different ideologies, as we saw in the discussion of true believers. *Ideology* is an academic word for belief systems or worldviews. We all have our own ideologies. We all look at the world through a lens shaped by our life's experiences. Our beliefs and values are shaped by our family background, our friends, our culture, our particular time in history, our race or ethnicity, our gender or sexual orientation, our social class, our religion, our education, and so forth. Because we tend to think that our particular lens for looking at the world is natural and universal rather than specific to ourselves, we must be aware that persons who disagree with us may not share our deepest assumptions and beliefs.

This lack of shared assumptions is evident in many disputes concerning politics or religion. For example, consider differences over how to interpret the Bible within communities identifying as Christian. Some Christian groups choose a straightforward, literal interpretation of the Bible as God's inerrant word, sometimes quoting Biblical passages as "proof texts" to support their stand on civic issues. Others believe the Bible is divinely inspired, meant to lead humans to a relationship with God, but transmitted through human authors. Other groups tend to read the Bible metaphorically or mythically, focusing on the paradoxes, historical contexts, and interpretive complexities of the Bible. Still other Christian groups read it as an ethical call for social justice. Members of these different Christian groups may not be able to argue rationally about, say, evolution or gay marriage because they have very different ways of reading Biblical passages and invoking the Bible's authority. Similarly, within other religious traditions, believers may also differ about the meaning and applicability of their sacred texts to scientific issues and social problems.

Similar disagreements about assumptions occur in the political arena as well. Our point is that certain religious or political beliefs or texts cannot be evoked for evidence or authority when an audience does not assume the belief's truth or does not agree on the way that a given text should be read or interpreted.

PSEUDO-ARGUMENTS CAUSED BY LACK OF CONFIDENCE IN EVIDENCE
Finally, pseudo-arguments arise when disputants can't agree about the trustworthiness of particular evidence or about the possibility of trustworthy evidence existing at all. Reasonable arguments must be grounded in evidence that can be verified and trusted. Sometimes unethical writers invent facts and data to create propaganda, advance a conspiracy theory, or make money from the sale of fake stories. Scientific fraud has also occasionally occurred wherein scientists have fudged their data or even made up data to support a claim. Tabloids and fringe news sites are notorious for spreading fake news, often in their attention-grabbing but bizarre headlines ("Farmer shoots 23-pound grasshopper").

For disputants with different ideologies, pseudo-arguments may even occur with issues grounded in science. Liberals may distrust scientific data about the safety of genetically modified organisms, whereas conservatives may distrust the scientific data about climate change. Genuine argument can emerge only when all sides of the dispute agree that any given evidence derives from verifiable facts or data. We don't mean that reasonable disputants must use the same facts: Arguers necessarily and always select and frame their evidence to support their points (see the discussion of *angle of vision* in Chapter 4). But no matter

---

For Writing and Discussion

Reasonable Arguments Versus Pseudo-Arguments

Individual task:

Which of the following questions will lead to reasonable arguments, and which will lead only to pseudo-arguments? Explain your reasoning.

1. Are the *Star Wars* films good science fiction?
2. Should cities subsidize professional sports venues?
3. Is this abstract oil painting created by a monkey smearing paint on a canvas a true work of art?
4. Are nose rings and tongue studs attractive?

Group task:

Working in pairs, small groups, or as a class, share your reasoning about these questions with classmates.

---

what evidence is chosen, disputants must agree that the evidence is verifiable—that it is real news or evidence, not fake news or evidence.

Frame of an Argument: A Claim Supported by Reasons

2.4   Describe the basic frame of an argument.

We said earlier that an argument originates in an *issue question,* which by definition is any question that provokes disagreement about the best answer. When you write an argument, your task is to take a position on the issue and to support it with reasons and evidence. The *claim* of your essay is the position you want your audience to accept. To put it another way, your claim is your essay's *thesis statement,* a one-sentence summary answer to your issue question. Your task, then, is to make a claim and support it with reasons.

What Is a Reason?

A *reason* (also called a *premise*) is a claim used to support another claim. In speaking or writing, a reason is usually linked to the claim with a connecting word such as *because, since, for, so, thus, consequently,* or *therefore,* indicating that the claim follows logically from the reason.

Let us take an example. In one of our recent classes, students heatedly debated the ethics of capturing wild dolphins and orcas (killer whales) and training them to perform in marine parks. This issue—made public in news stories and films such as *The Cove* (2009) and *Blackfish* (2013)–has many dimensions, including safety concerns for both the animals and their human trainers, as well as moral, scientific, legal, and economic considerations. Here are the frameworks the class developed for two alternative positions on this public issue:

One View

CLAIM: The public should not support marine parks.

REASON 1: Marine parks inhumanely separate dolphins and orcas from their natural habitats.

REASON 2: The education these parks claim to offer about marine mammals is just a series of artificial, exploitive tricks taught through behavior modification.

REASON 3: These parks are operated by big business with the goal of making large profits.

REASON 4: Marine parks encourage artificial breeding programs and cruel hunts and captures.

REASON 5: Marine parks promote an attitude of human dominance over animals.

Alternative View

CLAIM: The public should continue to enjoy marine parks.

REASON 1: These parks observe accreditation standards for animal welfare, health, and nutrition.

REASON 2: These marine parks enable scientists and veterinarians to study animal behavior in ways not possible with field studies in the wild.

REASON 3: These marine parks provide environmental education and memorable entertainment.

REASON 4: Marine parks use some of their profits to support research, conservation, and rescue and rehabilitation programs.

REASON 5: In their training of dolphins and orcas, these marine parks reinforce natural behaviors, exercise the animals' intelligence, and promote beneficial bonding with humans.

Formulating a list of reasons in this way breaks your argumentative task into a series of subtasks. It gives you a frame for building your argument in parts. In this example, the frame for the argument opposing commercial use of sea mammals suggests five different lines of reasoning a writer might pursue. You might use all five reasons or select only two or three, depending on which reasons would most persuade the intended audience. Each line of reasoning would be developed in its own separate section of the argument.

Expressing Reasons in *Because* Clauses

Chances are that when you were a child, the word *because* contained magical explanatory powers. (*I don't want that kind of butter on my toast! Why? Because. Because why? Just because.*) Somehow *because* seemed decisive. It persuaded people to accept your view of the world; it changed people's minds. Later, as you got older, you discovered that *because* only introduced your arguments and that it was the reasons following *because* that made the difference. Still, *because* introduced you to the powers potentially residing in the adult world of logic.

This childhood power of *because* perhaps explains why *because* clauses are the most common way of linking reasons to a claim. For example:

> The public should not support marine parks because these parks inhumanely separate dolphins and orcas from their natural habitats.

Of course, there are also many other ways to express the logical connection between a reason and a claim. Our language is rich in ways of stating *because* relationships:

- Marine parks inhumanely separate dolphins and orcas from their natural habitats. Therefore, the public should not support marine parks.
- Marine parks inhumanely separate dolphins and orcas from their natural habitats, so the public should not support these parks.
- One reason that the public should not support marine animal parks is that these parks inhumanely separate dolphins and orcas from their natural habitats.

Even though logical relationships can be stated in various ways, writing out one or more *because* clauses seems to be the most succinct and manageable way to clarify an argument for yourself. We therefore suggest that at some time in the writing process, you create a *working thesis statement* that summarizes your main reasons as *because* clauses attached to your claim.* *When* you compose your own working thesis statement depends largely on your writing process. Some writers like to plan their whole argument from the start and compose their working thesis statements with *because* clauses before they write their rough drafts. Others discover their arguments as they write. Composing *because* clauses can be a powerful discovery tool, causing you to think of many different kinds of arguments to support your claim. But it is often difficult to wrestle your ideas into the *because* clause shape, which may seem overly tidy for the complex network of ideas you are working with. Nevertheless, trying to summarize your argument as a single claim with reasons should help you see more clearly the emerging shape of your argument.

For Writing and Discussion

Developing Claims and Reasons

Try this group exercise to help you see how writing *because* clauses can be a discovery procedure. Divide into small groups. Each group member should contribute an issue with potentially opposing claims. While thinking of your issue, imagine a person who might disagree with you about it. This person will become your audience. Discussing each group member's issue in turn, help each member develop a claim supported by several reasons that might appeal to the imagined audience. Express each reason as a *because* clause. Then write out the working thesis statement for each person's argument by attaching the *because* clauses to the claim. Finally, try to create *because* clauses in support of an alternative claim for each issue. Each group should select two or three working thesis statements to present to the class.

---

* A working thesis statement opposing the commercial use of captured dolphins and orcas might look like this: The public should not support marine parks because marine parks inhumanely separate dolphins and orcas from their natural habitats; because marine parks are mainly big businesses driven by profit; because marine parks create inaccurate and incomplete educational information about dolphins and orcas; because marine parks encourage inhumane breeding programs, hunts, and captures; and because marine parks promote an attitude of human dominance over animals. You probably would not put a bulky thesis statement like this into your essay; rather, a working thesis statement is a behind-the-scenes way of summarizing your argument so that you can see it fully and clearly.

Writing Assignment

An Issue Question and Working Thesis Statements

Decide on an issue and a claim for a classical argument that you would like to write. Also imagine a reader who might be skeptical of your claim. Write a one-sentence question that summarizes the controversial issue that your claim addresses. Then draft a working thesis statement for your proposed argument. Organize the thesis as a claim with bulleted *because* clauses for reasons. You should have at least two reasons, but it is okay to have three or four. Also include an opposing thesis statement—that is, a claim with *because* clauses for an alternative position on your issue. Think of this opposing argument as your imagined reader's starting position.

Unless you have previously done research on an issue, it is probably best to choose an issue based on your personal experiences and observations. For example, you might consider issues related to your college or high school life, your work life, your experiences in clubs or family life, your prospective career, and so forth. (Part Two of this text introduces you to research-based argument.) As you think about your claim and *because* clauses for this assignment, take comfort in the fact that you are in a very early stage of the writing process: the brainstorming stage. Writers almost always discover new ideas when they write a first draft. As they take their writing project through multiple drafts and share their drafts with readers, their views may change substantially. In fact, honest writers can change positions on an issue by discovering that a counter-argument is stronger than their own. Thus the working thesis statement that you submit for this assignment may evolve when you begin to draft your essay.

Below, as well as in Chapters 3 and 4, we follow the process of student writer Carmen Tieu as she constructs an argument on violent video games. During a class discussion, Carmen mentioned a psychology professor who described playing violent video games as gendered behavior (overwhelmingly male). The professor indicated his dislike for such games, pointing to their antisocial, dehumanizing values. In class, Carmen described her own enjoyment of violent video games—particularly first-person-shooter games—and reported the pleasure that she derived from beating boys at Halo 2 and 3. Her classmates were interested in her ideas. She knew that she wanted to write an argument on this issue. The following is Carmen's submission for this assignment.

Carmen's Issue Question and Working Thesis Statements

Issue Question: Should girls be encouraged to play first-person-shooter video games?
My claim: First-person-shooter (FPS) video games are great activities for girls,
- because they empower girls when they beat guys at their own game.
    - because they equip girls with skills that free them from feminine stereotypes.
    - because they give girls a different way of bonding with males.
    - because they give girls new insights into a male subculture.
Opposing claim: First-person-shooter games are a bad activity for anyone, especially girls,
- because they promote antisocial values such as indiscriminate killing.
- because they amplify the bad, macho side of male stereotypes.
- because they waste valuable time that could be spent on something constructive.
- because FPS games could encourage women to see themselves as objects.

Chapter 3
The Logical Structure of Arguments

Logos

Learning Objectives

In this chapter you will learn to:

3.1 Explain the logical structure of argument in terms of claim, reason, and assumption granted by the audience.

3.2 Use the Toulmin system to describe an argument's logical structure.

3.3 Use the Toulmin system to generate ideas for your argument and test it for completeness.

In Chapter 2 you learned that the core of an argument is a claim supported by reasons and that these reasons can often be stated as *because* clauses attached to a claim. In this chapter, we examine the logical structure of arguments in more depth.

An Overview of *Logos*: What Do We Mean by the "Logical Structure" of an Argument?

3.1 Explain the logical structure of argument in terms of claim, reason, and assumption granted by the audience.

As you will recall from our discussion of the rhetorical triangle, *logos* refers to the strength of an argument's support and its internal consistency. *Logos* is the argument's logical structure. But what do we mean by "logical structure"?

Formal Logic Versus Real-World Logic

First of all, what we *don't* mean by logical structure is the kind of precise certainty you get in a philosophy class in formal logic. Logic classes deal with symbolic assertions that are universal and unchanging, such as "If all *p*s are *q*s and if *r* is a *p*, then *r* is a *q*." This statement is logically certain so long as *p*, *q*, and *r* are pure abstractions. But in the real world, *p*, *q*, and *r* turn into actual things, and the relationships among them suddenly become fuzzy. For example, *p* might be a class of actions called "Sexual Harassment," while *q* could be the class called "Actions That Justify Getting Fired from One's Job." If *r* is the class "Telling Off-Color Stories," then the logic of our *p–q–r* statement suggests that telling off-color stories (*r*) is an instance of sexual harassment (*p*), which in turn is an action justifying getting fired from one's job (*q*).

Now, most of us would agree that sexual harassment is a serious offense that might well justify getting fired. In turn, we might agree that telling off-color stories, if the jokes are sufficiently raunchy and are inflicted on an unwilling audience, constitutes sexual harassment. But few of us would want to say categorically that all people who tell off-color stories are harassing their listeners and ought to be fired. Most of us would want to know the particulars of the case before making a final judgment.

In the real world, then, it is difficult to say that *r*s are always *p*s or that every instance of a *p* results in *q*. That is why we discourage students from using the word *prove* in claims they write for arguments (as in "This paper will prove that euthanasia is wrong"). Real-world arguments seldom *prove* anything. They can only make a good case for something, a case that is more or less strong, more or less probable. Often the best you can hope for is to strengthen the resolve of those who agree with you or weaken the resistance of those who oppose you.

The Role of Assumptions

A key difference, then, between formal logic and real-world argument is that real-world arguments are not grounded in abstract, universal statements. Rather, as we shall see, they must be grounded in beliefs, assumptions, or values granted by the audience. A second important difference is that in real-world arguments, these beliefs, assumptions, or values are often unstated. So long as writer and audience share the same assumptions, it's fine to leave them unstated. But if these underlying assumptions aren't shared, the writer has a problem.

To illustrate the nature of this problem, suppose that you are an environmentalist opposed to the use of plastic bags in grocery stores. You have several reasons for opposing these bags, one of which is their role in polluting the oceans. You express this reason in a *because* clause as follows:

> States should ban plastic bags from grocery stores because banning bags will reduce plastic pollution in the ocean.

On the face of it, this is a plausible argument, but it depends on the audience's accepting the writer's assumption that it is good to reduce plastic pollution in the ocean. In other words, you might agree that plastics are polluting the ocean, but unless you also believe that this pollution is significantly harming the oceans, you might not automatically agree that plastic bags should be banned from grocery stores. What if you believe that pollution-caused damage to the ocean is not as severe as proponents claim? What if you believe that plastic bags account for only a small percentage of plastic pollution in the oceans? What if you believe that the harm to the oceans is outweighed by the environmental benefits of plastic bags, which are reusable, recyclable, and more ecofriendly to produce and transport than paper bags? What if you believe that harm to the oceans might soon be reduced by scientific advances in creating biodegradable plastics or in developing microorganisms that "eat" plastics? If these were your beliefs, the argument wouldn't work for you because you would reject its underlying assumption that plastic pollution is significantly harmful. To make this line of reasoning persuasive, the writer would have to provide evidence not only that plastic bags are polluting the ocean but also that this pollution is harmful enough to justify a ban.

The Core of an Argument: The Enthymeme

The previous core argument ("States should ban plastic bags from grocery stores because banning bags will reduce plastic pollution in the ocean") is an incomplete logical structure called an *enthymeme*. Its persuasiveness depends on an underlying assumption or belief that the audience must accept. To complete the enthymeme and make it effective, the audience must willingly supply a missing premise—in this case, that plastic pollution of the oceans is significantly harmful. The Greek philosopher Aristotle showed how successful enthymemes root the speaker's argument in assumptions, beliefs, or values held by the audience. The word *enthymeme* comes from the Greek *en* (meaning "in") and *thumos* (meaning "mind"). Listeners or readers must have in mind an assumption, belief, or value that lets them willingly supply the missing premise. If the audience is unwilling to supply the missing premise, then the argument fails. Our point is that successful arguments depend both on what the arguer says and on what the audience already has "in mind."

To clarify the concept of enthymeme, let's go over this same territory again, this time more slowly, examining what we mean by "incomplete logical structure." The sentence "States should ban plastic bags from grocery stores because banning bags will reduce plastic pollution in the ocean" is an enthymeme. It combines a claim (States should ban plastic bags from grocery stores) with a reason expressed as a *because* clause (because banning bags will reduce plastic pollution in the ocean). To render this enthymeme logically complete, the audience must willingly supply a missing assumption—that plastic pollution is harmful enough to the oceans to justify a ban on plastic bags. If your audience accepts this assumption, then you have a starting place on which to build an effective argument. If your audience doesn't accept this assumption, then you must supply another argument to support it, and so on until you find common ground with your audience.

To sum up:

1. Claims are supported with reasons. You can usually state a reason as a *because* clause attached to a claim.

2. A *because* clause attached to a claim is an incomplete logical structure called an enthymeme. To create a complete logical structure from an enthymeme, the underlying assumption (or assumptions) must be articulated.

3. To serve as an effective starting point for the argument, this underlying assumption should be a belief, value, or principle that the audience grants.

Let's illustrate this structure by putting the previous example into schematic form.

ENTHYMEME

CLAIM: States should ban plastic bags from grocery stores

REASON: because banning plastic bags will reduce plastic pollution in the ocean.

Audience must supply this assumption ⟶

UNDERLYING ASSUMPTION
Plastic pollution in the ocean is harmful enough to justify a ban.

The Power of Audience-Based Reasons

Aristotle's concept of the enthymeme focuses on the writer's need to create what we can now call "audience-based reasons" as opposed to "writer-based reasons." A reason that is persuasive to you as a writer might not be persuasive to your audience. Finding audience-based reasons means finding arguments effectively anchored within your audience's beliefs and values.

To illustrate the difference between an audience-based reason and a writer-based reason, suppose that you are a vegetarian persuaded mainly by ethical arguments against causing needless suffering to animals. Suppose further that you want to persuade others to become vegetarians or at least to reduce their consumption of meat. Your "writer-based reason" for vegetarianism could be stated as follows:

> You should become a vegetarian because doing so will help reduce the needless suffering of animals.

The underlying assumption here is that it is wrong to cause the suffering of animals. This writer-based reason might also be an audience-based reason for persons who are wrestling with the moral dimension of animal suffering. But this assumption might not resonate with people who have made their own peace with eating meat. How might you use audience-based reasons to appeal to these meat-eaters? Here are two more possible enthymemes:

> You should become a vegetarian because doing so may help you lower your cholesterol.
>
> You should become a vegetarian because doing so will significantly lower your carbon footprint.

These arguments hook into the assumption that it is good to lower one's cholesterol (health values) or that it is good to lower one's carbon footprint (environmental values). All three of the arguments—whether based on ethics, health, or the environment—might further the practice of vegetarianism or at least reduce the amount of meat consumed, but they won't appeal equally to all audiences. From the perspective of logic alone, all three arguments are equally sound. But they will affect different audiences differently.

For Writing and Discussion

Identifying Underlying Assumptions and Choosing Audience-Based Reasons

Working individually or in small groups, identify the unstated assumption that the audience must supply in order to make the following enthymemes persuasive.

Example

> **Enthymeme:** Rabbits make good pets because they are gentle.
> **Underlying assumption:** Gentle animals make good pets.

1. We shouldn't elect Joe as committee chair because he is too bossy.
2. The federal government should institute a carbon tax because doing so will reduce U.S. production of greenhouse gases.
3. The federal government should not institute a carbon tax because doing so will damage the economy.
4. We should strengthen the Endangered Species Act because doing so will preserve genetic diversity on the planet.
5. The Endangered Species Act is too stringent because it severely restricts the rights of property owners.

Adopting a Language for Describing Arguments: The Toulmin System

3.2   Use the Toulmin system to describe an argument's logical structure.

Understanding a new field usually requires you to learn a new vocabulary. For example, if you were taking biology for the first time, you'd have to learn hundreds and hundreds of new terms. Luckily, the field of argument requires us to learn a mere handful of new terms. A particularly useful set of argument terms, one we'll be using occasionally throughout this text, comes from philosopher Stephen Toulmin. In the 1950s, Toulmin rejected the prevailing models of argument based on formal logic in favor of a very audience-based courtroom model.

Toulmin's courtroom model differs from formal logic in that it assumes that (1) all assertions and assumptions are contestable by "opposing counsel" and that (2) all final "verdicts" about the persuasiveness of the opposing arguments will be rendered by a neutral third party, a judge, or a jury. As writers, keeping in mind the "opposing counsel" forces us to anticipate counterarguments and to question our assumptions. Keeping in mind the judge and jury reminds us to answer opposing arguments fully and without rancor, and to present positive reasons for supporting our case as well as negative reasons for disbelieving the opposing case. Above all else, Toulmin's model reminds us not to construct an argument that appeals only to those who already agree with us. In short, it helps arguers tailor arguments to their audiences.

The system we use for analyzing arguments combines Toulmin's language with Aristotle's concept of the enthymeme. It builds on the system you have already been practicing. We simply need to add a few key terms from Toulmin. The first term is Toulmin's *warrant*, the name we will now use for the underlying assumption that turns an enthymeme into a complete, logical structure as shown below.

Toulmin derives his term *warrant* from the concept of "warranty" or "guarantee." The warrant is the value, belief, or principle that the audience has to hold if the soundness of the argument is to be guaranteed or warranted. We sometimes make similar use of this word in ordinary language when we say "That is an unwarranted conclusion," meaning one has leaped from information about a situation to a conclusion about that situation without any sort of general principle to justify or "warrant" that move. Thus the warrant—once accepted by the audience—"guarantees" the soundness of the argument.

ENTHYMEME

CLAIM: States should ban plastic bags from grocery stores

REASON: because banning plastic bags will reduce plastic pollution in the ocean.

Audience must supply this warrant ⟶

WARRANT

Plastic pollution in the ocean is harmful enough to justify a ban.

But arguments need more than claims, reasons, and warrants. These are simply one-sentence statements—the frame of an argument, not a developed argument. To give body and weight to our arguments and make them convincing, we need what Toulmin calls *grounds* and *backing*. Let's start with grounds. Grounds are the supporting evidence that causes an audience to accept your reason. Grounds are facts, data, statistics, causal links, testimony, examples, anecdotes—the blood and muscle that flesh out the skeletal frame of your enthymeme. Toulmin suggests that grounds are "what you have to go on" in an argument—the stuff you can point to and present before a jury. Here is how grounds fit into our emerging argument schema:

> **ENTHYMEME**
>
> CLAIM: States should ban plastic bags from grocery stores
>
> REASON: because banning plastic bags will reduce plastic pollution in the ocean.

Grounds support the reason

> **GROUNDS**
>
> Evidence that a substantial percentage of thrown-away plastic bags end up as ocean pollution and could be reduced with bans:
>
> • According to the Earth Policy Institute, 100 billion plastic bags pass through the hands of U.S. consumers each year.
>
> • Plastic bags that don't end up in landfills often float into the oceans from river and stream pollution.
>
> • According to Ocean Crusaders, plastic bags are the most prevalent man-made thing that sailors see in the ocean.
>
> • A scientific study in 2014 estimated that there are 269,000 metric tons of plastic and 5.25 trillion plastic particles on the ocean's surface.
>
> • Plastics float on the surface, where they are concentrated by ocean currents. *National Geographic* has documented the "Pacific trash vortex"—a floating garbage patch the size of Texas.
>
> • Bans, which are becoming acceptable to consumers as shown by states and cities that have recently instituted bans on plastic grocery bags, have cut down on plastic bags in landfills and coastal areas.

In many cases, successful arguments require just these three components: a claim, a reason, and grounds. If the audience already accepts the unstated assumption behind the reason (the warrant), then the warrant can safely remain in the background, unstated and unexamined. But if there is a chance that the audience will question or doubt the warrant, then the writer needs to back it up by providing an argument in its support. *Backing* is the argument that supports the warrant. It may require as little as one or two sentences or as much as a major section in your argument. Its goal is to persuade the audience to accept the warrant. Here is how *backing* is added to our schema:

> **WARRANT**
>
> Plastic pollution in the ocean is harmful enough to justify a ban.

Backing supports the warrant

> **BACKING**
>
> Arguments that plastics, especially plastic bags, are significantly harmful to the oceans:
>
> • Plastics cause great harm to marine life (sea turtles eat plastic bags, which look like jellyfish; birds and surface-feeding fish ingest small pieces of plastic, which often results in death or starvation).
>
> • Toxins absorbed from digesting plastic work their way up the food chain, including into the fish we eat, jeopardizing food safety.
>
> • Plastic particles unbalance the ecosystem; for example, some ocean insect species breed more quickly where plastics are floating.
>
> • *National Geographic News* reports a study showing that "degrading plastics are leaching potentially toxic chemicals such as bisphenol A into the seas, possibly threatening ocean animals, and us."

Toulmin's system next asks us to imagine how a resistant audience would try to refute our argument. Specifically, an adversarial audience might challenge our reason and grounds by arguing that plastic bags are not polluting the oceans or that the pollution is not extensive. The adversary might also attack our warrant and backing by arguing that the harm caused by plastic pollution is not significant enough to justify a ban on plastic bags. These rebuttal strategies are outlined in the right-hand column of our schema as shown on the next page.

Toulmin's final term, used to limit the force of a claim and indicate the degree of its probable truth, is *qualifier*. The qualifier reminds us that real-world arguments almost never prove a claim. We may say things such as *very likely, probably,* or *maybe* to indicate the strength of the claim we are willing to draw from our grounds and warrant. Thus, if there are exceptions to your warrant or if your grounds are not very strong, you may have to qualify your claim. For example, you might say, "States should ban plastic bags from grocery stores because banning plastic bags would be a small first step toward reducing plastic pollution of the oceans" or "Except for limited cases of scientific research, dolphins and orcas should not be held in captivity." In our future displays of the Toulmin scheme we will omit the qualifiers, but you should always remember that no argument is 100 percent conclusive.

ENTHYMEME

CLAIM: States should ban plastic bags from grocery stores

REASON: because banning plastic bags will reduce plastic pollution in the ocean.

GROUNDS

Evidence that a substantial percentage of thrown-away plastic bags end up as ocean pollution:

- According to the Earth Policy Institute, 100 billion plastic bags pass through the hands of U.S. consumers each year.

- Plastic bags that don't end up in landfills often float into the oceans from river and stream pollu-tion.

- According to Ocean Crusaders, plastic bags are the most prevalent man-made thing that sailors see in the ocean.

- A scientific study in 2014 estimated that there are 269,000 metric tons of plastic and 5.25 trillion plastic particles on the ocean's surface.

- Plastics float on the surface, where they are con-centrated by ocean currents. *National Geographic* has documented the "Pacific trash vortex"—a floating garbage patch the size of Texas.

- Bans, which are becoming acceptable to consumers as shown by states and cities that have recently instituted bans on plastic grocery bags, have cut down on plastic bags in landfills and coastal areas.

Writer must anticipate these attacks from skeptics

POSSIBLE CONDITIONS OF REBUTTAL

A skeptic can attack the reason and grounds:

- Arguments that plastic bags from grocery stores comprise only a small proportion of plastic pollution in the ocean (far greater damage comes from plastic bottles, Styrofoam pellets, and floating fish nets)

- Arguments that the pollution is not extensive

- Arguments that banning plastic bags would eliminate all the ecological and consumer benefits of plastic bags

- Arguments that plastic bags are more eco-friendly to produce than paper bags and are completely recyclable

- Arguments that plastic bags are reusable, are better than paper for storing moist products, and save on use of plastic wrapping

- Arguments that bans don't work and that other polices would be more effective at tackling this problem, such as placing higher fees on plastic bags or implementing intensive recycling campaigns

(Continued)

WARRANT

Plastic pollution in the ocean is harmful enough to justify a ban.

BACKING

Arguments that plastics, especially plastic bags, are significantly harmful to the oceans:

- Plastics cause great harm to marine life (sea turtles eat plastic bags, which look like jellyfish; birds and surface-feeding fish ingest small pieces of plastic, which often results in death or starvation).
- Toxins absorbed from digesting plastic work their way up the food chain, including into the fish we eat, jeopardizing food safety.
- Plastic particles unbalance the ecosystem; for example, some ocean insect species breed more quickly where plastics are floating.
- *National Geographic News* reports a study showing that "degrading plastics are leaching potentially toxic chemicals such as bisphenol A into the seas, possibly threatening ocean animals, and us."

POSSIBLE CONDITIONS OF REBUTTAL

A skeptic could attack the warrant and backing:

- Arguments that data about harm to sea life are primarily anecdotal and amplified by photographs appealing to *pathos*
- Argument conceding that some harm is done to the ocean, but research has not yet documented the extent of the danger to marine life
- Arguments that ocean damage is not severe enough to justify a ban, especially when balanced against the ecological benefits of plastic bags
- Arguments that the problem of ocean pollution might soon be solved by science, which is on track to devise biological methods to "eat plastic" or to make plastic more biodegradable

For Writing and Discussion

Developing Enthymemes with the Toulmin Schema

Working individually or in small groups, imagine that you have to write arguments developing the five enthymemes listed in the first For Class Discussion exercise in this chapter. Use the Toulmin schema to help you determine what you need to consider when developing each enthymeme. We suggest that you try a four-box diagram structure as a way of visualizing the schema. We have applied the Toulmin schema to the first enthymeme: "We shouldn't elect Joe as committee chair because he is too bossy."

ENTHYMEME

CLAIM We shouldn't elect Joe as committee chair

REASON because he is too bossy.

GROUNDS

Evidence of Joe's bossiness:

- Examples of the way he dominates meetings—doesn't call on people, talks too much
- Testimony about his bossiness from people who have served with him on committees
- Anecdotes about his abrasive style

CONDITIONS OF REBUTTAL

Attacking the reason and grounds:

Evidence that Joe is not bossy or is only occasionally bossy:

- Counterevidence showing his collaborative style
- Testimony from people who have liked Joe as a leader and claim he isn't bossy; testimony about his cooperativeness and kindness
- Testimony that anecdotes about Joe's bossiness aren't typical

WARRANT	CONDITIONS OF REBUTTAL
Bossy people make bad committee chairs.	***Attacking the warrant and backing:***
BACKING	• Arguments that bossiness can be a good trait
Problems caused by bossy committee chairs:	◦ Sometimes bossy people make good chairpersons.
• Bossy people don't inspire cooperation and enthusiam.	◦ This committee needs a bossy person who can make decisions and get things done.
• Bossy people make others angry.	• Argument that Joe has other traits of good leadership that outweigh his bossiness
• Bossy people tend to make bad decisions because they don't incorporate advice from others.	

Using Toulmin's Schema to Plan and Test Your Argument

3.3 **Use the Toulmin system to generate ideas for your argument and test it for completeness.**

So far we have seen that a claim, a reason, and a warrant form the frame for a line of reasoning in an argument. Most of the words in an argument, however, are devoted to grounds and backing.

Hypothetical Example: Cheerleaders as Athletes

For an illustration of how a writer can use the Toulmin schema to generate ideas for an argument, consider the following case. In April 2005, the Texas House of Representatives passed a bill banning "sexually suggestive" cheerleading. Across the nation, evening TV comedians poked fun at the bill, while newspaper editorialists debated its wisdom and constitutionality. In one of our classes, however, several students, including one who had earned a high school varsity letter in competitive cheerleading, defended the bill by contending that provocative dance moves hurt the athletic image of cheerleading. In the following example, which draws on ideas developed in class discussion, we create a hypothetical student writer (we'll call her Chandale) who argues in defense of the Texas bill. Chandale's argument is based on the following enthymeme:

> The bill banning suggestive dancing for high school cheerleaders is a good law because it promotes a view of female cheerleaders as athletes.

Chandale used the Toulmin schema to brainstorm ideas for developing her argument. Here are her notes:

Chandale's Planning Notes Using the Toulmin Schema

Enthymeme: The bill banning suggestive dancing for high school cheerleaders is a good law because it promotes a view of female cheerleaders as athletes.

Grounds: First, I've got to use evidence to show that cheerleaders are athletes.

- Cheerleaders at my high school are carefully chosen for their stamina and skill after exhausting two-week tryouts.
- We begin all practices with a mile run and an hour of warm-up exercises—we are also expected to work out on our own for at least an hour on weekends and on days without practice.
- We learned competitive routines and stunts consisting of lifts, tosses, flips, catches, and gymnastic moves. This requires athletic ability! We'd practice these stunts for hours each week.
- Throughout the year cheerleaders have to attend practices, camps, and workshops to learn new routines and stunts.
- Our squad competed in competitions around the state.
- Competitive cheerleading is a growing movement across the country—the University of Maryland has made it a varsity sport for women.
- Skimpy uniforms and suggestive dance moves destroy the image of cheerleaders as athletes by making women eye candy (for example, the Dallas Cowboys cheerleaders).

Warrant: It is a good thing to view female cheerleaders as athletes.

Backing: Now I need to make the case that it is good to see cheerleaders as athletes rather than as eye candy.

- Athletic competition builds self-esteem, independence, and a powerful sense of achievement. It also contributes to health, strength, and conditioning.
- Competitive cheerleading is one of the few sports where teams are made up of both men and women. (Why is this good? Should I use this?)
- The suggestive dance moves turn women into sex objects whose function is to be gazed at by men, which suggests that women's value is based on their beauty and sex appeal.
- We are talking about HIGH SCHOOL cheerleading—it is a very bad early influence on girls to model themselves on Dallas Cowboys cheerleaders or sexy videos of rock stars.
- Junior-high girls want to do what senior-high girls do—suggestive dance moves promote sexuality way too early.

Conditions of Rebuttal: Would anybody try to rebut my reasons and grounds that cheerleading is an athletic activity?

- No. I think it is obvious that cheerleading is an athletic activity once they see my evidence.
- However, they might not think of cheerleading as a sport. They might say that the University of Maryland just declared it a sport as a cheap way to meet Title IX federal rules to have more women's sports. I'll have to make sure that I show that cheerleading is really a sport.
- They also might say that competitive cheerleading shouldn't be encouraged because it is too dangerous—lots of serious injuries, including paralysis, have been caused by mistakes in doing flips, lifts, and tosses. If I include this, maybe I could say that other sports are dangerous also, and it is in fact danger that makes this sport so exciting.

Would anyone doubt my warrant and backing that it is good to see female cheerleaders as athletes?

- Yes, all those people who laughed at the Texas legislature think that people are being too prudish and that banning suggestive dance moves violates free expression. I'll need to make my case that it is bad for young girls to see themselves as sex objects too early.

The information that Chandale lists under "grounds" is what she sees as the facts of the case—the hard data she will use as evidence to support her contention that cheerleading is an athletic activity. The following paragraph shows how this argument might look in a more formally written format.

First Part of Chandale's Argument

Although evening TV comedians have made fun of the Texas legislature's desire to ban "suggestive" dance moves from cheerleading routines, I applaud this bill because it promotes a healthy view of female cheerleaders as athletes rather than showgirls. I was lucky enough to attend a high school where cheerleading is a sport, and I earned a varsity letter as a cheerleader. To get on my high school's cheerleading squad, students have to go through an exhausting two-week tryout of workouts and instruction in the basic routines; then they are chosen based on their stamina and skill. Once on the squad, cheerleaders begin all practices with a mile run and an hour of grueling warm-up exercises, and they are expected to exercise on their own on weekends. As a result of this regimen, cheerleaders achieve and maintain a top level of physical fitness. In addition, to get on the squad, students must be able to do handstands, cartwheels, handsprings, high jumps, and splits. Each year the squad builds up to its complex routines and stunts consisting of lifts, tosses, flips, catches, and gymnastic moves that only trained athletes can do. In tough competitions at the regional and state levels, the cheerleading squad demonstrates its athletic talent. This view of cheerleading as a competitive sport is also spreading to colleges. As reported recently in a number of newspapers, the University of Maryland has made cheerleading a varsity sport, and many other universities are following suit. Athletic performance of this caliber is a far cry from the sexy dancing that many high school girls often associate with cheerleading. By banning suggestive dancing in cheerleading routines, the Texas legislature creates an opportunity for schools to emphasize the athleticism of cheerleading.

Summarizes opposing view

States her claim

For grounds, uses personal experience details to show that cheerleading is an athletic activity

Provides more grounds by showing emerging views of cheerleading as a competitive sport

---

As you can see, Chandale has plenty of evidence for arguing that competitive cheerleading is an athletic activity quite different from sexy dancing. But how effective is this argument as it stands? Is Chandale's argument complete? The Toulmin schema encourages writers to include—if needed for the intended audience—explicit support for their warrants as well as attention to conditions for rebuttal. Because the overwhelming national response to the Texas law was ridicule at the perceived prudishness of the legislators, Chandale decided to expand her argument as follows:

Continuation of Chandale's Argument

Supplies warrant: It is good to see cheerleaders as athletic and bad to see them as sex objects

Supplies backing: Shows benefits that come from seeing cheerleaders as athletes

Anticipates an objection

Responds to objection by supplying more evidence that cheerleading is a sport; in fact, it is a dangerous sport

Sums up by returning to claim

This emphasis on cheerleaders as athletes rather than sexy dancers is good for girls. The erotic dance moves that many high school cheerleaders now incorporate into their routines show that they are emulating the Dallas Cowboys cheerleaders or pop stars in music videos. Our already sexually saturated culture (think of the suggestive clothing marketed to little girls) pushes girls and women to measure their value by their beauty and sex appeal. It would be far healthier, both physically and psychologically, if high school cheerleaders were identified as athletes. For women and men both, competitive cheerleading can build self-esteem, pride in teamwork, and a powerful sense of achievement, as well as promote health, strength, and fitness.

Some people might object to competitive cheerleading by saying that cheerleading isn't really a sport. Some have accused the University of Maryland of making cheerleading a varsity sport only as a cheap way of meeting Title IX requirements. But anyone who has watched competitive cheerleading, and imagined what it would be like to be thrown high into the air, knows instinctively that this is a sport indeed. In fact, other persons might object to competitive cheerleading because it is too dangerous, with potential for very severe injuries, including paralysis. Obviously the sport is dangerous—but so are many sports, including football, gymnastics, diving, and trampoline. The danger and difficulty of the sport are part of its appeal. Part of what can make cheerleaders as athletes better role models for girls than cheerleaders as erotic dancers is the courage and training needed for success. Of course, the Texas legislators might not have had athleticism in mind when they banned suggestive dancing. They might only have been promoting their vision of morality. But at stake are the role models we set for young girls. I'll pick an athlete over a Dallas Cowboys cheerleader every time.

Our example suggests how a writer can use the Toulmin schema to generate ideas for an argument. For evidence, Chandale draws primarily on her personal experiences as a cheerleader/athlete and on her knowledge of popular culture. She also draws on her reading of several newspaper articles about the University of Maryland making cheerleading a varsity sport. (In an academic paper rather than a newspaper editorial, she would need to document these sources through formal citations.) Although many arguments depend on research, many can be supported wholly or in part by your own personal experiences, so don't neglect the wealth of evidence from your own life when searching for data. (Chapter 4 provides a more detailed discussion of evidence in arguments.)

Extended Student Example: Girls and Violent Video Games

Let's look at one more example of how the Toulmin system can help you generate ideas for your argument. In this case, we will look at a complete example from student writer Carmen Tieu, whose evolving argument about girls and violent video games was introduced in the last chapter. Carmen's assignment was to write a "supporting reasons" argument, which is a shortened form of the classical argument described at the beginning of Chapter 2. It has all the features of a classical argument except for the requirement to summarize and rebut opposing views. In planning her argument, Carmen decided to use four lines of reasoning, as shown in her *because* clauses listed at the end of Chapter 2. She then created a basic Toulmin frame for each reason and used these frames to plan out the needed examples and evidence. Here is her final argument:

Student Essay

Why Violent Video Games Are Good for Girls

Carmen Tieu

It is ten o'clock P.M., game time. My entire family knows by now that when I am home on Saturday nights, ten P.M. is my gaming night when I play my favorite first-person-shooter (FPS) games, usually *Halo 3*, on Xbox Live. Seated in my mobile chair in front of my family's 42-inch flat screen HDTV, I log onto Xbox Live. A small message in the bottom of the screen appears with the words "Kr1pL3r is online," alerting me that one of my male friends is online and already playing. As the game loads, I send Kr1pL3r a game invite, and he joins me in the pre-game room lobby.

In the game room lobby, all the players who will be participating in the match are chatting aggressively with each other: "Oh man, we're gonna own you guys so bad." When a member of the opposing team notices my gamer tag, "embracingapathy," he begins to insult me by calling me various degrading, gay-associated names: "Embracing apa-what? Man, it sounds so emo. Are you some fag? I bet you want me so bad. You're gonna get owned!" Players always assume from my gamer tag that I am a gay male, never a female. The possibility that I am a girl is the last thing on their minds. Of course, they are right that girls seldom play first-person-shooter games. Girls are socialized into activities that promote togetherness and talk, not high-intensity competition involving fantasized shooting and killing. The violent nature of the games tends to repulse girls. Opponents of violent video games typically hold that these games are so graphically violent that they will influence players to become amoral and sadistic. Feminists also argue that violent video games often objectify women by portraying them as sexualized toys for men's gratification. Although I understand these objections, I argue that playing first-person-shooter games can actually be good for girls.

First, playing FPS games gives girls the chance to beat guys at their own game. When I first began playing *Halo 2*, I was horrible. My male friends constantly put me down for my lack of skills, constantly telling me that I was awful, "but for a girl, you're good." But it didn't take much practice until I learned to operate the two joysticks with precision and with quick instinctual reactions. While guys and girls can play many physical games together, such as basketball or touch football, guys will always have the advantage because on average they are taller, faster, and stronger than

(continued)

Title makes persuasive claim

Attention-grabbing scene

Continues scene and provides more background

Sums up opposing views

States claim

States first reason

For grounds, uses personal narrative to show how she can beat guys females. However, when it comes to video games, girls can compete equally because physical strength isn't required, just quick reaction time and manual dexterity—skills that women possess in abundance. The adrenaline rush that I receive from beating a bunch of testosterone-driven guys at something they supposedly excel at is empowering and exciting; I especially savor the look of horror on their faces when I completely destroy them.

Because female video gamers are so rare, playing shooter games allows girls to be freed from feminine stereotypes and increases their confidence. Our culture generally portrays females as caring, nonviolent, and motherly beings who are not supposed to enjoy FPS games with their war themes and violent killings. I am in no way rejecting these traditional female values because I myself am a compassionate, tree-hugging vegan. But I also like to break these stereotypes. Playing video games offers a great way for females to break the social mold of only doing "girly" things and introduces them to something that males commonly enjoy. Playing video games with sexist males has also helped me become more outspoken. Psychologically, I can stand up to aggressive males because I know that I can beat them at their own game. The confidence I've gotten from excelling at shooter games may have even carried over into the academic arena because I am majoring in chemical engineering and have no fear whatsoever of intruding into the male-dominated territory of math and science. Knowing that I can beat all the guys in my engineering classes at *Halo* gives me that little extra confidence boost during exams and labs.

Another reason for girls to play FPS games is that it gives us a different way of bonding with guys. Once when I was discussing my latest *Halo 3* matches with one of my regular male friends, a guy whom I didn't know turned around and said, "You play *Halo*? Wow, you just earned my respect." Although I was annoyed that this guy apparently didn't respect women in general, it is apparent that guys will talk to me differently now that I can play video games. From a guy's perspective I can also appreciate why males find video games so addicting. You get joy from perfecting your skills so that your high-angle grenade kills become a thing of beauty. While all of these skills may seem trivial to some, the acknowledgment of my skills from other players leaves me with a perverse sense of pride in knowing that I played the game better than everyone else. Since I have started playing, I have also noticed that it is much easier to talk to males about lots of different subjects. Talking video games with guys is a great ice-breaker that leads to different kinds of friendships outside the realm of romance and dating.

Finally, playing violent video games can be valuable for girls because it gives them insights into a disturbing part of male subculture. When the testosterone starts kicking in, guys become blatantly homophobic and misogynistic. Any player, regardless of gender, who cannot play well (as measured by having a high number of kills and a low number of deaths) is made fun of by being called gay, a girl, or worse. Even when some guys finally meet a female player, they will also insult her by calling her a lesbian or an ugly fat chick who has no life. Their insults towards the girl will dramatically increase if she beats them because they feel so humiliated. In their eyes, playing worse than a girl is embarrassing because girls are supposed to be inept at FPS games. Whenever I play *Halo* better than my male friends, they often comment on how "it makes no sense that we're getting owned by Carmen."

Briefly backs warrant by showing the good feeling of empowerment

States second reason

Details focus on backing for warrant: It is good for girls to be freed from feminine stereotypes

Provides third reason

Uses a narrative example for grounds; shows how FPS games give her a different way of bonding with males

Backing for warrant: This new kind of bonding is good

Provides final reason

Provides grounds: gives examples of what she learned about male subculture

When males act like such sexist jerks it causes one to question if they are always like this. My answer is no because I know, firsthand, that when guys like that are having one-on-one conversations with a female, they show a softer side, and the macho side goes away. They don't talk about how girls should stay in the kitchen and make them dinner, but rather how they think it is cool that they share a fun, common interest with a girl. But when they are in a group of males their fake, offensive macho side comes out. I find this phenomenon troubling because it shows a real problem in the way boys are socialized. To be a real "man" around other guys, they have to put down women and gays in activities involving aggressive behavior where men are supposed to excel. But they don't become macho and aggressive in activities like reading and writing, which they think of as feminine. I've always known that guys are more physically aggressive than women, but until I started playing violent video games I had never realized how this aggression is related to misogyny and homophobia. Perhaps these traits aren't deeply ingrained in men but come out primarily in a competitive male environment. Whatever the cause, it is an ugly phenomenon, and I'm glad that I learned more about it. Beating guys at FPS games has made me a more confident woman while being more aware of gender differences in the way men and women are socialized. I joined the guys in playing *Halo*, but I didn't join their subculture of ridiculing women and gays.

> Provides backing for warrant: Shows value of learning about male subculture while keeping separate from it

> Sums up why her playing FPS games is valuable

The Thesis-Governed "Self-Announcing" Structure of Classical Argument

Like the complete classical argument explained at the beginning of Chapter 2, Carmen's supporting-reasons argument has a thesis-governed structure in which she states her claim near the end of the introduction, begins body paragraphs with clearly stated reasons, and uses effective transitions throughout to keep her reader on track. This kind of tightly organized structure is sometimes called a *self-announcing* or *closed-form* structure because the writer states his or her claim before beginning the body of the argument and forecasts the structure that is to follow. In contrast, an *unfolding* or *open-form* structure often doesn't give away the writer's position until late in the essay. (We discuss delayed-thesis arguments in Chapter 6.) A general rule of thumb for arguments using more than one line of reasoning is to place your most important or most interesting reason last, where it will have the greatest impact on your readers.

In writing a self-announcing argument, students often ask how much of the argument to summarize in the thesis statement. Consider Carmen's options:

- She might announce only her claim:

  Playing first-person-shooter games can be good for girls.

- She might forecast a series of parallel reasons:

  There are several reasons that playing first-person-shooter games can be good for girls.

- She might forecast the actual number of reasons:

  I will present four reasons that playing first-person-shooter games can be good for girls.

- Or she might forecast the whole argument by including her *because* clauses with her claim:

> Playing first-person-shooter games can be good for girls because it lets girls feel empowered by beating guys at their own game, because it frees girls from feminine stereotypes, because it gives girls a different way of bonding with guys, and because it gives girls new insights into a male subculture.

This last thesis statement forecasts not only the claim, but also the supporting reasons that will serve as topic sentences for key paragraphs throughout the body of the paper.

No formula can tell you precisely how much of your argument to forecast in the introduction. However, these suggestions can guide you: In writing a self-announcing argument, forecast only what is needed for clarity. In short arguments, readers often need only your claim. In longer arguments, however, or in especially complex arguments, readers appreciate your forecasting the complete structure of the argument (claim with reasons). Also, as we explain in later chapters, the directness of classical argument is not always the best way to reach all audiences. On many occasions more open-form or delayed-thesis approaches are more effective.

For Writing and Discussion
Reasons, Warrants, and Conditions of Rebuttal

Individual task:

1. Choose one of the following reasons. Then write a passage that provides grounds to support the reason. Use details from personal experience or imagine plausible, hypothetical details.
   a. Web surfing or checking social media can be harmful to college students because it wastes study time.
   b. Getting one's news from social media undermines informed citizenship because social media tend to sensationalize news events.
   c. The university's decision to raise parking fees for solo drivers is a good environmental plan because it encourages students to use public transportation.
2. Now create an argument to support the warrant for the reason you chose in task 1. The warrants for each of the arguments are stated below.

   a. Support this warrant: Wasting study time is harmful for college students.
   b. Support this warrant: Sensationalizing of the news is harmful to citizens' understanding.
   c. Support this warrant: It is good for the environment to encourage students to use public transportation.

Group task:
Working in pairs, small groups, or as a class, share your strategies for supporting your chosen reason and warrant.

Writing Assignment

Plan of an Argument's Details

This assignment asks you to return to the working thesis statement that you created for the brief writing assignment in Chapter 2. From that thesis statement extract one of your enthymemes (your claim with one of your *because* clauses). Write out the warrant for your enthymeme. Then use the Toulmin schema to brainstorm the details you might use (grounds, backing, conditions of rebuttal) to convert your enthymeme into a fleshed-out argument. Use as your model Chandale's planning notes or Carmen's planning notes earlier in this chapter. Note that this is a process-oriented brainstorming task aimed at helping you generate ideas for an argument in progress. You may end up changing your ideas substantially as you compose the actual argument. (An assignment to write a complete "supporting reasons" argument like Carmen's comes at the end of the next chapter, which explains the uses of evidence.)

Chapter 4
Using Evidence Effectively

Learning Objectives

In this chapter you will learn to:

4.1 Explain the different kinds of evidence

4.2 Make your evidence persuasive by using the STAR criteria and other strategies

4.3 Understand evidence rhetorically by explaining how the selection and framing of evidence reveal an angle of vision

In Chapters 2 and 3 we introduced the concept of *logos*—the logical structure of reasons and evidence in an argument—and showed how an effective argument advances the writer's claim by linking its supporting reasons to one or more assumptions, beliefs, or values held by the intended audience. In this chapter, we turn to the uses of evidence in argument. By *evidence*, we mean all the verifiable data and information a writer might use as support for an argument. In Toulmin's terms, evidence is part of the *grounds* or *backing* of an argument in support of reasons or warrants. By understanding evidence rhetorically, you will better understand how to use evidence ethically, responsibly, and persuasively in your own arguments.

Kinds of Evidence

4.1 **Explain the different kinds of evidence.**

You have numerous options for the kinds of evidence you can use in an argument, including personal experience, observations, interviews, questionnaires, field or laboratory research, or findings derived from researching primary or secondary sources found in libraries, databases, or the web. Carmen Tieu's argument in Chapter 3 is based on personal experience. More commonly, college arguments require library and Internet research—skills we teach in Part Two (Entering an Argumentative Conversation") and Part Five ("The Researched Argument"). This chapter focuses more basically on how evidence functions rhetorically in an argument and how it is selected and framed.

We begin by categorizing and evaluating different kinds of evidence, illustrating how each might be incorporated into an argument.

DATA FROM PERSONAL EXPERIENCE   One powerful kind of evidence comes from personal experience.

Example	Strengths and Limitations
Despite recent criticism that Ritalin is overprescribed for hyperactivity and attention deficit disorder, it can often seem like a miracle drug. My little brother is a perfect example. Before he was given Ritalin, he was a terror in school . . . . [Tell the "before" and "after" story of your little brother.]	• Personal-experience examples help readers identify with the writer; they show the writer's personal connection to the issue. • Vivid stories capture the imagination and appeal to *pathos*. • Skeptics may sometimes argue that personal-experience examples are insufficient (the writer is guilty of hasty generalization), not typical, or not adequately scientific or verifiable.

DATA FROM OBSERVATION OR FIELD RESEARCH   You can also develop evidence by personally observing a phenomenon or by doing your own field research.

Example	Strengths and Limitations
The intersection at Fifth and Montgomery is particularly dangerous because pedestrians almost never find a comfortable break in the heavy flow of cars. On April 29, I watched fifty-seven pedestrians cross the street. Not once did cars driving in either direction on Fifth Avenue stop before the pedestrian stepped off the sidewalk to cross Montgomery Street. [Continue with observed data about danger.]	• Field research imparts a sense of scientific credibility. • Observations and field research increase typicality by expanding the database beyond a single example. • Observation and field research enhance the *ethos* of the writer as personally invested and reasonable. • Skeptics may point to flaws in how observations were conducted, showing how data are insufficient, inaccurate, or nontypical.

DATA FROM INTERVIEWS, QUESTIONNAIRES, AND SURVEYS   You can also gather data by interviewing stakeholders in a controversy, creating questionnaires, or conducting surveys.

Example	Strengths and Limitations
Another reason to ban laptops from classrooms is the extent to which laptop users disturb other students. In a questionnaire that I distributed to fifty students in my residence hall, a surprising 60 percent said that they are annoyed by fellow students checking Instagram, sending e-mail, paying their bills, or surfing the Web while pretending to take notes in class. Additionally, I interviewed five students who gave me specific examples of how these distractions interfere with learning. [Report the examples.]	• Interviews, questionnaires, and surveys enhance the sufficiency and typicality of evidence by expanding the database beyond the experiences of one person. • Quantitative data from questionnaires and surveys often increase the argument's scientific feel. • Surveys and questionnaires often uncover local or recent data not available in published research. • Interviews can provide engaging personal stories, thus enhancing *pathos*. • Skeptics can raise doubts about research methodology, questionnaire design, or typicality of interview subjects.

DATA FROM LIBRARY OR INTERNET RESEARCH   For many arguments, evidence is derived from reading, particularly from library or Internet research. Appendix 2 helps you conduct effective research and incorporate research sources into your arguments.

Example	Strengths and Limitations
The belief that a high-carbohydrate, low-fat diet is the best way to lose weight has been challenged by research conducted by Walter Willett and his colleagues in the department of nutrition at the Harvard School of Public Health. Willett's research suggests that complex carbohydrates such as pasta and potatoes spike glucose levels, increasing the risk of diabetes. Additionally, some fats—especially monounsaturated and polyunsaturated fats found in nuts, fish, and most vegetable oils—help lower "bad" cholesterol levels (45).*	• Researched evidence is often powerful, especially when sources speak with verifiable authority/expertise on their subjects and are respected by your audience; writers can spotlight the source's credentials through attributive tags (see Appendix 2). • Researched data may take the form of facts, examples, quotations, summaries of research studies, and so forth. • Skeptics might doubt the accuracy of facts, the credentials of a source, or the research design of a study. They might also cite studies with different results. • Skeptics might raise doubts about sufficiency, typicality, or relevance of your research data.

TESTIMONY   Writers frequently use testimony when direct data are either unavailable or highly technical or complex. Testimonial evidence can come from research or from interviews.

Example	Strengths and Limitations
Although the Swedish economist Bjorn Lomborg claims that acid rain is not a significant problem, many environmentalists disagree. According to David Bellamany, president of the Conservation Foundation, "Acid rain does kill forests and people around the world, and it's still doing so in the most polluted places, such as Russia" (qtd. in *BBC News*).	• By itself, testimony is generally less persuasive than direct data. • Persuasiveness can be increased if the source has impressive credentials, which the writer can convey through attributive tags introducing the testimony. • Skeptics might undermine testimonial evidence by questioning the source's credentials, showing the source's bias, or quoting a countersource.

STATISTICAL DATA   Many contemporary arguments rely heavily on statistical data, often supplemented by graphics such as tables, pie charts, and graphs. (See Chapter 9 for a discussion of the use of graphics in argument.)

Example	Strengths and Limitations
After graduating from college, millennials aren't leaving their parents' homes the way college graduates used to. According to the U.S. Census Bureau's 2015 American Community Survey, 34.1 percent of people between the ages of eighteen and thirty-four lived in their parents' households, with the percentage even higher in states with high real-estate costs.	• Statistics can provide powerful snapshots of aggregate data from a wide database. • Statistics are often used in conjunction with graphics. • Statistics can be calculated and displayed in different ways to achieve different rhetorical effects, so the reader must be wary. • Skeptics might question statistical methods, research design, and interpretation of data.

HYPOTHETICAL EXAMPLES, CASES, AND SCENARIOS   Arguments occasionally use hypothetical examples, cases, or scenarios, particularly to illustrate conjectured consequences of an event or to test philosophical hypotheses.

---

*Parenthetical citations in this example and the next follow the MLA documentation system. See Appendix 2 for a discussion of how to cite and document sources.

Example	Strengths and Limitations
Consider what might happen if we continue to use biotech soybeans that are resistant to herbicides. The resistant gene, through cross-pollination, might be transferred to an ordinary weed, creating an out-of-control superweed that herbicides couldn't kill. Such a superweed could be an ecological disaster.	• Scenarios have strong imaginative appeal. • Scenarios are persuasive only if they seem plausible. • A scenario narrative often conveys a sense of "inevitability" even if the actual scenario is unlikely; hence, the rhetorical effect may be illogical. • Skeptics might show the implausibility of the scenario or offer an alternative scenario.

REASONED SEQUENCE OF IDEAS   Sometimes arguments are supported with a reasoned sequence of ideas rather than with concrete facts or other forms of empirical evidence. The writer's goal is to support a point through a logical progression of ideas. Such arguments are conceptual, supported by linked ideas, rather than evidential. This kind of support occurs frequently in arguments and is often intermingled with evidential support.

Example	Strengths and Limitations
Embryonic stem cell research, despite its promise in fighting diseases, may have negative social consequences. This research encourages us to place embryos in the category of mere cellular matter that can be manipulated at will. Currently we reduce animals to this category when we genetically alter them for human purposes, such as engineering pigs to grow more human-like heart valves for use in transplants. Using human embryos in the same way—as material that can be altered and destroyed at will—may benefit society materially, but this quest for greater knowledge and control involves a reclassifying of embryos that could potentially lead to a devaluing of human life.	• These sequences are often used in causal arguments to show how causes are linked to effects or in definitional or values arguments to show links among ideas. • A sequence of ideas has great potential to clarify values and show the belief structure on which a claim is founded. • A sequence of ideas can sketch out ideas and connections that would otherwise remain latent. • The effectiveness of this type of evidence depends on the audience's acceptance of each link in the sequence of ideas. • Skeptics might raise objections at any link in the sequence, often by pointing to different values or outlining different consequences.

The Persuasive Use of Evidence

4.2   **Make your evidence persuasive by using the STAR criteria and other strategies.**

We turn now from kinds of evidence to strategies for making evidence as convincing and persuasive as possible. Consider a target audience of educated, reasonable, and careful readers who approach an issue with healthy skepticism, open-minded but cautious. What demands would such readers make on a writer's use of evidence? To answer that question, let's look at some general principles for using evidence persuasively.

Apply the STAR Criteria to Evidence

Our open-minded but skeptical audience would expect the evidence to meet what rhetorician Richard Fulkerson calls the STAR criteria:*

---

*Richard Fulkerson, *Teaching the Argument in Writing* (Urbana, IL: National Council of Teachers of English, 1996), 44–53. In this section, we are indebted to Fulkerson's discussion.

Sufficiency: Is there enough evidence?

Typicality: Is the chosen evidence representative and typical?

Accuracy: Is the evidence accurate and up-to-date?

Relevance: Is the evidence relevant to the claim?

Let's examine each in turn.

SUFFICIENCY OF EVIDENCE   How much evidence you need is a function of your rhetorical context. In a court trial, opposing attorneys often agree to waive evidence for points that aren't in doubt in order to concentrate on contested points. The more contested a claim or the more skeptical your audience, the more evidence you may need to present. On the one hand, if you provide too little evidence you may be accused of *hasty generalization* (see Appendix 1), a reasoning fallacy in which you make a sweeping conclusion based on only one or two instances. On the other hand, if you provide too much evidence your argument may become overly long and tedious. You can guard against having too little or too much evidence by appropriately qualifying the claim your evidence supports.

Strong claim: Working full-time seriously harms a student's grade point average (much data needed—probably a combination of examples and statistical studies).

Qualified claim: Working full-time often harms a student's grade point average (a few representative examples may be enough).

TYPICALITY OF EVIDENCE   If readers are to trust your evidence, they need to be confident that you have chosen typical and representative cases rather than extreme or outlier cases. Suppose that you want to argue that students can successfully work full-time while going to college full-time. You cite the case of your friend Pam, who earned a straight-A grade point average while working forty hours per week as a night receptionist in a small hotel. Your audience might doubt the typicality of Pam's case because a night receptionist can often use work hours for studying. What about more typical jobs, they'll ask, where you can't study while you work?

ACCURACY OF EVIDENCE   Evidence can't be used ethically unless it is accurate and up-to-date, and it can't be persuasive unless the audience believes in the credibility of the writer's sources. This criterion is particularly important in an era of "fake news" and "alternative facts." Arguers need to evaluate their sources, analyzing where each source might be placed on the continuum from "truth-seeking" to "persuasion" (see Figure 1.2.) Ethical arguers must also develop an eye and ear for identifying reliable sources of data, distinguishing, for example, between widely respected news and public affairs sites and potential fake news sites. Later in this section, we illustrate our own fact-checking search to ensure the accuracy of a piece of evidence, explaining how we tracked down the original source for a piece of data cited in a *The New Yorker* article.

RELEVANCE OF EVIDENCE   Finally, evidence will be persuasive only if the reader considers it relevant to what is at stake in the dispute. Consider the following student argument: "I deserve an A in this course because I worked exceptionally hard." The student then cites substantial evidence of how hard he worked—a log of study hours, copies of multiple drafts of papers, testimony from friends, and so forth. But what is at stake here is the underlying assumption (warrant) that grades should be based on effort, not quality of work. The student provides ample evidence to support the reason ("I worked exceptionally hard"), but this evidence is irrelevant to the warrant ("People who work exceptionally hard deserve an A"). Although some instructors may give partial credit for effort, the criterion for grades is usually the quality of the student's performance, not the student's time spent studying.

Establish a Trustworthy *Ethos*

Besides supplying evidence that meets the STAR criteria, you can make your evidence more persuasive by being fair, honest, and open to uncertainty (the appeal to *ethos*—see Chapter 5). To establish your readers' confidence, you must first tell them the source of your evidence. If your evidence comes from personal experience or observation, your prose needs to make that clear. If your evidence comes from others (for example, through interviews or library/Internet research), you must indicate these sources through attributive tags (phrases like "according to T. Alvarez" or "as stated by a recent EPA report"). For academic papers, you must also cite and document your sources using an appropriate style for in-text citations and concluding bibliography (see Appendix 2). Finally, you need to be fair in the way you select evidence from your research sources. For example, it is unethical to take quotations out of context or to write an unfair summary that oversimplifies or distorts a source author's intended meaning.

Be Mindful of a Source's Distance from Original Data

When you support an argument through library/Internet research, you often encounter sources that report evidence from a second- or third-hand perspective. You need to imagine where your source author found the information that you now want to use in your own argument. How might you trace the process that led from the original data to your source author's use of it? Let's take as an example a passage from an article on the minimum wage by James Surowiecki writing for *The New Yorker*. (You can read the full article in Chapter 8.) Because the source is a magazine article rather than an academic paper, it contains no footnotes or bibliography, but the author nevertheless uses attributive tags to identify his main sources. Here is a passage from the article:

Passage from "The Pay Is Too Damn Low" by James Surowiecki

[O]ver the past three decades, the U.S. economy has done a poor job of creating good middle-class jobs; five of the six fastest-growing job categories today pay less than the median wage. That's why, as a recent study by the economists John Schmitt and Janelle Jones has shown, low-wage workers are older and better educated than ever. More important, more of them are relying on their paychecks not for pin money or to pay for Friday-night dates but, rather, to support families.

> Attributive tag (cites this study as his source)
>
> Purported factual statement that we are examining

Much of Surowiecki's argument for increasing the minimum wage depends on evidence that low-wage workers are "older and better educated than ever."

But we might ask: How does Surowiecki know about the age and education of low-wage workers? Why should we trust him? Using an attributive tag, he identifies his source as a recent study by economists John Schmitt and Janelle Jones. We conducted a Google search and quickly located the source: a working paper titled "Low-Wage Workers Are Older and Better Educated than Ever," dated April 2012. The paper was published by the Center for Economic and Policy Research, which, according to its Web site, is a nonprofit, nonpartisan research center aimed at providing factual economic data for public policy makers. So where did Schmitt and Jones get their data? They cite statistical tables compiled by the *Current Population Survey*, which is a joint effort of the Census Bureau and the Bureau of Labor Statistics. Based on these original data, Schmitt and Jones constructed two graphs showing shifts in the distribution of low-wage workers by age and then by education from 1971 to 2011. One of these graphs shows that in 1979, 26 percent of low-wage jobs were held by teenagers, but by 2011 only 12 percent of low-wage jobs were held by teenagers. (You can see this graph in Figure 8.2.) In contrast, Schmitt and Jones's second graph shows that in 1979 only 25 percent of low-wage job holders had completed at least some college, but by 2011, 43 percent had completed some college.

Let's summarize the process we have just traced. The original data came from government statistics collected by the Census Bureau and the Bureau of Labor Statistics. Schmitt and Jones then converted these data into detailed graphs. Surowiecki then summarized the graphs' message into a single sentence. If you were to cite Surowiecki as your source of this same information ("low-wage workers are older and better educated than ever"), you would be depending on a chain of trust stretching from the original data through Schmitt and Jones and Surowiecki to you. Of course, you can't be expected to trace all your research-gathered evidence back to the original data, but you need to imagine that it is possible to do so.

Rhetorical Understanding of Evidence

4.3   **Understand evidence rhetorically by explaining how the selection and framing of evidence reveal an angle of vision.**

In the previous section we presented some principles for persuasive use of evidence. We now ask you to look more closely at the rhetorical context in which evidence operates.

Angle of Vision and the Selection and Framing of Evidence

When we enter the argumentative arena, we arrive as complex, whole persons, not as disembodied computers that reach claims through a value-free calculus. We enter with our own ideologies, beliefs, values, and guiding assumptions as formed by our particular lived lives. These differences help explain why one person's terrorist might be another person's freedom fighter, or why a handgun in a drawer might be one person's defense against intruders and another person's accident waiting to happen. In writing about guns, a believer in Second Amendment rights is apt to cite evidence that having a gun can stop a violent intruder or prevent a rape. Conversely, proponents of gun control are apt to cite evidence about accidental deaths or suicides. In an argument, evidence is always selected to further the arguer's claim and is never simply an inert, neutral "fact."

These guiding beliefs and values work together to create a writer's *angle of vision*: a perspective, bias, lens, filter, frame, or screen that helps determine what a writer sees or doesn't see. This angle of vision makes certain items stand out in a field of data while other items become invisible. The angle of vision both determines and reveals the writer's view of which data are important and significant, and which data are trivial and can be ignored.

To help you better understand the concepts of selection and framing, we offer the following exercise based on different angles of vision regarding Uber, the ride-sharing company. Wildly popular in many cities, Uber has been accused of unfair or unsafe business practices causing dilemmas for city governments, regulatory agencies, insurance companies, and customers who want to avoid supporting socially irresponsible companies.

Suppose that your city has scheduled a public hearing on whether Uber needs stricter government regulations—either for public safety or for ensuring fair business practices. The following pieces of data and evidence are available to the people who plan to attend the hearing.

- Uber has provided income opportunity for over 1 million drivers.
- Customers generally love Uber for the ease of its rider experience. The rider is automatically billed through the mobile app without the need to pull out a credit card or pay a tip.
- Some Uber drivers have complained of low pay and stressful work conditions. Uber data show that 11 percent of Uber drivers quit within a month, and about half quit within a year.
- Uber classifies its drivers as independent contractors rather than employees. Therefore, Uber doesn't have to provide health insurance, overtime pay, and other benefits.
- As independent contractors, Uber drivers have the freedom to work any hours they wish, and they accept only the riders and destinations they choose.
- In San Francisco, an Uber driver who was watching his Uber app for a potential rider struck a six-year-old girl in a crosswalk. The parents sued Uber, but Uber lawyers claimed that the company bore no responsibility for the accident because the driver was an independent contractor and was not carrying a rider.
- Uber stores every user's ride-history data. If your Uber app is running, Uber can also track your location even if you aren't requesting an Uber ride. Uber has been accused of using its tracking data to dig up dirt on journalists who are critical of Uber and to spy on Uber's rivals.
- Several independent studies have shown that a rollout of Uber in new areas is frequently associated with a decrease in drunk driving incidents.
- Several American cities have reported instances of Uber drivers sexually assaulting passengers. Two lawsuits in California accuse Uber of misleading

customers about the quality of their background checks for drivers. As part of the suits, district attorneys cited findings that twenty-five Uber drivers in San Francisco and Los Angeles had criminal records.

- An Australian report found that Uber is less risky than a taxi because both passengers and drivers have profiles that can be checked before pickup. Unlike taxi services, Uber provides an online record of who the driver is.

- Taxicab drivers and union leaders complain that Uber's "surge pricing" policies are unfair to both regulated taxi companies and to customers. During low demand times, Uber is cheaper than taxis; during surge times, customers are often surprised by a bill that is higher than what a taxi company would charge.

- One union leader for taxi drivers said: "Either the city should deregulate us [taxis] completely, like them [Uber] . . . or regulate them at least closer to us, and let there be fair business competition."

For Writing and Discussion
Creating Contrasting Angles of Vision

Individual task:

Drawing on data that you select from the above list, compose two short speeches, one supporting the current Uber business model and one calling for more government regulation of Uber. Be ready to explain how you selected and framed data to create a pro-Uber angle of vision in one speech and an anti-Uber angle of vision in the other. How do data highlighted in one of your speeches become "less seen" or even "unseen" in the other?

Group task:

Working in pairs or as a whole class, share your speeches with classmates. Then, after you have shared examples, explain the approaches that different classmates employed. What principle of selection was used? If arguers included evidence contrary to their positions, how did they handle it, respond to it, minimize its importance, or otherwise channel its rhetorical effect?

Rhetorical Strategies for Framing Evidence

What we hope you learned from the preceding exercises is that an arguer consciously selects evidence from a wide field of data and then frames these data through rhetorical strategies that emphasize some data, minimize other data, and guide the reader's response. Now that you have a basic idea of what it means to frame evidence, here are some strategies you can use to guide what the reader sees and feels.

STRATEGIES FOR FRAMING EVIDENCE

- **Controlling the space given to supporting versus contrary evidence.** Depending on your audience and purpose, you can devote most of your space to supporting evidence and minimal space to contrary evidence (or omit it entirely). Thus, people arguing in favor of Uber's current business model may have used the pro-Uber evidence from the list while omitting (or summarizing very briefly) the negative data about Uber.

- **Emphasizing a detailed story versus presenting a lot of facts and statistics.** Often, you can choose to support a point with a memorable individual case or with aggregate data such as statistics or lists of facts. A memorable story can have a strongly persuasive effect. For example, to argue for more government regulation of Uber, you might tell the harrowing story of the parents who sued Uber when a distracted Uber driver killed their daughter in a crosswalk. In contrast, a supporter of Uber might tell stories of happy Uber customers using the Uber app instead of standing on a corner trying to hail a taxi.

  A different strategy is to use aggregate data such as facts and statistics rather than narratives. For example, a pro-regulation (anti-Uber) argument might use graphs to show how Uber has cut into the revenue stream of taxi companies, or it might use comparative data about the way different cities, states, or governments have tried to regulate ride-sharing companies like Uber and Lyft. In contrast, a pro-Uber argument might use data showing the cost savings of using uber rather than taxis.

  Each method has its own strengths and weaknesses. The narrative story often has a powerful rhetorical effect, but it is always open to the charge that it is an insufficient or nonrepresentative example. Vivid anecdotes make for engaging reading, but by themselves they may not be compelling logically. In contrast, aggregate data, often used in scholarly publications, can provide more compelling, logical evidence but sometimes make the prose wonkish and dense.

- **Providing contextual and interpretive comments when presenting data.** When citing data, you can add brief contextual or interpretive comments that act as lenses over the readers' eyes to help them see the data from your perspective. Suppose you want to support Uber, but you also want to admit that the Uber business model creates new problems. You could make these problems seem inconsequential with this sentence: "It is true that Uber has had occasional start-up problems, but that is to be expected whenever free enterprise creates a better business model." That sentence identifies Uber with creative free enterprise while minimizing Uber's problems as "typical" of all start-ups. An Uber supporter might also spin Uber positively through an interpretive analogy that positions Uber as "modern" and taxis as obsolete: "Protecting taxi companies by regulating Uber is like protecting stagecoaches by regulating trains."

- **Putting contrary evidence in subordinate positions.** Just as a photographer can emphasize or deemphasize an object by placing it in the center or the background of a photograph, you can place a piece of data in a subordinate or main clause of a sentence. Note how the structure of the following sentences changes the writer's angle of vision:

  - "Although Uber drivers sometimes complain of stressful work conditions and low pay, they are free as independent contractors to work any hours they wish and accept only the riders and destinations they choose." (negative data in subordinate clause deemphasizes it)

  - "Although Uber drivers are free to work any times they wish and to accept only the rides and destinations they choose, drivers' complaints about low pay and high stress are frequent." (negative data in main clause emphasizes it).

- **Choosing labels and names that guide the reader's response to data.** One of the most subtle ways to control your readers' response to data is to choose labels and names that prompt them to see the issue as you do. If you like Uber, you might call its business model "creative entrepreneurship," praising Uber for destroying the old, clunky regulations on taxis. In contrast, if you dislike Uber, you might call it a "dangerously unregulated predator" that steals fares from hardworking taxi drivers. The labels you choose, along with the connotations of the words you select, urge your reader to share your angle of vision.

- **Using images (photographs, drawings, other graphics) to guide the reader's response to data.** Another strategy for moving your audience toward your angle of vision is to include a photograph, drawing, or other graphic that portrays a contested issue from your perspective. Supporters of Uber might include an up-close photograph of an Uber app showing the location of the approaching driver. Anti-Uber images might depict taxi drivers participating in a protest demonstration. (See Chapter 9 for a complete discussion of using visuals in argument.)

- **Revealing the value system that determines the writer's selection and framing of data.** Ultimately, how you select and frame evidence is linked to the system of values that organizes your argument. If you admire Uber, you probably favor technological innovation and the "creative destruction" (of older business models) made possible by free markets. You might want government to require background checks for Uber drivers, but in general you likely want the government to stay out of the free market. If you don't admire Uber, you probably favor more government regulation aimed at ensuring consumer safety, enhancing workers' rights, and protecting consumers against fraud or false advertising. You may also have doubts about the sharing economy, which may benefit consumers but may have long-range negative effects on workers. If you are targeting an audience that shares your assumptions, you can frame your selected data by stating explicitly the values that guide your argument.

Strategies for Framing Statistical Evidence

Numbers and statistical data can be framed in so many ways that this category of evidence deserves a much closer look. By recognizing how writers frame numbers to support the story they want to tell, you will always be aware that other stories are also possible. Ethical use of numbers means that you use reputable sources for your basic data, that you don't invent or distort numbers to suit your own purposes, and that you don't ignore alternative points of view. Here are some of the choices you can make when framing statistical data:

- **Numbers versus percentages.** You can alter the rhetorical effect of a statistic by choosing between numbers and percentages. If your uncle reports a $5,000 drop in his retirement account, that sounds scary. It sounds much less scary if he reports a 1 percent drop. You can apply this framing option directly to the Uber case. To emphasize the danger of sexual assault by an Uber driver, you can say that in a given year eight persons filed sexual assault suits against Uber. This use of numbers emphasizes each reported case. To minimize this statistic, you could report it as a percentage of the total number of Uber rides within the United States in a given year. When reported as a percentage, the sexual assault rate by Uber drivers is a tiny fraction of 1 percent.

- **Median versus mean.** Another way to alter the rhetorical effect of numbers is to choose between the median and the mean. The *mean* is the average of all numbers in a list. The *median* is the middle number when all the numbers are arranged in order from high to low. In 2016 the mean annual income of retirees aged 70–74 in the United States was $38,000—not a large amount of income, but enough to live on comfortably if the retirees owned their own home. However, retirees' median income in 2016 was only $23,000, a figure that points to a much more unequal income distribution among older Americans. This median figure means that half of the retired persons in this age bracket had annual incomes of $23,000 or less—close to poverty level. The much higher mean income indicates that some retired Americans are very wealthy. This wealth raises the average of all incomes (the mean) but doesn't affect the median.

- **Unadjusted versus adjusted numbers.** Suppose your boss tells you that you are getting a 5 percent raise. You might be happy—unless inflation rates are running at 6 percent. Economic data can be hard to interpret across time unless the dollar amounts are adjusted for inflation. This same problem occurs in other areas. For example, comparing grade point averages of college graduates in 1970 versus 2016 means little unless one can somehow adjust the numbers for grade inflation.

- **Interval sizes on graphs.** Whenever you draw a line graph, you can manipulate a curve's slope (angle) by the intervals you choose on the vertical axis. If you want to make a graph showing that Earth's average temperature has increased by 1.5 degrees Fahrenheit since 1850, the curve will look steep if you choose ½ degree intervals on the vertical axis. However, if you choose five-degree intervals, the curve will look almost flat. You can see this difference by comparing graphs produced by climate scientists (where global warming is made to "pop out") versus those produced by climate skeptics (where global warming is made to seem nonexistent). For more on graphic display of data, see Chapter 9.

For Writing and Discussion
Using Strategies to Frame Statistical Evidence

A proposal to build a publicly funded sports stadium in a major American city yielded a wide range of statistical arguments. All of the following statements are reasonably faithful to the same facts:

- The stadium would be paid for by raising the sales tax from 8.2 percent to 8.3 percent for a twenty-year period.
- The sales tax increase is one-tenth of 1 percent.
- The sales tax increase represents an average of $7.50 per person per year—about the price of a special coffee drink and a pastry.
- The sales tax increase represents $750 per five-person family over the twenty-year period in which the higher tax is in effect.
- For a family building a new home in this city, this tax will increase building costs by $200.
- This is a $250 million tax increase for city residents.

How would you describe the costs of the proposed sports stadium if you opposed the proposal?
How would you describe the costs if you supported the proposal?

Creating a Plan for Gathering Evidence

As you begin contemplating an argument, you can use the following checklist to help you think of possible sources for evidence.

A CHECKLIST FOR BRAINSTORMING SOURCES OF EVIDENCE

- What personal experiences have you had with this issue? What details from your life or the lives of your friends, acquaintances, or relatives might serve as examples or other kinds of evidence?
- What observational studies would be relevant to this issue?
- Which people could you interview to provide insights or expert knowledge on this issue?
- Which questions about your issue could be researched with a survey or questionnaire?
- What useful information on this issue might encyclopedias or specialized reference works in your university library provide?
- What evidence might you seek on this issue using licensed databases to search for relevant articles from magazines, newspapers, and scholarly journals?
- How might an Internet search help you research this issue?
- What evidence might you find on this issue from reliable statistical resources such as the U.S. Census Bureau, the Centers for Disease Control, or the website USA.gov? (For more information on the last four points, see Chapter 16.)

Writing Assignment

A Supporting-Reasons Argument

Write an argument that uses at least two reasons to support your claim and appropriate evidence to develop your reasons. Your argument should include the features of a classical argument described at the beginning of Chapter 2 except that you can omit the section on summarizing and responding to opposing views, which we will cover in Chapter 6. This assignment builds on the brief writing assignments in Chapter 2 (create a thesis statement for an argument) and Chapter 3 (brainstorm support for one of your enthymemes using the Toulmin schema). Like a complete classical argument, a supporting-reasons argument has a thesis-governed structure in which you state your claim at the end of the introduction, begin body paragraphs with clearly stated reasons, and use effective transitions throughout to keep your reader on track. In developing your own argument, place your most important, persuasive, or interesting reason last, where it will have the greatest impact on your readers. A model for a supporting-reasons argument is Carmen Tieu's "Why Violent Video Games Are Good for Girls" in Chapter 3.

Chapter 5
Moving Your Audience

Ethos, Pathos, and Kairos

Learning Objectives

In this chapter you will learn to:

5.1 Explain how the classical appeals of *logos*, *ethos*, and *pathos* work together to move your audience.

5.2 Create effective appeals to *ethos*.

5.3 Create effective appeals to *pathos*.

5.4 Be mindful of *kairos* or the "timeliness" of your argument.

5.5 Explain how images make visual appeals to *logos*, *ethos*, *pathos*, and *kairos*.

5.6 Explain how audience-based reasons appeal to *logos*, *ethos*, *pathos*, and *kairos*.

In Chapters 3 and 4 we focused on *logos*—the logical structure of reasons and evidence in argument. Even though we have treated *logos* in its own chapters, an effective arguer's concern for *logos* is always connected to *ethos* and *pathos* (see the rhetorical triangle in Figure 2.2) and always considers the *kairos*, or timeliness of the argument. This chapter explains how arguers can create effective appeals from *ethos*, *pathos*, and *kairos*. It also explains the crucial role played by concrete language, examples, narrative stories, and use of images in enhancing ethical and emotional appeals. We conclude by showing how audience-based reasons enhance *logos* while also appealing to *ethos* and *pathos*.

Logos, *Ethos*, and *Pathos* as Persuasive Appeals: An Overview

5.1 **Explain how the classical appeals of *logos*, *ethos*, and *pathos* work together to move your audience.**

To see how *logos*, *ethos*, and *pathos* work together to create an impact on the reader, consider the different impacts of the following arguments, all having roughly the same logical appeal.

1. People should adopt a vegetarian diet because doing so will help prevent the cruelty to animals caused by factory farming.

2. If you are planning to eat chicken tonight, please consider how much that chicken suffered so that you could have a tender and juicy meal. Commercial growers cram the chickens so tightly together into cages that they never walk on their own legs, see sunshine, or flap their wings. In fact, their beaks must be cut off to keep them from pecking each other's eyes out. One way to prevent such suffering is for more people to become vegetarians.

3. People who eat meat are no better than sadists who torture other sentient creatures to enhance their own pleasure. Unless you enjoy sadistic tyranny over others, you have only one choice: Become a vegetarian.

4. People committed to justice might consider the extent to which our love of eating meat requires the agony of animals. A visit to a modern chicken factory—where chickens live their entire lives in tiny, darkened coops without room to spread their wings—might raise doubts about our right to inflict such suffering on sentient creatures. Indeed, such a visit might persuade us that vegetarianism is a more just alternative.

Each argument has roughly the same logical core:

But the impact of each argument varies. The difference between arguments 1 and 2, most of our students report, is the greater emotional power of argument 2. Whereas

---

ENTHYMEME

CLAIM: People should adopt a vegetarian diet

REASON: because doing so will help prevent the cruelty to animals caused by factory farming.

GROUNDS

- Evidence of suffering in commercial chicken farms, where chickens are crammed together and lash out at one another

- Evidence that only widespread adoption of vegetarianism will end factory farming

WARRANT

If we have an alternative to making animals suffer, we should use it.

argument 1 refers only to the abstraction "cruelty to animals," argument 2 paints a vivid picture of chickens with their beaks cut off to prevent their pecking each other blind. Argument 2 makes a stronger appeal to *pathos* (not necessarily a stronger argument), stirring feelings by appealing simultaneously to the heart and to the head.

The difference between arguments 1 and 3 concerns both *ethos* and *pathos*. Argument 3 appeals to the emotions through highly charged words such as *torture, sadists,* and *tyranny*. But argument 3 also draws attention to its writer, and most of our students report not liking that writer very much. His stance is self-righteous and insulting. In contrast, argument 4's author establishes a more positive *ethos*. He establishes rapport by assuming his audience is committed to justice and by qualifying his argument with the conditional term *might*. He also invites sympathy for the chickens' plight—an appeal to *pathos*—by offering a specific description of chickens crammed into tiny coops.

Which of these arguments is best? The answer depends on the intended audience. Arguments 1 and 4 seem aimed at receptive audiences reasonably open to exploration of the issue, whereas arguments 2 and 3 seem designed to shock complacent audiences or to rally a group of true believers. Even argument 3, which is too abusive to be effective in most instances, might work as a rallying speech at a convention of animal liberation activists.

Our point thus far is that *logos, ethos,* and *pathos* are different aspects of the same whole, different lenses for intensifying or softening the light beam you project onto the screen. Every choice you make as a writer affects in some way each of the three appeals. The rest of this chapter examines these choices in more detail.

How to Create an Effective *Ethos*: The Appeal to Credibility

5.2   Create effective appeals to *ethos*.

The ancient Greek and Roman rhetoricians recognized that an argument would be more persuasive if the audience trusted the speaker. Aristotle argued that such trust resides within the speech itself, not in the speaker's prior reputation. Speakers project their credibility through their manner and delivery, their tone, their word choice, their use of trustworthy evidence, and the sympathy and fairness with which they treat alternative views. Aristotle called the impact of the speaker's credibility the appeal from *ethos*. How does a writer create credibility? We suggest four ways:

- **Be knowledgeable about your issue.** The first way to gain credibility is to *be* credible—that is, to argue from a strong base of knowledge, to have at hand the examples, personal experiences, statistics, and other empirical data needed to make a sound case. If you have done your homework, you will command the attention of most audiences.

- **Be fair.** Besides being knowledgeable about your issue, you need to demonstrate fairness and courtesy to alternative views. Because true argument can occur only where people may reasonably disagree with one another, your *ethos* will be strengthened if you demonstrate that you understand and empathize with other points of view. There are times when you may appropriately scorn an opposing view. But these times are rare, and they mostly occur when you address audiences predisposed to your view. Demonstrating empathy to alternative views is generally the best strategy.

- **Build a bridge to your audience.** A third means of establishing credibility—building a bridge to your audience—has been treated at length in our earlier discussions of audience-based reasons. By grounding your argument in shared values and assumptions, you demonstrate your goodwill and enhance your image as a trustworthy person respectful of your audience's views. We mention audience-based reasons here to show how this aspect of *logos*—finding the reasons that are most rooted in the audience's values—also affects your *ethos* as a person respectful of your readers' views.

- **Demonstrate professionalism.** Finally, you can enhance your *ethos* by the professionalism revealed in your manuscript itself. Appropriate style, careful editing and proofreading, accurate documentation, and adherence to the genre conventions expected by your audience all contribute to the image of the person behind the writing. If your manuscript is sloppy, marred by spelling or grammatical errors, or inattentive to the tone and style of the expected genre, your credibility will be damaged.

How to Create *Pathos*: The Appeal to Beliefs and Emotions

5.3   Create effective appeals to *pathos*.

Although commonly defined as an "appeal to the emotions," *pathos* evokes effects that are subtler and more complex than the word *emotions* suggests. Arguers create pathetic appeals whenever they connect their claims to readers' values, thus triggering positive or negative feelings depending on whether these values are affirmed or transgressed. Because understanding is a matter of feeling as well as perceiving, *pathos* can give access to nonlogical, but not necessarily nonrational, ways of knowing. *Pathos* helps us see what is deeply at stake in an issue, what matters to the whole person. Appeals to *pathos* help readers walk in the writer's shoes. That is why arguments are often improved through stories that make issues come alive or sensory details that allow us to see, feel, and taste the reality of a problem.

Although it is difficult to classify all the ways that writers can create appeals from *pathos*, we will focus on four strategies: concrete language; specific examples and illustrations; narratives; and connotations of words, metaphors, and analogies.

Use Concrete Language

Concrete language—one of the chief ways that writers achieve voice—can increase the liveliness, interest level, and personality of a writer's prose. When used in argument, concrete language typically heightens *pathos*. For example, consider the differences between the first and second drafts of the following student argument:

FIRST DRAFT

People who prefer driving a car to taking a bus think that taking the bus will increase the stress of the daily commute. Just the opposite is true. Not being able to find a parking spot when in a hurry to be at work or school can cause a person stress. Taking the bus gives a person time to read or sleep, etc. It could be used as a mental break.

SECOND DRAFT (CONCRETE LANGUAGE ADDED)

> Taking the bus can be more relaxing than driving a car. Having someone else behind the wheel gives people time to chat with friends or study for an exam. They can check Instagram and Twitter, send text messages, doze off, read their favorite news website, or get lost in a novel rather than foam at the mouth looking for a parking space.

In this revision, specific details enliven the prose by creating images that evoke positive feelings. Who wouldn't want some free time to doze off or to get lost in a novel?

Use Specific Examples and Illustrations

Specific examples and illustrations serve two purposes in an argument: They provide evidence that supports your reasons; simultaneously, they give your argument presence and emotional resonance. Note the flatness of the following draft arguing for the value of multicultural studies in a university core curriculum:

FIRST DRAFT

> Another advantage of a multicultural education is that it will help us see our own culture in a broader perspective. If all we know is our own heritage, we might not be inclined to see anything bad about this heritage because we won't know anything else. But if we study other heritages, we can see the costs and benefits of our own heritage.

Now note the increase in presence and emotional resonance when the writer adds a specific example:

SECOND DRAFT (EXAMPLE ADDED)

> Another advantage of multicultural education is that it raises questions about traditional Western values. For example, owning private property (such as buying your own home) is part of the American dream. However, in studying the beliefs of American Indians, students are confronted with a very different view of private property. When the U.S. government sought to buy land in the Pacific Northwest from Chief Sealth, he is alleged to have replied:
>
>> The president in Washington sends words that he wishes to buy our land. But how can you buy or sell the sky? The land? The idea is strange to us. If we do not own the freshness of the air and the sparkle of the water, how can you buy them? [. . .] We are part of the earth and it is part of us. [. . .] This we know: The earth does not belong to man, man belongs to the earth.
>
> Our class was shocked by the contrast between traditional Western views of property and Chief Sealth's views. One of our best class discussions was initiated by this quotation from Chief Sealth. Had we not been exposed to a view from another culture, we would have never been led to question the "rightness" of Western values.

   The writer begins his revision by evoking a traditional Western view of private property, which he then questions by shifting to Chief Sealth's vision of land as open, endless, and unobtainable as the sky. Through the use of a specific example, the writer brings to life his previously abstract point about the benefit of multicultural education.

Use Narratives

A particularly powerful way to evoke *pathos* is to tell a story that either leads into your claim or embodies it implicitly and that appeals to your readers' feelings and imagination. Brief narratives—whether true or hypothetical—are particularly effective as opening attention grabbers for an argument. To illustrate how an introductory narrative (either a story or a brief scene) can create appeals to *pathos*, consider the following first paragraph to an argument opposing jet skis:

> I dove off the dock into the lake, and as I approached the surface I could see the sun shining through the water. As my head popped out, I located my cousin a few feet away in a rowboat waiting to escort me as I, a twelve-year-old girl, attempted to swim across the mile-wide, pristine lake and back to our dock. I made it, and that glorious summer day is one of my most precious memories. Today, however, no one would dare attempt that swim. Jet skis have taken over this small lake where I spent many summers with my grandparents. Dozens of whining jet skis crisscross the lake, ruining it for swimming, fishing, canoeing, rowboating, and even water-skiing. More stringent state laws are needed to control jet skiing because it interferes with other uses of lakes and is currently very dangerous.

This narrative makes a case for a particular point of view toward jet skis by winning our identification with the writer's experience. She invites us to relive that experience with her while she also taps into our own treasured memories of summer experiences that have been destroyed by change.

   Opening narratives to evoke *pathos* can be powerfully effective, but they are also risky. If they are too private, too self-indulgent, too sentimental, or even too dramatic and forceful, they can backfire. If you have doubts about an opening narrative, read it to a sample audience before using it in your final draft.

Use Words, Metaphors, and Analogies with Appropriate Connotations

Another way of appealing to *pathos* is to select words, metaphors, or analogies with connotations that match your aim. We have already described this strategy in our discussion of the "framing" of evidence in Chapter 4. By using words with particular connotations, a writer guides readers to see the issue through the writer's angle of vision. Thus, if you want to create positive feelings about a recent city council decision, you can call it "bold and decisive"; if you want to create negative feelings, you can call it "short-sighted and autocratic." Similarly, writers can use favorable or unfavorable metaphors and analogies to evoke different imaginative or emotional responses. A tax bill might be viewed as a "potentially fatal poison pill" or as "unpleasant but necessary economic medicine." In each of these cases, the words create an emotional as well as intellectual response.

For Writing and Discussion

Incorporating Appeals to *Pathos*

Outside class, rewrite the introduction to one of your previous papers (or a current draft) to include more appeals to *pathos.* Use any of the strategies for giving your argument presence: concrete language, specific examples, narratives, metaphors, analogies, and connotative words. Bring both your original and your rewritten introductions to class. In pairs or in groups, discuss the comparative effectiveness of these introductions in trying to reach your intended audience.

Kairos: The Timeliness and Fitness of Arguments

5.4 Be mindful of *kairos* or the "timeliness" of your argument.

To increase your argument's effectiveness, you need to consider not only its appeals to *logos, ethos,* and *pathos,* but also its *kairos*—that is, its timing, its appropriateness for the occasion. *Kairos* is one of those wonderful words adopted from another language (in this case, ancient Greek) that is impossible to define, yet powerful in what it represents. In Greek, *kairos* means "right time," "season," or "opportunity." It differs subtly from the ordinary Greek word for time, *chronos,* the root of our words "chronology" and "chronometer." You can measure *chronos* by looking at your watch, but you measure *kairos* by sensing the opportune time through psychological attentiveness to situation and meaning. To think *kairotically* is to be attuned to the total context of a situation in order to act in the right way at the right moment. By analogy, consider a skilled base runner who senses the right moment to steal second, a wise teacher who senses the right moment to praise or critique a student's performance, or a successful psychotherapist who senses the right moment to talk rather than listen in a counseling session. *Kairos* reminds us that a rhetorical situation is not stable and fixed, but evolves as events unfold or as audiences experience the psychological ebbs and flows of attention and care. Here are some examples that illustrate the range of insights contained by the term *kairos:*

- If you write a letter to the editor of a newspaper or post a response to a blog, you usually have a one- or two-day window before a current event becomes "old news" and is no longer interesting. An out-of-date response will go unread, not because it is poorly written or argued but because it misses its *kairotic* moment.

- Similar instances of lost timeliness occur in class discussions: On how many occasions have you wanted to contribute an idea to class discussion, but the professor doesn't acknowledge your raised hand? When you finally are called on, the *kairotic* moment has passed.

- A sociology major is writing a senior capstone paper as a graduation requirement. The due date for the paper is fixed, so the timing of the paper isn't at issue. But *kairos* is still relevant. It urges the student to consider what is appropriate for such a paper. What is the "right way" to produce a sociology paper at this moment in the history of the discipline? Currently, what are leading-edge versus trailing-edge questions in sociology? What theorists are now in vogue? What research methods would most impress a judging committee? How would a good capstone paper written in 2019 differ from one written a decade earlier?

As you can see from these examples, *kairos* concerns a whole range of questions connected to the timing, fitness, appropriateness, and proportions of a message within an evolving rhetorical context. There are no rules to help you determine the *kairotic* moment for your argument, but being attuned to *kairos* will help you "read" your audience and rhetorical situation in a dynamic way.

For Writing and Discussion

Analyzing an Argument from the Perspectives of *Logos, Ethos, Pathos,* and *Kairos*

Your instructor will select an argument for analysis. Working in small groups or as a class, analyze the assigned argument first from the perspective of *kairos* and then from the perspectives of *logos, ethos,* and *pathos.*

Using Images to Appeal to *Logos, Ethos, Pathos,* and *Kairos*

5.5 Explain how images make visual appeals to *logos, ethos, pathos,* and *kairos.*

One of the most powerful ways to move your audience is to use photos or other images that can appeal to *logos, ethos, pathos,* and *kairos* in one glance. (Chapter 9 focuses exclusively on visual rhetoric—the persuasive power of images.) Although many written arguments do not lend themselves to visual illustrations, we suggest that when you construct arguments you consider the potential of visual support. When images work well, they make particularly powerful appeals to *pathos* analogous to the verbal strategies of concrete language, specific illustrations, narratives, and connotative words. The challenge in using visuals is to find material that is straightforward enough to be understood without elaborate explanations, that is timely and relevant, and that clearly adds impact to a specific part of your argument. As an example, suppose you are writing an argument supporting fund-raising efforts to help a developing country that has recently experienced a natural catastrophe. To add a powerful appeal to *pathos,* you might consider incorporating into your argument the photograph shown in Figure 5.1 of the devastation and personal loss caused by Typhoon Haiyan in the Philippines in 2013. A photograph such as this one can evoke a strong emotional and imaginative response as well as make viewers think.

For Writing and Discussion

Analyzing Images as Appeals to *Pathos*

Use the following questions to analyze the photo in Figure 5.1.

1. How would you describe the emotional/imaginative impact of Figure 5.1? What specific details of the photo create its appeal to *pathos*?
2. Many disaster-relief photos seek to convey the magnitude of the destruction and suffering, sometimes shockingly, by depicting destroyed buildings, mangled bodies, and images of human misery. How is your response to Figure 5.1 similar to or different from your response to commonly encountered close-up photographs of grief-stricken victims or to distance shots of widespread destruction? To what extent is Figure 5.1's story—told from the perspective of a child—different from the more typical photographs of destroyed buildings or anguished faces?

Figure 5.1 Photo after Typhoon Haiyan in the Philippines

How Audience-Based Reasons Appeal to *Logos, Ethos, Pathos,* and *Kairos*

5.6 Explain how audience-based reasons appeal to *logos, ethos, pathos,* and *kairos.*

We conclude this chapter by returning to the concept of audience-based reasons that we introduced in Chapter 3. Audience-based reasons enhance *logos* because they build on underlying assumptions (warrants) that the audience is likely to accept. But they also enhance *ethos, pathos,* and *kairos* by helping the audience identify with the writer, by appealing to shared beliefs and values, and by conveying a shared sense of an issue's timeliness. To consider the needs of your audience, you can ask yourself the questions in Table 5.1.

To see how a concern for audience-based reasons can enhance *ethos* and *pathos,* we ask you to role play a student in the following hypothetical scenario. Interested in a career in public health, you are a nursing major who has done research on the obesity crisis in the United States. You have also researched the role of sugary soda and energy drinks in promoting heart disease and diabetes. Recently health advocates in your city have teamed with preschool education advocates to persuade the city council to propose a soda tax. Revenue from the tax would be used to improve the city's preschool programs. Your city council points to nationwide precedents for soda taxes, citing Philadelphia; Berkeley, California; and Cook County, Illinois, which includes Chicago. Other cities, such as Seattle, are on the verge of creating such a tax. The tax being proposed in your city would raise the price of a twelve-pack of soda by four dollars; the price of a large fountain soda at a fast-food restaurant would go up 35 cents.

Table 5.1 Questions for Analyzing Your Audience

What to Ask	Why to Ask It
1. *Who is your audience? What are their values and beliefs?*	Your answer will help you think about audience-based reasons.
2. *How much does your audience know or care about your issue?*	Your answer can especially affect your introduction and conclusion. The less the audience knows, the more background you will have to provide. The less your audience already cares, the more you may need to appeal to *pathos.*
3. *What is your audience's current attitude toward your issue?*	Your answer will help you decide the structure and tone of your argument.
4. *What will be your audience's likely objections to your argument?*	Your answer will help determine the content of your argument and will alert you to extra research you may need to conduct.
5. *What values, beliefs, or assumptions about the world do you and your audience share?*	Your answer will help you find common ground with your audience.

As you can expect, the proposed tax is controversial. Opponents include the beverage industry, grocery store owners, fast-food restaurants, truck drivers (who deliver soda to the stores), and citizens who oppose the government's telling private citizens what they should or should not buy. Proponents include health advocates and education advocates. Medical and nursing associations point to the long-range health benefits of reducing consumption of sugary drinks. Meanwhile, education advocates point to the value of improved and extended preschool programs made possible by revenue from the soda tax.

Your school's student nurse association is scheduling a meeting next week to produce an advocacy piece in favor of the soda tax. Here is your dilemma: You are opposed to the soda tax, not from the perspective of business owners but from the perspective of disproportionate costs to lower-income city residents. What bothers you is the fact that the soda tax is regressive, meaning that it will hit low-income consumers harder than wealthier consumers. Will you have enough courage to speak out at the nursing association meeting? After all, your anti-tax stance will be unpopular among other nursing students, even though it might be applauded by business owners, truck drivers, and the beverage industry.

As you think about your upcoming speech, you formulate your audience-based problem like this:

Problem: How can I create an argument rooted in shared values with my fellow nursing students? How can I reduce my audience's fear that I am becoming an advocate for the beverage industry? How can I make the case that I share my audience's goals of reducing sugar consumption and improving preschool education? How can I show that these goals might be accomplished in a fairer way?

Possible bridge-building strategies:

- Show that I support the health goals of our nursing association—to fight obesity-related diseases by reducing consumption of sugary drinks.

- Show that I support the educational goals made reachable by revenue from the tax. This revenue will make improved preschool education available for all children's in the city.

- Stress that both my audience and I share a concern for the welfare of the poorest citizens, who will be hit hardest by the tax.

- Make the case that the tax will eat up a higher proportion of poor people's income than wealthier people's income. Research shows that poorer people buy more soda than wealthy people. Paying an extra four dollars for a 12-pack of soda puts a substantial strain on a poor family's budget. (Wealthy people often choose diet soda or get their sugar fix from syrups in their espresso coffee drinks). The cost of improving the city's preschools will thus be borne disproportionately by the poor.

- Show that the values underlying the tax are incoherent: If the tax truly reduces consumption of soda (the goal of health advocates), then it will not generate enough revenue to achieve the goals of the education advocates. In sum, the goals of one set of tax proponents are in conflict with the goals of the other set of proponents.

- Show that the goal of reducing sugar consumption might be better achieved through an aggressive educational campaign. Putting a "sin tax" on soda won't be as effective in the long run as raising public awareness about healthy diets and the danger of wasted calories.

- Show that the goal of improving preschool education can be achieved by establishing a fairer tax that puts a higher burden on wealthier people who can afford it.

These thinking notes allow you to develop the following plan for your argument:

Our nursing association should take a courageous stand against the soda tax

- because a soda tax places a disproportionate burden on low-income consumers. (*WARRANT: Taxes that primarily burden low-income consumers are unfair.*)

- because preschool revenue can be raised by a more equitable tax that burdens the wealthy more than the poor. (*WARRANT: It is fair for wealthier people to pay a greater proportion of their income on taxes than the poor.*)

- because an educational campaign may be more effective than a soda tax in changing long-range diet behaviors. (*WARRANT: If alternative solutions can be applied to a problem, the one promoting long-range change is better.*)

As this plan shows, your strategy is to seek reasons whose warrants your audience will accept. Even though you oppose the soda tax, your argument differs significantly from the pro-business arguments mounted by the beverage industry. Whereas their arguments are aimed at undecided voters, your argument is aimed specifically at supporters of the tax. You can hope to persuade them only if you can build bridges to them with audience-based reasons and appeals to shared values.

For Writing and Discussion

Planning an Audience-Based Argumentative Strategy

Working individually or in small groups, plan an audience-based argumentative strategy for one or more of the following tasks. Follow the thinking process used by the writer of the anti-soda tax argument: (1) state several problems that the writer must solve to reach the audience, and (2) develop possible solutions to those problems.

1. An argument for the right of software companies to continue making and selling violent video games: Aim the argument at parents who oppose their children's playing these games.
2. An argument to reverse grade inflation by limiting the number of As and Bs a professor can give in a course: Aim the argument at students who fear getting lower grades.
3. An argument supporting the legalization of cocaine: Aim the argument at readers of *Reader's Digest*, a conservative magazine that supports the current war on drugs.

Writing Assignment

Revising a Draft for *Ethos, Pathos*, and Audience-Based Reasons

Part 1:

Choose an argument that you have previously written or that you are currently drafting. Revise the argument with explicit focus on increasing its appeals to *logos, ethos, pathos,* and *kairos* via audience-based reasons and other strategies. Consider especially how you might improve *ethos* by building bridges to the audience or improve *pathos* through concrete language, specific examples, metaphors, or connotations of words. Finally, consider the extent to which your reasons are audience-based.

Or

Create a multimodal argument by adding effective photographs or images to an argument that you have previously written or are currently drafting that could be enhanced with effective photographs or images. Revise your argument to include these images, perhaps creating a desktop-published document that wraps text around visuals chosen to enhance *pathos.* Other multimodal possibilities include transforming your argument into a speech supported by PowerPoint images (see Chapter 15, into a poster argument (see Chapter 9), or even into a podcast that includes music.

Part 2:

Attach to your revision or transformed project a reflective letter explaining the choices you made in revising your original argument or in transforming it using a multimodal approach. Describe for your instructor the changes or transformations you made, and explain how or why your new version enhances your argument's effectiveness at moving its audience.

Chapter 6
Responding to Objections and Alternative Views

Learning Objectives

In this chapter, you will learn to:

6.1 Explain the differences between one-sided, multisided, and delayed-thesis arguments.

6.2 Determine the degree of your audience's resistance to your views in order to shape the content, structure, and tone of your argument.

6.3 Use one-sided argument to appeal to supportive audiences.

6.4 Use classical argument to appeal to neutral or undecided audiences, using refutation and concession.

6.5 Consider using delayed- thesis argument to appeal to resistant audiences.

Chapter 5 discussed strategies for moving your audience through appeals to *ethos*, *pathos*, and *kairos*. In this chapter we examine strategies for addressing opposing or alternative views—whether to omit them, refute them, concede to them, or incorporate them through compromise and conciliation.

One-Sided, Multisided, and Delayed-Thesis Arguments

6.1 **Explain the differences between one-sided, multisided, and delayed-thesis arguments.**

Arguments can be one-sided, multisided, or delayed thesis:

- **A one-sided argument** presents only the writer's position on the issue without summarizing and responding to alternative viewpoints.

- **A multisided argument** presents the writer's position, but it also summarizes and responds to possible objections and alternative views.

- **A delayed thesis argument** has a strong component of inquiry in which writers present themselves as uncertain and invite resistant readers to become partners in the dialogue. By keeping the question open (and not presenting the writer's own view until later), the writer considers and values multiple perspectives. However, if an issue is heatedly contested, it may be fruitful to move beyond argument altogether and to use instead the listening and negotiating strategies of collaborative rhetoric explained in Chapter 10.

How can you determine the kind of argument that would be most effective in a given case? As a general rule, if an issue is highly contested, one-sided arguments tend to strengthen the convictions of those who are already in the writer's camp but alienate those who aren't. In contrast, for those initially opposed to a writer's claim, a multisided argument shows that the writer has considered other views and thus reduces some initial hostility. An especially interesting effect can occur with neutral or undecided audiences. In the short run, one-sided arguments are often persuasive to a neutral audience, but in the long run, multisided arguments have more staying power. Neutral audiences who have heard only one side of an issue tend to change their minds when they hear alternative arguments. By anticipating and rebutting opposing views, a multisided argument diminishes the surprise and force of subsequent counterarguments. If we move from neutral to highly resistant audiences, adversarial approaches—even multisided ones—are seldom effective because they increase hostility and harden the differences between writer and reader. In such cases, a delayed thesis argument can be helpful. When conflict is emotionly heated, we may even choose to turn from argument to collabortive rhetoric, where we simply listen to those with whom we disagree in an effort to open up channels of communication and consensual problem-solving (see Chapter 10).

In the rest of this chapter we will show you how your choice of writing one-sided, multisided, or delayed-thesis arguments is a function of how you perceive your audience's resistance to your views, your level of confidence in your own views, and your purpose—to persuade your audience or open up dialogue.

Determining Your Audience's Resistance to Your Views

6.2 Determine the degree of your audience's resistance to your views in order to shape the content, structure, and tone of your argument.

When you write an argument, you must always consider your audience's point of view. One way to imagine your relationship to your audience is to place it on a scale of resistance ranging from strong support of your position to strong opposition (Figure 6.1). At the "Accord" end of this scale are like-minded people who basically agree with your position on the issue. At the "Resistance" end are those who strongly disagree with you, perhaps unconditionally, because their values, beliefs, or assumptions sharply differ from your own. Between "Accord" and "Resistance" lies a range of opinions. Close to your position will be those leaning in your direction but with less conviction than you have. Close to the resistance position will be those basically opposed to your view but willing to listen to your argument and perhaps willing to acknowledge some of its strengths. In the middle are those undecided people who are still sorting out their feelings, seeking additional information, and weighing the strengths and weaknesses of alternative views.

Seldom, however, will you encounter an issue in which the range of disagreement follows a simple line from accord to resistance. Often, resistant views fall into different categories so that no single line of argument appeals to all those whose views are different from your own. You thus have to identify not only your audience's resistance to your ideas but also the causes of that resistance.

Figure 6.1 Scale of resistance

Accord	Undecided/Neutral	Resistance

| strongly supportive | supportive with conditions | uncertain | mostly opposed | strongly opposed |

Appealing to a Supportive Audience: One-Sided Argument

6.3 Use one-sided argument to appeal to supportive audiences.

One-sided arguments may occur early in an argumentative conversation when a writer's aim is merely to put forth a new or different point of view. When an issue is highly contested, however, or when the targeted audience is indifferent, one-sided arguments are used mainly to stir the passions of supporters or to inspire the apathetic—for example, to convert belief into action by inspiring a party member to contribute to a senator's campaign or a bored office worker to sign up for a change-your-life weekend seminar.

Typically, appeals to a supportive audience are structured as one-sided arguments that either ignore opposing views or reduce them to "enemy" stereotypes. Filled with motivational language, these arguments list the benefits that will follow from the reader's donations to the cause and the horrors just around the corner if the other side wins. One of the authors of this text received a fund-raising letter from an environmental lobbying group declaring, "It's crunch time for the polluters and their pals on Capitol Hill." The "corporate polluters" and "anti-environment politicians," the letter continues, have "stepped up efforts to roll back our environmental protections—relying on large campaign contributions, slick PR firms, and well-heeled lobbyists to get the job done before November's election." This letter makes the reader feel like part of an in-group of good guys fighting the big business "polluters." Nothing in the letter examines environmental issues from business's perspective or attempts to examine alternative views fairly. Because the intended audience already believes in the cause, nothing in the letter invites readers to consider the issues more thoroughly. Rather, the letter's goal is to solidify support, increase the fervor of belief, and inspire action. Most appeal arguments make it easy to act, ending with an 800 phone number to call, a website to visit, an online petition to sign, or a congressperson's address to write to.

Appealing to a Neutral or Undecided Audience: Classical Argument

6.4   Use classical argument to appeal to neutral or undecided audiences, using refutation and concession.

The in-group appeals that motivate an already supportive audience can repel a neutral or undecided audience. Because undecided audiences are like jurors weighing all sides of an issue, they distrust one-sided arguments that caricature other views. Generally the best strategy for appealing to undecided audiences is the classically structured argument described in Chapter 2.

What characterizes the classical argument is the writer's willingness to summarize opposing views fairly and to respond to them openly—either by trying to refute them or by conceding to their strengths and then shifting to a different field of values. Let's look at these strategies in more depth.

Summarizing Opposing Views

The first step toward responding to opposing views in a classical argument is to summarize them fairly. Follow the *principle of charity*, which obliges you to avoid loaded, biased, or "straw man" summaries that oversimplify or distort opposing arguments, making them easy to knock over.

Consider the difference between an unfair and a fair summary of an argument. In the following example, a hypothetical supporter of genetically engineered foods intends to refute the argument of organic-food advocate Lisa Turner, who opposes all forms of biotechnology.

UNFAIR SUMMARY OF TURNER'S ARGUMENT

> In a biased article lacking scientific understanding of biotechnology, natural-foods huckster Lisa Turner parrots the health food industry's party line that genetically altered crops are Frankenstein's monsters run amok. She ignorantly claims that consumption of biotech foods will lead to worldwide destruction, disease, and death, ignoring the wealth of scientific literature showing that genetically modified foods are safe. Her misinformed attacks are scare tactics aimed at selling consumers on overpriced "health food" products to be purchased at boutique organic-food stores.

FAIR SUMMARY OF TURNER'S ARGUMENT

> In an article appearing in a nutrition magazine, health-food advocate Lisa Turner warns readers that much of our food today is genetically modified using gene-level techniques that differ completely from ordinary crossbreeding. She argues that the potential, unforeseen, harmful consequences of genetic engineering offset the possible benefits of increasing the food supply, reducing the use of pesticides, and boosting the nutritional value of foods. Turner asserts that genetic engineering is imprecise, untested, unpredictable, irreversible, and also uncontrollable because of animals, insects, and winds.

In the unfair summary, the writer distorts and oversimplifies Turner's argument, creating a straw man argument that is easy to knock over because it doesn't make the opponent's best case. In contrast, the fair summary follows the principle of charity, allowing the strength of the opposing view to come through clearly.

Refuting Opposing Views

Once you have summarized opposing views, you can either refute them or concede to their strengths. In refuting an opposing view, you attempt to convince readers that its argument is logically flawed, inadequately supported, or based on erroneous assumptions. In refuting an argument, you can rebut (1) the writer's stated reason and grounds, (2) the writer's warrant and backing, or (3) both. Put in less specialized language, you can rebut a writer's reasons and evidence or the writer's underlying assumptions. Suppose, for example, that you wanted to refute this hypothetical argument from a writer we'll call Jason Jones:

> Students should limit the number of internships they take because internships are time-consuming. (Warrant: Time-consuming internships are bad for students.)

One way to refute this argument is to rebut the stated reason that internships are time-consuming. Your rebuttal might go something like this:

> I disagree with Jones' argument that internships are time-consuming. In fact, organizations and businesses are usually very upfront, realistic, and flexible in the weekly hours that they ask of students. The examples that Jones cites of overly demanding internships are exceptions. Furthermore, these internships have since been retailored to students' schedules. [The writer could then provide examples of effective, limited-time internships.]

Or you could concede that internships are time-consuming but rebut the argument's warrant that a time-consuming internship is bad for students:

> I agree that internships take sizable chunks of students' time, but investment in real-world work environments is a worthwhile use of students' time. Through this investment, students clarify their professional goals, log work experience, and gain references. Without interning in these work environments, students would miss important career preparation.

Let's now illustrate these strategies in a more complex situation. Consider the controversy inspired by a *New York Times Magazine* article titled "Recycling Is Garbage." Its author, John Tierney, argued that recycling is not environmentally sound and that it is cheaper to bury garbage in a landfill than to recycle it. Tierney argued that recycling wastes money; he provided evidence that "every time a sanitation department crew picks up a load of bottles and cans from the curb, New York City loses money."

A number of environmentalists responded angrily to Tierney's argument, challenging either his reason, his warrant, or both. Those refuting the reason offered counterevidence showing that recycling isn't as expensive as Tierney claimed. Those refuting the warrant said that even if the costs of recycling are higher than the costs of burying wastes in a landfill, recycling still benefits the environment by reducing the amount of virgin materials taken from nature. These critics, in effect, offered a new warrant: Conserving the world's resources is an important goal of garbage disposal.

Strategies for Rebutting Evidence

Whether you are rebutting an argument's reasons or its warrant, you will frequently need to question a writer's use of evidence. Here are some strategies you can use:

- **Deny the accuracy of the data.** Arguers can disagree about the facts of a case. If you have reasons to doubt a writer's facts, call them into question.

- **Cite counterexamples and countertestimony.** You can often rebut an argument based on examples or testimony by citing counterexamples or countertestimony that denies the conclusiveness of the original data.

- **Cast doubt on the representativeness or sufficiency of examples.** Examples are powerful only if they are believed to be representative and sufficient. Many environmentalists complained that John Tierney's attack on recycling was based too largely on data from New York City and that it didn't accurately take into account the more positive experiences of other cities and states. When data from outside New York City were examined, the cost-effectiveness and positive environmental impact of recycling seemed more apparent.

- **Cast doubt on the relevance or recency of the examples, statistics, or testimony.** The best evidence is up-to-date. In a rapidly changing universe, data that are even a few years out-of-date are often ineffective. For example, as the demand for recycled goods increases, the cost of recycling will be reduced. Out-of-date statistics will skew any argument about the cost of recycling.

- **Question the credibility of an authority.** If an opposing argument is based on testimony, you can undermine its persuasiveness if you show that a person being cited lacks current or relevant expertise in the field.

- **Question the accuracy or context of quotations.** Evidence based on testimony is frequently distorted by being either misquoted or taken out of context. Often scientists qualify their findings heavily, but the popular media omit these qualifications. You can thus attack the use of a quotation by putting it in its original context or by explaining how scientists qualified their findings in the original source.

- **Question the way statistical data were produced or interpreted.** Chapter 4 provides fuller treatment of how to question statistics. In general, you can rebut statistical evidence by calling into account how the data were gathered, treated mathematically, or interpreted. It can make a big difference, for example, whether you cite numbers or percentages or whether you choose large or small increments for the axes of graphs.

Conceding to Opposing Views

In writing a classical argument, a writer must sometimes concede to an opposing argument rather than refute it. Sometimes you encounter portions of an argument that you simply can't refute. For example, suppose that you are a libertarian who supports the legalization of hard drugs such as cocaine and heroin. Adversaries argue that legalizing hard drugs will increase the number of drug users and addicts. You might dispute the size of their numbers, but you reluctantly agree that they are right. Your strategy is thus not to refute the opposing argument but to concede to it by admitting that legalization of hard drugs will promote heroin and cocaine addiction. Having made that concession, your task is then to show that the benefits of drug legalization, such as a reduction in crime and fewer people serving time in America's prisons, still outweigh the costs you've just conceded.

As this example shows, the strategy of a concession argument is to switch from the field of values employed by the writer you disagree with to a different field of values more favorable to your position. You don't try to refute the writer's stated reason and grounds (by arguing that legalization will *not* lead to increased drug usage and addiction) or the writer's warrant (by arguing that increased drug use and addiction is not a problem). Rather, you shift the argument to a new field of values by introducing a new warrant, one that you think your audience can share (that the benefits of legalization outweigh the costs of increased addiction). To the extent that opponents of legalization share your desire to stop drug-related crime, shifting to this new field of values is a good strategy. Although it may seem that you weaken your own position by conceding to an opposing argument, you may actually strengthen it by increasing your credibility and gaining your audience's goodwill. Moreover, conceding to one part of an opposing argument doesn't mean that you won't refute other parts of that argument.

Example of a Student Essay Using Refutation Strategy

The following essay by student writer Trudie Makens grew out of her research into the issue of raising the minimum wage to a living wage. Trudie's essay illustrates how a classical argument appealing to a neutral or even mildly resistant audience engages with alternative views. Note the use of both concession and rebuttal strategies. (Trudie's in-text parenthetical citations and her Works Cited list follow the MLA documentation style explained in Appendix 2.)

Student Essay

Bringing Dignity to Workers: Make the Minimum Wage a Living Wage

Trudie Makens

Having worked as a busser in a pizza restaurant, a part-time barista, and a server at a dumpling café, I have worked a number of minimum-wage jobs. My coworkers have ranged from students like myself to single parents and primary providers for their families. As a student, I have always had my parents as a safety net protecting me from financial hardship. However, my coworkers whose only income is their minimum wage endured financial hardships daily. I witnessed one of my coworkers, Maria, lose her home trying to balance supporting her two children and paying her rent. At work, Maria would describe her anxiety as she bounced from relative to relative, straining her family relations and image of herself as an able provider. Without a living wage or the government's providing social insurance programs to ensure financial security for all citizens, families like Maria's are locked into poverty. Raising the federal minimum wage to a livable standard is an important and necessary step to eradicate poverty and ensure dignified living for individuals and families.

Yet some argue that a higher federal minimum wage will do more harm than good. Michael Saltsman, the research director of the Employment Policy Institute, elaborates the pro-business objections to a minimum wage in several op-ed pieces published in national print or online newspapers. Saltsman primarily makes three arguments against raising the minimum wage. Each of them, I contend, is weak or flawed.

First, Saltsman warns that raising the minimum wage will force businesses to cut jobs. In order to maintain profit and to keep prices low, Saltsman argues, businesses will pay for a higher wage by slashing the number of workers. Worse, businesses may cut entire departments in favor of automation, such as having fast-food customers order their meals from computer touch screens. Saltsman's argument, however, depends on older studies that, according to University of California economist Michael Reich, are "fundamentally flawed" (Maclay). In a study published in 2010, Reich and his coauthors find that these earlier studies fail to account for all the critical variables besides wages that influence employment levels. By comparing employment levels between states with higher versus lower minimum-wage levels, Reich and his colleagues provide empirical evidence that raising the minimum wage produces no "adverse employment effects" (954).

Saltsman's second objection to a higher minimum wage is that it targets the wrong people and thus won't reduce overall poverty levels. According to Saltsman, a majority of people living in poverty are unemployed while a majority of minimum-wage workers are from households above the poverty line. Although Saltsman may be correct that a higher minimum wage won't help a jobless person, he ignores the benefits of a living wage to the working poor who would be lifted out of poverty. Moreover, a higher minimum wage might itself stimulate jobs because minimum-wage workers with more money in their pockets are apt to spend it, increasing demand for goods.

(continued)

Uses personal example to illustrate problems of low-wage workers

Thesis statement

Forecasts rebuttal of three opposing views raised by Saltsman

Summarizes Saltsman's first objection to minimum wage

Rebuts argument by citing more recent research

Summarizes Saltsman's second objection

Concedes that higher minimum wage won't help jobless, but shifts to other benefits that Saltsman ignores

5

Summarizes Saltsman's last argument

Finally, Saltsman argues that the minimum wage is less effective at reducing poverty than the Earned Income Tax Credit, which boosts the income of low-wage workers while not giving any income boost to workers who are already above the poverty level. However, the Earned Income Tax Credit, like the minimum wage, does nothing for the jobless poor. Moreover, the Earned Income Tax Credit puts the burden of poverty relief on taxpayers rather than employers and corporate shareholders, doing little to shift the economy in an equitable direction. We need both an increased minimum wage and the Earned Income Tax Credit.

Rebuts this argument by showing weaknesses in the Earned Income Tax Credit approach

Uses conclusion to summarize additional measures (besides higher minimum wage) to combat poverty

It seems clear that to combat poverty, the United States needs a many-pronged effort, with a hike in the minimum wage being only one of the prongs. Although a higher minimum wage will not by itself eliminate poverty, it will certainly help. It needs to be combined with investments in infrastructure to create jobs, with affordable higher education, with better job training, and with other safety-net systems such as those in place in Europe to give dignity to all citizens. Rather than our government and market system prioritizing corporations and profit, the rights and dignity of workers should be held foremost important. Raising the minimum wage to a living wage will help change the structure of a market system that often exploits workers.

Works Cited

Maclay, Kathleen. "Minimum Wage Hikes Don't Eliminate Jobs, Study Finds." *UC Berkeley News Center*, 1 Dec. 2010, news.berkeley.edu/2010/12/01/minimumwagejobs.

Reich, Michael, et al. "Minimum Wage Effects Across State Borders: Estimates Using Contiguous Counties." *Review of Economics and Statistics*, vol. 92, no. 4, 2010, pp. 945–64.

Saltsman, Michael. "The Wrong Way to Reduce Poverty." *USA Today*, 20 Sept. 2013, www.usatoday.com/story/opinion/2013/09/20/minimum-wages-poverty-column/2839003.

---. "To Help the Poor, Move Beyond 'Minimum' Gestures." *The Huffington Post*, 26 Apr. 2013, updated 26 June 2013, www.huffingtonpost.com/michael-saltsman/earned-income-tax-credit-minimum-wage_b_3165459.html.

For Writing and Class Discussion

Refutation Strategies

Individually or in groups, examine each of the following arguments, imagining how the claim and reason could be fleshed out with grounds and backing. Then attempt to refute each argument. Suggest ways to rebut the reason, or the warrant, or both, or to concede to the argument and then switch to a different field of values.

a. The criminal justice system should reduce sentences for low-level, nonviolent offenders because this change will save taxpayers' money.

b. Majoring in engineering is better than majoring in music because engineers make more money than musicians.

c. The United States should build more nuclear reactors because nuclear reactors will provide substantial electrical energy without emitting greenhouse gases.

Appealing to a Resistant Audience: Delayed-Thesis Argument

6.5 **Consider using delayed-thesis argument to appeal to resistant audiences.**

Whereas classical argument is effective for neutral or undecided audiences, it is often less effective for audiences strongly opposed to the writer's views. Because resistant audiences hold values, assumptions, or beliefs widely different from the writer's, they are often unswayed by classical argument, which attacks their worldview too directly. Unlike a classical argument, a delayed-thesis argument assumes either an initial exploratory approach to a subject or an approach that focuses on shared values, evoking sympathy for the audience's views. With some issues, you may want to convey that you are still thinking out your position, finding your way through a thicket of alternative views and the complexities of the issue. On other issues, you might simply want to focus first on shared values. Under these rhetorical conditions, a delayed-thesis argument enables you to establish initial rapport with your audience. Instead of declaring a claim and reasons early in the argument, you may work your way slowly to your claim, often delaying your thesis until the end.

Let's look at an example of a delayed-thesis argument, examining its form and its emotional impact. (For another example of a delayed-thesis argument, see Ellen Goodman's "Womb for Rent—for a Price" in Chapter 7.) The following essay, by British journalist Alexander Chancellor, appeared in the conservative British magazine *The Spectator*:

Oh, How I Will Miss the Plastic Bag

Alexander Chancellor

Title shows fondness for plastic bags

It has taken years, but finally England has joined the rest of the United Kingdom and other countries around the world in declaring war on the plastic carrier bag. This week for the first time English supermarkets are being forbidden by law to give plastic bags away for free. From now on they will have to charge 5p for every one of them. It is the beginning of the end. The plastic bag is heading for oblivion. The most useful shopping tool of the last half-century will soon, I imagine, be extinct.

Provides context and explains new law requiring stores to charge for plastic bags

It seems only appropriate at this point to say how wonderful plastic bags have been. They are the most useful carriers ever invented — strong, light, capacious, and absurdly cheap to produce. Life without them will never be so easy again. In future, anyone wanting to buy a few things from the supermarket on the way home from work will have to remember to take a reusable shopping bag out with him in the morning. Anyone stocking up with food at the weekend will have to set out with a supply of his own bags in the car. I already try to do this, but usually forget. Oh, how I will miss the plastic bag.

Establishes rapport with audience by praising the usefulness of plastic bags

Elaborates his shared view with the audience—the value of plastic bags

Surprises reader by acknowledging that British citizens, not the government, voted to ban the bags

Credits the ban to the unselfishness of people, who put the environment ahead of convenience

Provides evidence of the environmental damage caused by discarded plastic bags

Provides more evidence of the damage caused to oceans and marine life

Shows the dramatic power of a visual image to turn citizens against plastic bags

States his thesis: Plastic bags "are not a good thing"

But the remarkable thing is that the end of the plastic bag, when it happens, will not have been an imposition from above but a fulfilment of the popular will. A consultation exercise carried out eight years ago found, for example, that 90 percent of Londoners were in favor of banning plastic bags altogether. Ninety percent of Londoners wanted to abolish one of the greatest conveniences of their everyday lives! Who can say that people are always selfish?

The popularity of the new measure against plastic bags, the docile acceptance of having to pay for something that always used to be free, is evidence of how responsive people can be to campaigns for the wider public good. The campaign against smoking has been successful, too, but smoking kills individuals, which is rather different. Plastic bags just threaten the world.

That threat, however, is impressive. The statistics are enough to alarm anyone. Hitherto in Britain, billions of plastic bags have been given to shoppers each year, and they have all got thrown away. About 60,000 tons of them have ended up in landfills, where they can take more than 400 years to decompose—a process that promotes climate change by releasing carbon dioxide into the atmosphere.

Throughout the world, between 500 and 1,000 billion plastic bags are thought to be consumed annually, more than a million a minute. And those that don't reach landfill sites get blown about on the wind from the North Pole to the South, littering every continent and polluting every sea.

Those floating out at sea have a devastating effect on marine life. Turtles eat them, thinking they are jellyfish, and die in consequence. Altogether, more than 100,000 mammals, including whales and seals, and up to one million seabirds are thought to be killed each year from eating or getting tangled up in plastic. And like the poignant photograph of a dead child on a beach in Turkey that got the campaign to admit refugees to Britain going, it took a distressing image to spark the revolution against plastic bags.

It was the sight of some albatross chicks dying from eating plastic on a beach in Devon that eight years ago upset Rebecca Hosking, a BBC camerawoman, so much that she persuaded shopkeepers in her hometown of Modbury to give up plastic bags altogether, thus launching the campaign of which we are seeing the results today.

Discarded plastic bags may occasionally have their uses. I am told that in some parts of Africa there has developed a cottage industry in which people turn them into hats. But on the whole I have to say that even I am convinced that they are not a good thing. So I will try not to mourn them. I will stock up on sturdy canvas bags and try to remember to take them with me to the supermarket. Or maybe I should do the sensible thing and start getting my groceries delivered to my home instead.

If Chancellor had chosen to write a classical argument, he might have declared his position in the first paragraph, perhaps with a thesis statement like this:

> The forthcoming British ban on plastic bags is a good thing because the ban will help reduce the plastic pollution of oceans and other environmental damage caused by discarded bags.

He would have then presented his evidence about environmental damage caused by plastic bags, particularly to marine life. Near the end of his argument, he might have summarized an opposing view ("Of course, many people like plastic bags . . . "), conceded that the plastic bags had many uses, but then switched to another field of values: "However, the environmental harm caused by pollution outweighs the benefits to consumers." Organized as a classical argument, Chancellor's essay would use a Toulmin schema similar to our plastic bag example in Chapter 3.

But Chancellor delays stating his thesis until the last paragraph and instead begins his argument with what looks like a lament for the loss of the plastic bag—"the most useful shopping tool of the last half-century." As a cultural conservative writing for a conservative British magazine, he imagines his readers being angry at the government for banning these wonderful plastic bags. He assumes that his readers will expect him to oppose the ban on plastic bags, viewing the ban as an example of an overreaching liberal government. But instead he surprises them halfway through by supporting the ban.

His delayed thesis structure allows him to bring in a second argument in favor of the ban—an argument praising the unselfishness of British citizens who voted overwhelmingly to go against their own selfish interests. The actor in this happy story is not an overreaching liberal government but rather the average British citizen, whose unselfishness is made more vivid by the writer's and readers' shared love of the plastic bag. The title of the essay and the opening paragraphs give readers a chance to identify first with their beloved plastic bags and then second with the unselfishness of good people acting to save the world. Whereas the classical argument can often seem to divide stakeholders into pro and con camps, Chancellor's delayed-thesis approach unites writer and readers as unselfish, good people placing the needs of the world above themselves. Conservatives' grumbles against an overreaching government dissolve into warm feelings about being unselfish and doing good for the world.

Writing a Delayed-Thesis Argument

Clearly, where you place your claim can affect your argument's impact on its audience. We should note, however, that a delayed-thesis argument is not simply a classical argument turned upside down. Instead, it promotes empathy for the audience's views, inviting rather than compelling them toward the writer's stance. It places value on enriching and complicating the discussion by exploring different perspectives. It entails some risk to the writer because it leaves space only at the end of the argument for developing the writer's claim. Moreover, it can backfire in a confusing way if the writer simply seems to change positions without explanation. When done well, however, it may lead the writer and readers to a deeper understanding of the issue, provide clarification, and promote further discussion. Although there is no set form, the organization plan in Figure 6.3 shows characteristic elements often found in delayed-thesis arguments.

Figure 6.3 Organizational plan for a delayed-thesis argument

Organization Plan for a Delayed-Thesis Argument

Introduction	• Establish the problem under discussion and (when appropriate) the occasion that makes the issue timely (*kairos*).
Option 1: Truth-seeking exploration of issue*	• Explore the problem from multiple perspectives, showing the validity of different views • Show how you are wrestling with the problem • For a good portion of the argument, keep the problem open, building some suspense about what your thesis will be
Option 2: Establishment of shared values**	• Focus on values or beliefs that you share with the resistant audience • Show openness and sympathy toward your audience's view of the issue
Delayed thesis and support	• Present your thesis-claim later in the argument • If you present your thesis at the end, it should grow out of reasons and evidence presented earlier • If you present your thesis in the middle, then support it with reasons and evidence
Conclusion	• Leave a last impression favoring your thesis

*This exploratory approach is illustrated by Ellen Goodman's "Womb for Rent—For a Price" in Chapter 7.

**The shared values approach is illustrated by Alexander Chancellor's "Oh How I Will Miss the Plastic Bag" in this chapter.

Writing Assignment
A Classical Argument or a Delayed Thesis Argument

Option 1: A Classical Argument

Write a classical argument following the explanation in Section 2.1 at the beginning of Chapter 2 and using the guidelines for developing such an argument throughout Chapters 2–6. Consider carefully how you will handle alternative views in your argument, based on your awareness of your audience's degree of resistance to your claim and reasons. How will you rebut opposing views? Where will you concede to them? Depending on your instructor's preferences, this argument could be on a new issue, or it could be a final stage of an argument in progress. For an example of a classical argument, see "The Dangers of Digital Distraction" by Lauren Shinozuka (below). Note how Lauren uses research to show that she is joining a larger public conversation on her generation's use of digital technology.

Option 2: A Delayed-Thesis Argument

If you imagine a strongly resistant audience, write a delayed-thesis argument following the model of either Alexander Chancellor in this chapter or of Ellen Goodman in Chapter 7.

Reading

The following essay, by student writer Lauren Shinozuka, illustrates a classical argument. This essay grew out of Lauren's own wrestling with her immersion in social media. She decided to persuade her peers to see the problem her way with the goal that they will join her in new awareness and new habits.

Student Essay

The Dangers of Digital Distractedness

Lauren Shinozuka

We are the Net Generation, the Facebook Generation—digital natives. Cultural critics praise us for our digital skills, our facility with multimedia, and our ability to interact electronically with others through collaboration and co-creation. But at what cost? If we are honest, the following antisocial scene is familiar. You are sitting at a table with friends, and then you hear various pings and look up to see every one of your friends with squinted eyes, checking social media apps and text messages, scrolling away on their phones and furiously punching a reply. What kind of togetherness is this? We seem to feel some urgency or need to know what the world wants from us in that moment, prompting us to check our smartphones every six and a half minutes a day. Although we may seem to be skillfully interactive technologically, I argue that our behavior represents dependence, even addiction, that has deep, pervasive consequences. It harms us by promoting an unproductive habit of multitasking, by dehumanizing our relationships, and by encouraging a distorted self-image.

I can hear my peers immediately rejecting these claims as too extreme and too critical, and I acknowledge that a good case can be made for our digital savvy and the benefits that it brings. Armed with smartphones and laptops, we believe we are masters of technology because we can access so much information easily and immediately. Thanks to our cell phones, all of our friends are only a mere click or swipe away for starting a conversation or sending an invitation to meet up. I also have to admit that our digital knowledge gives us on-the-job advantages. At my part-time job at a

(continued)

high-end retail store, I constantly use a mobile point-of-sale system to ring up customers for fast and easy "on-the-spot checkout," receiving compliments for my competence. With my comfort with the company's technology, I can troubleshoot easily and help other employees. Because technology facilitates much of what we do and keeps us plugged into the rest of the world, I recognize that it can be difficult to see the negative aspects of our relationship to digital technology, but it is time for serious self-examination.

In college, we tell ourselves that multitasking with technology helps us use our time wisely, but in actuality we become even less productive. I notice that while I study, I feel the need to stop every five or ten minutes to check my phone, or log onto a website and allow myself to get distracted before going back to my task. These momentary distractions eat away at my time; when I sit down to write a paper at 9 P.M. I am often startled to find that it is suddenly 12 A.M. and I have less than a page written. We Millennials think we are so cutting edge with our multitasking, yet we get little done with our time. We submerge ourselves into a technological bubble consisting of laptops and music and cell phones, convinced that by arming ourselves with these tools, we can really do it all. In actuality, as writer John Hamilton explains in his report for National Public Radio, our brains cannot "focus on more than one thing at a time." Hamilton cites MIT neuroscientist Earl Miller, who says that our minds are "not paying attention to . . . two things simultaneously, but switching between them very rapidly"; thus, multitasking in itself is a myth. Furthermore, as we continue to overload our brains with multiple tasks, we also begin to reshape our thought processes. Technology—the Internet in particular—helps us avoid the hard work of concentration and contemplation. In the article "Is Google Making Us Stupid?" nonfiction business and technology writer Nicholas Carr describes this way we take in and distribute information as a "swiftly moving stream of particles." We skim rather than read; we rapidly switch tasks rather than truly multitask. I recognize this superficial way of operating in the world in my own behavior. I often turn to Google for an immediate answer to a question I have: Who's the current Speaker of the House? How many ounces are in a cup? Then I click on the first link I see, and more often than not, I see the little subheading that states, "You've visited this page X times." I realize my mental instincts tell me that it's much easier to Google an answer multiple times rather than just *learn* the information. Because I constantly overindulge in my technology, I have engrained the habits of skimming streams of information, constantly bouncing from one task to another, but never stopping to bask in its depths.

Our obsession with technology and social media not only reshapes the way we think, but also fosters a type of false superficial friendship with people we barely know, dehumanizing the kinds of relationships we have. Since coming to college, I've made hundreds of new Facebook friends and attracted dozens of new followers on Twitter. To be fair, a number of these people are truly my good friends, but most of these "friendships" came from a one-time meeting at a party or a class I had with them during my sophomore year. Although some will insist on the vital role social media plays in keeping them connected to distant family and friends, we need to address more directly the extent and pervasive effects of our more common arbitrary cyber friendships. Last summer, while I taught a program at a local elementary school, I would occasionally post a Facebook status of something funny that happened that day, or a picture of my class. Back home later for a short vacation, I ran into a girl from high school whom I hadn't seen in four years and barely knew then. When we stopped to chat, she asked me all about my summer program, and she commented that all my students were so cute! After our chat, I left feeling perturbed and uneasy. Immediately, I thought she was so "creepy," but I realized that ultimately I chose to share my life with the rest of the world. Speaking about these digital relationships, Sherry Turkle, MIT professor and author of *Alone Together: Why We Expect More from Technology and Less from Each Other,* labels our behavior "a Goldilocks effect": "We can't get enough of one another if we can use technology to keep one another at distances we can control: not too close, not too far, just right." That moment when my distant "friend" reached out to me about my summer felt so disturbing because she crossed that Goldilocks line through a personal face-to-face conversation. I am embarrassed to say that I was comfortable only when she was one of the masses; I didn't want to engage in a true interpersonal connection.

This lack of intimacy through false relationships leads to the creation of a distorted identity. We begin to form a social identity through our conscious decisions of what we choose to share with the rest of the digital world. We want to post pretty pictures that will garner us a number of "likes," and we want to tweet something witty or profound so others will retweet us. When I began to reevaluate my own social media identity, I found that I consciously try to word my Facebook status in order for people to find it funny, and I'm obsessed with editing my pictures with the right filters to achieve that hipster artist effect. I realized that I was interpreting my own life experiences in such a way that I would seem interesting or entertaining to all of my "friends," as if I were performing for an audience I was trying to please. That image of myself is dishonest: It conveys the person I want people to think I am, not the real me.

We see this willful self-distortion in a growing trend called "catfishing": an Internet phenomenon where one person creates a false online identity to engage in a romantic relationship with another person physically far removed. Instead of using his or her own photo, the "catfisher" substitutes photos of attractive, talented people to create a false identity. A documentary named for this phenomenon, *Catfish,* features these long-distance lovers traveling across the country for a chance to meet the person who is really on the other side of the screen. Often that person's appearance and even gender and motives are strikingly at odds with the self-portrayal. While it is easy for us to judge negatively these extreme cases of catfishing, Molly McHugh, writer for *Digital Trends,* points out what she calls the "slippery slope of catfishdom." These cases may seem extreme, but to an extent, all of us who embrace social media are indeed "catfish" as well. We succumb to what McHugh calls the "aspirational beast" of social media, bending the truth online to some degree in order to portray the self that we want to be. With our growing reliance on social media and technology, the tendency for our romantic relationships to blend into our digital selves becomes even

5

more prevalent. When we continue to mix this intimate, personal self with the demands and desires of social media, we produce tragic, ill-formed identities that no longer resemble our true selves.

Of course, we may draw a sharp distinction between our own digital dependence and the growing number of young users who are actual technological addicts. (According to Carolyn Gregoire's *Huffington Post* article, there is now an inpatient Internet rehabilitation center designed specifically for true addicts.) However, our own participation in the more widespread digital craze remains a serious problem too. Yet by taking the first step of making the unconscious conscious, I believe we can combat the digital damage in our lives. I have begun by taking several steps. I purposefully put my phone across the table so I physically need to get up to check it; I let myself binge-check all my social media apps only once, just before going to bed, rather than ten times a day, and I have stopped trying to take pictures of every pretty meal I consume or sunset I see because I know that those are my own special moments, not some glamorous, envy-inducing image I want to project. I have begun to avoid friends who find their phones more interesting than the immediate world around them, and this new company has made it easier to break away from my own addiction. I am trying to rehumanize my friendships, and I am finding solace in deep reading once more without the distractions of cell phone vibrations. I invite members of my generation to join me, so we can be together, no longer alone together.

Works Cited

Carr, Nicholas. "Is Google Making Us Stupid? What the Internet Is Doing to Our Brains." *The Atlantic*, July-Aug. 2008, www.theatlantic.com/magazine/archive/2008/07/is-google-making-us-stupid/306868.

Gregoire, Carolyn. "Welcome to Internet Rehab." *The Huffington Post*, 25 Sept. 2013, updated 25 Oct. 2013, www.huffingtonpost.com/2013/09/25/this-is-where-people-are-_n_3976240.html.

Hamilton, John. "Think You're Multitasking? Think Again." *National Public Radio*, 2 Oct. 2008, www.npr.org/templates/story/story.php?storyId=95256794.

McHugh, Molly. "It's Catfishing Season! How to Tell Lovers from Liars Online, and More." *Digital Trends*, 23 Aug. 2013, www.digitaltrends.com/web/its-catfishing-season-how-to-tell-lovers-from-liars-online-and-more.

Turkle, Sherry. "The Flight from Conversation." *The New York Times*, 21 Apr. 2012, www.nytimes.com/2012/04/22/opinion/sunday/the-flight-from-conversation.html.

PART TWO
Entering an Argumentative Conversation

Across the country, protests like this one are raising awareness of the poverty-level wages of fast-food workers, who are not represented by unions and who often depend on public assistance such as food stamps to get by every month. While protestors argue for a minimum wage of $15 per hour, opponents argue that raising the minimum wage would increase food prices and reduce the number of jobs. If you were making a brochure or poster in favor of an increased minimum wage for fast-food workers, how effective would this realistic, low-key photo be in raising sympathy for the cause? Chapter 8 explores the issue of a living wage for unskilled workers.

Chapter 7
Analyzing Arguments Rhetorically

Learning Objectives

In this chapter you will learn to:

7.1 Explain what it means to think rhetorically about texts.

7.2 Reconstruct a source text's rhetorical context by analyzing the text's author, purpose, motivating occasion, audience, genre, and angle of vision.

7.3 Ask questions that promote rhetorical thinking.

7.4 Conduct a rhetorical analysis of a source text.

In Part One of this textbook, we explained the principles of argument—identifying an issue, making a claim, supporting the claim with reasons and evidence (and perhaps supporting the underlying warrants also), summarizing and responding to opposing views, and paying attention to the rhetorical appeals of *logos, ethos,* and *pathos*.

In Part Two we shift attention to the critical thinking skills you will need when, as a researcher and a reader of arguments, you begin exploring a new issue. By emphasizing exploration and inquiry, Part Two focuses on the truth-seeking aim of argument as the entry point into a new issue.

To engage thoughtfully in inquiry, you need to analyze arguments rhetorically—that is, to examine an argument closely to understand the author's purpose and intended audience, to evaluate the author's choices, and to determine what makes the argument effective or ineffective for its targeted audience. A rhetorical analysis identifies the text under scrutiny, summarizes its main ideas, presents some key points about the text's rhetorical strategies for persuading its audience, and elaborates on these points.

Becoming skilled at analyzing arguments rhetorically will have multiple payoffs for you. This skill helps you become an inquisitive, truth-seeking reader. It also plays a major role in helping you construct your own arguments. Particularly, analyzing sources rhetorically helps you determine the reliability of the evidence you might draw from other sources while also helping you summarize and respond to opposing views. In this chapter, we explain what it means to think "rhetorically" about other people's arguments (and your own). Chapter 8 then teaches you to apply rhetorical thinking to an actual issue; there, you will draw on your own critical skills to summarize other stakeholders' arguments, analyze their strengths and weaknesses, and begin formulating your own stance.

Thinking Rhetorically about a Text

7.1   Explain what it means to think rhetorically about texts.

To become an effective reader of arguments and to construct effective arguments yourself, you need to think of all arguments as voices in ongoing conversations about issues. Invested stakeholders construct arguments in order to move their audiences to see the issues their way. To understand these arguments fully, you need to think about them rhetorically.

Let's look more closely at what we mean by "thinking rhetorically." At the broadest level, *rhetoric* is the study of how human beings use language and other symbols to influence the attitudes, beliefs, and actions of others. In a narrower sense, rhetoric is the art of making messages persuasive. Perhaps the most famous definition comes from Aristotle, who defined rhetoric as "the ability to see, in any particular case, all the available means of persuasion."

Thinking rhetorically means determining what "available means of persuasion" a writer is using in a particular argument. You can do this by getting inside an argument, listening carefully to what the writer is arguing, and determining *how* this argument has been constructed to reach its audience. To think rhetorically, you should imagine stakeholders as real persons who were motivated to write by some occasion and to achieve some real purpose.

Reconstructing a Text's Rhetorical Context

7.2   Reconstruct a source text's rhetorical context by analyzing the text's author, purpose, motivating occasion, audience, genre, and angle of vision.

To enter an argumentative conversation, you need to think rhetorically about each stakeholder's argument. A first step in doing so is to reconstruct the text's rhetorical context by asking questions about the author and then about the author's purpose, motivating occasion, audience, genre, and angle of vision. Let's look at each of these in turn.

Author, Motivating Occasion, and Purpose

The first three questions you should ask about a source text are these: Who is the author? What motivates the author to write? What is the author's purpose? In real life, writers are motivated to write because some occasion prompts them to do so. In most cases, the writer's purpose is to bring about some desirable change in the targeted audience's actions, beliefs, or views. However, if you are entering an argumentative conversation for the first time–say as part of a research project–you may have difficulty imagining the author of a blog post or a magazine article as a real person writing for a real purpose sparked by a real occasion. The following list identifies some of the categories of real-world people who are apt to write arguments about civic issues.

Typical Stakeholders in Argumentative Discussion of Civic Issues

- **Lobbyists and advocacy groups.** Lobbyists and advocacy groups commit themselves to a cause, often with passion, and produce avidly partisan arguments aimed at persuading voters, legislators, government agencies, and other decision makers. They often maintain advocacy websites; buy advertising space in newspapers, magazines, and online; and lobby legislators face to face.

- **Legislators, political candidates, and government officials.** Whenever new laws, regulations, or government policies are proposed, staffers do research and write arguments recommending positions on an issue. Often these arguments are available on the web.

- **Business professionals and labor union leaders.** Business spokespeople often address public issues in ways that support corporate or business interests. In contrast, labor union officials support wage structures or working conditions favorable to workers.

- **Lawyers and judges.** Lawyers write briefs supporting their clients' cases or file "friend-of-the-court" briefs aimed at influencing a judge's decision. Also, judges write opinions explaining their decisions on a case.

- **Journalists, syndicated columnists, and media commentators.** Many controversial issues attract the attention of media commentators (journalists, columnists, bloggers, political cartoonists) who write editorials, blogs, or op-ed pieces on the issue or produce editorial cartoons, filtering their arguments through the perspective of their own political views.

- **Professional freelance or staff writers.** Some of the most thoughtful analyses of public issues are composed by freelance or staff writers for public forum magazines such as *Atlantic Monthly* or *The National Review* or for online news sites or blogs such as *The Daily Kos* or *The Drudge Report*. These can range from in-depth background pieces to arguments with a highly persuasive aim.

- **Think tank members.** Because many of today's political, economic, and social issues are very complex, policy makers and commentators often rely on research institutions or think tanks to supply statistical studies and in-depth investigation of problems. These think tanks range across the political spectrum from conservative or libertarian to centrist or liberal.

- **Scholars and academics.** College professors play a public role through their scholarly research, contributing data, studies, and analyses to public debates. Scholarly research differs substantially from advocacy argument in that scholarly research is a systematic attempt to arrive at the best answers to questions based on the full examination of relevant data. Scholarly research is usually published in refereed academic journals rather than in popular magazines.

- **Documentary filmmakers.** Testifying to the growing popularity of film and its power to involve people in issues, documentary filmmakers often embed their point of view into their dramatic storytelling to create persuasive arguments on public issues. The global film industry is adding international perspectives as well.

- **Citizens and students.** Engaged citizens influence social policy through e-mails to legislators, letters to the editor, contributions to advocacy websites, guest editorials for newspapers, blogs, and speeches in public forums. Students also write for university communities, present their work at undergraduate research conferences, and influence public opinion by writing to political leaders and decision makers.

Audience

Effective argument depends on the writer's rhetorical understanding of audience. A writer's analysis of a targeted audience often includes demographic data (income, geographic region, typical occupations), political ideology (liberal, centrist, libertarian, conservative, populist), and what scholars call *intersectional positioning* (race, class, gender, ethnicity, sexual orientation, gender identity), and other factors. The writer's goal is to walk in his or her audience's shoes, to see where they are coming from, to understand their values, assumptions, and beliefs. Although writers of arguments occasionally preach to the choir (that is, address people who already agree with them), they usually want to reach people who hold alternative views or are otherwise skeptical of the writer's position. As we saw throughout Part One, effective arguers try to base their arguments on *audience-based reasons* that appeal to the targeted audience's underlying beliefs, values, and assumptions.

Genre

Genres, or types of writing, emerge from specific social contexts and represent social actions. Think of these genres, for example: billboard ads, infomercials, product reviews, and letters to the editor. The term *genre* refers to recurring categories of writing that follow certain conventions of style, structure, approach to subject matter, and document design. The genre of any given argument helps determine its length, tone, sentence complexity, level of informality or formality, use of visuals, kinds of evidence, and the presence or absence of documentation.

Consider, for example, the difference between a tweet and a letter to the editor. Both genres are short (a tweet is limited to 140 characters, a letter to about 200 words). The initial audience for a tweet are the tweeter's followers; the size of the audience depends on the number of followers and on the number of those who retweet the message to their own followers. (During his presidential candidacy, Donald Trump—a master user of Twitter—was able to reach millions of potential voters in seconds.) Because a tweet is self-published with no editor or fact checker, the reader must be especially wary. A tweet's shortness allows no space for a complete argument, only for an opinion or claim. In contrast, letters to the editor have quite different features. The audience for a letter are those newspaper subscribers who follow the editorial pages. Unlike tweets, letters to the editor are just long enough to allow a mini-argument, letting writers support their claims with brief reference to reasons and evidence. Also, unlike a tweet, there is some editorial review of a letter because editors must read many competing submissions for the limited space and choose letters that contribute something valuable to a conversation.

The concept of genre creates strong reader expectations, placing specific demands on writers. Genres are social practices that arise out of particular social

Table 7.1 Frequently Encountered Genres of Argument

Genre	Explanation and Examples	Stylistic Features
Newspaper editorials and op-ed pieces	• Published on the editorial or op-ed ("opposite-editorial") pages • Editorials promote the views of the newspaper's owners/editors • Op-ed pieces, usually written by professional columnists or guest writers, range in bias from ultraconservative to socialist • Often written in response to political events or social problems in the news	• Usually short (500–1,000 words) • Vary from explicit thesis-driven arguments to implicit arguments with stylistic flair • Have a journalistic style (short paragraphs) without detailed evidence • Sources are usually not documented
Blogs and postings to chat rooms and electronic bulletin boards	• Web-published commentaries, usually on specific topics and often intended to influence public opinion • Blogs (weblogs) are gaining influence as alternative commentaries to the established media	• Often blend styles of journalism, personal narrative, and formal argument • Often difficult to determine identity and credentials of blogger
Magazine articles	• Reflect a wide range of perspectives • Usually written by staff writers or freelancers • Appear in public-affairs magazines such as *National Review* or *The Progressive* or in niche magazines for special-interest groups such as *Rolling Stone* (popular culture), *Minority Business Entrepreneur* (business), or *The Advocate* (gay and lesbian issues) • Often reflect the magazine's political point of view	• Often provide hyperlinks to related sites on the web • Frequently include narrative elements rather than explicit thesis-and-reasons organization • Often provide well-researched coverage of various perspectives on a public issue
Articles in scholarly journals	• Peer-reviewed articles published by nonprofit academic journals subsidized by universities or scholarly societies • Characterized by scrupulous attention to completeness and accuracy in treatment of data	• Usually employ a formal academic style • Include academic documentation and bibliographies • May reflect the biases, methods, and strategies associated with a specific school of thought or theory within a discipline

needs and conditions. How you write any given grant proposal, op-ed piece, bumper sticker, or academic argument depends on the structure and style of hundreds of previous grant applications, op-ed pieces, bumper stickers, or academic articles written before yours. Table 7.1 identifies some of the important genres of argument that you will encounter as part of an argumentative conversation.

In addition to these commonly encountered print genres, arguments are also carried on in multimedia genres such as advocacy advertisements, advocacy websites, political cartoons, PowerPoint speeches, and documentary films.

Angle of Vision

Angle of vision, as we explained in Chapter 4, refers to the way that writers frame an issue through their own ideological perspective. Rhetoricians often use an optical metaphor: A writer looks at an issue through a lens that colors or filters the subject matter in a certain way. This lens causes the writer to select certain details while omitting others or to choose words with connotations that reflect the writer's view (whether to say, for example, "greedy capitalist" or "job creator"). A writer's angle of vision is persuasive because it controls what the reader "sees." Unless readers are rhetorically savvy, they can lose awareness that they are seeing the writer's subject matter through a lens that both reveals and conceals.

Closely connected to angle of vision is a writer's degree of advocacy along the continuum from "truth seeking" to "persuasion" (see Chapter 1, Figure 1.2). The more writers are trying to persuade readers toward their view, the more the reader has to recognize angle of vision at work. When doing research, for example, you should be aware of the angle of vision taken by many media outlets themselves—journals, magazines, newspapers, blogs, and websites—that may be associated with a political ideology. It is important to know, for example, whether an article you are reading came from *Mother Jones* (a liberal magazine), *National Review* (a conservative magazine), or *infowars.com* (an alt-right site often associated with "fake news").

Asking Questions That Promote Rhetorical Thinking

7.3   Ask questions that promote rhetorical thinking.

At an operational level, seeing arguments rhetorically means posing certain kinds of questions that uncover the rhetorical context and position of each stakeholder in the conversation. When you hear or read someone else's argument (let's call this argument a "source" written by a "source author"), you need to ask rhetorically focused questions about the source author's argument. If you seek answers to the list of questions shown in Table 7.2, you will be thinking rhetorically about arguments. Although a rhetorical analysis will not include answers to all these questions, using some of these questions in your thinking stages can give you a thorough understanding of the argument while helping you generate insights for your own rhetorical analysis essay.

Table 7.2 Questions for Rhetorical Analysis

What to Focus on	Questions to Ask	Applying These Questions
The *kairotic* moment and writer's motivating occasion	• What motivated the writer to produce this piece? • What social, cultural, political, legal, or economic conversations does this argument join?	• Is the writer responding to a bill pending in Congress, a speech by a political leader, or a local event that provoked controversy? • Is the writer addressing cultural trends such as the impact of science or technology on values?
Rhetorical context: Writer's purpose and audience	• What is the writer's purpose? • Who is the intended audience? • What assumptions, values, and beliefs would readers have to hold to find this argument persuasive? • How well does the text suit its particular audience and purpose?	• Is the writer trying to change readers' views by offering a new interpretation of a phenomenon, calling readers to action, or trying to muster votes or inspire further investigations? • Does the audience share a political or religious orientation with the writer?
Rhetorical context: Writer's identity and angle of vision	• Who is the writer and what is his or her profession, background, and expertise? • How does the writer's personal history, education, ethnicity, age, class, sexual orientation, gender identity, and political leaning influence the angle of vision? • What is emphasized and what is omitted in this text? • How much does the writer's angle of vision dominate the text?	• Is the writer a scholar, researcher, scientist, policy maker, politician, professional journalist, or citizen blogger? • Is the writer affiliated with conservative or liberal, religious or lay publications? • Is the writer advocating a stance or adopting a more inquiry-based mode? • What points of view and pieces of evidence are "not seen" by this writer?

(continued)

Table 7.2 Continued

What to Focus on	Questions to Ask	Applying These Questions
Rhetorical context: Genre	• What is the argument's original genre? • What is the original medium of publication? How do the genre and the argument's place of publication influence its content, structure, and style?	• How popular or scholarly, informal or formal is this genre? • Does the genre allow for in-depth or only sketchy coverage of an issue?
Logos **of the argument**	• What is the argument's claim, either explicitly stated or implied? • What are the main reasons in support of the claim? Are the reasons audience-based? • How effective is the writer's use of evidence? How is the argument supported and developed? • How well has the argument recognized and responded to alternative views?	• Is the core of the argument clear and soundly developed? Or do readers have to unearth or reconstruct the argument? • Is the argument one-sided, multisided, or delayed-thesis? • Does the argument depend on assumptions the audience may not share? • What evidence does the writer employ? Does this evidence meet the STAR criteria?
Ethos **of the argument**	• What *ethos* does the writer project? • How does the writer try to seem credible and trustworthy to the intended audience? • How knowledgeable does the writer seem in recognizing opposing or alternative views, and how fairly does the writer respond to them?	• If you are impressed or won over by this writer, what has earned your respect? • If you are filled with doubts or skepticism, what has caused you to question this writer? • How important is the character of the writer in this argument?
Pathos **of the argument**	• How effective is the writer in using audience-based reasons? • How does the writer use concrete language, word choice, narrative, examples, and analogies to tap readers' emotions, values, and imaginations?	• What examples, connotative language, and uses of narrative or analogy stand out for you in this argument? • Does this argument rely heavily on appeals to *pathos?* Or is it more brainy and logical?
Writer's style	• How do the writer's language choices and sentence length and complexity contribute to the impact of the argument? • How well does the writer's tone (attitude toward the subject) suit the argument?	• How readable is this argument? • Is the argument formal, scholarly, journalistic, informal, or casual? • Is the tone serious, mocking, humorous, exhortational, confessional, urgent, or something else?
Design and visual elements	• How do design elements—layout, font sizes and styles, and use of color—influence the effect of the argument? (See Chapter 9 for a detailed discussion of these elements.) • How do graphics and images contribute to the persuasiveness of the argument?	• Do design features contribute to the logical or the emotional/imaginative appeals of the argument? • How would this argument benefit from visuals and graphics or some different document design?
Overall persuasiveness of the argument	• What features of this argument contribute most to making it persuasive or not persuasive for its target audience and for you yourself? • How would this argument be received by different audiences? • What features contribute to the rhetorical complexity of this argument? • What is particularly memorable, disturbing, or problematic about this argument? • What does this argument contribute to its *kairotic* moment and the argumentative controversy of which it is a part?	• Are appeals to *pathos* legitimate and suitable? Do the quality and quantity of the evidence help build a strong case, or do they fall short? • What specifically would count as a strength for the target audience? • If you differ from the target audience, how do you differ and where does the argument derail for you? • What gaps, contradictions, or unanswered questions are you left with? • How does this argument indicate that it is engaged in a public conversation? How does it "talk" to other arguments you have read on this issue?

Conducting a Rhetorical Analysis of a Source Text

7.4   Conduct a rhetorical analysis of a source text.

To illustrate rhetorical analysis, we will analyze two articles on reproductive technology, a subject that continues to generate arguments in the public sphere. (The first article is in this section; the second is in the student example at the end of this chapter.) By *reproductive technology* we mean scientific advances in the treatment of infertility, such as egg and sperm donation, artificial insemination, in vitro fertilization, and surrogate motherhood. Our first article, written over a decade ago, springs from the early and increasing popularity of these technological options. Our second article—to be used in our later student example—responds to the recent globalization of this technology.

At this point, please read the first article, "Egg Heads" by Kathryn Jean Lopez (immediately following), and then proceed to the discussion questions that follow. Lopez's article was originally published in the conservative news commentary magazine *National Review*.

Egg Heads

KATHRYN JEAN LOPEZ

Filling the waiting room to capacity and spilling over into a nearby conference room, a group of young women listen closely and follow the instructions: Complete the forms and return them, with the clipboard, to the receptionist. It's all just as in any medical office. Then they move downstairs, where the doctor briefs them. "Everything will be pretty much normal," she explains. "Women complain of skin irritation in the local area of injection and bloating. You also might be a little emotional. But, basically, it's really bad PMS."

This is not just another medical office. On a steamy night in July, these girls in their twenties are attending an orientation session for potential egg donors at a New Jersey fertility clinic specializing in in-vitro fertilization. Within the walls of IVF New Jersey and at least two hundred other clinics throughout the United States, young women answer the call to give "the gift of life" to infertile couples. Egg donation is a quietly expanding industry, changing the way we look at the family, young women's bodies, and human life itself.

It is not a pleasant way to make money. Unlike sperm donation, which is over in less than an hour, egg donation takes the donor some 56 hours and includes a battery of tests, ultrasound, self-administered injections, and retrieval. Once a donor is accepted into a program, she is given hormones to stimulate the ovaries, changing the number of eggs matured from the usual one per month up to as many as fifty. A doctor then surgically removes the eggs from the donor's ovary and fertilizes them with the designated sperm.

Although most programs require potential donors to undergo a series of medical tests and counseling, there is little indication that most of the young women know what they are getting themselves into. They risk bleeding, infection, and scarring. When too many eggs are matured in one cycle, it can damage the ovaries and leave the donor with weeks of abdominal pain. (At worst, complications may leave her dead.) Longer term, the possibility of early menopause raises the prospect of future regret. There is also some evidence of a connection between the fertility drugs used in the process and ovarian cancer.

5 But it's good money—and getting better. New York's Brooklyn IVF raised its "donor compensation" from $2,500 to $5,000 per cycle earlier this year in order to keep pace with St. Barnabas Medical Center in nearby Livingston, New Jersey. It's a bidding war. "It's obvious why we had to do it," says Susan Lobel, Brooklyn IVF's assistant director. Most New York–area IVF programs have followed suit.

Some infertile couples and independent brokers are offering even more for "reproductive material." The International Fertility Center in Indianapolis, Indiana, for instance, places ads in the *Daily Princetonian* offering Princeton girls as much as $35,000 per cycle. The National Fertility Registry, which, like many egg brokerages, features an online catalogue for couples to browse in, advertises $35,000 to $50,000 for Ivy League eggs. While donors are normally paid a flat fee per cycle, there have been reports of higher payments to donors who produce more eggs.

College girls are the perfect donors. Younger eggs are likelier to be healthy, and the girls themselves frequently need money—college girls have long been susceptible to classified ads offering to pay them for acting as guinea pigs in medical research. One 1998 graduate of the University of Colorado set up her own website to market her eggs. She had watched a television show on egg donation and figured it "seemed like a good thing to do"—especially since she had spent her money during the past year to help secure a country music record deal. "Egg donation would help me with my school and music expenses while helping an infertile couple with a family." Classified ads scattered throughout cyberspace feature similar offers.

The market for "reproductive material" has been developing for a long time. It was twenty years ago this summer that the first test-tube baby, Louise Brown, was born. By 1995, when the latest tally was taken by the Centers for Disease Control, 15 percent of mothers in this country had made use of some form of assisted-reproduction technology in conceiving their children. (More recently, women past menopause have begun to make use of this technology.) In 1991 the American Society for Reproductive Medicine was aware of 63 IVF programs offering egg donation. That number had jumped to 189 by 1995 (the latest year for which numbers are available).

Defenders argue that it's only right that women are "compensated" for the inconvenience of egg donation. Brooklyn IVF's Dr. Lobel argues, "If it is unethical to accept payment for loving your neighbor, then we'll have to stop paying baby-sitters." As long as donors know the risks, says Glenn McGee of the University of Pennsylvania's Center for Bioethics, this transaction is only "a slightly macabre version of adoption."

10 Not everyone is enthusiastic about the "progress." Egg donation "represents another rather large step into turning procreation into manufacturing," says the University of Chicago's Leon Kass. "It's the dehumanization of procreation." And as in manufacturing, there is quality control. "People don't want to say the word any more, but there is a strong eugenics issue inherent in the notion that you can have the best eggs your money can buy," observes sociology professor Barbara Katz Rothman of the City University of New York.

The demand side of the market comes mostly from career-minded baby-boomers, the frontierswomen of feminism, who thought they could "have it all." Indeed they *can* have it all—with a little help from some younger eggs. (Ironically, feminists are also among its strongest critics; *The Nation*'s Katha Pollitt has pointed out that in egg donation and surrogacy, once you remove the "delusion that they are making babies for other women," all you have left is "reproductive prostitution.")

Unfortunately, the future looks bright for the egg market. Earlier this year, a woman in Atlanta gave birth to twins after she was implanted with frozen donor eggs. The same technology has also been successful in Italy. This is just what the egg market needed, since it avoids the necessity of coordinating donors' cycles with recipients' cycles. Soon, not only will infertile couples be able to choose from a wider variety of donor offerings, but in some cases donors won't even be needed. Young women will be able to freeze their own eggs and have them thawed and fertilized once they are ready for the intrusion of children in their lives.

There are human ovaries sitting in a freezer in Fairfax, Virginia. The Genetics and IVF Institute offers to cut out and remove young women's ovaries and cryopreserve the egg-containing tissue for future implantation. Although the technology was originally designed to give the hope of fertility to young women undergoing treatment for cancer, it is now starting to attract the healthy. "Women can wait to have children until they are well established in their careers and getting a little bored, sometime in their forties or fifties," explains Professor Rothman. "Basically, motherhood is being reduced to a good leisure-time activity."

Early this summer, headlines were made in Britain, where the payment of egg donors is forbidden, when an infertile couple traveled to a California clinic where the woman could be inseminated with an experimental hybrid egg. The egg was a combination of the recipient's and a donor's eggs. The clinic in question gets its eggs from a Beverly Hills brokerage, the Center for Surrogate Parenting and Egg Donation, run by Karen Synesiou and Bill Handel, a radio shock-jock in Los Angeles. Miss Synesiou recently told the London *Sunday Times* that she is "interested in redefining the family. That's why I came to work here."

The redefinition is already well under way. Consider the case of Jaycee Buz- 15
zanca. After John and Luanne Buzzanca had tried for years to have a child, an embryo was created for them, using sperm and an egg from anonymous donors, and implanted in a surrogate mother. In March 1995, one month before the baby was born, John filed for divorce. Luanne wanted child support from John, but he refused—after all, he's not the father. Luanne argued that John is Jaycee's father legally. At this point the surrogate mother, who had agreed to carry a baby for a stable two-parent household, decided to sue for custody.

Jaycee was dubbed "Nobody's Child" by the media when a California judge ruled that John was not the legal father nor Luanne the legal mother (neither one was genetically related to Jaycee, and Luanne had not even borne her). Enter Erin Davidson, the egg donor, who claims the egg was used without her permission. Not to be left out, the sperm donor jumped into the ring, saying that his sperm was used without his permission, a claim he later dropped. In March of this year, an appeals court gave Luanne custody and decided that John is the legal father, making him responsible for child support. By contracting for a medical procedure resulting in the birth of a child, the court ruled, a couple incurs "the legal status of parenthood." (John lost an appeal in May.) For Jaycee's first three years on earth, these people have been wrangling over who her parents are.

In another case, William Kane left his girlfriend, Deborah Hect, 15 vials of sperm before he killed himself in a Las Vegas hotel in 1991. His two adult children (represented by their mother, his ex-wife) contested Miss Hect's claim of ownership. A settlement agreement on Kane's will was eventually reached, giving his children 80 percent of his estate and Miss Hect 20 percent. Hence she was allowed three vials of his sperm. When she did not succeed in conceiving on the first two tries, she filed a petition for the other 12 vials. She won, and the judge who ruled in her favor wrote, "Neither this court nor the decedent's adult children possess reason or right to prevent Hect from implementing decedent's pre-eminent interest in realizing his 'fundamental right' to procreate with the woman of his choice." One day, donors may not even have to have lived. Researchers are experimenting with using aborted female fetuses as a source of donor eggs.

And the market continues to zip along. For overseas couples looking for donor eggs, Bill Handel has the scenario worked out. The couple would mail him frozen sperm of their choice (presumably from the recipient husband); his clinic would use it to fertilize donor eggs, chosen from its catalogue of offerings, and reply back within a month with a frozen embryo ready for implantation. (Although the sperm does not yet arrive by mail, Handel has sent out embryos to at least one hundred international customers.) As for the young women at the New Jersey clinic, they are visibly upset by one aspect of the egg-donation process: they can't have sexual intercourse for several weeks after the retrieval. For making babies, of course, it's already obsolete.

For Writing and Discussion

Identifying Rhetorical Features

Working in groups or as a class, develop responses to the following questions:

1. How does Lopez appeal to *logos*? What is her main claim, and what are her reasons?
2. What does she use for evidence? What ideas would you have to include in a short summary of "Egg Heads"?
3. What appeals to *pathos* does Lopez make in this argument? How well are these suited to the conservative readers of the *National Review*?
4. How would you characterize Lopez's *ethos*? Does she seem knowledgeable and credible? Does she seem fair to stakeholders in this controversy?
5. Choose an additional focus from the "Questions for Rhetorical Analysis" (Table 7.2) to apply to "Egg Heads." How does this question expand your understanding of Lopez's argument?
6. What strikes you as problematic, memorable, or disturbing in this argument?

Our Own Rhetorical Analysis of "Egg Heads"

Now that you have identified some of the rhetorical features of "Egg Heads," we offer our own notes for a rhetorical analysis of this argument.

RHETORICAL CONTEXT   As we began our analysis, we reconstructed the rhetorical context in which "Egg Heads" was published. In the late 1990s, a furious debate about egg donation rippled through college and public newspapers, popular journalism, websites, and scholarly commentary. This debate had been kicked off by several couples placing ads in the newspapers of the country's most prestigious colleges, offering up to $50,000 for the eggs of brilliant, attractive, athletic college women. Coinciding with these consumer demands, advances in reproductive technology provided an increasing number of complex techniques to surmount the problem of infertility, including fertilizing eggs in petri dishes and implanting them into women through surgical procedures. These procedures could use either a couple's own eggs and sperm or donated eggs and sperm. All these social and medical factors created the *kairotic* moment for Lopez's article and motivated her to protest the increasing use of these procedures. (Egg donation, concerns for the long-term health of egg donors, surrogate motherhood, and the potential dehumanizing of commercial reproduction continue to be troubling and unresolved controversies across many genres, as you will see when you read Ellen Goodman's op-ed piece at the end of this chapter and student Zachary Stumps's rhetorical analysis of it.)

GENRE AND WRITER   When we considered the genre and writer of this article and its place of publication, we noted that this article appeared in the *National Review*, which describes itself as "America's most widely read and influential magazine and website for Republican/conservative news, commentary, and opinion." It reaches "an affluent, educated, and highly responsive audience of corporate and government leaders, the financial elite, educators, journalists, community and association leaders, as well as engaged activists all across America" (http://www.nationalreview.com). According to our Internet search, Kathryn Jean Lopez is known nationally for her conservative journalistic writing on social and political issues. Currently the editor-at-large of *National Review Online*, she has also published in *The Wall Street Journal*, the *New York Post*, and the *Washington Times*. This information told us that in her article "Egg Heads," Lopez is definitely on home territory, aiming her article at a conservative audience.

LOGOS   Turning to the *logos* of Lopez's argument, we decided that the logical structure of Lopez's argument is clear throughout the article. Her claim is that egg donation and its associated reproductive advances have harmful, long-reaching consequences for society. Basically, she argues that egg donation and reproductive technology represent bad scientific developments for society because they are potentially harmful to the long-range health of egg donors and because they lead to an unnatural dehumanizing of human sexuality. She states a version of this last point at the end of the second paragraph: "Egg donation is a quietly expanding industry, changing the way we look at the family, young women's bodies, and human life itself."

The body of her article elaborates on each of these reasons. In developing her reason that egg donation endangers egg donors, Lopez lists the risks but doesn't supply supporting evidence about the frequency of these problems: damage to the ovaries, persistent pain, early menopause, possible ovarian cancer, and even death. She supports her claim about "the expanding industry" by showing how the procedures have become commercialized. To show the popularity of these procedures as well as their commercial value, she quotes a variety of experts such as directors of in vitro clinics, fertility centers, bioethicists, and the American Society for Reproductive Medicine. She also cleverly bolsters her own case by showing that even liberal cultural critics agree with her views about the big ethical questions raised by the reproductive-technology business. In addition to quoting experts, Lopez has sprinkled impressive numbers and vivid examples throughout the body of her argument; these numbers and examples give her argument momentum as it progresses from the potential harm to young egg donors to a number of case studies that depict increasingly disturbing ethical problems.

PATHOS   Much of the impact of this argument, we noted, comes from Lopez's appeals to *pathos*. By describing in detail the waiting rooms for egg donors at fertility clinics, Lopez relies heavily on pathetic appeals to move her audience to see the physical and social dangers of egg donation. She conveys the growing commercialism of reproductive technology by giving readers an inside look at the egg-donation process as these young college women embark on the multistep process of donating their eggs. These young women, she suggests in her title "Egg Heads," are largely unaware of the potential physical dangers to themselves and of the ethical implications and consequences of their acts. She asserts that they are driven largely by the desire for money. Lopez also appeals to *pathos* in her choice of emotionally loaded and often cynical language, which creates an angle of vision opposing reproductive technology: "turning procreation into manufacturing"; "reproductive prostitution"; "the intrusion of children in their lives"; "motherhood . . . reduced to a good leisure-time activity"; "aborted female fetuses as a source of donor eggs"; and intercourse as an "obsolete" way to make babies.

AUDIENCE   Despite Lopez's success at spotlighting serious medical and ethical questions, her lack of attention to alternative views and the alarmism of her language caused us to wonder: Who might find this argument persuasive, and who would challenge it? What is noticeably missing from Lopez's argument—and apparently from her worldview—is the perspective of infertile couples hoping for a baby. Pursuing our question, we decided that a provocative feature of this argument—one worthy of deeper analysis—is the disparity between how well this argument is suited to its target audience and yet how unpersuasive it is for readers who do not share the assumptions, values, and beliefs of this primary audience.

To Lopez's credit, she has attuned her reasons to the values and concerns of her conservative readers of the *National Review*, who believe in traditional families, gender differences, and gender roles. Opposed to feminism as they understand it, this audience sanctions careers for women only if women put their families first. Lopez's choice of evidence and her orchestration of it are intended to play to her audience's fears that science has fallen into the hands of those who have little regard for the sanctity of the family or traditional motherhood. For example, in playing strongly to the values of her conservative readers, Lopez belabors the physical, social, and ethical dangers of egg donation, mentioning worst-case scenarios; however, these appeals to *pathos* will most likely strike other readers who do some investigating into reproductive technology as overblown. She emphasizes the commercialism of the process as her argument moves from college girls as egg donors to a number of sensationalist case studies that depict intensifying ethical and legal ambiguity. In other words, both the *logos* and the *pathos* of her argument skillfully focus on details that tap her target audience's values and beliefs, feeding that audience's fears and revulsion.

USE OF EVIDENCE   For a broader or skeptical audience, the alarmism of Lopez's appeals to *pathos*, her use of atypical evidence, and her distortion of the facts weaken the *logos* and *ethos* of her argument. First, Lopez's use of evidence fails to measure up to the STAR criteria (that evidence should be sufficient, typical, accurate, and relevant). She characterizes all egg donors as young women seeking money. But she provides little evidence that egg donors are only out to make a buck. She also paints these young women as shortsighted, uninformed, and foolish. As a gap in her evidence, she neglects to examine the potential for long-term health consequences to egg donors. Lopez would rather toss out threats and criticize the young women than really explore this issue. Lopez also weakens her *ethos* by not considering the young women who may be motivated, at least in part, by compassion for couples who can't conceive on their own.

Lopez also misrepresents the people who are using egg donation, placing them all into two groups: (1) wealthy couples eugenically seeking designer babies with preordered special traits and (2) feminist career women. She directs much of her criticism toward this latter group: "The demand side of the market comes mostly from career-minded baby-boomers, the frontierswomen of feminism, who thought they could 'have it all.'" However, readers who do a little research on their own, as we did, will learn that infertility affects one in seven couples; that it is often a male and a female problem, sometimes caused by an incompatibility between the man's and the woman's reproductive material; and that most couples who take the big step of investing in these expensive efforts to have a baby have been trying to get pregnant for a number of years. Rather than being casual about having children, they are often deeply desirous of children and depressed about their inability to conceive. In addition, far from being the sure thing and quick fix that Lopez suggests, reproductive technology has a success rate of only 50 percent overall and involves a huge investment of time, money, and physical discomfort for women receiving donor eggs.

Another way that Lopez violates the STAR criteria is her choice of extreme cases. For readers outside her target audience, her argument appears riddled with straw man and slippery-slope fallacies. (See Appendix 1, "Informal Fallacies.") Her examples become more bizarre as her tone becomes more hysterical. Here are some specific instances of extreme, atypical cases:

- her focus on career women casually and selfishly using the service of young egg donors

- the notorious case of Jaycee Buzzanca, dubbed "Nobody's Child" because her adoptive parents who commissioned her creation divorced before she was born

- the legal contest between a dead man's teen girlfriend and his ex-wife and adult children over his vials of sperm

- the idea of taking eggs from aborted female fetuses

By keeping invisible the vast majority of ordinary couples who go to fertility clinics out of last-hope desperation, Lopez uses extreme cases to create a "brave new world" intended to evoke a vehement rejection of these reproductive advances. Skeptical readers would offer the alternative view of the sad, ordinary couples of all ages sitting week after week in fertility clinics, hoping to conceive a child through the "miracle" of these reproductive advances and grateful to the young women who have contributed their eggs.

CONCLUDING POINTS   In short, we concluded that Lopez's angle of vision, although effectively in sync with her conservative readers of the *National Review,* exaggerates and distorts her case against these reproductive advances. Lopez's traditional values and slanting of the evidence undermine her *ethos,* limit the value of this argument for a wider audience, and compel that audience to seek out alternative sources for a more complete view of egg donation.

Writing Assignment

A Rhetorical Analysis

Write a thesis-driven rhetorical analysis essay in which you examine the rhetorical effectiveness of an argument specified by your instructor. Unless otherwise stated, direct your analysis to an audience of your classmates. In your introduction, establish the argumentative conversation to which this argument is contributing. Briefly summarize the argument and present your thesis highlighting the rhetorical features of the argument that you find central to its effectiveness or ineffectiveness. Zachary Stumps's analysis of Ellen Goodman's "Womb for Rent" (reproduced at the end of this chapter) is an example of this assignment.

Generating Ideas for Your Rhetorical Analysis

To develop ideas for your essay, you might follow these steps:

Step	How to Do It
Familiarize yourself with the article you are analyzing.	Read the article several times. Divide it into sections to understand its structure.
Place the article in its rhetorical context.	Reconstruct the article's rhetorical context following the advice in this chapter. Use the list of questions in Table 7.2, "Questions for Rhetorical Analysis."
Summarize the article.	If you have never written a summary before, you can find specific instruction in Chapter 8.
Reread the article, identifying "hot spots."	Note hot spots in the article—points that impress you, disturb you, confuse you, or puzzle you.
Use the list of questions in Table 7.2, "Questions for Rhetorical Analysis"	Choose several of these questions and freewrite responses to them.
From your notes and freewriting, identify the focus for your analysis.	Choose several features of the article that you find particularly important and that you want to discuss in depth in your essay. Identify points that will bring something new to your readers and that will help them see this article with new understanding. You may want to list your ideas and then look for ways to group them together around main points.
Write a thesis statement for your essay.	Articulate your important points in one or two sentences, setting up these points clearly for your audience.

In finding a meaningful focus for your rhetorical analysis essay, you will need to create a focusing thesis statement that avoids wishy-washy formulas such as, "This argument has some strengths and some weaknesses." To avoid a vapid thesis statement, focus on the complexity of the argument, the writer's strategies for persuading the target audience, and the features that might impede its persuasiveness for skeptics. The best thesis statements articulate how their writers see the inner workings of these arguments as well as the arguments' contributions to their public conversations. For example:

> Lopez's angle of vision, although effectively in sync with her conservative readers of the *National Review*, exaggerates and distorts her case against certain reproductive advances, weakening her *ethos* and the value of her argument for a wider audience. [This is the thesis we would use if we were writing a stand-alone essay on the Lopez article.]

To make your rhetorical analysis of your article persuasive, you will need to develop each of the points stated or implied in your thesis statement using textual evidence, including short quotations. Your essay should show how you have listened carefully to the argument you are analyzing, summarized it fairly, and probed it deeply.

Organizing Your Rhetorical Analysis

The organization plan in Figure 7.1 provides a possible structure for your rhetorical analysis.

Figure 7.1 Organizational plan for a rhetorical analysis of an argument

Organization Plan for a Rhetorical Analysis of an Argument

Introduction	• Present the *kairos* of the article • Engage reader's interest in the issue of the article • Indicate your interest and investment • Present a thesis with three or four rhetorical points about the article you will analyze in depth
Summary of Argument	• Briefly present the claim and main points of the article you are analyzing to help readers understand your analysis • [Possibly include the summary of the article in your introduction]
Rhetorical Analysis	• Explain, develop, and discuss the rhetorical points in your thesis, examining the author's rhetorical strategies • Use examples and quotations from the article's argument you are analyzing to make your points clear to your readers
Conclusion	• Wrap up your analysis • Perhaps mention the stakes or importance of this article's contribution to the public conversation on this issue

Readings

Our first reading is by Pulitzer Prize–winning columnist, author, and speaker Ellen Goodman. In our second reading, student Zachary Stumps analyzes Goodman's op-ed piece rhetorically.

Womb for Rent

ELLEN GOODMAN

By now we all have a story about a job outsourced beyond our reach in the global economy. My own favorite is about the California publisher who hired two reporters in India to cover the Pasadena city government. Really.

(continued)

There are times as well when the offshoring of jobs takes on a quite literal meaning. When the labor we are talking about is, well, labor.

In the last few months we've had a full nursery of international stories about surrogate mothers. Hundreds of couples are crossing borders in search of lower-cost ways to fill the family business. In turn, there's a new coterie of international workers who are gestating for a living.

Many of the stories about the globalization of baby production begin in India, where the government seems to regard this as, literally, a growth industry. In the little town of Anand, dubbed "The Cradle of the World," 45 women were recently on the books of a local clinic. For the production and delivery of a child, they will earn $5,000 to $7,000, a decade's worth of women's wages in rural India.

5 But even in America, some women, including Army wives, are supplementing their income by contracting out their wombs. They have become surrogate mothers for wealthy couples from European countries that ban the practice.

This globalization of baby-making comes at the peculiar intersection of a high reproductive technology and a low-tech work force. The biotech business was created in the same petri dish as Baby Louise, the first IVF baby. But since then, we've seen conception outsourced to egg donors and sperm donors. We've had motherhood divided into its parts from genetic mother to gestational mother to birth mother and now contract mother.

We've also seen the growth of an international economy. Frozen sperm is flown from one continent to another. And patients have become medical tourists, searching for cheaper health care whether it's a new hip in Thailand or an IVF treatment in South Africa that comes with a photo safari thrown in for the same price. Why not then rent a foreign womb?

I don't make light of infertility. The primal desire to have a child underlies this multinational Creation, Inc. On one side, couples who choose surrogacy want a baby with at least half their own genes. On the other side, surrogate mothers, who are rarely implanted with their own eggs, can believe that the child they bear and deliver is not really theirs.

As one woman put it, "We give them a baby and they give us much-needed money. It's good for them and for us." A surrogate in Anand used the money to buy a heart operation for her son. Another raised a dowry for her daughter. And before we talk about the "exploitation" of the pregnant woman, consider her alternative in Anand: a job crushing glass in a factory for $25 a month.

10 Nevertheless, there is—and there should be—something uncomfortable about a free-market approach to baby-making. It's easier to accept surrogacy when it's a gift from one woman to another. But we rarely see a rich woman become a surrogate for a poor family. Indeed, in Third World countries, some women sign these contracts with a fingerprint because they are illiterate.

For that matter, we have not yet had stories about the contract workers for whom pregnancy was a dangerous occupation, but we will. What obligation does a family that simply contracted for a child have to its birth mother? What control do—should—contractors have over their "employees'" lives while incubating "their" children? What will we tell the offspring of this international trade?

"National boundaries are coming down," says bioethicist Lori Andrews, "but we can't stop human emotions. We are expanding families and don't even have terms to deal with it."

It's the commercialism that is troubling. Some things we cannot sell no matter how good "the deal." We cannot, for example, sell ourselves into slavery. We cannot sell our children. But the surrogacy business comes perilously close to both of these deals. And international surrogacy tips the scales.

So, these borders we are crossing are not just geographic ones. They are ethical ones. Today the global economy sends everyone in search of the cheaper deal as if that were the single common good. But in the biological search, humanity is sacrificed to the economy and the person becomes the product. And, step by step, we come to a stunning place in our ancient creation story. It's called the marketplace.

Our second reading shows how student writer Zachary Stumps analyzed the Ellen Goodman article.

Student Essay

A Rhetorical Analysis Of Ellen Goodman's "Womb For Rent"

Zachary Stumps

With her op-ed piece "Womb for Rent," published in the *Seattle Times* (and earlier in *The Washington Post*), syndicated columnist Ellen Goodman enters the murky debate about reproductive technology gone global. Because Americans are outsourcing everything else, "Why not then rent a foreign womb?" she asks. Goodman, a Pulitzer Prize–winning columnist for the Washington Post Writers Group, is known for helping readers understand the "tumult of social change and its impact on families," and for shattering "the mold of men writing exclusively about politics" ("Ellen Goodman"). This op-ed piece continues her tradition of examining social change from the perspective of family issues.

Introduction provides context and poses issue to be addressed

Provides background on Goodman

Goodman launches her short piece by asserting that one of the most recent and consequential "jobs" to be outsourced is having babies. She explains how the "globalization of baby production" is thriving because it brings together the reproductive desires of people in developed countries and the bodily resources of women in developing countries such as India. Briefly tracing how both reproductive technology and medical tourism have taken advantage of global possibilities, Goodman acknowledges that the thousands of dollars Indian women earn by carrying the babies of foreign couples represent a much larger income than these women could earn in any other available jobs.

Summarizes the op-ed piece

(continued)

After appearing to legitimize this global exchange, however, Goodman shifts to her ethical concerns by raising some moral questions that she says are not being addressed in this trade. She concludes with a full statement of her claim that this global surrogacy is encroaching on human respect and dignity, exploiting business-based science, and turning babies into products.

Thesis paragraph

In this piece, Goodman's delay of her thesis has several rhetorical benefits: It gives Goodman space to present the perspective of poor women, enhanced by her appeals to *pathos*, and it invites readers to join her journey into the complex contexts of this issue. However, this strategy is also risky because it limits the development of her own argument.

Develops first point 5 in thesis: use of pathos in exploring perspective of poor women

Instead of presenting her thesis up front, Goodman devotes much of the first part of her argument to looking at this issue from the perspective of foreign surrogate mothers. Using the strategies of *pathos* to evoke sympathy for these women, she creates a compassionate and progressive-minded argument that highlights the benefits to foreign surrogate mothers. She cites factual evidence showing that the average job for a woman in Anand, India, yields a tiny "$25 a month" gotten through the hard work of "crushing glass in a factory," compared to the "$5,000 to $7,000" made carrying a baby to term. To carry a baby to term for a foreign couple represents "a decade's worth of women's wages in rural India." Deepening readers' understanding of these women, Goodman cites one woman who used her earnings to finance her son's heart operation and another who paid for her daughter's dowry. In her fair presentation of these women, Goodman both builds her own positive *ethos* and adds a dialogic dimension to her argument by helping readers walk in the shoes of impoverished surrogate mothers.

Develops second point in thesis: the complex contexts of this issue—outsourcing and medical tourism

The second rhetorical benefit of Goodman's delayed thesis is that she invites readers to explore this complex issue of global surrogacy with her before she declares her own view. To help readers understand and think through this issue, she relates it to two other familiar global topics: outsourcing and medical tourism. First, she introduces foreign surrogacy as one of the latest forms of outsourcing: "This globalization of baby-making comes at the peculiar intersection of a high reproductive technology and a low-tech work force." Presenting these women as workers, she explains that women in India are getting paid for "the production and delivery of a child" that is analogous to the production and delivery of sneakers or bicycle parts. Goodman also sets this phenomenon in the context of global medical tourism. If people can pursue lower-cost treatment for illnesses and health conditions in other countries, why shouldn't an infertile couple seeking to start a family not also have such access to these more affordable and newly available means? This reasoning provides a foundation for readers to begin understanding the many layers of the issue.

Shows how the delayed-thesis structure creates two perspectives in conflict

The result of Goodman's delayed-thesis strategy is that the first two-thirds of this piece seem to justify outsourcing surrogate motherhood. Only after reading the whole op-ed piece can readers see clearly that Goodman has been dropping hints about her view all along through her choice of words. Although she clearly sees how outsourcing surrogacy can help poor women economically, her use of market language such as "production," "delivery," and "labor" carry a double meaning. On first reading of this op-ed piece, readers don't know if Goodman's punning is meant to be catchy and entertaining or serves another purpose. This other purpose becomes clear in the last third of the article when Goodman forthrightly asserts her criticism of the commercialism of the global marketplace that promotes worldwide searching for a "cheaper deal": "humanity is sacrificed to the economy and the person becomes the product." This is a bold and big claim, but does the final third of her article support it?

In the final five paragraphs of this op-ed piece, Goodman begins to develop the rational basis of her argument; however, the brevity of the op-ed genre and her choice not to state her view openly initially have left Goodman with little space to develop her own claim. The result is that she presents some profound ideas very quickly. Some of the ethically complex ideas she introduces but doesn't explore much are these:

Restates the third point in his thesis: lack of space limits development of Goodman's argument

- The idea that there are ethical limits on what can be "sold"
- The idea that surrogate motherhood might be a "dangerous occupation"
- The idea that children born from this "international trade" may be confused about their identities.

Goodman simply has not left herself enough space to develop these issues and perhaps leaves readers with questions rather than with changed views. I am particularly struck by several questions. Why have European countries banned surrogacy in developing countries, and why has the United States not banned this practice? Does Goodman intend to argue that the United States should follow Europe's lead? She could explore more how this business of finding illiterate women to bear children for the wealthy continues to exploit third-world citizens much as sex tourism exploits women in the very same countries. It seems to perpetuate a tendency for the developed world to regard developing countries as poor places of lawlessness where practices outlawed in the rest of the world (e.g., child prostitution, slave-like working conditions) are somehow tolerable. Goodman could have developed her argument more to state explicitly that a woman who accepts payment for bearing a baby becomes an indentured servant to the family. Yet another way to think of this issue is to see that the old saying of "a bun in the oven" is more literal than metaphorical when a woman uses her womb as a factory to produce children, a body business not too dissimilar to the commercialism of prostitution. Goodman teases readers by mentioning these complex problems without producing an argument.

Discusses examples of ideas raised by Goodman but not developed

Still, although Goodman does not expand her criticism of outsourced surrogate motherhood or explore the issues of human dignity and rights, this argument does introduce the debate on surrogacy in the global marketplace, raise awareness, and begin to direct the conversation toward a productive end of seeking a responsible, healthy, and ethical future. Her

10 Conclusion

(continued)

op-ed piece lures readers into contemplating deep, perplexing ethical and economic problems, and it lays a foundation for readers to create an informed view of this issue.

Works Cited

Uses MLA format to list sources cited in the essay

"Ellen Goodman." *Washingtonpost.com*, www.washingtonpost.com/
    wp-srv/post/writersgroup/biogoodman.htm. Accessed 8 Apr. 2016.
Goodman, Ellen. "Womb for Rent." *The Washington Post*, 11 Apr.
    2008, p. B6.

Chapter 8

Argument as Inquiry

Reading, Summarizing, and Speaking Back

Learning Objectives

In this chapter, you will learn to:

8.1 Use exploratory strategies to find an engaging issue.

8.2 Summarize a stakeholder's argument as an entry into the issue.

8.3 Respond to a stakeholder's argument through believing, doubting, and dialectic thinking.

8.4 Delay closure by thinking dialectically.

This chapter, like the preceding one, focuses on the inquiring or truth-seeking aim of argument. Truth-seeking is an antidote to locking ourselves up in echo chambers of like-minded individuals who have little interest in other people's views because they believe they already know the truth. Dismayed by these echo chambers, cultural critic Matt Miller recently posed the questions: "Is it possible in America today to convince anyone of anything he doesn't already believe? . . . [A]re there enough places where this mingling of minds occurs to sustain a democracy?"*

Miller's "mingling of minds" is essential for the truth-seeking process to work. Argument as truth-seeking depends on the willingness of stakeholders to listen to one another and to change their views in the face of new reasons and evidence. We value the insight of rhetorician Wayne Booth, who proposes that when we enter an argumentative conversation, we should not ask first "How can I change your mind?" but rather "When should I change my mind?"**

---

*Matt Miller, "Is Persuasion Dead?" *The New York Times*, 4 June 2005, A29.
**Wayne Booth raised these questions in a featured session with Peter Elbow titled "Blind Skepticism vs. the Rhetoric of Assent: Implications for Rhetoric, Argument, and Teaching," presented at the CCCC annual convention, Chicago, Illinois, March 2002.

Argument as truth-seeking is not easy because argumentative conversations always entail disagreements. Whenever you argue, you necessarily bring your view into tension with some alternative view: *"Although some stakeholders think X, I am arguing Y."* Your view on an issue (which you will need to support with your own reasons and evidence) pushes against an alternative view (which you must be able to summarize fairly). When you first begin exploring an issue, you may not know where you stand on the issue, and even if you do know, you should be willing to change your mind as your research takes you deeper into the issue. To participate thoughtfully in this inquiry process, you need two high-level skills: (1) the ability to summarize each stakeholder's view as you encounter it and (2) the ability to formulate your own thoughtful response to that view. Eventually this exploratory process of summary and response can help you stake out your own claim in the conversation and determine your best means of supporting it.

This chapter teaches you these summary/response skills. After presenting strategies to help you discover an engaging issue, we show you how to summarize a stakeholder's argument and then respond to it through believing, doubting, and dialectic thinking. To illustrate argument as inquiry, we follow the thinking process of student writer Trudie Makens as she explores the problem of whether fast-food workers and other low-wage laborers should be paid a "living wage" of $15 per hour.

Finding Issues to Explore

8.1   Use exploratory strategies to find an engaging issue.

Your engagement with a controversial issue might be sparked by personal experience, by conversations with others, or by something you listen to, see, or read. Sometimes you will be confused about the issue, unable to take a stand. At other times, you will have a visceral gut reaction that causes you to take an immediate position, even though you haven't thought through the issue in depth. At the start of the arguing process, the confused or puzzled position is often the stronger one because it promotes inquiry as truth-seeking. If you start with a firm stand, you might be less disposed to uncover your issue's complexity and let your position evolve. In this section we examine some strategies you can use to find issues worth exploring.

Do Some Initial Brainstorming

As a first step, make an inventory of issues that interest you. Many of the ideas you develop may become subject matter for arguments that you will write later in this course. The strategies suggested in Table 8.1 (Brainstorming Issues to Explore) will help you generate a productive list.

Once you've made a list, add to it as new ideas strike you and return to it each time you are given a new argumentative assignment.

Be Open to the Issues All Around You

We are surrounded by argumentative issues. You'll start noticing them everywhere once you get attuned to them. You will be invited into argumentative

Table 8.1 Brainstorming Issues to Explore

What You Can Do	How It Works
Make an inventory of the communities to which you belong. Consider classroom communities; clubs and organizations; residence hall, apartment, neighborhood, or family communities; church/synagogue or work communities; communities related to your hobbies or avocations; your city, state, region, nation, and world communities.	Because arguments arise out of disagreements within communities, you can often think of issues for argument by beginning with a list of the communities to which you belong.
Identify controversies within those communities. Think both big and small: • Big issue in world community: What is the best way to prevent destruction of rain forests? • Small issue in residence-hall community: Should quiet hours be enforced?	To stimulate thinking, use prompts such as these: • People in this community frequently disagree about ____. • Within my work community, Person X believes ____; however, this view troubles me because ____.
Narrow your list to a handful of problematic issues for which you don't have a position; share it with classmates. Identify a few issues that you would like to explore more deeply. When you share your list with classmates, add their list of issues to yours.	Sharing your list with classmates stimulates more thinking and encourages conversations. The more you explore your views with others, the more ideas you will develop. Good writing grows out of good talking.
Brainstorm a network of related issues. Any given issue is always embedded in a network of other issues. To see how open-ended and fluid an argumentative conversation can be, try connecting one of your issues to a network of other issues, including subissues and side issues.	Brainstorm questions that compel you to look at an issue in a variety of ways. For example, if you explored the controversy over whether states should legalize marijuana (see Chapter 1), you might generate these questions about related issues: • Is marijuana a gateway drug toward cocaine or heroin? • How will legalizing marijuana affect the black market in drugs? • What has been the experience of states that have already legalized marijuana?

conversations by posters, bumper stickers, tweets, blog sites, newspaper editorial pages, magazine articles, the sports section, movie reviews, and song lyrics. When you read or listen, watch for "hot spots"—passages or moments that evoke strong agreement, disagreement, or confusion. As an illustration of how arguments are all around us, try the following exercise on the issue of a living wage for low-wage workers.

Explore Ideas by Freewriting

Freewriting is useful at any stage of the writing process. When you freewrite, you put fingers to keyboard (or pen to paper) and write rapidly *nonstop*, usually five to ten minutes at a stretch, without worrying about structure, grammar, or correctness. Your goal is to generate as many ideas as possible without stopping to edit your work. If you can't think of anything to say, write "relax" or "I'm stuck" over and over until new ideas emerge. Here is Trudie Makens's freewrite in response to the protest photo that introduces Part 2.

For Writing and Discussion

Responding to Visual Arguments About a Living Wage

Suppose, in your initial search for a controversial issue, you encounter the following visual texts related to raising the minimum wage for fast-food workers: the photo of protesters (beginning of Part 2), the cartoon (Figure 8.1), and the graph (Figure 8.2). Working individually or in small groups, generate exploratory responses to these questions:

1. What claim is each of these visual texts making?
2. What background information about the problems of minimum-wage workers do these visual texts assume?
3. What network of issues do these visual texts suggest?
4. What puzzling questions do these visual texts raise for you?

Figure 8.1 Political cartoon on minimum wage

Figure 8.2 Graph offering employment statistics relevant to minimum wage controversy

Adapted from Schmitt, John, and Janelle Jones, "Low-Wage Workers Are Older and Better Educated than Ever." Center for Economic and Policy Research. April 2012.

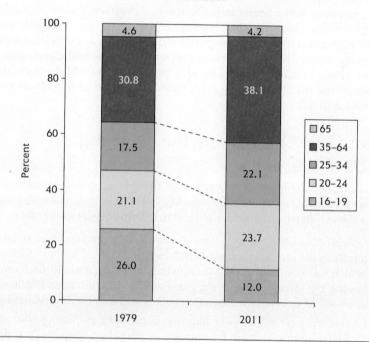

Percentage of Low-Wage Workers By Age Group, 1979 and 2011

TRUDIE'S FREEWRITE

Working in the food and service industry as a busser, I relate to the people in the picture wearing union T-shirts and arguing for a $15/hour minimum wage. It's hard to live off of minimum wage, and if it weren't for my tips, I wouldn't be able to pay some of my bills. And that is with help from my parents because I am a college student. I can't imagine what it would be like for full-time workers in the fast-food industry where orders are taken via counter. I remember when I worked counter service jobs, as a barista and at a dumpling café, no one ever tipped. They didn't feel like they needed to because it was not formal wait service. My work, and my coworkers' work, was not valued. What some people don't realize is that whether you are working at McDonald's or in an upscale restaurant, you are still working hard to provide good service. If anything, it is harder to work jobs like McDonald's where customers are dismissive and don't value the service they are receiving. Think, relax. Why do people not value the work of fast-food and counter service workers? Because it is considered unskilled labor? A lot of the people I have worked with didn't have the time or money to go to college because they were burdened with the financial strains of having children or caring for sick or elderly relatives. I remember my coworker Maria who was always stressed out because she couldn't pay her rent and had a child to support. A living wage would help people who haven't been lucky enough to inherit wealth to pull themselves out of poverty. And it wouldn't hurt corporations like McDonald's to live with a little less profit.

Explore Ideas by Idea Mapping

Another good technique for exploring ideas is *idea mapping*. To make an idea map, draw a circle in the center of a page and write some trigger idea (a broad topic, a question, or working thesis statement) in the center of the circle. Then record your ideas on branches and subbranches extending from the center circle. As long as you pursue one train of thought, keep recording your ideas on that branch. But when that line of thinking gives out, start a new branch. Often your thoughts will jump back and forth between branches. That's a major advantage of "picturing" your thoughts; you can see them as part of an emerging design rather than as strings of unrelated ideas.

Idea maps usually generate more ideas, though less well-developed ones, than freewrites. Figure 8.3 shows an idea map that Trudie Makens created on the issue of the minimum wage after class discussion of the visual texts in Figures 8.1 and 8.2.

Explore Ideas by Playing the Believing and Doubting Game

The believing and doubting game, a critical-thinking strategy developed by rhetorician Peter Elbow that systematically stretches your thinking, is an excellent way to imagine views different from your own and to anticipate responses to those views.

- *As a believer, your role is to be wholly sympathetic to an idea.* You must listen carefully to the idea and suspend all disbelief. You must identify all the ways in which the idea may appeal to different audiences and all the reasons for believing the idea. The believing game can be difficult, even frightening, if you are asked to believe an idea that strikes you as false or threatening.
- *As a doubter, your role is to be judgmental and critical, finding fault with an idea.* The doubting game is the opposite of the believing game. You do your

Figure 8.3 Trudie's idea map

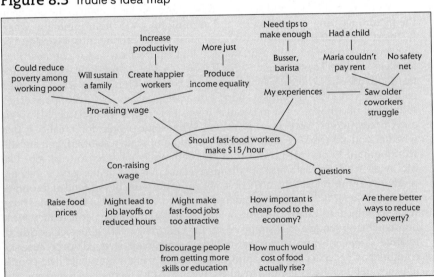

best to find counterexamples and inconsistencies that undermine the idea you are examining. Again, it can be threatening to doubt ideas that you instinctively want to believe.

When you play the believing and doubting game with an assertion, simply write two different chunks, one chunk arguing for the assertion (the believing game) and one chunk opposing it (the doubting game). Freewrite both chunks, letting your ideas flow without censoring them. Or, alternatively, make an idea map with believing and doubting branches. Here is how Trudie Makens played the believing and doubting game with the assertion "Fast-food workers should be paid $15 per hour."

Trudie's Believing and Doubting Game

Believing: I doubt anyone strives to become a full-time fast-food worker, but many people become stuck in those jobs and can't advance because they don't have a college education or because there are no better jobs available. Sometimes the workers are college students, so an increase in minimum pay would help them not accrue so much debt and perhaps have more time to study because they wouldn't have to work so many hours. But the real benefit would come to the uneducated, unskilled fast-food worker whose financial situation has led him or her to the fast-food job. The current minimum wage is barely livable. If fast-food workers were to receive $15 per hour, there is far more of a chance for them to support themselves and their family comfortably without the stress of poverty. Even if full-time fast-food workers do not go on to get more skills or go to college, it becomes more likely their children will be able to go to college if the fast-food worker is receiving a higher wage. Thus, the cycle of poverty as it is inherited generationally is, at least mildly, disrupted.

Doubting: If a $15 per hour minimum wage were to be implemented, the fast-food corporations would have to find ways to compensate for the loss of profits. The most obvious way would be to raise food prices. If prices were to rise, fast food would no longer be affordable. This could have damaging and reversing effects on the working class, which may rely on cheap fast food. Another problem is that the $15 per hour minimum wage may encourage workers to stay put in their jobs and not strive for a career. Student workers may no longer see the benefit of going into debt to get a degree and be satisfied with their current fast-food job. The effect of more desirable fast-food jobs may put pressure on other companies to raise the hourly wage of their entry-level positions. The rise in wage may, again, have the ripple effect of higher-priced products, thus reducing sales and forcing these companies to lay off some workers. No matter what scenario is dreamt up, it would seem that raising the minimum wage to $15 per hour, even if just for fast-food workers, might have damaging effects on the economy that would diminish any benefits or advantages that theoretically come from receiving a higher wage.

Although Trudie sees the injustice of paying low wages to fast-food workers, she also sees that paying such workers $15 per hour might raise the cost of food, reduce the number of jobs available, or have other negative consequences. Playing the believing and doubting game has helped her articulate the dilemma and see the issue in more complex terms.

For Writing and Discussion

Playing the Believing and Doubting Game

Individual task:

Choose one or more of the following controversial claims and play the believing and doubting game with it, through either freewriting or idea mapping.

1. A student should report a fellow student who is cheating on an exam or plagiarizing an essay.
2. Federal law should forbid the purchase of assault weapons or other firearms with high-capacity magazines.
3. Athletes should be allowed to take steroids and human growth hormone under a doctor's supervision.

Group task:

Working in pairs, in small groups, or as a class, share your results with classmates.

Summarizing a Stakeholder's Argument

8.2 **Summarize a stakeholder's argument as an entry into the issue.**

When you research an issue, you will encounter the conflicting views of many different stakeholders. You will eventually push against some of these stakeholders with your own claim and reasons (*"Although Jones and Lopez argue X, I argue Y"*). But you may also be in full or partial agreement with other stakeholders, drawing on them for support or evidence. In either case, you have to understand thoroughly the sources you are engaging with.

One way to show this understanding is to summarize a stakeholder's argument in your own words. A summary (also called an *abstract*, a *précis*, or a *synopsis*) presents only a text's major points and eliminates supporting details. Summaries can be any length, depending on the writer's purpose, but usually they range from several sentences to one or two paragraphs. To maintain your own credibility, your summary should be as neutral and fair to that piece as possible.

To explain how to write a summary, we will continue with our example of raising the minimum wage. The following article, "The Pay Is Too Damn Low," appeared in *The New Yorker*, a magazine with a liberal perspective. It was written by James Surowiecki, an American journalist who writes the "Financial Page" column for *The New Yorker*. Please read this article carefully in preparation for the exercises and examples that follow.

The Pay Is Too Damn Low

JAMES SUROWIECKI

A few weeks ago, Washington, D.C., passed a living-wage bill designed to make Walmart pay its workers a minimum of $12.50 an hour. Then President Obama called on Congress to raise the federal minimum wage (which is currently $7.25 an hour). McDonald's was widely derided for releasing a budget to help its employees plan financially, since that only underscored how brutally hard it is to live on a McDonald's wage. And last week fast-food workers across the country staged walkouts, calling for an increase in their pay to fifteen dollars an hour. Low-wage earners have long been the hardest workers to organize and the easiest to ignore. Now they're front-page news.

The workers' grievances are simple: low wages, few (if any) benefits, and little full-time work. In inflation-adjusted terms, the minimum wage, though higher than it was a decade ago, is still well below its 1968 peak (when it was worth about $10.70 an hour in today's dollars), and it's still poverty-level pay. To make matters worse, most fast-food and retail work is part time, and the weak job market has eroded what little bargaining power low-wage workers had: their earnings actually fell between 2009 and last year, according to the National Employment Law Project.

Still, the reason this has become a big political issue is not that the jobs have changed; it's that the people doing the jobs have. Historically, low-wage work tended to be done either by the young or by women looking for part-time jobs to supplement family income. As the historian Bethany Moreton has shown, Walmart in its early days sought explicitly to hire underemployed married women. Fast-food workforces, meanwhile, were dominated by teenagers. Now, though, plenty of family breadwinners are stuck in these jobs. That's because, over the past three decades, the U.S. economy has done a poor job of creating good middle-class jobs; five of the six fastest-growing job categories today pay less than the median wage. That's why, as a recent study by the economists John Schmitt and Janelle Jones has shown, low-wage workers are older and better educated than ever. More important, more of them are relying on their paychecks not for pin money or to pay for Friday-night dates but, rather, to support families. Forty years ago, there was no expectation that fast-food or discount-retail jobs would provide a living wage, because these were not jobs that, in the main, adult heads of household did. Today, low-wage workers provide 46 percent of their family's income. It is that change which is driving the demand for higher pay.

The situation is the result of a tectonic shift in the American economy. In 1960, the country's biggest employer, General Motors, was also its most profitable company and one of its best-paying. It had high profit margins and real pricing power, even as it was paying its workers union wages. And it was not alone: firms such as Ford, Standard Oil, and Bethlehem Steel employed huge numbers of well-paid workers while earning big profits. Today, the country's biggest employers are retailers and fast-food chains, almost all of which have built their businesses on low pay—they've striven to keep wages down and unions out—and low prices.

5   This complicates things, in part because of the nature of these businesses. They make plenty of money, but most have slim profit margins: Walmart and Target earn between three and four cents on the dollar; a typical McDonald's franchise restaurant earns around six cents on the dollar before taxes, according to an analysis from Janney Capital Markets. In fact, the combined profits of all the major retailers, restaurant chains, and supermarkets in the Fortune 500 are smaller than the profits of Apple alone. Yet Apple employs just 76,000 people, while the retailers, supermarkets, and restaurant chains employ 5.6 million. The grim truth of those numbers is that low wages are a big part of why these companies are able to stay profitable while offering low prices. Congress is currently considering a bill increasing the minimum wage to $10.10 over the next three years. That's an increase that the companies can easily tolerate, and it would make a significant difference in the lives of low-wage workers. But that's still a long way from turning these jobs into the kind

of employment that can support a middle-class family. If you want to accomplish that, you have to change the entire way these companies do business. Above all, you have to get consumers to accept significantly higher, and steadily rising, prices. After decades in which we've grown used to cheap stuff, that won't be easy.

Realistically, then, a higher minimum wage can be only part of the solution. We also need to expand the Earned Income Tax Credit and strengthen the social-insurance system, including child care and health care (the advent of Obamacare will help in this regard). Fast-food jobs in Germany and the Netherlands aren't much better-paid than in the United States, but a stronger safety net makes workers much better off. We also need many more of the "middle-class jobs" we're always hearing about. A recent McKinsey report suggested that the government should invest almost a trillion dollars over the next five years in repairing and upgrading the national infrastructure, which seems like a good place to start. And we really need the economy as a whole to grow faster, because that would both increase the supply of good jobs and improve the bargaining power of low-wage workers. As Jared Bernstein, an economist at the Center for Budget and Policy Priorities told me, "The best friend that low-wage workers have is a strong economy and a tight job market." It isn't enough to make bad jobs better. We need to create better jobs.

Thinking Steps for Writing a Summary

To help you write an effective summary, we recommend the following steps:

Step 1: *Read the argument for general meaning*. Don't judge it. Put your objections aside; just follow the writer's meaning, trying to see the issue from the writer's perspective. Try to adopt the writer's values and belief system. Walk in the writer's shoes.

Step 2: *Reread the article slowly, writing brief* does *and* says *statements for each paragraph (or group of closely connected paragraphs)*. A *does* statement identifies a paragraph's function, such as "summarizes an opposing view," "introduces a supporting reason," "gives an example," or "uses statistics to support the previous point." A *says* statement summarizes a paragraph's content. Your challenge in writing *says* statements is to identify the main idea in each paragraph and translate that idea into your own words, most likely condensing it at the same time. This process may be easier with an academic article that uses long, developed paragraphs headed by clear topic sentences than with more informal, journalistic articles that use shorter, less developed paragraphs. What follows are *does* and *says* statements for the first three paragraphs of Surowiecki's article:

Does/Says Analysis of Surowiecki's Article

Paragraph 1: *Does*: Gives examples of recent news stories about protests of low-wage workers. *Says*: Hard-to-organize, low-wage earners are now in the news demanding an increase in the minimum wage.

Paragraph 2: *Does*: Provides details about the workers' grievances. *Says*: A weakening job market combined with low wages, lack of benefits, and mainly part-time hours keeps low-wage workers at poverty levels.

Paragraph 3: *Does*: Explains the changing demographics of those who hold low-wage jobs. *Says*: In the past, minimum-wage jobs were held primarily by teenagers or by women desiring part-time work to supplement family incomes, but today many primary breadwinners depend on minimum-wage jobs to support a family.

For Writing and Discussion

Does/Says Statements

Working individually or in small groups, write *does* and *says* statements for the remaining paragraphs of Surowiecki's article.

Step 3: *Examine your* does *and* says *statements to determine the major sections of the argument.* Create a list of the major points (and subpoints) that must appear in a summary in order to represent that argument accurately. If you are visually oriented, you may prefer to make a diagram, flowchart, or scratch outline of the sections of Surowiecki's argument.

Step 4: *Turn your list, outline, flowchart, or diagram into a prose summary.* Typically, writers do this in one of two ways. Some start by joining all their *says* statements into a lengthy paragraph-by-paragraph summary and then prune it and streamline it. They combine ideas into sentences and then revise those sentences to make them clearer and more tightly structured. Others start with a one-sentence summary of the argument's thesis and major supporting reasons and then flesh it out with more supporting ideas. Your goal is to be as neutral and objective as possible by keeping your own response to the writer's ideas out of your summary. To be fair to the writer, you also need to cover all the writer's main points and give them the same emphasis as in the original article.

Step 5: *Revise your summary until it is the desired length and is sufficiently clear, concise, and complete.* Your goal is to spend your words wisely, making every word count. In a summary of several hundred words, you will often need transitions to indicate structure and create a coherent flow of ideas: "Surowiecki's second point is that . . . " or "Surowiecki concludes by . . . ." However, don't waste words with meaningless transitions such as "Surowiecki goes on to say . . . ." When you incorporate a summary into your own essay, you must distinguish the author's views from your own by using *attributive tags* (expressions such as "Surowiecki asserts" or "according to Surowiecki"). You must also put any directly borrowed wording in quotation marks. Finally, you must cite the original author using appropriate conventions for documenting sources.

Examples of Summaries

What follows are two summaries of Surowiecki's article—a one-paragraph version and a one-sentence version—by student writer Trudie Makens. Trudie's one-paragraph version illustrates the MLA documentation system, with complete bibliographic information placed in a Works Cited list at the end of the paper. The in-text citations do not have page numbers because the work cited is from a web source. See Appendix 2 for an explanation of the MLA and APA documentation systems.

TRUDIE'S ONE-PARAGRAPH SUMMARY OF SUROWIECKI'S ARGUMENT

> In his *The New Yorker* article "The Pay Is Too Damn Low," James Surowiecki analyzes the grievances of workers at fast-food franchises, Walmart, or Target. In the past, it didn't matter that these jobs were low-pay, part-time, and without benefits because they were held mainly by teenagers or married women seeking to supplement a husband's wages. But today, says Surowiecki, a growing number of primary breadwinners rely on these poverty-level wages to support families. The problem stems from a "tectonic shift in the American economy." While in 1960, "firms such as Ford, Standard Oil, and Bethlehem Steel employed huge numbers of well-paid workers while earning big profits," nowadays America's biggest employers are fast-food and retail companies with low profit margins. These companies depend on low-wage workers to keep prices cheap for the American consumer. Paying living wages to workers would completely change the business model, resulting in steadily rising prices. According to Surowiecki, raising the minimum wage is only one tool for fighting poverty. America also needs to create a social insurance system like that of Germany or the Netherlands. Surowiecki calls for an increase in the Earned Income Tax Credit, universal health insurance, affordable child care, and investment of almost a trillion dollars in infrastructure to create good middle-class jobs.

Works Cited

Surowiecki, James. "The Pay Is Too Damn Low." *The New Yorker*, 12 Aug. 2013, www.newyorker.com/magazine/2013/08/12/the-pay-is-too-damn-low.

TRUDIE'S ONE-SENTENCE SUMMARY OF SUROWIECKI'S ARGUMENT

> In his *The New Yorker* article, "The Pay Is Too Damn Low," James Surowiecki argues that raising the minimum wage is only a partial solution to the problem of poverty and needs to be supplemented with a European-style social security network including an increase in the Earned Income Tax Credit, universal health insurance, affordable child care, and investment of almost a trillion dollars in infrastructure to create good middle-class jobs.

Responding to a Stakeholder's Argument

8.3 Respond to a stakeholder's argument through believing, doubting, and dialectic thinking.

Once you have summarized an argument, you need to respond to it in thoughtful ways that go beyond simple agreement ("I like it"), disagreement ("I don't like it"), or partial agreement ("It has good parts and bad parts"). To help you resist these simple responses, we urge you to follow the spirit of the believing and doubting game, which will stretch your critical thinking in powerful ways.

Practicing Believing: Willing Your Own Acceptance of the Writer's Views

A powerful strategy for reading an argument rhetorically is to will yourself to "believe" a stakeholder's argument even if you tend to doubt it. When you read to believe an argument, you practice what psychologist Carl Rogers calls *empathic listening*. Empathic listening requires that you see the world through the author's eyes, temporarily adopt the author's beliefs and values, and suspend your skepticism and biases in order to hear what the author is saying.

Although writing an accurate summary of an argument shows that you have listened to it effectively and understood it, summary writing by itself doesn't mean that you have actively tried to enter the writer's worldview. Rhetorician Peter Elbow reminds us that before we doubt a text, we should try to "dwell with" and "dwell in" the writer's ideas—play the believing game—in order to "earn" our right to criticize.* To help you "believe" a writer, find places in the text that resonate positively for you, look for values and beliefs you hold in common (however few), and search for personal experiences and values that affirm his or her argument.

Practicing Doubting: Willing Your Own Resistance to the Writer's Views

After willing yourself to believe an argument, will yourself to doubt it. Turn your mental energies toward raising objections, asking questions, expressing skepticism, and withholding your assent. When you read as a doubter, you question the writer's logic, the writer's evidence and assumptions, and the writer's strategies for developing the argument. You also think about what is *not* in the argument by noting what the author has glossed over, left unexplained, or left out entirely. You add a new layer of marginal notes, articulating what is bothering you, demanding proof, doubting evidence, and challenging the author's assumptions and values. Writing your own notes helps you read a text actively, bringing your own voice into conversation with the author.

For Writing and Discussion

Raising Doubts About Surowiecki's Argument

Return now to Surowiecki's article and read it skeptically. Raise questions, offer objections, and express doubts. Then, working as a class or in small groups, list all the doubts you have about Surowiecki's argument.

Now that you have doubted Surowiecki's article, compare your questions and doubts to some raised by Trudie Makens.

Trudie's Doubts about Surowiecki's Article

- In his second paragraph, Surowiecki outlines three workers' grievances: "low wages, few (if any) benefits, and little full-time work." But increasing the minimum wage addresses only one of the grievances. A higher minimum wage might make it less likely for a worker to receive benefits or obtain full-time rather than part-time

---

*Peter Elbow, "Bringing the Rhetoric of Assent and the Believing Game Together—Into the Classroom," *College English*, 67.4 (March 2005), 389.

work. Moreover, with a higher wage, large companies may try to maintain profits by cutting jobs.

- Surowiecki asserts that large retailers and fast-food companies would absorb the cost of a higher minimum wage by raising prices on consumer goods. But if low-wage workers are also consumers, won't higher prices on previously cheap products defeat the benefits of a higher wage?
- Though he ends his article by calling for a multifaceted solution to poverty, he does so without offering a way to accomplish this goal. Where would the money come from in order to expand the Earned Income Tax Credit, strengthen the United States' current social insurance system, or invest in infrastructure? Further, how would the United States effectively implement and sustain these nationwide social programs without upsetting the already delicate economy?
- In his article, Surowiecki mentions several studies, but there is no way to tell if these are widely respected studies or controversial ones. Would other studies, for example, conclude that low-wage workers today are responsible for 46 percent of their family's income?

These are only some of the objections that might be raised against Surowiecki's argument. The point here is that doubting as well as believing is a key part of the exploratory process and purpose. *Believing* takes you into the views of others so that you can expand your views and perhaps see them differently and modify or even change them. *Doubting* helps protect you from becoming overpowered by others' arguments and teaches you to stand back, consider, and weigh points carefully. It also leads you to new questions and points you might want to explore further.

Thinking Dialectically

8.4 Delay closure by thinking dialectically.

This chapter's final strategy—thinking dialectically to bring texts into conversation with one another—encompasses all the previous strategies and can have a powerful effect on your growth as a thinker and arguer. The term *dialectic* is associated with the German philosopher Georg Wilhelm Friedrich Hegel, who postulated that each thesis prompts an opposing thesis (which he calls an "antithesis") and that the conflict between these views can lead thinkers to a new claim (a "synthesis") that incorporates aspects of both views. Dialectic thinking is the philosophical underpinning of the believing and doubting game, pushing us toward new and better ideas. As Peter Elbow puts it, "Because it's so hard to let go of an idea we are holding (or more to the point, an idea that's holding us), our best hope for leverage in learning to doubt such ideas is *to take on different ideas.*"* Dialectic thinking means playing ideas against one another, creating a tension that forces you to keep expanding your perspective. It helps you achieve the "mingling of minds" that we discussed in the introduction to this chapter.

As you consider multiple points of view on an issue, try using the questions in Table 8.2 to promote dialectic thinking:

---

*Peter Elbow, "Bringing the Rhetoric of Assent and the Believing Game Together—Into the Classroom," *College English* 67.4 (March 2005), 390.

Table 8.2 Questions to Promote Dialectic Thinking

1. What would writer A say to writer B?

2. After I read writer A, I thought _____; however, after I read writer B, my thinking on this issue had changed in these ways: _____.

3. To what extent do writer A and writer B disagree about facts and interpretations of facts?

4. To what extent do writer A and writer B disagree about underlying beliefs, assumptions, and values?

5. Can I find any areas of agreement, including shared values and beliefs, between writer A and writer B?

6. What new, significant questions do these texts raise for me?

7. After I have wrestled with the ideas in these two texts, what are my current views on this issue?

Responding to questions like these—either through class discussion or through exploratory writing—can help you work your way into a public controversy. Earlier in this chapter you read James Surowiecki's article expressing liberal support for raising the minimum wage and enacting other government measures to help the poor. Now consider an article expressing a quite different point of view, an opinion piece appearing in *The Huffington Post* written by Michael Saltsman, the research director at the Employment Policies Institute—a pro-business, free-market think tank opposed to raising the minimum wage. We ask you to read the article and then use the questions in Table 8.2 to stimulate dialectic thinking about Surowiecki versus Saltsman.

For Writing and Discussion
Practicing Dialectic Thinking with Two Articles

Individual task:

Freewrite your responses to the questions in Table 8.2, in which Surowiecki is writer A and Saltsman is writer B.

Group task:

Working as a class or in small groups, share your responses to the two articles, guided by the dialectic questions.

To Help the Poor, Move Beyond "Minimum" Gestures

MICHAEL SALTSMAN

Actor and director Ben Affleck made news this week with the announcement that he'll spend five days living on just $1.50—the U.S.-dollar daily equivalent of extreme poverty, according to the Global Poverty Project.

Affleck's heart is in the right place, but his actions won't provide a measurable benefit for people who actually live in poverty. On that score, Affleck's actions are not unlike a series of recently-introduced proposals to raise the federal minimum wage—well-intentioned but ultimately empty gestures that will do little to raise poor families out of poverty.

For poverty-reducing policies to benefit the poor, the benefits first have to be properly targeted to people living in poverty. On this count, a higher minimum wage fails miserably. Census Bureau data shows that over 60 percent of people living below the poverty line don't work. They don't need a raise—they need a job.

Among those who do earn the minimum wage, a majority actually don't live in poverty. According to a forthcoming Employment Policies Institute analysis of Census Bureau data, over half of those covered by President Obama's $9 proposal live in households with income at least twice the poverty level—and one-third are in households with an income three times or greater than the poverty level.

5   That's because nearly 60 percent of affected employees aren't single earners, according to the EPI report—they're living in households where a parent or a spouse often earns an income far above the minimum. (The average family income of this group is $50,789.) By contrast, we found that only 9 percent of people covered by President Obama's $9 minimum wage are single parents with children.

It's for reasons like these that the majority of academic research shows little connection between a higher minimum wage and reductions in poverty. For instance, economists from American and Cornell Universities examined data from the 28 states that raised their minimum wages between 2003 and 2007, and found no associated reductions in poverty.

Of course, poor targeting isn't the only problem. The vast majority of economic research—including 85 percent of the most credible studies from the last two decades—finds that job loss for the least-skilled employees follows on the heels of minimum wage hikes.

That's why better-targeted policies like the Earned Income Tax Credit (EITC) deserve the support of politicians and public figures who want to do something about poverty. It's been empirically proven to boost employment and incomes, without the unintended consequences of a wage hike. Accounting for the EITC, the full-time hourly wage for many minimum wage earners is already above the $9 figure that President Obama has proposed.

Three Ways to Foster Dialectic Thinking

In this concluding section, we suggest three ways to stimulate and sustain the process of dialectic thinking.

EFFECTIVE DISCUSSIONS   Good, rich talk is one of the most powerful ways to stimulate dialectic thinking and foster a "mingling of minds." The key is to keep these discussions from becoming shouting matches or bully pulpits for those who like to dominate the airtime. Discussions are most productive if people are willing to express different points of view or to role-play those views for the purpose of advancing the conversation. Good discussions can occur in class, in late-night coffee shops, or in online chat rooms or on discussion boards.

READING LOGS   In our classes, we require students to keep reading logs or journals in which they use freewriting and idea mapping to explore their ideas as they encounter multiple perspectives on an issue. One part of a journal or reading log should include summaries of each article you read. Another part should focus on your own dialectic thinking as you interact with your sources while you are reading them. Adapt the questions in Table 8.2 for promoting dialectic thinking.

A FORMAL EXPLORATORY ESSAY A formal exploratory essay tells the story of an intellectual journey. It is both a way of promoting dialectical thinking and a way of narrating one's struggle to negotiate multiple views. The keys to writing successful exploratory essays are: (1) choosing an issue to explore on which you don't yet have an answer or position (or on which you are open to changing your mind); (2) wrestling with an issue or problem by resisting quick, simple answers and by exploring diverse perspectives; and (3) letting your thinking evolve and your own stance on the issue grow out of this exploration.

Exploratory essays can be powerful thinking and writing experiences in their own right, but they can also be a valuable precursor to a formal argument. Many instructors assign a formal exploratory paper as the first stage of a course research project—what we might call a "thesis-seeking" stage. (The second stage is a formal argument that converts your exploratory thinking into a hierarchically organized argument using reasons and evidence to support your claim.) Although often used as part of a research project, exploratory essays can also be low-stakes reflective pieces narrating the evolution of a writer's thinking.

An exploratory essay includes these thinking moves and parts:

- The essay is opened and driven by the writer's issue question or research problem—not a thesis.

- The introduction to the essay presents the question and shows why it interests the writer, why it is significant, and why it is problematic rather than clear-cut or easy to resolve.

- The body of the essay shows the writer's inquiry process. It demonstrates how the writer has kept the question open, sincerely wrestled with different views on the question, accepted uncertainty and ambiguity, and possibly redefined the question in the midst of reading and reflecting on multiple perspectives.

Writing Assignment
An Argument Summary or a Formal Exploratory Essay

Option 1: An Argument Summary

Write a 250-word summary of an argument selected by your instructor. Then write a one-sentence summary of the same argument. Use as models Trudie Makens's summaries of James Surowiecki's argument on raising the minimum wage earlier in this chapter.

Option 2: A Formal Exploratory Essay

Write an exploratory essay in which you narrate in first-person, chronological order the evolution through time of your thinking about an issue or problem. Rather than state a thesis or claim, begin with a question or problem. Then describe your inquiry process as you worked your way through sources or different views. Follow the guidelines for an exploratory paper shown in Figure 8.4. When you cite the sources you have considered, be sure to use attributive tags so that the reader can distinguish between your own ideas and those of the sources you have summarized. If you use research sources, use MLA documentation for citing ideas and quotations and for creating a Works Cited at the end of your essay (see Appendix 2).

(continued)

Figure 8.4 Organization plan for an exploratory essay

Introduction (one to several paragraphs)	• Establish that your question is complex, problematic, and significant. • Show why you are interested in it. • Present relevant background on your issue. Begin with your question or build up to it, using it to end your introductory section.
Body section 1: First view or source	• Introduce your first source and show why you started with it. • Provide rhetorical context and information about it. • Summarize the source's content and argument. • Offer your response to this source, including both believing and doubting points. • Talk about what this source contributes to your understanding of your question: What did you learn? What value does this source have for you? What is missing from this source that you want to consider? Where do you want to go from here?
Body section 2: Second view or source	• Repeat the process with a new source selected to advance the inquiry. • Explain why you selected this source (to find an alternative view, pursue a subquestion, find more data, and so forth). • Summarize the source's argument. • Respond to the source's ideas. Look for points of agreement and disagreement with other sources. • Show how your cumulative reading of sources is shaping your thinking or leading to more questions.
Body sections 3, 4, 5, etc.	• Continue exploring views or sources.
Conclusion	• Wrap up your intellectual journey and explain where you are now in your thinking and how your understanding of your problem has changed. • Present your current answer to your question based on all that you have learned so far, or explain why you still can't answer your question, or explain what research you might pursue further.

- The body of the essay includes summaries of the different views or sources that the writer explored and often includes believing and doubting responses to them.

- In the essay's conclusion, the writer may clarify his or her thinking and discover a thesis to be developed and supported in a subsequent argument. But the conclusion can also remain open because the writer may not have discovered his or her own position on the issue and may acknowledge the need or desire for more exploration.

One of the writing assignment options for this chapter is a formal exploratory paper. Trudie Makens's exploratory essay at the end of this chapter shows how she explored different voices in the controversy over raising the minimum wage to $15 per hour.

Reading

What follows is Trudie Makens's exploratory essay on the subject of raising the minimum wage. Her research begins with the articles by Surowiecki and Saltsman that you have already read and discussed. She then moves off in her own direction.

Student Essay

Should Fast-Food Workers Be Paid $15 per Hour?

Trudie Makens

Having worked as a busser in a pizza restaurant, a part-time barista, and a server at a dumpling café, I was immediately attracted to our class discussions of minimum wage, sparked by recent protests of fast-food workers demanding pay of $15 per hour. My first job as a barista exposed me to the harsh reality of living on today's existing minimum wage as I witnessed my coworker Maria lose her home because she couldn't pay rent and support her kids at the same time. As a single mother of two, Maria had to bounce from relative to relative, which put a strain on her family relations, her image of herself as an able provider, and her children. I am lucky because, as a student, I am blessed to have my family operate as a safety net for me. If I am ever short on a bill or get sick or hurt, my parents will assist me financially. Many of the individuals I have worked with do not have that same safety net. These individuals are often older and have children or are beginning a family. Understanding the hardships of minimum-wage jobs, I entered our class discussions in support of the $15/hour demand because this pay rate would give workers a living wage. However, despite my personal affinities with these workers, I also understood that raising the minimum wage might have negative consequences for our economy. I wanted to explore this issue in more depth so I decided to pose my research question as "Should fast-food workers be paid a living wage of $15 per hour?"

(continued)

Title as question indicates an exploratory purposec

Introduction identifies the issue, explains the writer's interest in it, and acknowledges its complexity

Writer states her research question

Writer identifies her first source

Writer summarizes the article

My exploration began with an article that our instructor assigned to the whole class: "The Pay Is Too Damn Low" by James Surowiecki from *The New Yorker*. In the past, according to Surowiecki, it didn't matter that jobs at Walmart, Target, or fast-food franchises were low-pay, part-time, and without benefits because they were held mainly by teenagers or married women seeking to supplement a husband's wages. But today, says Surowiecki, a growing number of primary breadwinners rely on these poverty-level wages to support families. The problem stems from a "tectonic shift in the American economy." While in 1960, "firms such as Ford, Standard Oil, and Bethlehem Steel employed huge numbers of well-paid workers while earning big profits," nowadays America's biggest employers are fast-food and retail companies with low profit margins. While Surowiecki acknowledges that these retail companies and food franchises depend on low-wage workers to keep prices cheap for the American consumer, he still supports increasing the minimum wage but sees it as only one tool for fighting poverty. He argues that America also needs to create a European-style safety-net system and calls for an increase in the Earned Income Tax Credit, universal health insurance, affordable child care, and investment of almost a trillion dollars in infrastructure to create good middle-class jobs.

Surowiecki's concluding remarks about a safety net system resonated with me. I understood that what protected me from a financial crisis was my family acting as a safety net. The government, Surowiecki argues, should perform the same function for low-wage earners through such programs as child care and health care. He points to Germany and the Netherlands, arguing the stronger safety net put in place for workers by these European governments provides a better economic and social situation for low-wage workers, even though they are paid around the same amount as U.S. low-wage workers. Surowiecki also addressed some of my concerns regarding the economic consequences of implementing a living wage. Even though some low-wage jobs might be eliminated and food costs might go up, government investment in infrastructure might create more high-paying, middle-class jobs, resulting in a net benefit. But I still wasn't convinced or completely satisfied. How exactly would the government raise the money for a redesigned social insurance system? Would the country accept the needed higher taxes? While Surowiecki had convinced me that the government had an important role to play in creating the conditions for a living wage, I still was unclear on how the government could effectively do so without having a negative impact on the economy.

I wanted to know more about raising the minimum wage from the business perspective, so I Googled "living wage" and found an anti-minimum wage article from Michael Saltsman, the research director of the Employment Policy Institute. The opinion piece was published online in *The Huffington Post* and entitled "To Help the Poor, Move Beyond 'Minimum' Gestures." I also found a full-page ad from the same conservative institute depicting a robot doing the work of a fast-food employee. Saltsman believes that despite the good intentions of living-wage proponents, a higher federal minimum wage will do more harm than good. Within his piece, Saltsman equates the symbolic value of Ben Affleck's pledge to live five days on $1.50, "the U.S.-dollar equivalent of extreme poverty," to proposals for a higher federal minimum wage. Both, according to Saltsman, are "ultimately empty gestures" that do little to lift families out of poverty. What the poor need, Saltsman asserts, is "not a raise" but a job. Saltsman claims that over "60% of people living below the poverty line don't work," and those who do earn a minimum wage don't live in households whose total wages are below the poverty line. Even if a member of the working poor were to receive a living wage, Saltsman argues, "job loss for the least-skilled employees follows on the heels of a minimum wage hike." What helps to reduce poverty, according to Saltsman, is not a higher minimum wage but the Earned Income Tax Credit, "empirically proven to boost employment and incomes" and thus providing "a measurable difference for the poor."

Prior to reading Saltsman, I had not fully considered the potential that workers would be laid off because it would be cheaper for businesses to use robots or other automation than to employ higher-wage workers. Though Saltsman got me thinking about the dangers of job displacement, I wasn't convinced by his argument that an increased minimum wage would primarily benefit people who didn't need it, such as teenagers or second earners in an already middle-class family. I could see that an increased minimum wage wouldn't help the 60 percent of the poor who are unemployed, but I also realized that the Earned Income Tax Credit wouldn't help the unemployed either because it goes only to poor people who report income. (I Googled "earned income tax credit" just to make sure I understood how it works by giving a boost of income to poor but working tax filers.) Though Saltsman persuaded me to consider the negative economic consequences of a living wage, I wasn't convinced the living wage was entirely ineffective. I thought back to Surowiecki who, unlike Saltsman, saw a living wage as one component in a larger solution to reduce poverty. Both recommended an expanded Earned Income Tax Credit, but Surowiecki went further and also encouraged a stronger social-insurance system in addition to a higher minimum wage. Neither article persuaded me the living wage was either fully beneficial or fully injurious. To clarify my position, I needed to do more research.

I wanted another economist's perspective, so I typed "economic impact and living wage" into ProQuest, an interdisciplinary research database. One of the articles that caught my attention was "Living Wage: Some Gain, Neediest Lose Out." The article was an interview with labor economist Richard Toikka by author Charles Oliver featured in *Investor's Business Daily*, a conservative financial newspaper focused on stock and bond investments. In the interview, Oliver prompts Toikka to discuss the unintended consequences of a higher minimum wage. Toikka asserts that in order to absorb the cost of a higher wage, companies seek to hire higher-skilled workers who require less training, and thus cost the company less money. With a higher wage offered, Toikka argues, more high-skilled workers, such as college students, seek these jobs, increasing "the competition low-skilled workers face." Thus an increased minimum wage reduces the number of low-skilled jobs available. Toikka also makes the same argument as Saltsman, concluding that the benefits of a higher wage don't go towards the families who need it, but instead to second-earners who aren't living below the poverty line. Toikka cites a survey among labor economists asked to rate the efficiency of anti-poverty measures,

Writer summarizes second source

Writer includes both believing and doubting points

5

Writer shows dialectic thinking by comparing and contrasting views of first two sources

Writer again seeks sources purposefully; she shows how she found the source and places it in rhetorical context

Writer summarizes the article

(continued)

and "69% said living wages weren't at all efficient in meeting the needs of poor families." The more efficient way to combat poverty, Toikka argues, is not a living wage but an expansion of the Earned Income Tax Credit.

Putting Oliver/Toikka in conversation with Saltsman, I began to understand and heed the warnings of both economists. Though well-intentioned, increasing the minimum wage by itself is not apt to reduce poverty and would ultimately injure the poor rather than helping them. If a living wage does lead to heightened competition and employers slashing jobs, then perhaps a living wage is ineffective and therefore should be abandoned in favor of the Earned Income Tax Credit. So far, all the articles agreed the Earned Income Tax Credit is a good way to reduce poverty, even though it too benefits only those with jobs. Even so, I couldn't help but think that abandoning a living wage was a concession to a flawed economic system that doesn't value the working poor or impoverished, unemployed people enough. I thought back to Surowiecki when he praised Germany and the Netherlands for providing a strong social-insurance system that serves as a safety net for those in low-wage jobs. If Europe can ensure dignity and security to its citizens, then why can't the United States? Although 69 percent of labor economists say that a living wage is an inefficient way to alleviate poverty, we don't know what they would say if the government also invested in infrastructure to create well-paying jobs. Right now, it seems from my readings, that the current market doesn't value low-wage workers. What is valued in our economy is capital, profit, and cheap goods, all of which come at the expense of millions of workers. Is the structure of the economy where wealth is unequally distributed and workers are exploited really inevitable? Or is it an economic trend that can be reversed? I wanted to believe the latter, so I returned to ProQuest to find another article addressing the economic impact of a living wage but from a pro-labor perspective.

In my search, I found an article entitled "The Task Rabbit Economy," authored by Robert Kuttner and published in the progressive magazine *The American Prospect*. Kuttner begins by describing a successful San Francisco company whose website matches people who have an odd job they need done with people who will do the work for a fee. The company, named Task Rabbit, is like an online temp agency that operates by having would-be workers bid against one another, driving the price down for their labor. Kuttner argues that Task Rabbit's business model, which produces cheap labor, is analogous to our current economy, where workers have lost "bargaining power" and work has become casual and unstable (46). Kuttner argues that this low-wage economy has produced less economic growth, less prosperity, and more unemployment than earlier eras when there was more job stability and higher wages. According to Kuttner, the claim made by labor economists that a higher minimum wage leaves low-skilled workers without a job ignores how an unregulated labor market has allowed corporations to "weaken labor . . . and extract abnormal profits" (47). Kuttner draws on the economy of Sweden to provide an example where a living wage, full employment, and a "deliberate effort to narrow wage gaps" has been implemented effectively (48). What's more, Kuttner addresses the concern of rising prices by citing a Demos study that found raising wages so retail workers "earned at least $25,000 a year" only cost large retailers "1 percent of their $2.17 trillion annual sales" (52). Kuttner closes his article by emphasizing that "organized labor" is what will change the labor market, using both collective bargaining and "political force" (55).

Kuttner's article moved me in a way that Oliver/Toikka and Saltsman's pieces could not. Instead of accepting an economic system where low-wage workers are exploited for stockholder profits and cheap goods, Kuttner criticizes the labor market for its failure to value workers. Kuttner acknowledges that a higher minimum wage will upset the present economy, but he argues that the present economic system isn't inevitable but rather the result of large employers choosing to value capital over people in the absence of strong governmental policies protecting labor and the poor. Moreover, Kuttner's article illuminates the inefficiency of our economy. The studies Kuttner references reveal that the United States was better off in the years after World War II, when jobs were stable, plentiful, and paid a living wage. Most of all, I appreciated Kuttner's concluding call to action, and his assurance that such action will not lead to economic suicide but instead create the "dynamic, supple, and innovative" economy our nation strives for. According to Kuttner, we can choose to allow the market to continue unregulated, or, through organizing workers, we can push towards policies that value people—their rights, health, and dignity. As I read Kuttner, I wondered what current labor movements are in existence today and the progress they are making in their fight to gain rights and a living wage. I again turned to ProQuest.

My search handed me a long list of results, but I found one article that provided a relevant look into a labor campaign organized by Walmart sales associates. Titled "Job Insecurity," the article was written by Kevin Clarke and published in the Catholic magazine *America*. Clarke begins by introducing William Fletcher, a twenty-three-year-old retail sales associate at Walmart. According to Fletcher, he loves his job and "working with the public" but, he says, he and other employees constantly struggle with "low wages, chaotic scheduling, and insensitive management." Both Fletcher and Clarke wonder why being a retail sales associate for Walmart warrants not receiving enough to "have a home, have health insurance, have all the basic things in life." In order to improve his working conditions, Fletcher joined Organization United for Respect at Walmart, or OUR Walmart. OUR Walmart, Clarke states, is "part of an emerging labor phenomenon of non-union activism against Walmart and other powerful, profitable U.S. corporations that maintain large, low-paid work forces." Walmart, according to both Fletcher and Clarke, is a trend-setting company. If labor conditions improve at Walmart, other companies could follow suit. The organization draws from the tactics of "community organizing and the civil rights movement." Unfortunately, Clarke states, Walmart management continues to thwart protests or walkouts. Despite obstacles, OUR Walmart persists, marking a major moment in the contemporary labor movement. The article ends with Clarke's appeal to the Catholic social justice tradition of solidarity with the poor. He notes that Walmart sales associates depend on government support programs such as food stamps and housing assistance. He reminds his readers that our continual search for the cheapest goods makes us partially guilty of the exploitation of workers. He urges us to shop conscientiously and thoughtfully.

(continued)

Writer shows how this source has advanced and solidified her own thinking

Writer again shows purposeful search for next source

10

Writer identifies next source and places it in rhetorical context

I reached the end of the article feeling shocked. I was amazed that Walmart could dismiss the demands of OUR Walmart. Clarke states the owners of Walmart, the Walton family, possess "48% of Walmart stock and [are] the richest family on earth, with over $107 billion in net worth." Hearing numbers like these confirmed my forming conviction that the unregulated labor market dangerously exploits workers in order to gain cheap labor, cheap goods, and bloated profits. What's more, Walmart actively tries to scare workers from organizing—threatening to take away their jobs. Though there is much more to read and learn about the growing labor movement in the United States, Clarke's article, as well as Surowiecki, Saltsman, Oliver/Toikka, and Kuttner's pieces, allowed me to round out my position on a higher minimum wage. As I end my exploratory paper, I understand that a living wage is possible and should be provided to service workers as a basic human right. But it also needs to be supplemented with the kinds of social insurance systems stressed by Surowiecki and Kuttner.

Writer pulls together the results of her dialectic thinking, which has resulted in a synthesis

Final sentences reveal synthesis that goes beyond original leanings in first paragraph

Works Cited

Clarke, Kevin. "Job Insecurity." *America*, 18 Feb. 2013, americamagazine .org/issue/article/job-insecurity.

Kuttner, Robert. "The Task Rabbit Economy." *The American Prospect*, 24 Sept. 2013, pp. 45-55.

Oliver, Charles. "Living Wage: Some Gain, Neediest Lose Out." *Investor's Business Daily*, 5 Sept. 2000. *ProQuest*, 10 Jan. 2014, search.proquest .com/docview/1026806044/fulltext/DA48476F0F254E4CPQ/1?accou ntid=10226.

Saltsman, Michael. "To Help the Poor, Move Beyond 'Minimum' Gestures." *The Huffington Post*, 26 Apr. 2013, updated 26 June 2013, www .huffingtonpost.com/michael-saltsman/earned-income-tax-credit-minimum-wage_b_3165459.html.

Surowiecki, James. "The Pay Is Too Damn Low." *The New Yorker*, 12 Aug. 2013, www.newyorker.com/magazine/2013/08/12/ the-pay-is-too-damn-low.

Writer compiles an MLA-formatted "Works Cited" page that lists alphabetically all the sources discussed in the paper. Page numbers are included only for sources in print format; most web articles do not have page numbers

PART THREE

Expanding Our Understanding of Argument

Increasingly, countries are employing hydraulic fracturing (called fracking), which extracts natural gas from deeply buried shale, to meet their energy needs. Burning natural gas is cleaner than burning gasoline, oil, and coal and emits less carbon dioxide. However, each fracking site uses millions of gallons of water, leaves contaminated waste water, and often emits methane. Also environmentalists fear that fracking may contaminate aquifers. This photo depicts anti-fracking views in a protest near Manchester, England, in January 2014. To what extent does the garb of the protestors make effective appeals to *logos* and *pathos* to turn viewers against fracking?

Chapter 9
Making Visual and Multimodal Arguments

Learning Objectives

In this chapter you will learn to:

9.1 Explain the visual design elements in multimodal arguments.

9.2 Analyze the compositional features of photographs and drawings rhetorically.

9.3 Explain the genres of multimodal argument.

9.4 Construct your own multimodal arguments.

9.5 Use information graphics rhetorically in arguments.

This chapter focuses on the rhetorical persuasiveness of images, either by themselves or in combination with words to create multimodal arguments. A **multimodal** argument combines two or more modes of communication, such as words, images, sounds, or numerical graphics.

To appreciate the power of multimodal arguments, consider Figure 9.1—a photo of demonstrators protesting a federal travel ban on persons from certain Muslim-majority countries. The photograph contains several layers of multimodal arguments. The protest itself is a multimodal argument in which the protestors shout slogans, sing chants, and wave banners emphasizing the value of cultural and religious diversity. In this photograph, the poster carried by one of the protestors is also a multimodal argument combining words ("We the people are greater than fear"—set in different type sizes for rhetorical effect) with the drawing of a Muslim woman wearing the American flag as a hijab. The poster

Figure 9.1 A multimodal argument about cultural and religious diversity

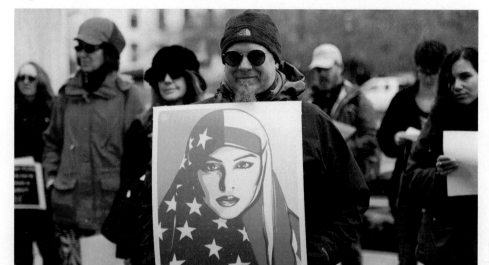

visually identifies and welcomes the Muslim woman as an American whose flag hijab is just as legitimate as a flag cowboy hat or a flag T-shirt.

The poster in Figure 9.1 makes use of all three classical appeals. It appeals to *logos* by arguing that this woman is one of the "us" in "we the people" (highlighted in bold capital letters) based on the constitutional claim that the United States is a nation of diverse peoples. It appeals to *pathos* by taking a patriotic symbol beloved by Americans (the flag) and associating it with groups of people whom the government has labeled as a threat. It also appeals to *ethos* by showing citizens courageously protesting and rejecting fear. The striking multimodal poster and the surrounding protesters in the photo create a memorable social and political argument.

Understanding Visual Design Elements in Multimodal Argument

9.1   Explain the visual design elements in multimodal arguments.

To understand how visual images can produce an argument, you need to understand the design elements that work together to create a visual text.

The Components of Visual Design

There are four basic components of visual design: use of type, use of space and layout, use of color, and use of images and graphics. The most important considerations in using these design features are shown in Table 9.1.

Table 9.1 Components of Visual Design

Design Component	Key Variables	Key Principles
Use of type	• Font style ranging from conservative (Times New Roman, Courier) to playful and decorative (Zapf Chancery and other specialty fonts) • Font size • Variables for emphasis (**boldface**, *italics*, underlining, ALL CAPS)	• For headings, titles, and slogans, choose sans serif type (without the little extensions on letters) like Century Gothic and Ariel. • For body text within a document, choose serif type (with the little extensions on letters) like Times New Roman and Courier New. • Make type functional and appealing by using only two or three type styles per document. • Use consistent patterns of type to indicate relationships among items. • Choose type to project a specific impression. To create a formal, businesslike impression, as in scholarly publications, use a structured combination of serif and sans serif type. To create an informal look, as in popular magazine publications and highly visual posters and fliers, use sans serif and specialty type.
Use of space and layout	• Page size and type of paper • Proportion of text to white space • Arrangement of text on page (space, margins, columns, size of paragraphs, spaces between paragraphs, justification of margins) • Use of highlighting elements such as bulleted lists, tables, sidebars, boxes • Use of headings and other means of breaking text into visual units	• Use layout to make documents highly readable and to guide readers with structural clues (headings, paragraph breaks, and bulleted lists). • Focus on creating meaning and coherence with layout. • For academic arguments, use simple, functional layouts. For popular magazine arguments and visual arguments, vary the layout and make the page visually attractive. However, for visual arguments, avoid clutter and confusion by limiting the amount of text and the number of visual items on a page.
Use of color	• Variations in font color for effect • Use of color in images and graphics • Use of background tints and colored shading	• Use color to meet audience and genre expectations (minimal use in academic argument and often lavish color in popular magazines). • For visual arguments, use color functionally to indicate relationships or decoratively to create visual appeal. • For visual arguments, decide whether color will be used to make images look documentary-like (realistic) or to create symbolic associations (for example, psychedelic colors and the 1960s) or to create a specific aesthetic effect (for example, pleasing, disturbing, or soothing).
Images and graphics	• Photographs • Drawings • Numeric graphics	• For visual argument, consider the image's function (to convey an idea, provide evidence, evoke emotions). • For multimodal arguments combining words and images, make sure that the words and images work together for mutual reinforcement.

An Analysis of a Multimodal Argument Using Type and Spatial Elements

To illustrate the persuasive power of type and layout, we ask you to consider Figure 9.2, which reproduces a public affairs ad sponsored by the Ad Council and an advocacy organization, StopBullying.gov. This advocacy piece, which is part of an ongoing campaign to curtail bullying among young people, is aimed at parents, urging them to encourage their children to actively oppose bullying.

This ad demonstrates how the use of type can create powerful visual effects that combine with the words to convey its argument. The ad's creators chose to use lettering—rather than a photograph or a drawing—to illustrate bullying. The type style, presentation of the letters, and words themselves create a strange rhetorical effect—simultaneously personal and impersonal—that draws viewers into the ad more than an image would. The type style and font make strong appeals

Figure 9.2 Anti-bullying public affairs ad

to *pathos* through the blend of the shocking abusive language and disturbing lettering style. The words "dumb," "piece," and "trash" are all harshly derogatory. The direct address to the viewer in the word "you" conveys that bullying is an attack, sometimes verbal and often physical.

Note how the blurring of the message in the large bold type makes a visual statement about the act of bullying, how bullying is perceived, and the psychological damage it causes. These large, heavy, blurred letters convey multiple messages. Bullying can be crude and forceful, but it is often carried on covertly where authority figures cannot see or stop it. The lettering itself bullies the viewers while at the same time reinforcing the idea that not everyone is aware of bullying. The blurring of these letters also suggests that bullying washes out the personhood of its victims. In addition, the ad makes it look as though these dark letters have smudged and stained the yellow background, suggesting that bullying also harms society.

The layout of this ad also contributes to its *logos* and *ethos*. The shock of reading the bold message propels readers to the black sidebar in the ad's lower right side, where the message in smaller type interprets and explains the message of the blurred letters. The text speaks directly to parents' unawareness of the hostility in their kids' environment and makes an urgent appeal to parental responsibility. While the lettering and layout convey the causal reasons behind the need for action, the message in the smaller letters states the proposal claim: Instruct your kids how to become more than passive observers of bullying: "Teach your kids to be more than a bystander." In addition to delivering a strong message, this ad conveys a positive *ethos* by demonstrating knowledge of the problem and directing readers to authoritative sources of information that will help them engage with this serious social issue.

An Analysis of a Multimodal Argument Using All the Design Components

Before we discuss the use of images and graphics in detail, we illustrate how all four of the design components—use of type, layout, color, and images—can reinforce and support one another to achieve a rhetorical effect in a multimodal argument as shown in the advocacy ad in Figure 9.3. Because the intricacies of copyright law restrict our reproduction of advertisements in this textbook, we commissioned an ad team to create this advocacy piece for a fictitious organization, "Morementum." This ad is intended for publication in a regional magazine or in the ad insert of a major regional newspaper. It highlights the design features of image, color, and layout, with type used to interpret and reinforce the message delivered by the other features.

Let's examine the ad in more detail. The layout highlights the connection between the wheel-chair-bound person in the lower-left center of the ad, the scene he is viewing, and readers who take in the whole scene. The text in the band of color at the top ("Mobility is more than an app") arouses curiosity and plays on words: For many people, mobility *is* an app—simply touch Uber or Lyft on your smartphone. However, the words "more than" suggest that this ad looks more deeply at the idea of "mobility." What is at stake, as the "story" of the ad makes clear, is a different kind of dependence and independence. The ad's story is suggested by the text in smaller print at the bottom of the ad, which leads readers to reconsider the person in the wheelchair: "Morementum provides care, training, and specialized equipment for injured vets." The next line of text further interprets the African American man as a military hero and clarifies the purpose

Figure 9.3 Advocacy ad: Morementum

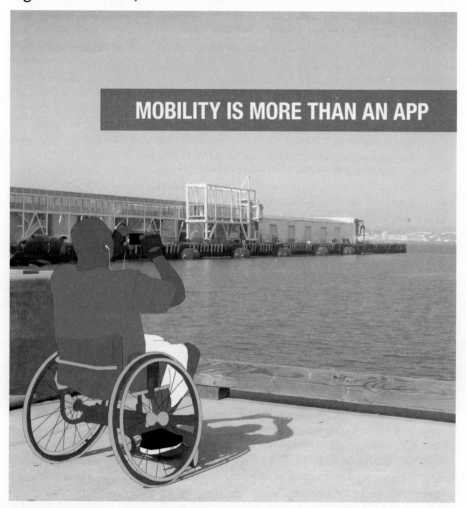

Morementum provides care, training, and specialized equipment for injured vets.
Your donation can help a hero find a new horizon.

MOREMENTUM. *THE DIFFERENCE IS US.*

of the ad: to elicit donations to help these vets enlarge their options and expand their quality of life It says, "Your donation can help a hero find a new horizon."

This advocacy ad works on readers by blending three themes—the hope for mobility and independence in the face of disability; a subtle patriotic appeal; and the symbolic meaning of "new horizons"—to convey how people's support of Morementum can empower veterans with disabilities to help themselves. These themes are portrayed through various visual strategies. The focus on one figure—a man in a wheelchair on a boardwalk—underscores the fact that he has maneuvered himself to the spot on his own. He sits in the kind of athletic wheelchair used in basketball games, and his special leather gloves highlight his ability to roll this wheelchair himself, emphasizing his desire to be independent, active, and mobile. He is out and about on a nice day, listening to music and taking photos of the attractive view from the side of the lake. This equipment has opened up activities for him.

The man's identity as a veteran is further developed by the ad's color scheme, which is both realistic and symbolic in its subtle patriotism. The white lettering on a red background relates well with the deep blue of the man's shirt and the white of his shorts, framing the ad in America's colors: red, white, and blue. Finally, the symbolism of horizons infuses this whole advocacy ad. For the photo of the scene itself, the ad designers positioned the camera behind the man in the wheelchair so that the scene includes the disabled veteran but also reaches outward to the view that the man sees, compelling readers to consider the whole scene. The fact that the man takes up much of the foreground makes him central to the ad's message. However, the camera's position behind the man also forces readers' gaze out to what the man sees, converting the disabled veteran from a particular individual into an "every veteran."

Note that the man is looking off to the horizon on the other side of the lake. Even the industrial pier with refueling and loading stations for boats and the buildings in the distance across the lake have a subtle symbolism: This is not a resort or vacation setting, but rather a place for jobs and productive activity. The brightness of the scene and the deep aqua color of the water combined with the man's engagement with the scene capture the sense of hope and new possibilities inherent in the concept of horizon. The text itself ties the whole ad together. The organization's title, "Morementum," encompasses the concept of momentum— moving—and the altering of "momentum" to include the word "more" suggests a reaching forward to a better and bigger life, not one restricted by disability. It also asks readers to participate by adding something "more" to these veterans' lives through awareness, concern, and donations.

The rhetorical design choices in the construction of this advocacy ad explain its positive effect on readers. The ad portrays an upbeat scene of a veteran enjoying his ability to get around on a city boardwalk to experience the nice weather and lake view. The image, layout, and color scheme work in conjunction with the positive words "help," "hero," and "new horizon." The tagline of the piece— "MOREMENTUM. THE DIFFERENCE IS US"—continues the positive feelings by encouraging readers to contribute money so that more veterans can find pleasure in life and move forward.

For Writing and Discussion

Analyzing an Advocacy Ad

Individual Task

Using your knowledge of type, layout, color, and image, analyze the Buzzed Driving advocacy ad sponsored by the Ad Council and the National Highway and Traffic Safety Administration in Figure 9.4. The following questions can guide your response:

1. What story does this ad tell? What is the ad's core argument?
2. How does this ad use type, layout, image, and color for persuasive effect?
   - Layout and Image: Does the image convey an idea, illustrate a point, or evoke an emotional response? Why do you think the ad designer chose to give spatial preference to the image?

Figure 9.4 Advocacy ad against drunk driving

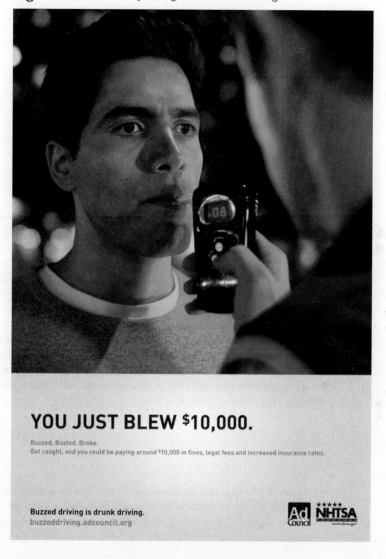

- **Color:** Is the use of color in this ad decorative, realistic, aesthetic, or some combination of these? Explain. How does the use of color contribute to the ad's message?
- **Type:** What is the relationship between the image and the type? Look at the words and ideas in each line of type. What is the effect of using different font sizes?

3. How does this ad appeal to *logos, ethos,* and *pathos*?

Group Task:

Working in pairs or as a class, share your analysis of this multimodal advocacy ad. Consider alternative designs for ads warning against driving under the influence of alcohol. What other images, layouts, use of type, and color might be effective in conveying the same message as this ad?

The Compositional Features of Photographs and Drawings

9.2   Analyze the compositional features of photographs and drawings rhetorically.

Now that we have introduced you to the four major elements of visual design—type, layout, color, and images—we turn to an in-depth discussion of photographic images and drawings. Used with great shrewdness in most product advertisements, photos and drawings can be employed with equal shrewdness in posters, fliers, advocacy ads, and websites. When an image is created specifically for the purpose of advancing an argument, almost nothing is left to chance. Although such images are often made to seem spontaneous and "natural," they are almost always composed. That is, designers consciously select the details of staging and composition. They also use camera techniques (filters, camera angle, lighting) and digital or chemical development techniques (airbrushing, merging of images) to control the message.

Even news photography can have a composed feel. For example, public officials often try to control the effect of photographs by creating "photo opps" (photographing opportunities), wherein reporters are allowed to photograph an event only during certain times and only from certain angles. Political photographs appearing in newspapers often come from press releases officially approved by the politician's staff.

To analyze a photograph or drawing, or to create visual images to include with your own arguments, you need to think both about the composition of the image and about the camera's relationship to the subject. Because drawings produce a perspective on a scene analogous to that of a camera, you can apply design considerations for photographs to drawings as well. The following list can guide your analysis of any persuasive image.

Compositional Features to Examine in Photos and Drawings

- **Type of photograph or drawing:** Is the image documentary-like (representing a real event), fiction-like (intending to tell a story or dramatize a scene), or conceptual (illustrating or symbolizing an idea or theme)? The photo of factory farming at the start of Part 1, the photo of the protest for higher wages for fast-food workers at the start of Part 2, and the photo of the anti-fracking march at the start of Part 3 are documentary photos capturing real events in action. In contrast, the vaping ad at the start of Part 4 is yet another type of drawing. The drawing of a woman's face, showing her perfect make-up, healthy skin, and vapor-wreathed lips, tries to persuade us visually that vaping is safer and healthier than smoking cigarettes.

- **Distance from the subject:** Is the image a close-up, medium shot, or long shot? Close-ups tend to increase the image's intensity and suggest its importance; long shots tend to blend the subject into the background. The intensifying effect of a close-up is shown in Figure 9.4, where the camera focuses on the apprehended young man's face, particularly his eyes, lighted up by the police vehicle of the officer who has pulled him over. In contrast, the medium shot of the boy holding the toy he has found in the wreckage caused by Typhoon Haiyan (Figure 5.1) focuses on both the boy and his surroundings. While the photo captures the magnitude of the disaster, it also shows the child's interests and his attempt to recover some of his past life.

- **Image orientation and camera angle:** Is the camera (or artist) positioned in front of or behind the subject? Is the camera positioned below the subject, looking up (a low-angle shot)? Or is it above the subject, looking down (a high-angle shot)? Front-view shots (for example, the photo of the fracking protestor at the start of Part 3) tend to emphasize the persons being photographed. In contrast, rear-view shots often emphasize the scene or setting. A low-angle perspective tends to make the subject look superior and powerful, whereas a high-angle perspective can reduce the size—and by implication, the importance—of the subject. A level angle tends to imply equality.

- **Point of view:** Does the camera or artist stand outside the scene and create an objective effect? Or is the camera or artist inside the scene as if the photographer or artist is an actor in the scene, creating a subjective effect?

- **Use of color:** Is the image in color or in black and white? Is this choice determined by the restrictions of the medium (such as images designed to run in black-and-white in newspapers), or is it the choice of the photographer or artist? Are the colors realistic or muted? Have special filters been used (for example, a photo made to look old through the use of brown tints)? Are bright colors intended to be catchy, attractive, dominant, or disturbing?

- **Compositional special effects:** Is the entire image clear and realistic? Is any portion of it blurred? Is it blended with other realistic or nonrealistic images (for example, a car ad that blends a city and a desert; a body lotion ad that merges a woman and a cactus)? Is the image an imitation of some other famous image such as a classic painting (as in parodies)? The image of the Muslim woman wearing the American flag (Figure 9.1) as a hijab makes a visual association between an image of a beautiful woman and American patriotism.

- **Juxtaposition of images:** Are several different images juxtaposed (that is, placed closed together or side by side), suggesting relationships between them? Juxtaposition can suggest sequential or causal relationships, or it can metaphorically transfer the identity of a nearby image or background to the subject (as when a bath soap is associated with a meadow). Juxtaposition of images is frequently used to shape viewers' perceptions of political figures, as when political figures are photographed with patriotic monuments.

- **Manipulation of images:** Are staged images made to appear real, natural, or documentary-like? Are images altered with airbrushing? Are the images a series of composites of a number of images (for instance, using images of different women's bodies to create one perfect model in an ad or film)? Are images *cropped* for emphasis? That is, has any part of the original photo been cut out? If so, what is left out? Are images downsized or enlarged?

- **Settings, furnishings, props:** Is the photo or drawing an outdoor scene or an indoor scene? What is in the background and foreground? What furnishings and props (such as furniture, objects in a room, pets, and landscape features) help create the scene? What social associations of class, race, and gender are attached to these settings and props?

- **Characters, roles, actions:** Does the photo or drawing tell a story? Are the people in the scene models? Are the models instrumental (acting out real-life roles), or are they decorative (extra and included for visual or sex appeal)? What are the people's facial expressions, gestures, and poses? What are the figures' spatial relationships? (Who is in the foreground, center, and background? Who is large and prominent?) What social relationships are implied by these poses and positions? In the "Morementum" advocacy ad in Figure 9.3, the solitary man in the wheelchair enjoying the view from the wooden boardwalk tells the story of hoped-for independence.

- **Presentation of images:** Are images separated from one another in a larger composition or connected to one another? Are the images large in proportion to written text? How are images labeled, if at all? How does the text relate to the image(s)? Does the image illustrate the text? Does the text explain or comment on the image?

An Analysis of a Multimedia Video Argument Using Words, Images, and Music

To show you how to analyze a multimodal argument with images and text, let's examine a student advocacy video, "It's a Toilet, Not a Trash Can," made for a first-year inquiry seminar on water and citizenship. Eight stills from this advocacy video are shown in Figures 9.5–9.12. The assignment asked students to construct an advocacy video addressing a public problem related to water, inviting them to explore questions such as: What should responsible citizens know about where their water comes from, where it goes, and what it costs? How should we manage water to be certain that it is clean, safe, and available? How do we allot available water to different stakeholders such as households, industry, agriculture, and recreation? For this assignment, students were asked to construct a video to encourage a specific audience to act responsibly in their water usage. Having taken a class trip to a local wastewater treatment plant, the students in this class became aware of how nonbiodegradable trash enters the wastewater system instead of going to a landfill or a recycling plant. One group of students chose to attack one cause of this problem: the casual flushing of trash items down residence hall toilets.

This video uses humorous exaggeration to underscore its serious point. The video begins with scenes from a windy fall day, with different groups of students returning to a residence hall with what seem to be full grocery bags. Students walk and talk with friends, take the residence hall elevator, and walk down their hallway toward their rooms (Figures 9.5 and 9.6). At this point, the advocacy video

Figure 9.5 Students carrying plastic bags into a residence hall elevator

Figure 9.6 Students in residence hallway carrying the same bags spins off into hyperbole (exaggeration) and absurdity. Some students, instead of carrying groceries in their shopping bags, have been carrying garbage, which they proceed to dump into the toilet (Figure 9.7). The humorous shock value of this action is intensified through close-ups of a large amount of garbage emptied into the toilet (Figures 9.8 and 9.10). Interspersed between action scenes are a few verbal text screens that explain the problem of trash in the sewage system and drive home the costs of the problem (such as the verbal text screen in Figure 9.9). The final screens use text to state the video's message explicitly (Figures 9.11 and 9.12).

Figure 9.7 Student dumping garbage in residence hall toilet

Figure 9.8 Garbage filling the toilet

Figure 9.9 Screen explaining why this trash is harmful

"Tampons and other commonly flushed products including wipes and condoms cannot be broken down in the sewage System."
Tara Johnson (EPA)

Figure 9.10 Hand adding more garbage to the toilet

Figure 9.11 Screen stating the absurdity of the actions in the video

You wouldn't empty your garbage in the toilet.

Figure 9.12 Final screen with tagline that summarizes the advocacy video's point

It's a toilet, not a trash can.

As the story builds intensity, this advocacy video combines appeals to *pathos*, *ethos*, and *logos*. The appeals to *pathos* begin with the simple, fast-paced, haunting instrumental music that plays in the background throughout the video; the music is both pleasant and somewhat disturbing, the kind that lingers in the mind. Student viewers can also easily relate to the characters in the video (a quality of *pathos*) in that the student actors wear ordinary clothing and the residence hall elevator and hallway are so generic that they could be found anywhere in the country. Once the surprise of the garbage dumping starts, the mild shock and humor stir different kinds of emotions. Viewers can no longer predict where the video is going. The dumping of garbage into the toilet is so puzzling and so over the top that it elicits both laughs and gasps from the audience. Close-ups of toilets filled with floating bottles and garbage are ridiculously distressing.

In addition to appeals to *pathos*, the video includes appeals to *logos* through the interspersed text-based screens (stark in their white type on a black background) that explain the harm done by trash in the sewage system. Several of these screens also appeal to *ethos* by citing facts from authorities such as the Environmental Protection Agency (as in Figure 9.9) and the Clean Watersheds Needs Survey (not shown in the sequence of still photos), which explain the burden and cost of garbage in waste-water treatment plants. In fact, all kinds of items—pieces of clothing and plastic, combs, condoms, sanitary products, diapers, even dollar bills—find their way into these treatment systems and need to be fished out. The message conveyed by the video emerges from the actions portrayed and confronts readers directly in the final screens. The video does not state its proposal claim initially because the creators of the video did not want viewers to dismiss the claim outright or arouse defensiveness. The final tagline ("It's a toilet, not a trash can") plays on viewers' emotions through its memorable, catchy alliteration ("toilet" and "trash can"). This line just might come to mind the next time someone is about to drop a piece of trash in the toilet.

The Genres of Multimodal Argument

9.3 **Explain the genres of multimodal argument.**

In some cases, multimodal texts are primarily written text with inserted photographs or drawings that enhance the *logos* or *pathos* of the argument. For example, a verbal argument promoting help for AIDS victims in Africa might be accompanied by a photograph of a dying mother and child. In contrast, in some multimodal genres the visual design carries most of the argumentative weight; verbal text is used primarily for labeling, for focusing the argument's claim, or for commenting on the images. In this section, we describe a variety of multimodal genres that rely primarily on visual elements.

Posters and Fliers

To persuade audiences, an arguer might create a poster or flier to rally support for a cause. For example, during World War II, posters asked Americans to invest in war bonds and urged women to join the workforce in order to free men for active combat. During the Vietnam War, famous posters used slogans such as "Make Love, Not War" or "Girls say yes to boys who say no" to increase national resistance to the war.

The hallmark of an effective poster is the way it uses a visual-verbal text to focus and encode a complex meaning, often with one or more striking images. These images are often symbolic—for example, using children to symbolize family and home, a soaring bird to symbolize freedom, or three firefighters raising the American flag over the World Trade Center rubble on September 11, 2001, to symbolize American heroism, patriotism, and resistance to terrorism. These symbols derive potency from the values they share with their target audience. Posters tend to use words sparingly, either as slogans or as short, memorable directives. This concise verbal text augments the message encoded in an eye-catching, dominant image.

As an example of a contemporary poster urging people to see a recent independent film, consider *The Humble Assessment* poster in Figure 9.13. Because this film is new and unknown, the poster must arouse curiosity and elicit interest. In this poster, the text creates the context—the competitive job market and the financial anxieties of applicants. The poster shows a man in a business suit, white shirt, and tie in a sitting position, possibly waiting for an interview. However, the poster leaves viewers with many questions: Is the man sitting on a chair or cramped into a coffin-like space? Why doesn't the man have a head? Why is he playing with a Rubik's cube? Why do his hands look tense? Why are the clock's hands replaced by a spider whose eight legs point to a bewildering number of time possibilities? Why are the clock with the spider and the line "The job market has gone to hell" placed between the man's knees? How do the wavering letters of the film's title contribute to the claustrophobic, unsettling impression produced by the text and image? How

Figure 9.13 Poster for *The Humble Assessment*

does the use of the words "stomach for it," "you," "we," and "gone to hell" both draw viewers in and put them on edge? "Assessment" means a judgment of value. What does that word have to do with "humble," and why would a job interview be called "an assessment"? In short, this film poster uses text and image to pique curiosity and suggest disturbing content in this absurdist, surreal postmodern depiction of the demoralizing and dehumanizing corporate job market.

Public Affairs Advocacy Advertisements

Public affairs advocacy advertisements share with posters an emphasis on visual elements, but they are designed specifically for publication in newspapers and magazines (and are often reproduced on websites). In their persuasive strategies, they are very similar to product advertisements. Public affairs advocacy ads are usually sponsored by a corporation or an advocacy organization, often are part of a particular campaign with a theme, and have a more immediate and defined target audience than posters do. Designed as condensed arguments aimed at influencing public opinion on civic issues, these ads are characterized by their brevity, audience-based appeals, and succinct, "sound bite" style. Often, in order to put forth their claim and reasons clearly and concisely, they employ headings and subheadings, bulleted lists, different sizes and styles of type, and a clever, pleasing layout on the page. They usually have an attention-getting slogan or headline such as "MORE KIDS ARE GETTING BRAIN CANCER. WHY?" or "STOP THE TAX REVOLT JUGGERNAUT!" And they usually include a call to action, such as a donation, a letter of protest to legislators, or an invitation to join the advocacy group.

The balance between verbal and visual elements in an advocacy advertisement varies. Some advocacy ads are verbal only, with visual concerns focused on document design (for example, an "open letter" from the president of a corporation appearing as a full-page newspaper ad). Other advocacy ads are primarily visual, using images and other design elements with the same shrewdness as advertisements.

This text reproduces a variety of public affairs advocacy ads across chapters. We have already examined the anti-bullying ad in Figure 9.2, the anti-drunk driving ad in Figure 9.4, and the fictionalized Morementum ad in Figure 9.3. These ads use text and images in different ways to present their messages.

For Writing and Discussion

Analyzing Posters Rhetorically

Working individually or in groups, examine the the poster shown in Figure 9.14, which shows a photo of an attractive girl behind the line "HEATHER'S LIFE ENDED TOO SOON." This poster, which appears on the TxtResponsibly.org website, reaches out to young drivers and their parents, using both images and text.

a. What visual features of this poster immediately attract your attention? What principles for the effective use of type, layout, color, and image does this ad exemplify?

b. What is this ad's core argument?

c. Why did Heather's parents choose a large photo of her? How does that photo work with the other photo of a mangled car?

d. How does the frankness of the text and the size and use of color lettering combine to convey the ad's message?

e. How would you design a poster warning against texting while driving? Consider the use of type, layout, and image; the core of its argument; and its appeals to *ethos*, *pathos*, and *kairos*.

Figure 9.14 Poster argument warning against texting while driving

Cartoons

An especially charged kind of visual argument is the editorial or political cartoon and its extended forms, the comic strip and the graphic novel. Here we focus on political cartoons, which are often mini-narratives portraying an issue dramatically, compactly, and humorously, through images and a few well-chosen words that dramatize conflicts and problems. Using caricature, exaggeration, and distortion, a cartoonist distills an issue down to an image that boldly reveals the cartoonist's perspective on the issue. The purpose of political cartoons is usually satirical, often criticizing some groups of people or ideas while delighting and inspiring those who agree with the cartoonist's viewpoint. Because they are so condensed and are often connected to current affairs, political cartoons are particularly dependent on the audience's background knowledge of cultural and political events. When political cartoons work well, their perceptive combination of images and words flashes a brilliant, clarifying light or opens a new lens on an issue, often giving readers a shock of insight.

As an example, note the cartoon by Milt Priggee in Figure 9.15. The setting of the cartoon envisions a humorous blend of prehistoric and contemporary times. This cartoon responds to recent scientific discussions of the creation and development of the universe and the age of the Earth. (Note the mention of dark matter, which is an energy-mass concept from physics and astronomy.) However, the main story of the cartoon connects the dinosaur characters with the behavior of people today who go about walking and tweeting, oblivious to everything around them, including dangerous environments. Thus, the cartoon links discussions of evolution to discussions of the contemporary obsession with smartphones and social media.

Figure 9.15 Tweeting and evolution cartoon

For Writing and Discussion

Analyzing Cartoons

Cartoons can provide insight into how the public is lining up on issues. Choose a current issue such as healthcare reform, use of drones, immigration policy, tax policy, or identity theft. Then, using an online cartoon index such as Daryl Cagle's Professional Cartoonists Index (www.cagle.com) or a web search of your own, find several cartoons that capture different perspectives on your issue.

1. What is the mini-narrative in each cartoon? What is the main claim? How are caricature, exaggeration, and/or distortion used in each cartoon?
2. How is *kairos*, or timeliness, important to each cartoon?

Websites

So far we have only hinted at how the World Wide Web has accelerated the use of visual images in argument. Multimodal websites exhibit the web's complex mix of text and image, a mix that has changed the way many writers think of argument. For example, the home page of an advocacy site often has many features of a poster argument, with hypertext links to galleries of images on the one hand and to verbal arguments on the other. These verbal arguments themselves often contain photographs, drawings, and graphics. The strategies discussed in this chapter for analyzing and interpreting visual texts also apply to websites.

Because the web is such an important tool in research, we have placed our main discussion of websites in Appendix 2. There you will find detailed explanations for reading, analyzing, and evaluating websites.

Advocacy Videos

Advocacy videos, often posted on YouTube, are perhaps the most influential of all multimodal arguments. Whether professionally made or quickly planned and produced by amateurs using video production software, advocacy videos allow powerful combinations of sounds, images, and verbal text (either as spoken dialogue, as voice-overs, or as inserted written text). Advocacy websites (and their parallel Facebook, Twitter, or Instagram sites) frequently link to advocacy videos. Earlier in this chapter, we described and analyzed a student advocacy video, "It's a Toilet, Not a Trash Can," and reproduced stills from the video. In the next section we offer guidelines for constructing your own advocacy video.

Constructing Your Own Multimodal Arguments

9.4   **Construct your own multimodal arguments.**

The most common multimodal arguments you are likely to create are posters, fliers, public affairs advocacy ads, and advocacy videos. The following guidelines will help you apply your understanding of visual elements to the construction of your own multimodal arguments.

Guidelines for Creating the Visual Elements in Posters, Fliers, and Advocacy Ads

1. **Genre:** Determine where this visual argument is going to appear (on a bulletin board, circulated as a flier, on one page of a magazine or newspaper, or on a website).

2. **Audience-based appeals:** Determine who your target audience is.
   - What values and background knowledge regarding your issue can you assume that your audience has?
   - What specifically do you want your audience to think or do after reading your visual argument?
   - If you are promoting a specific course of action (sign a petition, send money, vote for or against a bill, attend a meeting), how can you make that request clear and direct?

3. **Core of your argument:** Determine what clear claim and reasons will form the core of your argument; decide whether this claim and these reasons will be explicitly stated or implicit in your visuals and slogans.
   - How much verbal text will you use?
   - If the core of your argument will be largely implicit, how can you make it readily apparent and clear for your audience?

4. **Visual design:** What visual design and layout will grab your audience's attention and be persuasive?
   - How can font sizes and styles, layout, and color be used in this argument to create a strong impression?
   - What balance and harmony can you create between the visual and verbal elements of your argument? Will your verbal elements be a slogan, express the core of the argument, or summarize and comment on the image(s)?

5. **Use of images:** If your argument lends itself to images, what photo or drawing would support your claim or have emotional appeal? (If you want to use more than one image, be careful that you don't clutter your page and confuse your message. Simplicity and clarity are important.)
   - What image would be memorable and meaningful to your audience? Which would be more effective: a photo or a drawing?
   - Will your image(s) be used to provide evidence for your claim, illustrate a main idea, evoke emotions, or enhance your credibility and authority?

Guidelines for Creating Video Arguments

1. **Rhetorical situation:** Consider your purpose and audience, your core argument, and the effect you want your video to have on your targeted audience.
   - What is your core argument?
   - Are you imagining a sympathetic, neutral, or opposing audience?

- How do you plan to appeal to *logos*, *ethos*, and *pathos*?
- What role will you assume? Will you stay behind the scenes or appear in the video?
- Does your rhetorical purpose call for one point of view or multiple points of view to move your audience toward your view?

2. **Use of a storyboard to map out scenes:** Storyboards (rough sketch drawings of intended scenes) are like graphic organizers that help you plan your video scene by scene. When creating a storyboard, you plan the scenes you will use to tell a story and plan the camera angles you will use to create the visual narrative.

   - How will you organize individual shots?
   - How will you use camera angles to create a narrative story?
   - How would zooming, fading, or rapid cuts to a different angle help you create transitions between scenes?

3. **Priority on visual elements:** Audiences of video texts expect to be engaged visually at all times.

   - How will your sequence of scenes convey your message visually? Consider using different camera angles—establishing shots (medium or long shots), point-of-view shots (through a character's eyes), and reaction shots (close-ups of faces)—to tell a story.
   - While keeping priority on images, how might you use words to help readers interpret images? Consider using captions, inserted text screens, or voice-overs.
   - Have you paced your video effectively so that it leaves your audience neither confused nor bored?

4. **Incorporation of effective verbal and written text:** You can incorporate verbal text into a video through spoken dialogue, voice-overs, or printed text inserted as captions or as separate screens. Video technology allows for more versatile text options than just about any other multimodal form.

   - How might spoken or written text underscore the intended rhetorical effect of images by emphasizing main points and highlighting important information?
   - If you use voice-overs, how will you avoid using monotonous or uninteresting visuals as filler during stretches of spoken text?
   - If you insert written text, how will you make your points vivid and clear, avoiding both text density and vagueness?

5. **Use of musical elements and other sound options:** Sound options can underscore important rhetorical goals with auditory effects. Sound or the choice of silence can have a subtle but powerful impact on the viewers of a video text.

   - Have you matched sound effects to the meaning and rhetorical effect you want to achieve? Consider how you will use music, background sounds (street noise, café buzz, bird chirps, sudden silence), and voice qualities (accent, pitch, emotional emphasis).
   - If you have used separate microphones, are they well placed? Is the sound too soft or too loud? Is voice audible rather than muffled?

For Writing and Discussion

Developing Ideas for an Advocacy Ad or Poster Argument

This exercise asks you to do the thinking and planning for an advocacy ad, poster argument, or advocacy video for your college or university campus. Working individually, in small groups, or as a class, choose an issue that is controversial on your campus (or in your town or city), and follow the Guidelines for Creating Visual Arguments or the Guidelines for Creating Advocacy Videos to envision the view you want to advocate on that issue. For an advocacy video, map your argument as scenes using a storyboard. What might the core of your argument be? Who is your target audience? Are you representing a group, club, or other organization? What image(s) might be effective in attracting and moving your audience? Possible issues might be commuter parking; poor conditions in the computer lab; student reluctance to use the counseling center; problems with residence hall life; financial aid programs; intramural sports; ways to improve orientation programs for new students; work-study programs; travel-abroad opportunities; or new initiatives such as study groups for big lecture courses or new service-learning opportunities.

Using Information Graphics in Arguments

9.5   Use information graphics rhetorically in arguments.

Besides images in the form of photographs and drawings, writers often use quantitative graphics to support number-based arguments. In Chapter 4 we introduced the use of quantitative data in arguments, showing how stakeholders can use numbers for evidence, often framing those numbers to support their angle of vision. Using spreadsheet and presentation programs, today's writers often create and import quantitative graphics into their documents. These visuals—such as tables, pie charts, and line graphs or bar graphs—can have great rhetorical power by using numbers to tell a story at a glance. In this section, we show you how to make numbers speak with quantitative graphics. We also show you how to analyze graphics, incorporate them into your text, and reference them effectively.

How Tables Contain a Variety of Stories

Data used in arguments usually have their origins in raw numbers collected from surveys, questionnaires, observational studies, scientific experiments, and so forth. Through a series of calculations, the numbers are combined, sorted, and arranged in a meaningful fashion, often in detailed tables. Some of the tables published by the U.S. Census Bureau, for example, stretch across dozens of pages. The denser the table, the more its use is restricted to statistical experts who pore over the data to analyze and interpret them. More useful to the public are shorter tables contained on one or two pages that report data at a higher level of abstraction.

Consider, for example, Table 9.2, which reproduces data from a more detailed table published by the U.S. Energy Information Administration. This table shows the amount of energy consumed in the United States during selected years from 1950 to 2016 from specified primary sources such as coal, natural gas, nuclear power, wind, or the sun (solar energy).

Take a few moments to peruse the table and be certain you know how to read it. You read tables in two directions: from top to bottom and from left to right. Always begin with the title, which tells you what the table contains by including elements from the table's vertical and horizontal dimensions and by indicating the table's unit(s) of measure. In Table 9.2, the unit of measure is a quadrillion British thermal units (BTU). (A *quadrillion* is one million billions—that is, a 1 followed by 15 zeros. A BTU is the amount of energy needed to raise the temperature of one pound of water one degree Fahrenheit.) In Table 9.2, the vertical dimension shows years (every fifth year from 1950 to 2015, plus 2016). The horizontal dimension shows various sources of energy. The highest level of this horizontal dimension identifies the three primary energy sources: fossil fuels, nuclear energy, and renewable sources. Fossil fuels and renewable sources are then further divided into subcategories.

To make sure you know how to read the table, pick a couple of rows at random and explain what each number means. For example, the 1970 row shows that in 1970 Americans consumed 12.27 quadrillion BTUs of energy from coal, 21.8 quadrillion BTUs from natural gas, and 29.52 quadrillion BTUs from petroleum for a total of 63.52 quadrillion BTUs of fossil fuel energy. That same year,

Table 9.2 U.S. Primary Energy Consumption by Source, 1950 to 2016 (Quadrillion BTUs)

	Fossil Fuels			Nuclear Energy	Renewable Sources						Grand Total*
	Coal	Natural Gas	Petro-leum	Total	Nuclear Electric Power	Hydro-Electric Power	Geo-Thermal	Solar	Wind	Bio-mass	Total	
1950	12.35	5.97	13.32	31.63	0.00	1.42	-	-	-	1.56	2.98	34.62
1955	11.17	9.00	17.26	37.41	0.00	1.36	-	-	-	1.42	2.78	40.21
1960	9.84	12.39	19.92	42.14	0.01	1.61	-	-	-	1.32	2.93	45.09
1965	11.58	15.77	23.25	50.58	0.04	2.06	-	-	-	1.34	3.40	54.02
1970	12.27	21.80	29.52	63.52	0.24	2.63	0.01	-	-	1.43	4.07	67.84
1975	12.66	19.95	32.73	65.36	1.90	3.16	0.03	-	-	1.50	4.69	71.97
1980	15.42	20.24	34.21	69.83	2.74	2.90	0.05	-	-	2.48	5.43	78.07
1985	17.48	17.70	30.93	66.09	4.08	2.97	0.10	-	-	3.02	6.08	76.39
1990	19.17	19.60	33.55	72.33	6.10	3.05	0.17	0.06	0.03	2.74	6.04	84.48
1995	20.09	22.67	34.44	77.26	7.08	3.21	0.15	0.07	0.03	3.10	6.56	91.03
2000	22.58	23.82	38.27	84.74	7.86	2.81	0.16	0.06	0.06	3.01	6.10	98.82
2005	22.80	22.57	40.30	85.71	8.16	2.70	0.18	0.06	0.18	3.11	6.23	100.19
2010	20.83	24.58	35.49	80.89	8.43	2.54	0.21	0.09	0.92	4.27	8.03	97.45
2015	15.55	28.20	35.60	79.33	8.34	2.32	0.21	0.43	1.78	4.73	9.47	97.37
2016	14.23	28.42	35.94	78.57	8.42	2.48	0.23	0.59	2.11	4.76	10.16	97.40

*Note: Grand totals may not sum exactly due to rounding.

Americans used .24 quadrillion BTUs from nuclear energy and a total of 4.07 quadrillion BTUs from renewable energy. Renewable energy in 1970 was limited to hydropower (2.63 quadrillion BTUs), geothermal (.01 quadrillion BTUs) and biomass (1.43 quadrillion BTUs). (In 1970, *biomass* meant primarily the burning of wood and charcoal; in more recent years it has included the use of biofuels such as ethanol.) The total U.S. consumption of energy from that year—obtained by adding fossil fuels, nuclear energy, and renewable sources—is shown in the far right column: 67.84 quadrillion BTUs.

Now that you know how to read the table, examine it carefully to identify the kinds of questions it raises and stories it tells. What does the table show us, for example, about trends in total energy consumption in the United States? Is our use of natural gas increasing or decreasing? How about our use of nuclear energy or solar energy? In addition to looking just at the numbers on the table, you could convert numbers to percentages. For example, in any given year, what percent of total energy consumption came from renewable sources versus fossil fuels? Table 9.2 can also initiate interesting causal questions: In 2005, Americans consumed 22.8 quadrillion BTUs of coal energy. But by 2016 that number dropped to 14.23 quadrillion BTUs. Why has the use of coal declined? (Some people attribute the decline to anti-coal environmental regulations imposed by the Obama administration. Others attribute the decline to cheap natural gas made possible by fracking.)

Using a Graph to Tell a Story

Table 9.2 has many embedded energy stories, but you must tease them out from the dense columns of numbers. If you want to make a story pop out for readers, you can convert it to a graph. Three common types of graphs are bar graphs, pie charts, and line graphs.

BAR GRAPHS   Bar graphs use bars of varying length, extending either horizontally or vertically, to contrast two or more quantities. As with any graphic presentation, you must create a comprehensive title. In the case of bar graphs, titles tell readers what is being compared. Most bar graphs also have *legends*, which explain what the different features on the graph represent. Bars are typically distinguished from one another by use of different colors, shades, or patterns of crosshatching.

Bar graphs can help readers make quick comparisons. Suppose you want to link the recent decline in coal consumption to increased use of natural gas. You could tell this story at a glance with a bar graph, as in Figure 9.16. The first set of bars shows that in 2005 Americans used almost equal amounts of coal and natural gas. However, in the second set of bars (2016), the bar for coal has shrunk significantly while the bar for natural gas has grown.

PIE CHARTS   Another vivid kind of graph is a pie chart or circle graph, which depicts different percentages of a total (the pie) in the form of slices. Pie charts are often used to show how a whole is divided up into parts. For example, suppose that you wanted your readers to notice the percentage of U.S. energy consumption that came from each of the primary sectors in 2016. You could use a pie chart to make that percentage quickly visible through a pie chart like the one shown in Figure 9.17, which is based on the data in Table 9.2 As you can see, a pie chart shows at a glance how the whole of something is divided into segments. In this case there are only three segments.

Figure 9.16 U.S. consumption of energy from coal and natural gas, 2005 and 2016 (quadrillion BTUs)

SOURCE: United States Energy Information Agency

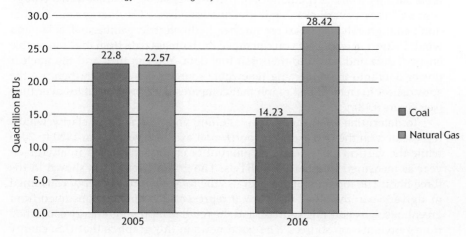

Figure 9.17 Consumption of energy by percentage from fossil fuel, nuclear, and renewal sources, 2016

SOURCE: United States Energy Information Agency.

A general note: The effectiveness of pie charts diminishes as you add more slices. In most cases, a pie chart becomes ineffective if you include more the five or six slices.

LINE GRAPHS   Another powerful quantitative graphic is a line graph, which converts numerical data into a series of points on a grid and then connects them to create flat, rising, or falling lines. The result is a picture of the relationship between the variables represented on the horizontal and vertical axes. By convention, the horizontal axis of a line graph contains the predictable, known variable, which has no surprises—what researchers call the *independent variable*. The vertical axis contains the unpredictable variable (what researchers call the *dependent variable*), which tells the graph's story.

Imagine that you want to create a line graph that compares use of energy sources that emit greenhouse gases with those that don't. Greenhouse-gas-emitting sources include both fossil fuels and biomass fuels. (Although biomass fuels such as wood and ethanol are listed in Table 9.2 as "renewable energy sources," they nevertheless emit greenhouse gases.) The energy sources that don't emit greenhouse gases are nuclear, hydroelectric, geothermal, solar, and wind. Using a spreadsheet you can move the biomass data from the "renewable energy" data and add it to the fossil fuel data. You can then add the nuclear power data into the remaining renewable sources data. You can then use the spreadsheet to create a line graph that compares these two variables over time (see Figure 9.18).

To determine what this graph is telling you, you need to clarify what's represented on the two axes. The horizontal axis lists years from 1950 to 2016 while the vertical axis shows the amount of energy consumed in any given year as measured in quadrillion BTUs. The graph's "story" is shown in the three lines: The top line (in gray) shows the total amount of energy consumed in a given year; the blue line below it represents the amount consumed from greenhouse-gas-emitting sources, and the red line represents energy consumed from zero-emission sources. The good news in this graph is that U.S. energy consumption appears to have peaked around 2005 and then declined slightly despite increases in population. Another piece of good news is that the consumption of zero-emission sources is slowly increasing while the use of greenhouse-gas-emitting sources is slowly decreasing. The bad news is that the gap between them is still huge.

Figure 9.18 U.S. energy consumption from greenhouse-gas-emitting sources versus zero emission sources, 1950–2016 (quadrillion BTUs)

NOTE: "Greenhouse-gas-emitting" sources of energy are fossil fuels and biomass fuels. "Zero emission" sources of energy are nuclear, geothermal, hydroelectric, solar, and wind power.

SOURCE: United States Energy Information Agency

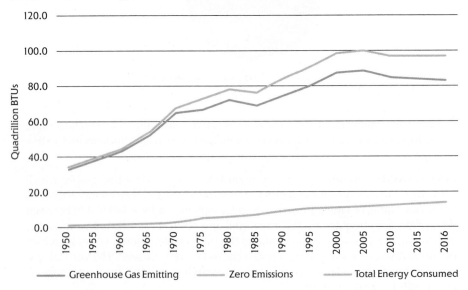

Incorporating Graphics into Your Argument

Today, writers working with quantitative data usually use graphing software that automatically creates tables, graphs, or charts from data entered into the cells of a spreadsheet. For college papers, some instructors may allow you to make your graphs with pencil and ruler and paste them into your document. The following suggestions will be helpful as you think about the best ways to incorporate graphics into your argument.

DESIGNING THE GRAPHIC   When you design your graphic, your goal is to have a specific rhetorical effect on your readers, not to demonstrate all the bells and whistles available on your software. Adding extraneous data to the graph or chart, or using such features as a three-dimensional effect, can often distract from your graph's story. Keep the graphic as uncluttered and simple as possible, and design it so that it reinforces the point you are making.

NUMBERING, LABELING, AND TITLING THE GRAPHIC   In newspapers and popular magazines, writers often include graphics in boxes or sidebars without specifically referring to them in the text itself. However, in academic and professional workplace writing, graphics are always labeled, numbered, titled, and referred to directly in the text. By convention, tables are listed as "Tables," whereas line graphs, bar graphs, pie charts, and any other kinds of drawings or photographs are labeled as "Figures." Suppose you create a document that includes four graphics—a table, a bar graph, a pie chart, and a photograph. The table would be labeled as Table 1. The others would be labeled as Figure 1, Figure 2, and Figure 3.

In addition to numbering and labeling, every graphic needs a comprehensive title that explains fully what information is being displayed. In a line graph showing changes over time, for example, a typical title will identify the information on both the horizontal and vertical axes (including the years covered). Bar graphs may also include a legend explaining how the bars are coded. When you import the graphic into your own text, be consistent in where you place the title—either above the graphic or below it.

Look again at the tables and figures in this chapter and compare their titles to the information in the graphics.

REFERENCING THE GRAPHIC IN YOUR TEXT   Academic and professional writers follow a referencing convention called *independent redundancy*. The general rule is this: The graphic should be understandable without the text; the text should be understandable without the graphic; the text should repeat the most important information in the graphic. Figure 9.19 provides an example.

A Note on How Graphics Frame Data Rhetorically

Note that graphs are designed to tell a story hidden in a much larger set of data. Any graph necessarily selects some data from a larger set and omits other data. Because no graph can tell the whole story, it always frames its designer's selected data for rhetorical emphasis. The graph shown in the student example in Figure 9.19 (called Figure 1 in the example) tells a true story about the rapid increase in the use of wind and solar energy. But that graph doesn't tell the whole story. One of the things it omits is the gap between solar and wind production and the total energy needs of the United States. A graph telling this larger story appears in Figure 9.20.

Figure 9.19 Example of a student text with a referenced graph

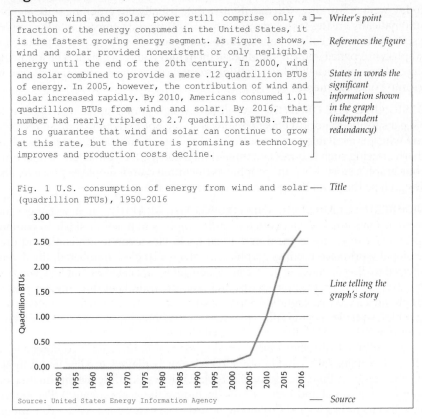

Although wind and solar power still comprise only a]— *Writer's point*
fraction of the energy consumed in the United States, it
is the fastest growing energy segment. As Figure 1 shows, — *References the figure*
wind and solar provided nonexistent or only negligible ⌉
energy until the end of the 20th century. In 2000, wind
and solar combined to provide a mere .12 quadrillion BTUs   *States in words the*
of energy. In 2005, however, the contribution of wind and   *significant*
solar increased rapidly. By 2010, Americans consumed 1.01]— *information shown*
quadrillion BTUs from wind and solar. By 2016, that   *in the graph*
number had nearly tripled to 2.7 quadrillion BTUs. There   *(independent*
is no guarantee that wind and solar can continue to grow   *redundancy)*
at this rate, but the future is promising as technology
improves and production costs decline. ⌋

Fig. 1 U.S. consumption of energy from wind and solar — *Title*
(quadrillion BTUs), 1950-2016

Line telling the graph's story

Source: United States Energy Information Agency — *Source*

Figure 9.20 Total U.S. energy consumption versus consumption of energy from wind and solar (quadrillion BTUs), 1950–2016

This graph no longer emphasizes the steep upward slope of solar and wind power usage. Rather, it emphasizes the huge difference between the total energy consumed in the United States and the comparatively tiny amount of wind and solar usage. Note that the vertical axis in Figure 9.20 goes from 0 to 120 quadrillion BTUs in increments of 20, while the same axis in the student graph in Figure 9.19 goes from 0 to 3 in increments of .5. The result in Figure 9.20 is to flatten out the wind/solar line until it is almost a straight, horizontal line. Both of these graphs (Figures 9.19 and 9.20) accurately use the original data in Table 9.2. Both are "true," but they tell different stories.

Writing Assignment

A Rhetorical Analysis of a Visual Argument, a Multimedia Poster, a Cartoon, or a Short Argument Using Quantitative Data

Option 1:
Writing a Rhetorical Analysis of a Visual Argument
Write a thesis-driven rhetorical analysis essay in which you examine the rhetorical effectiveness of a visual argument, either one of the visual arguments in this text or one specified by your instructor. Unless otherwise stated, direct your analysis to an audience of your classmates. In your introduction, establish the argumentative conversation to which this argument is contributing. Briefly summarize the argument and describe the visual text. Present your thesis, highlighting two or more rhetorical features of the argument—such as the way the argument appeals to *logos, ethos,* and *pathos*—that you find central to the effectiveness or ineffectiveness of this argument. To develop and support your own points, you will need to include visual features and details (such as color, design, camera angle, framing, and special effects) as well as short quotations from any verbal parts of the argument.

Option 2:
Multimodal Assignment: A Public Affairs Advocacy Ad, a Poster Argument, or an Advocacy Video
Working with the idea of an advocacy ad or poster argument that you explored in the For Writing and Discussion activity earlier in this chapter, use the visual design principles throughout the chapter; your understanding of visual argument and its genres; the Guidelines for Creating the Visual Elements in Posters, Fliers, and Advocacy Ads; the Guidelines for Creating Video Arguments; and your own creativity to produce a visual argument that can be displayed on your campus or in your town or city and/or posted somewhere on the web. Consider whether you will use photos or drawings. Try out the draft of your advocacy ad, poster, or video argument on people who are part of your target audience. Based on these individuals' suggestions for improving the clarity and impact of this visual argument, prepare a final version of your multimodal argument.

Option 3:
Multimodal Assignment: Cartoon
Choose a controversial issue important to you and create a single-frame political cartoon that presents your perspective on the issue in a memorable way. Use the cartoon strategies of mini-narrative, caricature, exaggeration, distortion, and the interaction between image and text.

Option 4:
A Short Argument Using a Quantitative Graphic
Write a short argument of one to two paragraphs that tells a story based on data you select from Table 9.2 or from some other table provided by your instructor or located by you. Include in your argument at least one quantitative graphic (table, line graph, bar graph, pie chart), which should be labeled and referenced according to standard conventions. Use as a model the short piece shown in Figure 9.19.

Chapter 10

An Alternative to Argument

Collaborative Rhetoric

Learning Objectives

In this chapter, you will learn to:

10.1 Explain the appropriateness and usefulness of collaborative rhetoric.

10.2 Explain the principles of collaborative rhetoric.

10.3 Prepare for collaborative rhetoric through reflective writing and discussion.

10.4 Write an open letter that demonstrates collaborative rhetoric by addressing and listening to someone who disagrees with you on an emotionally laden issue in order to open channels of communication and promote problem solving.

In Chapter 6, we introduced you to one-sided, multisided, and delayed-thesis arguments as strategies for persuading audiences with different degrees of resistance to your views. However, many argumentative situations you will encounter will not be conducive to persuasion. In such situations, you can turn to communication that does not seek to persuade but rather to promote listening.

This chapter focuses on rhetorical situations in which speakers and writers face emotionally laden issues with substantial disagreement among stakeholders. The most hopeful strategy is to switch from argument toward communication that listens, seeks clarification and understanding, and explores common ground. People facing emotionally laden issues often find opposing perspectives highly threatening. At stake for all involved are our deep-seated values, strong emotions, and even our identities. To change our positions on some issues, we may think, is to change who we are. Therefore, instead of argument that seeks to change people's views, the goal of communication shifts to listening to one another, opening channels of exchange, and seeking mutual growth in perspectives.

The Appropriateness and Usefulness of Collaborative Rhetoric

10.1 **Explain the appropriateness and usefulness of collaborative rhetoric.**

Much public communication today is mired in cross-purpose exchanges between people who don't "hear" opposing views. Stakeholders, who often have their emotions and identities entangled in issues and are wedded to their own sacred values, may not be willing to stop expressing their own views long enough to listen to other views. You will recognize situations like the following that involve clashing views and values.

- In one city community that has a "green belt" with a creek running through it, the question of land development has become an emotional issue. One group of people wants to widen and pave a path through the woods, turning this "wild" area into a park for all city residents. Another group opposes this development, believing that it will increase the volume of traffic in the neighborhood and disrupt the bird sanctuary. Several community meetings have ended in angry expressions of these clashing values, with some adamant about increasing accessibility to the public and others defending community safety and environmental preservation.

- Across the country, opinions of Planned Parenthood vary greatly. Some people view Planned Parenthood as an important healthcare provider and community service for women's overall health needs. They note that Planned Parenthood provides screenings for breast and cervical cancer, tests and treatment for STDs, and contraception. Others view Planned Parenthood mainly as an organization that provides abortions. Here, commitment to healthcare as a public good (including the right to preventive care) clashes with sacred pro-life values.

Impasses like these meet us at every turn in our public lives, and we could also find similar substantial disagreements in our personal lives.

Scholars who study political communication have demonstrated that our positions on conflicted issues are powerfully influenced by our emotions. In such situations, where our values and identities are at stake, we are unlikely to be persuaded by logical arguments. In the words of social psychologist Jonathan Haidt, "You can't change people's minds by utterly refuting their arguments."[1] So what kind of alternative communication is possible?

An approach developed by scholars, professionals, and organizations across disciplines focuses on *collaborative rhetoric* rather than adversarial argument. The goal of collaborative rhetoric in speech and writing is to open dialogue by listening to others' perspectives in order to increase mutual understanding and enlarge vision. Collaborative rhetoric also promotes seeking common ground by identifying places where parties might find agreement. For example, pro-choice and pro-life advocates may never agree on a woman's right to an abortion, but they may share common ground in wanting to reduce teenage pregnancy. By relinquishing persuasion as a goal, collaborative rhetoric finds value simply in continuing the conversation, keeping channels of communication open in a search for a more complex view of the problem and provisional solutions.

---

[1] *The Righteous Mind: Why Good People Are Divided by Politics and Religion.* Vintage, 2012, p. 57.

The Principles of Collaborative Rhetoric

10.2 **Explain the principles of collaborative rhetoric.**

Current understanding of collaborative rhetoric has emerged from a convergence of many disciplines and organizations: rhetoric and composition scholars studying Rogerian communication based on the work of psychotherapist Carl Rogers; practitioners of intergroup dialogue who seek to promote social justice; leaders in nonviolent communication; leaders in conflict resolution such as the Harvard Negotiation Project and the Compassionate Listening Project; and feminist scholars such as Krista Ratcliffe, who focus on rhetorical listening as a means of ethical growth. All of these approaches teach constructive communication practices suited to situations of high emotional investment, friction, and difference. While many of these theorists emphasize face-to-face oral communication, others explore how collaborative rhetoric can involve reading and writing. Despite the different work these theorists and practitioners do, they all subscribe to four main principles: nonjudgmental listening; identifying how values, emotions, and identities are involved; seeking common ground; and promoting openness to ongoing communication and change. We will explain each in turn.

Practicing Nonjudgmental Listening

The most important component of collaborative rhetoric is *nonjudgmental listening*: a commitment to listening to others' views for the purpose of simply understanding other perspectives. Because people are often threatened by other perspectives, the starting place must be an attitude of listening without judging and evaluating. As the manual for the Compassionate Listening Project states, "Everyone has a partial truth, and we must listen to, discern, and acknowledge this partial truth in everyone—particularly those with whom we disagree."[2] To help us appreciate each other's truths, to achieve the other's "frame of reference," Carl Rogers focuses on "empathic listening" between listeners to create a context "in which I see how the problem appears to you, as well as to me, and you see how it appears to me, as well as to you."[3] All proponents of collaborative rhetoric would agree with the Harvard Negotiation Project writers Douglas Stone, Bruce Patton, and Sheila Heen, who believe that the biggest attitudinal change with collaborative rhetoric is the shift from a *message-delivery stance* (speaking to tell others what we think, to prove a point, and to shape them to match our vision) to a *learning stance* (seeking to understand the other person's point of view, to initiate sharing conversations, and to learn from one another).[4]

---

[2] * Carol Hwoschinsky. *Listening with the Heart: A Guide for Compassionate Listening*. 3rd Ed. Compassionate Listening Project, p. xii.

[3] Rogers, *On Becoming a Person: A Therapist's View of Psychotherapy*. Houghton Mifflin, 1961, p. 336.

[4] We are indebted to the approaches explained in Douglas Stone, Bruce Patton, and Sheila Heen's, *Difficult Conversations: How to Discuss What Matters Most*, 10th Anniversary Ed., Penguin, 2010. This book, an outgrowth of the Harvard Negotiation Project, has had years of success in helping people who are in business, professional, and personal conflicts communicate to improve their relationships and the quality of their lives.

To demonstrate that you are listening nonjudgmentally, with understanding and empathy, Rogerian scholars emphasize the importance of the *say back* practice, which obligates a listener to summarize a previous speaker's views fairly and accurately before speaking his or her own views. The *say back* principle is comforting to all participants because it ensures that all speakers are being listened to and understood.

Identifying Values, Emotions, and Identities

Not only does collaborative rhetoric ask us to acknowledge the validity of others' feelings and views, it also asks us to reflect on our own values, emotions, and identities. Because conflicts threaten us on multiple levels, we need to use the reflective process to get in touch with our own emotional investments in issues. To truly listen, we must acknowledge our own feelings. We must recognize how our own identities are involved in the conflict. What is at stake for us? Why are we threatened by the other's perspective? In trying to understand someone else's threatening view, we are invited to enlarge our own view, to role-play new perspectives, to turn walls into windows. Collaborative rhetoric urges writers to play Peter Elbow's "believing game," where the writer must try to see from the perspective of someone who holds unwelcome ideas. (See our discussion of the believing and doubting game in Chapter 8.) This living within an unappealing idea (Elbow calls it "dwelling in") often compels writers to articulate their own values and to achieve a new understanding of them. Collaborative rhetoric thus promotes a writer's self-examination, exploration of multiple perspectives on a problem, and a willingness to consider change. This double process of reflection and exploration can in turn lead to a change of mind or at least to a deeper understanding of a problem.

Seeking Common Ground

Collaborative rhetoric also involves seeking common ground. By addressing a problem of mutual concern, speakers/writers need to discover and highlight areas of agreement. We have stressed this search for common ground in earlier chapters in our discussions of truth-seeking and audience-based reasons. But in classical argument, the goal is to use these audience-based reasons to further a claim. In collaborative rhetoric, the goal is simply to put multiple perspectives side by side with the goal of creating a foundation for ongoing conversation and problem solving.

For example, suppose that you are an environmentalist in conversation with a pro-oil-and-coal advocate with a "Drill, baby, drill" bumper sticker. Do you share any common ground that might reduce tension and establish conditions for continued conversation and problem solving? Collaborative rhetoric urges you first to summarize the other person's position empathically. You need to walk in that person's shoes, understanding his or her concern for the jobs of oil workers, coal miners, highway construction workers, and owners of local gas stations. You must also appreciate that this person views fracking as an engineering wonder that recovers natural gas and promotes energy independence. Finally, you must feel this person's anger at the way government regulations stifle energy production and at the hypocrisy of environmentalists who drive cars and fly on airplanes.

Once you understand these views, your own reflective practice urges you to find (or grow toward) some common ground. Perhaps you might show this person that you too value people's jobs, that you agree with the importance of energy independence (so that we don't have to import foreign oil), that you appreciate recent advances in safe drilling technology, and that you are disturbed by people who deny our country's vast energy needs. You also agree that it is unrealistic to pretend that we can dispense with our fossil fuel needs overnight. Your effort to understand your audience's views and to build bridges between you and your audience will encourage dialogue and make your audience more likely to listen when you offer your perspective.

Promoting Openness to Ongoing Communication and Change

Finally, collaborative rhetoric emphasizes negotiation and mutual openness to change. It aims to keep the conversation going. Contrary to adversarial argument, which rebuts opposing views and seeks to win others over, collaborative rhetoric takes what Stone, Patton, and Heen call an "And Stance"—the ability to hold different views in mind without pressuring any parties to give up their views. According to Stone, Patton, and Heen, instead of feeling forced to choose between these two stories, we can use the And Stance to recognize the complexity of the world and "embrace both" stories.[5] Think in terms of learning and opportunity, not pressure. The act of listening, seeking to understand, and being heard yourself will often lead to an enlarged vision that reflects the input of both perspectives.

Consequently, collaborative rhetoric often does result in changed perspectives. We feel as if we have "grown" into a new perspective without persuasive pushing on either side, which is often threatening. As Peter Elbow says in reference to the believing game, sometimes ideas hold onto us too tightly, and we can let go only by entering into the perspective of those who think differently. From the vantage point of the other, we gain a fresh perspective on our own position. For scholar-teacher Krista Ratcliffe, who uses the terms "rhetorical listening" and "standing under" other perspectives (instead of simply "understanding"), collaborative rhetoric opens up awareness so we can "consciously integrat[e] this information into our world views and decision making."[6] As psychologists note, the experience of feeling heard, understood, and respected can often result in change. Indeed, collaborative rhetoric has potential to bring about change in both parties. Thus, we see how collaborative rhetoric becomes a foundation for further discussion and for problem solving.

All four of these principles concentrate on reducing antagonism toward those with different beliefs, initiating steps in understanding, cultivating mutual respect, and encouraging further problem-solving—in short, nurturing conditions for future exchanges. Collaborative rhetoric is appropriate and possible whenever speakers or writers seek to open up dialogue with people who hold quite different views and are themselves willing to work toward a bigger picture, a synthesis of views, or at least future exchanges.

---

[5] Douglas Stone, Bruce Patton, and Sheila Heen, *Difficult Conversations: How to Discuss What Matters Most*, 10th Anniversary Ed., Penguin, 2010, pp. 39-40.

[6] Krista Ratcliffe, *Rhetorical Listening: Identification, Gender, Whiteness*. Carbondale, Southern Illinois University Press, p. 29.

For Writing and Discussion

Listening Empathically and Seeking Common Ground

The heated national debate over travel bans on immigrants and refugees from Muslim-majority countries is highlighted in the photos shown in Figures 10.1–10.3. The debate taps into deep-seated emotions of fear, anger, patriotism, and frustration. Should the United States take stringent measures to reduce the flow of immigrants and refugees into the United States, or should it rely on the already existing vetting process? Should the United States target travelers from specific countries? What will be the consequences to immigrants and refugees who already have family members residing in the United States? How do travel bans conflict with the premise of the United States as a nation of immigrants?

Individual Task:

From the three photos, choose one that represents the position on immigration with which you most disagree. Then imagine that you are conducting a collaborative discussion with the people in the photo (or the people who made the banners or signs) and follow these thinking and writing steps:

1. What feelings and values of your own are bound up in your views on U.S. immigration policies? What aspects of your identity does this issue touch? Where might you feel threatened by this issue and the controversies it has spawned? Explore your own values and personal investment.
2. Employing nonjudgmental listening and the *say back practice*, summarize the views you think the people in your chosen photo hold. Write your summary in fair, neutral language that indicates your understanding and that would make your summary acceptable to the people with whom you disagree.
3. Finally, write a common-grounds paragraph in which you go beyond summary to show your respectful understanding of the values held by these people. Consider how these views might be valid. Demonstrate your empathy, and add an example of your own that shows how your views and those of the people in the photo could intersect.

Group Task:

As you share your summaries and common-grounds paragraphs with members of your class, role-play the people in the photo with whom the writer is trying to seek common values and a basis for collaborative problem solving. From your assumed role, comment on how well the writer has understood and identified with your views and values.

Figure 10.1 Immigration ban protest

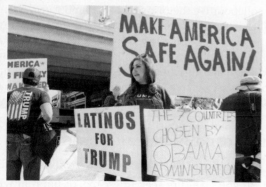

Figure 10.2 Immigration ban protest

(continued)

Figure 10.3 Immigration ban protest

Preparing for Collaborative Rhetoric Through Reflective Writing and Discussion

10.3 Prepare for collaborative rhetoric through reflective writing and discussion.

We now turn to steps you can take to learn and feel comfortable with this mode of communication and to put the principles of collaborative rhetoric into practice.

Preparing for Collaborative Rhetoric Through Reflective Writing

Reflective writing can develop your understanding of your personal communication style, a step that can be important for your growth as a collaborative thinker, speaker, and writer. Because collaborative rhetoric seeks to promote growth in all parties, reflective writing, which is a quiet, introspective, and exploratory activity, can play a vital role in preparing speakers and writers to participate in collaborative rhetoric. Reflective writing can help you understand what you as a communicator bring to situations where major disagreement is involved. For example, you might reflect on how you usually behave in the midst of these difficult conversations. The following questions can serve as a preliminary self-inventory to prompt reflective writing.

REFLECTIVE SELF-INVENTORY OF COMMUNICATION HABITS

1. How would you assess your ability to listen in situations involving conflict?
2. In the midst of conflict, do you clam up, seek to escape, or jump in when you find yourself feeling threatened by a conversation? Think of an example.

3. When have you felt the need to speak out forcefully to defend your views? When have you listened calmly and nonjudgmentally to others' perspectives?

4. Can you remember a time when you changed your views as a result of listening to someone else? If so, how did your change come about?

Achieving self-awareness about how you tend to listen can help you prepare for conversations or group discussions where nonjudgmental listening is critical.

You might also employ reflective writing to prepare to enter a specific situation where you need to use collaborative rhetoric. Think of this reflective writing, most likely freewriting or short informal writing, as a valuable opportunity for you to explore your personal relationship with the controversial issue and with the people who disagree with you. Take stock of your past experiences, your feelings, your values, your identity, and your investment in the issue. For example, after reading a controversial article that you know your class will be discussing, you might write a reflection that enables you to probe and pour out your responses. Your reflection might even be a short narrative. Or you might try freewriting about your own investment in an issue before you conduct library research on it. The following questions may help you discover and reflect on what matters to you in this issue and why.

REFLECTING ON YOUR PERSONAL ENGAGEMENT IN AN ISSUE

1. How do thinking about this issue and hearing what others think about it make you feel?

2. Why do you think you feel concerned, bothered, anxious, or angry?

3. Can you identify the values you hold that are engaged in this conflict?

4. What aspects of your identity are involved in this conflict? What is particularly threatening to you?

The reflective writing that you do might be entirely for yourself, or your instructor might assign it as a preparation for a collaborative discussion or a lead-in to formal writing. Either way, it can help you achieve more self-understanding, which will in turn make you a more effective participant in collaborative rhetoric.

Practicing Collaborative Rhetoric in Discussion

For most of us, collaborative rhetoric challenges our inclinations, our habits, our past communication backgrounds, and our contemporary culture. It also steps outside our experience of formal argumentation. Therefore, it is useful to practice collaborative rhetoric principles, sometimes as incremental steps. This practice could take the form of trying out nonjudgmental listening when you listen to a friend or to a controversial campus speaker. It could entail making a conscious effort to seek out common ground with someone who challenges your views, or it could simply involve imagining respectful, unemotional ways to state your own views to people who disagree with you. It could also involve holding discussions with groups of people in which you practice the "say back" rule. Before you add your own voice to the conversation, each participant would summarize the views of the preceding speaker to that speaker's satisfaction before offering his or her different view of the subject. This form of linked conversation compels participants to listen carefully to each other and respond calmly. These examples represent components of collaborative rhetoric. Practicing them can be useful in helping you develop communication skills for use in volatile situations.

Writing an Open Letter as Collaborative Rhetoric

10.4 **Write an open letter that demonstrates collaborative rhetoric by addressing and listening to someone who disagrees with you on an emotionally laden issue in order to open channels of communication and promote problem solving.**

The main setting for collaborative rhetoric in writing is two parties in conversation. Most practitioners of collaborative rhetoric focus on face-to-face conversations between disputants with the aim of reducing emotional threat and fear by abandoning the desire to persuade. The goal is to take the *And Stance*, wherein your view and the other person's view are both on the table for validation and respect. Rogerian psychotherapy, nonviolent communication workshops, and many negotiation processes are all rooted in this approach.

When we move from speaking to writing, it is easy to imagine this kind of face-to-face conversation carried on in real-time chat rooms or even by text or e-mail (although you lose all the important cues of body language, facial expressions, and tone of voice, though emojis can help). It is harder to imagine collaborative rhetoric in a stand-alone longer essay going in just one direction—from writer to reader/audience. However, the genre of the personal letter is quite conducive to collaborative rhetoric. The personal letter can also be converted into an "open letter" that can be read by a larger audience. In that case, the writer addresses a particular person but understands that a larger audience will also read this letter, including many people who agree with the person the writer is addressing in the letter. We now show you an example of an open letter written as collaborative rhetoric and then provide further instructions on how to write a letter like this yourself.

How do you find an issue and an audience for practicing collaborative rhetoric? In a classroom setting, a common way is for students to select an issue of their choice and then find an argument that strongly opposes their own stance on the issue. In the following example of an open letter written as collaborative rhetoric, student writer Colleen Fontana responds to an article written by Robert A. Levy, a senior fellow for constitutional studies at the Cato Institute, a libertarian think tank. In this open letter, Colleen conducts a collaborative discussion directed toward solving the problem of gun violence.[7] Annotations in the margins indicate how Colleen is practicing collaborative rhetoric principles.

---

[7] We are indebted to Doug Brent for his insight that Rogerian communication can take the form of a letter addressed to the author of an article that a reader finds disturbing. See "Rogerian Rhetoric: Ethical Growth Through Alternative Forms of Argumentation." In *Argument Revisited; Argument Redefined*, eds. Barbara Emmel, Paula Resch, and Deborah Tenney (Thousand Oaks, CA: Sage, 1996), p. 81.

Student Essay

An Open Letter to Robert Levy in Response to His Article "They Never Learn"

Colleen Fontana

Dear Robert Levy,

My recent interest in preventing gun violence led me to find your article "They Never Learn" in *The American Spectator* about the mass shooting at Virginia Tech in 2007. I was struck by the similarities between that incident and the recent shooting in Tucson, Arizona, where a young man gunned down U.S. Representative Gabrielle Giffords and nineteen others in a supermarket parking lot. Although your article came several years before this Arizona incident, we can see that gun violence remains an enduring issue. I have long struggled with the question of how we can reduce gun-related violence without detracting from an individual's right to own a gun. Your article shed new light on this question for me.

Your article stresses the need for something different from our nation's current gun policies. You assert that the solution lies not in stricter gun control policies, but rather in "liberalized laws." According to you, Mr. Levy, it was primarily the existence of anti-gun laws on the Virginia Tech campus that prevented an armed citizen from saving the victims of the 2007 shooting. You comment that "gun control does not work. It just prevents weaker people from defending themselves against stronger predators." Your article gives detailed examples of studies that have substantiated that stricter gun laws have not resulted in lower murder rates. You also cite evidence that fewer crimes are likely to happen if the victim brandishes a gun, even if he or she never fires it. According to your article, stricter gun laws are doing nothing to help society, and your solution lies in relaxed laws, allowing more responsible citizens to carry concealed weapons.

Living on a college campus myself, I identify immediately with your concern for preventing school shootings. I appreciate that you are concerned with the safety of the students and the public, and I agree that there exists a need for greater safety on school campuses. I also agree that current gun laws are not effective, as is shown by the number of gun-related deaths that happen annually. Even though such laws exist, they are not likely to stop "crazed fanatics undeterred by laws against murder," as you say, from committing certain crimes. I particularly agree with you when you discuss the right of self-defense. I struggle with laws that forbid carrying a gun because I believe in the right of self-defense. As you mentioned in your article, instances do occur in which civilians carrying guns have the ability to save themselves and others. Although I have not experienced this situation personally, I have read of brave acts of self-defense and intervention. For example, my research turned up an article by John Pierce on *MonachusLex.com*, "It Takes a Gun to Stop a Gunman." In this article Pierce describes an occurrence in Richmond, Virginia, in July of 2009 where a store owner and several customers were saved from an armed robber by a civilian in the store who happened to be

Writer addresses the audience

Writer identifies the problem, shows its current timeliness (kairos), and establishes a cordial relationship with the audience

In neutral, fair terms, the writer demonstrates nonjudgmental listening as she summarizes the audience's previous argument without evaluation

Common ground: Writer identifies common values that she shares with her audience; she demonstrates empathic listening; she imagines instances where the audience's values make the most sense

carrying a firearm. Even though Pierce is a long-time gun rights advocate and an NRA-certified instructor, the points he brought up were striking. If that civilian hadn't been carrying a gun in that store on that day, then everyone in the store might have been killed by the robber. This realization resonates with me. I imagine myself in that store, and I know I would have been quite grateful that he was carrying a weapon that saved my life. Reading this story has forced me to think of the responsibility many gun-owning citizens must feel—a responsibility to protect not only themselves but those around them as well. A similar event happened recently in New York where a person attempting to rob a jewelry shop was shot by the owner in an act of self-defense. His neighbors regard him as a hero (Kilgannon).

Writer moves respectfully to an And Stance. She presents her own questions and differing perspectives on the problem. Note her tone of negotiation and her willingness to engage in further discussion

While I agree with you that self-defense is an important right and that armed citizens can sometimes prevent the death of innocent people, I wonder whether the possibility of allowing more guns in public through liberalized gun laws is the best solution. Is there a chance more guns in the hands of more people would foster a more danger-prone climate both from accidents and from sudden fits of rage? I was surprised to learn from a recent *New York Times* article by Charles M. Blow that for every ten people in America there are nine guns. Among major nations, according to a U.N. study, we have both the highest ratio of guns to people and the highest incidence of violence. If liberalizing gun ownership will lead to even more guns, then my concern is that there will be a higher chance of children finding a loaded gun in a parent's bed stand or of deaths caused by gang warfare or from momentary rage in an escalating fight between neighbors. Such danger could also exist on school campuses if guns were allowed. On a campus where drinking nurtures the party scene, I worry that rowdy people waving a gun perhaps as a joke might turn a party into a tragedy. Do you have any ideas, Mr. Levy, for reducing gun accidents or irresponsible use of firearms if they are widely available?

5

I found your point about owning a firearm for self-defense really thought provoking. But even if Virginia Tech had allowed guns on campus, what are the odds that an armed student or teacher would have been at the right place at the right time with an actual chance of shooting the gunman? Only in the movies are good guys and heroes *always* on the spot and capable of taking the right action to protect potential victims. Although I can really see your point about using handguns for self-defense, I don't think self-defense can be used as a justification for assault weapons or automatic weapons with large clips. If guns were freely allowed on campuses, perhaps massacres such as the one at Virginia Tech might occur more often. Or is there a way to allow people to carry concealed handguns on campus but still to forbid rifles, shotguns, or other weapons more useful for massacres than for self-defense?

Writer expresses a second concern, one that Levy did not mention: assault weapons

After reading your article I have more understanding of the arguments in favor of guns, and I continue to ponder the ethical and practical issues of gun control versus the right to self-defense. You have underscored for me the importance of our continuing to seek means of preventing these terrible massacres from happening in our nation's schools. You have also opened my eyes to the fact that no amount of enforcement of gun laws can deter

(continued)

determined people from using guns to harm others. I am not sure, however, that your proposal to eliminate gun-control laws is the best solution, and I am hoping that you might be willing to consider some of my reasons for fearing guns, especially assault weapons and automatic weapons that can be fired like machine guns. Perhaps we could both agree that pursuing responsible gun ownership is a step in the right direction so that we reduce the number of accidents, keep guns away from children, and reduce access to guns capable of unleashing mass murder. I am hopeful that with our common concern over the current ineffectiveness of gun laws and the desire for safety in our schools, we can find a reasonable solution while still preserving the human right of self-defense.

Sincerely,

Colleen Fontana

Writer concludes her letter with a reiteration of the mutual concerns she shares with her audience; she acknowledges how her perspectives have been widened by Levy's views; she seeks to keep the channel of communication open; and she expresses interest in further problem solving

Works Cited

Blow, Charles M. "Obama's Gun Play." *The New York Times*, 21 Jan. 2011, www.nytimes.com/2011/01/22/opinion/22blow.html?_r=0.

Kilgannon, Cory. "After Shooting, Merchant Is Hero of Arthur Avenue." *The New York Times*, 12 Feb. 2011, www.nytimes.com/2011/02/18/nyregion/18arthur.html.

Levy, Robert A. "They Never Learn." *The American Spectator*, 25 Apr. 2007, spectator.org/articles/45477/they-never-learn.

Pierce, John. "It Takes a Gun to Stop a Gunman." *MonachusLex.com*, 15 July 2009, monachuslex.com/?p=262.

As Figure 10.4 shows, the open letter usually begins with context, a respectful address to the audience, and an expression of the problem of mutual concern. It adopts and maintains a *learning stance* by beginning with an empathic summary of the reader's view on the issue and then tries to articulate the writer's and reader's common ground of shared values or beliefs. Both the summary and the common grounds section allow you to hear the other story. The entire letter must be a *learning conversation*, not a *message-delivery* one. Ideally, the letter will help you loosen your hold on your own perspectives (how else will you grow?) while inviting readers to loosen theirs.

The *And Stance* enables you to fully engage with another view without compromising your values. In keeping with the And Stance, the open letter also has room for your own views, but it presents these views as "both/and" rather than "either/or." The conclusion of the open letter should demonstrate how sharing perspectives has enlarged your view of the problem as you have seen it through another's eyes. Remember that you don't have to abandon your values, but you do need to acknowledge that no one has the total perspective, the whole story. The concluding section of the letter should invite the audience to continue the conversation by writing back (or perhaps by meeting up somewhere for face-to-face conversation).

Using collaborative rhetoric requires writers (and speakers) to use language carefully, respectfully, and provisionally. Therefore, throughout the whole letter

Figure 10.4 Organization plan for an open letter as collaborative rhetoric

Introduction	• Address the audience and identify the problem that you and your audience want to solve. • Possibly show the timeliness (*kairos*) of the problem. • Try to establish a friendly or cordial relationship with the audience. • Possibly include information that shows your familiarity with the audience.
Summary of the Audience's Views	• Summarize the audience's views in a fair and neutral way that the audience would accept. • Show that you understand the audience's position. • Also show an understanding of, and respect for, the audience's values and beliefs; the goal of this "saying back" (Rogers' term) is to summarize these views in a way that will be entirely acceptable to the audience.
Common Ground	• Identify common ground you share with your audience. • Demonstrate your growth through empathic consideration of views that you would otherwise find threatening or unwelcome. • Show understanding of the audience's views by "indwelling" with them and perhaps by extending them to other situations through new examples. • Show how your views have been enlarged by empathic listening to the audience's ideas.
Contribution of New Points to the Negotiation	• Respectfully propose your own way of looking at this issue. • Through a respectful and inquiring tone, encourage the audience to listen and work with you to solve the problem.
Conclusion	• Possibly propose a synthesis of the two positions, discuss how both parties gain from an enlarged vision, or invite the audience to ongoing negotiation.

your language should be exploratory and negotiating. You are sharing, inviting, and considering. You are saying, "Let's share our perspectives and think this problem out together." Because you must stay in this listening/learning/loosening mode while focusing on collaboration and ongoing dialogue about a problem, you use a different vocabulary and sentence structure than you do when you argue. You are suggesting, offering, inviting, proposing, and encouraging your audience to consider the perspective that you are bringing to this conversation. You stay in this mode by asking questions, using language that is more tentative and provisional than you would if you were arguing. For example, collaborative rhetoric often uses what psychotherapists call "I statements" that avoid blaming the other party.

> **Blaming statement:** Your pro-oil views are destroying the earth.
>
> **I statement:** When I think of how much we all drive our cars, I fear that the earth is at risk.

In addition to "I" statements, you can focus on word choices that don't imply anger or blame and that ask questions rather than make strong assertions. You can offer your own view along with examples to support it, but you must treat these as points of consideration, not as rebuttals to the other party. Your sign-off in your letter must maintain a *learning stance*, keeping the door open for future dialogue.

The following guidelines can help you engage in collaborative rhetoric by preparing you to assume a *learning stance* rather than an argumentative stance. These guidelines can serve as reminders in situations that involve either speaking or writing. We suggest you focus on them in writing your open letter as collaborative rhetoric.

Guidelines for Practicing Collaborative Rhetoric

1. Demonstrate nonjudgmental listening.

   - Assume a *learning stance*, giving space and time to the other party's expression of ideas.

   - Employ the Rogerian *say back* rule by accurately summarizing what you have heard from or read by the other party.

   - Ask questions but resist all evaluations.

   - Show a desire to understand the other's position logically and emotionally.

2. Reflect on the way your own values, feelings, and identity are involved.

   - Identify either in your own mind or by articulating orally or on paper your own investment in the issue.

   - What is potentially threatening to you in this issue? What emotions does this issue arouse in you? What values does it tap?

   - How is your identity involved?

3. Seek common ground in a problem-solving spirit.

   - What similarities can you find between your views and that of the other party?

   - Under what conditions can you imagine the other party's perspective making sense to you?

   - How can you show that you have seen the issue sympathetically from the other party's perspective or *frame of reference*?

   - Can you add examples of your own to the other party's position?

4. Practice the *And Stance* and open channels for mutual change and further conversation.

- What points of your own do you want to contribute to the discussion? Ask questions about particularly difficult points of disagreement and lay your view side-by-side rather than falling into assertive *message-delivery mode*.
- How have your views been influenced by those of the other party?
- What can you integrate into your own perspective?
- How can you imagine steps toward problem-solving and further exchanges?

Writing Assignment

An Open Letter as Collaborative Rhetoric

Write an open letter employing collaborative rhetoric addressed to a specific person, either someone you know, someone you have heard deliver a speech, or the author of an article that has disturbed you. As you generate ideas for your letter, take stock of what you know about your own feelings and values on the issue on which you and your audience disagree. Think about your audience and summarize the person's views in a way that your audience would find satisfactory. Demonstrate nonjudgmental listening as you adopt a learning stance. As you explore what your audience values and believes in, also explore how your own values differ. Where do you agree with your audience? Under what conditions would you find your audience's values acceptable? How might the *And Stance* serve you? Follow the suggestions in the Guidelines for Practicing Collaborative Rhetoric in your open letter. Can you envision a synthesis of views, or depending on the distance between your views and your audience's, your goal may be simply to put your different perspectives into conversation, to encourage mutual listening, and to open up a discussion.

Imagine that your letter will be printed in a newspaper, so keep in mind that a larger audience beyond the person addressed in the letter will read it. In addition to Colleen Fontana's open letter on gun issues, we offer an additional example, Monica Allen's "An Open Letter to Christopher Eide in Response to His Article 'High-Performing Charter Schools Can Close the Opportunity Gap'" as a reading. Your instructor may ask you to attach a reflective response in which you describe how your experience of writing collaborative rhetoric in your open letter differed from your experience of writing classical arguments.

Reading

Student writer Monica Allen wrote her open letter as collaborative rhetoric as part of her larger research project to understand the stakes involved in her state's expansion of charter schools. Her instructor asked her to provide a Works Cited list to document all the sources she draws on in the letter.

Student Essay

An Open Letter to Christopher Eide in Response to His Article "High-Performing Charter Schools Can Close the Opportunity Gap"

Monica Allen

Dear Mr. Eide,

I want to thank you for your article "High-Performing Charter Schools Can Close the Opportunity Gap," which contributes to the national conversation about the role of charter schools in education reform. Like you, I am concerned about whether publicly funded, privately run charter schools can provide innovative new approaches to increase the quality of education for minority and economically disadvantaged students. I have been wrestling with the claims that charter schools can help reduce this troubling opportunity gap. Your helpful article has deepened my understanding of charter schools and has given me much to think about.

Your article proposes legislation specifically designed to create high-performing, effective charter schools. What is most exciting in your article is your suggestion that this legislation has the potential to close the opportunity gap. Citing the Stanford Center for Research on Education (CREDO) study and national charter efforts like the Knowledge is Power Program (KIPP), which focus on achievement gains for low-income students in some charter schools, you believe that increased charter education will enable our nation to better educate academically underserved students. Ultimately, you want to look beyond the inconsistent results charter schools have historically shown nationwide and urge our state to focus its charter-school innovation on improving opportunities for its students suffering most from the opportunity gap.

Your encouraging article speaks to the belief I share with you that the highest priority in educational innovation needs to be closing the opportunity gap. As education researcher Sean Reardon has shown in "The Widening Income Achievement Gap," the differences in opportunities and outcomes between low- and high-income background students have continued to widen throughout the past three decades. Clearly, we are in desperate need of more and better educational improvement. I share your concern that charter schools, focusing on the wrong objectives, could become a force that widens, rather than narrows, the opportunity gap. I particularly appreciate your commitment to concentrating reform efforts where they are needed most—with students from low-income backgrounds who are disproportionately left behind in traditional public schools. As an English Language Learning (ELL) tutor and teacher, I am encouraged that the CREDO study you cite indicates that some charter schools produce better gains for ELL students than do traditional public schools. I am grateful that you advocate for underserved students, such as English Language Learners, and am now much more interested in understanding the charter movement because of your conviction that it can address our most pressing educational issue.

(continued)

Your article also answers some of my prior concerns about charter schools, making me more open to charter education. In particular, I have been wary of the inconsistent performance of charter schools nationwide, and so I appreciate that you support rigorous legislation to hold charter schools accountable to the highest standards possible. Your article also helped dispel some of my concerns that charter schools tend to serve disproportionately higher-income students and thereby segregate our schools into high-income charters and low-income traditional public schools. It led me to do more research about charter schools' student demographics and to find that there are many examples of charters serving primarily low-income groups of students. Finally, I appreciated your article's urgency. I, too, believe that the needs of disproportionally poorly educated, low-income students today make this issue a pressing one that calls for immediate action.

5   Because your article awakened me to the social benefits that charter schools can provide, I'd like to share with you four reservations in the hopes that, together, people like us who hold different perspectives on charter schools can learn from one another and better close our education opportunity gap.

First, I share your belief that charter schools offer needed opportunities to be education laboratories—places whose freedom from bureaucracy enables them to test out new strategies that can inform widespread practices. However, are charter schools really experimental? Adamant charter school supporter and Columbia University researcher Priscilla Wohlstetter writes that despite her belief in the prospects of charter schools generally, "most [charter schools] do little to tap the potential of unique, innovative strategies. For all the hype, charters typically borrow familiar classroom strategies (back-to-basics, project-based learning, college prep) from private and traditional public schools." I share Wohlstetter's concern that while the education laboratory concept has popularized charter schools, research demonstrates they have not functioned as such in our education system. Though I am encouraged by your commitment to highly regulated charter schools, I am unsure whether state legislation that regulates only based on the test results of charter-school students really ensures that charters deliver what they intend to. Perhaps we should explore other means to measure innovation to ensure that the investment of public funds in charter schools results in gains for the education system as a whole, in part by demonstrating that charter schools can teach us how to teach better. That would be a partnership between public and charter education that I believe we all hope to see.

A second question I have is whether charter schools will make innovative learning more accessible to students who are traditionally underserved. While the CREDO study you cite shows some promising results, Jean Allen, head of the Center for Education Reform, has questioned the conclusiveness of the data (Sanchez). Indeed, researchers across the board believe that the jury is very much still out on the question of whether charter-school students really learn as much as traditional public-school students, which is why the National Alliance for Public Charter Schools and Harvard University just started afresh with a comprehensive study last fall. I am concerned

(continued)

that we may be implementing a system that has yet to be effectively tested. I do think the anecdotal evidence you cite about KIPP schools is extremely exciting and deserves public attention, because KIPP schools serve a majority of low-income student populations *and* are outperforming traditional public schools near them. But shouldn't we also consider that KIPP schools rely heavily on significant private donations and are unique among charters in this way? To me, it makes sense that KIPP schools outperform other local schools when their operating budgets are 30–50 percent higher (Di Carlo). Could we agree that the results of this disparity in school funding call for more investigation?

I also have a third, more fundamental question with respect to charter schools. I wonder whether in the enthusiasm to innovate our schools, we will lose sight of that which makes American education innovative at its core—its commitment to democratic education. I am concerned that charter schools focusing on low-income student bodies might contribute to the non-democratic socioeconomic and ethnic segregation of our schools. I believe that the segregation of schools into the haves and have-nots is one of the largest issues facing our national education system. Could charter schools that concentrate on serving low-income and traditionally underserved ethnic groups unintentionally widen the gap? Along with education activist and writer Jonathan Kozol (Cody), I fear that charter schools with names like "Black Success Academy" and "The African-American Academy for Leadership and Enterprise" divert attention from what really needs to be attended to—the de-segregating of our already divided schools and our school funding along lines of race and socioeconomic status. While I, like you, want us to do everything we can immediately to improve the chances for underserved students, I am most interested in focusing our efforts on equalizing our schools' demographics and budgets. How can charters and traditional public schools work together to do this?

Finally, Mr. Eide, I also wonder whether privatizing education will ultimately be in the best interest of students on the low spectrum of the opportunity gap. Public education promises public responsibility to educate each of its students for successful vocational and civic lives. Right now, you and I both know that the American public has not been living up to that responsibility. How can we do better? I am concerned that privatizing education removes not only the public investment in education (namely, tax dollars) from public hands, but also diminishes our sense of responsibility and capacity to be a nation that educates all its citizens. I wonder whether, in the long run, the students who stand to lose the most from the public's loss of responsibility to educate all are those who are the most vulnerable. How can charter and traditional schools work together to build public confidence in the civic power of education?

Because my own home state will soon be instituting new charter schools, I am thankful for having read your article. Clearly, people who hold different views about the potential of charter schools have much to learn from one another. I hope to see my home state pioneer cutting-edge methods for charter-school regulation and to build relationships between charter- and public-school communities so that the existence of charter

10

(continued)

schools in our state has a large-scale impact. I am very glad to have read your article and to know that many advocates of charter schools are committed to equalizing opportunity in education.

Regards,

Monica Allen

Works Cited

Cody, Anthony. "Confronting the Inequality Juggernaut: A Q&A with Jonathan Kozol." *Education Week: Teacher*, 18 July 2011, blogs.edweek.org/teachers/living-in-dialogue/2011/07/time_to_get_off_our_knees_why.html.

Di Carlo, Matthew. "Controversial Consensus on KIPP Charter Schools." *Albert Shanker Institute*, 12 Mar. 2013, www.shankerinstitute.org/blog/controversial-consensus-kipp-charter-schools.

Eide, Christopher. "High-Performing Charter Schools Can Close the Opportunity Gap." *The Seattle Times*, 11 July 2012, www.seattletimes.com/opinion/high-performing-charter-schools-can-close-the-opportunity-gap.

Reardon, Sean F. "The Widening Income Achievement Gap." *Educational Leadership*, vol. 70, no. 8, 2013, pp. 10-16.

Sanchez, Claudio. "The Charter School vs. Public School Debate Continues." *NPR Education*, 16 July 2013, www.npr.org/2013/07/16/201109021/the-charter-school-vs-public-school-debate-continues.

Wohlstetter, Priscilla. "The Debate Must Move On: Charter Schools Are Here to Stay." *WNYC: School Book*, 9 Dec. 2013, www.wnyc.org/story/charter-schools-are-here-stay-now-lets-have-useful-conversation-about-them.

PART FOUR
Arguments in Depth:
Types of Claims

This advertisement for Nicolites is one voice in the public controversy over e-cigarettes. The ad claims that e-cigarettes are safer than regular cigarettes but chooses to use the word "smoking" rather than the more sanitized word "vaping." The vapor from e-cigarettes usually has nicotine (and may have added flavors or aromas) but not the tar that cigarettes have. However, as the discussion in Chapter 11 shows, the safety, healthfulness, and advisability of e-cigarettes are hotly debated. Think about the strategies from Chapter 9 on analyzing visual texts. How do the words and images in this ad work together to make positive claims about e-cigarettes?

Chapter 11
An Introduction to the Types of Claims

Learning Objectives

In this chapter you will learn to:

11.1 Identify different claim types and their characteristic patterns of development.

11.2 Use strategies based on claim types to help focus an argument, generate ideas for it, and structure it persuasively.

11.3 Be mindful of how different claim types work together in hybrid arguments.

In Parts One, Two, and Three of this text, we showed how argument entails both inquiry and persuasion. We explained strategies for creating a compelling structure of reasons and evidence for your arguments (*logos*), for linking your arguments to the beliefs and values of your audience (*pathos*), and for establishing your credibility and trustfulness (*ethos*). We also showed you how to think about arguments rhetorically, how to do a rhetorical analysis of both verbal and visual texts, and how to use collaborative rhetoric as an alterative to classical argument.

Now, in Part Four, we examine arguments in depth by explaining five types of claims. Each type has its own characteristic patterns of development and support. Because almost all arguments use one or more of these types of claims as "moves" or building blocks, knowing how to develop each claim type will advance your skills in argument. The claims we examine in Part Four are related to an ancient rhetorical concept called *stasis*, from a Greek term meaning "stand," as in "to take a stand on something." There are many competing theories of stasis, so no two rhetoricians discuss stasis in exactly the same way. In Part Four, we present a version of stasis theory based on five types of claims. Studying these claim types will increase your flexibility and sophistication as an arguer.

The Types of Claims and Their Typical Patterns of Development

11.1 Identify different claim types and their characteristic patterns of development.

To appreciate what a study of claim types can do, imagine one of those heated but frustrating arguments in which the question at issue keeps shifting. Everyone talks at cross-purposes, with each speaker's point unconnected to the previous speaker's. Suppose your heated discussion is about the use of steroids. You might get such a discussion back on track if you say: "Hold it for a moment. What are we actually arguing about here? Are we arguing about whether steroids are a health risk or whether steroids should be banned from sports? These are two different issues. We can't debate both at once." Whether you recognize it or not, you are applying the concept of claim types to focus the argument.

To understand how claim types work, let's return to the concept of stasis. A stasis is an issue or question that focuses a point of disagreement. You and your audience may agree on the answer to question A and so have nothing to argue about. Likewise, you may agree on the answer to question B. But on question C you disagree. Question C constitutes a stasis where you and your audience diverge. It is the place where disagreement begins, where as an arguer you take a stand against another view. Thus you and your audience may agree that steroids, if used carefully under a physician's supervision, pose few long-term health risks but still disagree on whether steroids should be banned from sports. This last issue constitutes a stasis, the point where you and your audience part company.

Rhetoricians have discovered that the kinds of questions that divide people have classifiable patterns. In this text we identify five broad types of claims—each type originating in a different kind of question. Table 11.1 gives you an overview of these five types of claims, each of which is developed in more detail in subsequent chapters. It also shows you a typical structure for each type of argument. Note that the first three claim types concern questions of truth or reality, whereas the last two concern questions of value. You'll appreciate the significance of this distinction as you proceed through this chapter.

Table 11.1 Five Types of Claims about Truth or Value

Claim Type and Generic Question	Examples of Issue Questions	Typical Methods for Structuring an Argument
Claims about Truth (Reality or the Way Things Are)		
Definitional arguments: *In what category does this thing belong?* (Chapter 12)	• Is solitary confinement cruel and unusual punishment? • Is a skilled video game player an athlete?	• Create a definition that establishes criteria for the category. • Use examples to show how the contested case meets the criteria.
Resemblance arguments: *To what is this thing similar?* (Chapter 12)	• Is requiring someone to buy medical insurance like requiring him or her to buy car insurance? • Is addiction to sugar like addiction to tobacco?	• Let the analogy or precedent itself create the desired rhetorical effect. [or] • Elaborate on the relevant similarities between the given case and the analogy or precedent.

(Continued)

Claim Type and Generic Question	Examples of Issue Questions	Typical Methods for Structuring an Argument
Causal arguments: *What are the causes or consequences of this phenomenon?* (Chapter 13)	• What are the causes of bee colony collapse disorder? • What might be the consequences of raising the minimum wage to a living wage?	• Explain the links in a causal chain going from cause to effect, or summarize experimental studies showing cause or consequence.
Claims About Values		
Evaluation and ethical arguments: *What is the worth or value of this thing?* (Chapter 14)	• Is talk therapy a good approach for treating anxiety? • Is it ethical to use reproductive technology to make "designer babies"?	• Establish the criteria for a "good" or "ethical" member of this class or category. • Use examples to show how the contested case meets the criteria.
Proposal arguments: *What action should we take?* (Chapter 15)	• Should medical insurance policies be required to cover contraception? • Should the federal government enact a carbon tax?	• Make the problem vivid. • Explain your solution. • Justify your solution by showing how it is motivated by principle, by good consequences, or by resemblance to a previous action that the audience approves of.

For Writing and Discussion

Identifying Types of Claims

Working as a class or in small groups, read the following questions and decide which claim type is represented by each. Sometimes there are several different ways to classify a claim, so if you believe that the question fits two categories, explain your reasoning.

1. Should the U.S. president be authorized to employ weaponized drones to kill terrorists?
2. Is taking Adderall to increase concentration on an exam a form of cheating?
3. What would be the economic consequences of a carbon tax aimed at reducing carbon emissions?
4. Is burning the U.S. flag an act of free speech?
5. Is fighting the war on drugs like fighting an actual war?
6. How effective is acupuncture in reducing morning sickness?

Using Claim Types to Focus an Argument and Generate Ideas: An Example

11.2 Use strategies based on claim types to help focus an argument, generate ideas for it, and structure it persuasively.

Having provided an overview of the types of claims, we now show you some of the benefits of this knowledge. First of all, understanding claim types will help you focus an argument by asking you to determine what's at stake between you and your audience. Where do you and your audience agree and disagree? What are the questions at issue? Second, it will help you generate ideas for your argument by suggesting the kinds of reasons, examples, and evidence you'll need.

To illustrate, let's take the recent public controversy about e-cigarettes, which use a battery-powered heating element to vaporize the liquid in a small cartridge. The user inhales the vapor (an act often called "vaping"). Cartridges can be purchased containing various amounts of nicotine or no nicotine at all; flavored liquids (such as apple cinnamon or peach cobbler) are also available. Although there is debate about whether the vapors from e-cigarettes are harmful, everyone agrees that the nicotine-laced liquid itself is poisonous if ingested in its liquid form. In the absence of federal regulations, many states and cities have enacted their own laws about e-cigarettes, often treating them exactly as if they were real cigarettes—banning them from bars, restaurants, and other public places; forbidding their sale to minors; and restricting the ways they can be advertised.

Let's now take the hypothetical case of a city debating a policy on e-cigarettes. Imagine three different writers. Writer 1 wants to ban e-cigarettes, making them subject to the same restrictions as real cigarettes. Writer 2 wants to promote e-cigarettes as a preferred alternative to real cigarettes. Writer 3, a libertarian opposed to the nanny state, wants no restrictions on e-cigarettes other than forbidding sale of nicotine cartridges to minors and making sure that the liquid-containing cartridges are childproof. Let's consider how familiarity with claim types can help each writer generate ideas for his or her argument.

Writer 1: Ban E-Cigarettes

Writer 1, who believes that e-cigarettes are harmful, imagines a somewhat live-and-let-live audience inclined to take no action against e-cigarettes. Her goal is to portray e-cigarettes negatively in order to persuade this audience that e-cigarettes should be banned.

- **Definition argument:** Because regular cigarettes are already banned in public places, Writer 1 wants to place e-cigarettes in the same category as real cigarettes. For part of her argument she can use a definitional strategy, showing that e-cigarettes and regular cigarettes belong in the same category because both deliver nicotine extracted from tobacco leaves. She can argue that the differences between regular cigarettes and e-cigarettes, such as one producing smoke and the other vapor, are superficial. What makes them the same is the delivery of nicotine.

- **Resemblance argument:** Using a resemblance strategy, Writer 1 can also show how e-cigarettes are designed to look like regular cigarettes and make smoking look cool again. You can blow "smoke" rings with the exhaled vapor, just as you can with real tobacco smoke.

- **Causal argument:** To increase her negative portrayal of e-cigarettes, Writer 1 can also use a causal strategy. She can argue that e-cigarettes will hook children and teenagers on real cigarettes. She can show how flavored vapors such as "bubble gum" or "pancake" seem marketed to children and how the availability of cartridges that combine flavored vapors with nicotine give Big Tobacco a new way to create the next generation of nicotine addicts.

- **Evaluation argument:** Here Writer 1 will have to summarize and rebut counterviews that e-cigarettes are a good replacement for regular cigarettes. Supporters will say the e-cigarettes are better than regular cigarettes because e-cigarettes contain fewer carcinogens (cancer-causing agents) and are thus safer. Writer 1 will need to argue that the negative aspects of e-cigarettes—nicotine addiction and the enticement of children toward smoking—outweigh their increased safety. She can also argue that the propellant ingredients in the cartridges have not yet been proven safe, and she can refer to research showing that the liquid itself is extremely poisonous if ingested directly.

- **Proposal argument:** The city council should ban e-cigarettes.

This example shows that writers often need to argue issues of reality and truth in order to make claims about values. In this case, Writer 1's proposal claim to ban e-cigarettes is based on reasons that are themselves derived from definition, resemblance, and cause: "E-cigarettes should be banned because they contain the same tobacco-derived nicotine as real cigarettes (definition), because they are advertised to make smoking look cool again (resemblance), and because they will hook kids on smoking (cause)."

Writer 2: Promote E-Cigarettes as a Preferred Alternative to Real Cigarettes

Writer 2 shares with his audience a belief that cigarettes are harmful and that smoking should be banned. However, he wants to emphasize the benefits of e-cigarettes to people who already smoke. Like Writer 1, he can use the five claim types to generate strategies for his argument.

- **Definition argument:** To portray e-cigarettes more positively, Writer 2 can make the definitional claim that e-cigarettes are *not* the same as real cigarettes and thus belong in a different category. He can argue that the essential trait of real cigarettes is cancer-causing tar derived from the combustion of tobacco leaves. It is the danger of the tar and secondhand smoke, not the nicotine, that gave rise to the anti-smoking movement in the first place. By arguing that the delivery of nicotine is a superficial rather than essential criterion for defining cigarettes, Writer 2 can show that e-cigarettes' absence of tar and secondhand smoke makes them essentially different from real cigarettes.

- **Resemblance argument:** Using a resemblance strategy, Writer 2 can show that although e-cigarettes are essentially different from real cigarettes, the two have pleasing similarities. Vaping provides the same physical and social pleasures as does smoking, but without the harm to self and others.

- **Causal argument:** Writer 2 can also portray e-cigarettes positively through the causal argument that they can save current smokers' lives by converting them from a dangerous way of getting nicotine to a less dangerous way of getting nicotine. Without condoning nicotine addiction, Writer 2 can point to the positive health consequences of getting a nicotine hit without the carcinogens. Writer 2 can also argue that e-cigarettes can help people stop smoking because vapers can gradually reduce the nicotine content in the cartridges they purchase.

- **Evaluation argument:** Here Writer 2 can claim that e-cigarettes are better than real cigarettes by arguing that the health benefits of no smoke and no tar outweigh the drawbacks of an addiction to nicotine, which in itself causes little health risk.

- **Proposal argument:** E-cigarettes should be promoted as a safe alternative to real cigarettes.

Writer 3: Place No Restrictions on E-Cigarettes

Writer 3 is a libertarian who dislikes nanny-state restrictions on our individual freedoms. She wants to argue that the only restrictions on e-cigarettes should be federally mandated childproofing of the cartridges, truth-in-labeling requirements about what the cartridges contain, and banning sales of nicotine-containing cartridges to minors.

- **Definition argument:** Writer 3, like Writer 2, can argue that e-cigarettes are in a different category from regular cigarettes. Unlike regular cigarettes, e-cigarettes present no proven dangers either to self or to others through secondhand smoke.

- **Resemblance argument:** To celebrate the libertarian endorsement of individual freedom, Writer 3 can show the resemblance between taking a pleasurable hit on an e-cigarette and other pleasures frowned upon by the nanny state—drinking sugary sodas, buying a Big Mac, or owning a muscle car.

- **Causal argument:** Whereas Writer 2 argues that e-cigarettes are safer than regular cigarettes, Writer 3 can argue that nobody has demonstrated any firsthand or secondhand health hazards for e-cigarettes. She can make the additional causal argument that government wants to treat e-cigarettes like regular cigarettes so that they can tax them heavily to produce "sin-tax" revenue. She can also argue that nanny-state regulations lead to the loss of personal freedoms and the shutting down of free enterprise.

- **Evaluation argument:** Writer 3 can argue that people should be free to make their own evaluations of e-cigarettes.

- **Proposal argument:** The city should place no restrictions on sales of e-cigarettes to adults.

Hybrid Arguments: How Claim Types Work Together in Arguments

11.3 **Be mindful of how different claim types work together in hybrid arguments.**

As the e-cigarette example shows, hybrid arguments can be built from different claim types. A writer might develop a proposal argument with a causal subargument in one section, a resemblance subargument in another section, and an evaluation subargument in still another section. Although the overarching proposal argument follows the typical structure of a proposal, each of the subsections follows a typical structure for its own claim type.

Some Examples of Hybrid Arguments

The following examples show how these combinations of claim types can play out in actual arguments. (For more examples of hybrid arguments, see Chapter 15, Tables 15.1 and 15.2, where we explain how lower-order claims about reality and truth can support higher-order claims about values.)

An Extended Example of a Hybrid Argument

As the previous examples illustrate, different claim types often serve as building blocks for larger arguments. We ask you now to consider a more extended example. Read the following argument from *Outside Magazine* aimed at enthusiasts of

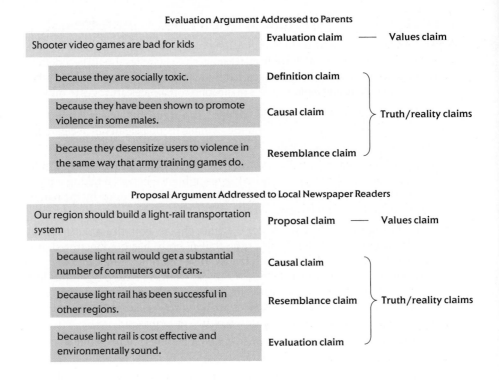

For Writing and Discussion

Exploring Different Claim Types and Audiences

Working in small groups or as a whole class, try to develop hybrid arguments for each of the authorial purposes below. How might supporting reasons for each argument be based on different claim types (definition, resemblance, cause, evaluation, proposal)? Use our example arguments about e-cigarettes as your models. Imagine an audience skeptical of your chosen position.

1. Carbon footprint: You want (do not want) the Environmental Protection Agency to regulate the amount of carbon dioxide that power plants can emit.
2. Gun restrictions: You want (do not want) the federal government to ban assault rifles and high-volume ammunition cartridges.
3. Diet: You want your classmates to adopt (or not to adopt) the paleo diet.

outdoor sports such as hiking, camping, mountain climbing, skiing, biking, and distance running. The magazine's readers are often health-conscious consumers of multivitamins and other dietary supplements such as minerals, fish oils, herbals, botanicals, enzymes, antioxidants, amino acids, and other substances often ingested as tablets, capsules, powders, energy drinks, or energy bars. In this startling article, the writer uses recent scientific studies to make the evaluation claim that these supplements are either "useless" or "worse than useless." Notice how this overall evaluation claim is supported by claims from definition, resemblance, and cause.

Your Daily Multivitamin May Be Hurting You

ALEX HUTCHINSON

In June, at this year's European College of Sport Science conference in Barcelona, Mari Carmen Gomez-Cabrera, a physiologist at the University of Valencia and one of the world's leading experts on antioxidants, was debating the merits of supplements with two top researchers. For more than 90 minutes they went back and forth, parsing the accumulated evidence in front of a packed auditorium. Finally, Gomez-Cabrera landed on a provocative question that summarized her position.

Introduces the evaluation issue "Are supplements good/bad?"

The debate, she explained, isn't whether supplements are good or bad for athletes. Rather, it's "are they useless, or are they worse than useless?"

*Restates **evaluation** issue with implied claim: Supplements are either useless or worse than useless*

The question may come as a shock to the more than half of Americans who take some sort of dietary supplement—a vast catch-all term that includes everything from vitamins and minerals to herbal remedies to exotic performance boosters like deer-antler spray and glutamine. It's no surprise that the purported muscle-building supplements make unproven claims and may come with hazardous side effects. But in the past few years, Gomez-Cabrera and a growing number of researchers have come to believe that even respectable mainstream supplements such as vitamins C and E suffer from the same basic flaw: few apparent benefits and increasing evidence of negative effects. For example, in July's issue of the *Journal of Physiology*, researchers discovered that resveratrol, an antioxidant in red wine, actually limited the positive effects of cardiovascular exercise—like an increased VO2 max—when taken daily in high concentrations. In July, scientists at the Fred Hutchinson Cancer Research Center found that men with high levels of the omega-3 fatty acid DHA in their blood, often from fish-oil supplements, had a significantly greater risk of prostate cancer.

*Further develops **evaluation** claim: Supplements are bad because they make unproven claims and because they may come with hazardous side effects*

*Uses **causal arguments** to illustrate bad side effects*

According to Pieter Cohen, a professor at Harvard Medical School, there are really only two types of sports supplements: those that are safe but don't work, and those that might work but have side effects, especially at higher than normal levels. "If any supplement, no matter how beneficial, has a pharmaceutical effect, it's also got a downside," he says. "There's no way to get around that basic principle."

Definition claim: Supplements belong to one of two categories: (1) safe but don't work or (2) work but have bad side effects

Most supplements stay firmly in the first category. Taking a daily multivitamin, Cohen emphasizes, won't harm you, but it usually won't help either, which is why major health organizations such as the American Heart Association and the American College of Sports Medicine don't recommend supplements to healthy people.

*Develops **definition** argument by showing how supplements fit first category of being safe but useless*

It's not that vitamins and minerals aren't important. If you don't get enough vitamin C, you can get scurvy; without enough iron, you can become anemic; and if you live far enough north to see Russia from your backyard, you may need some extra vitamin D. But all three of these substances have also been linked to negative effects at high doses. Same goes for prolonged use of other common supplements such as vitamin E and calcium. In short, unless tests have shown that you're low in a particular vitamin or mineral, there's no evidence to suggest that you should take a daily supplement.

Causal argument showing bad side effects (places supplements in second category of being harmful)

Causal argument showing still more bad side effects

That rule also applies if you're an athlete who takes supplements because, say, you assume your training requires an antioxidant boost to speed recovery. Gomez-Cabrera and her colleagues at the University of Valencia have shown that antioxidant supplements suppress the oxidative stress that signals your body to adapt and get stronger. The result: regular use of something seemingly innocuous such as vitamin C can actually block gains in endurance-boosting mitochondria.

Causal argument from psychology showing different bad effect: People who take supplements feel they are healthier and thus actually act in less healthy ways

The balance between risk and return also works in subtler ways, as Wen-Bin Chiou, a psychologist at National Sun Yatsen University in Taiwan, has shown in a series of experiments on a phenomenon called the licensing effect. As part of a battery of tests, subjects were asked to take a pill; half were told the pill was a multivitamin, while the other half were told it was a placebo. In truth, they were all placebos.

In subsequent tests, the subjects who thought they'd taken a vitamin consistently behaved in less healthy ways. When asked to try out a pedometer, they were more likely to choose a shorter walking route; at lunch, they chose less healthy food. In follow-up studies, Chiou has also discovered that smokers who think they've been given a vitamin smoke more, and people who are given a weight-loss supplement are less likely to stick to their diet. The same thing happens when you go to the gym or eat a plate of spinach. The difference is that exercise and vegetables have real benefits, so you've still got a chance to come out ahead. If you take a pill with no benefits, the best you can do is break even.

Brief resemblance argument: Taking a vitamin is NOT like eating spinach or going to the gym

Conclusion

Which brings us back to Gomez-Cabrera in Barcelona. She, of all people, has enormous respect for the powers of micronutrients such as antioxidants—she has devoted her life to studying them. "But if you eat enough fruits and vegetables, five servings a day," she says, "I don't think you need anything else." And if you're not eating like that, then taking a pill isn't a solution. In fact, it may be part of the problem.

As this editorial demonstrates, awareness of different kinds of claims can help you increase your flexibility and effectiveness as an arguer. In the following chapters, we discuss each of the claim types in more detail, showing how they work and how you can develop skills and strategies for supporting each type of claim.

Chapter 12
Definition and Resemblance Arguments

Learning Objectives

In this chapter, you will learn to:

12.1 Explain what is at stake in arguments about definition and resemblance.

12.2 Explain four types of categorical arguments.

12.3 Explain the criteria-match structure of categorical arguments based on definition.

12.4 Use criteria-match reasoning to generate ideas for your own definition argument.

12.5 Write your own definition argument.

Arguments about definition or resemblance concern disputes about what category something belongs to, either directly by definition or indirectly or metaphorically through comparison or resemblance. They are among the most common argument types you will encounter.

Case 1: In What Category Does My Wad of Gum (Wrapped in Mustard-Stained Tissue) Belong?

This cartoon by Rina Piccolo poses a definitional issue. The ethically motivated hero of this cartoon, trying valiantly to do the right thing, ponders the criteria for each bin. Is her wad of tissue-wrapped gum "just plain old garbage"? Or is it perhaps "organic waste"? (The answer depends on how you define "garbage" versus "organic waste.") While pointing to the challenges of classifying waste, the cartoon gently mocks the bureaucratic mind that invents all these categories and then has to define them. In the wonderful way that cartoons can work, the cartoon's categorical choices can even define human actors. As long as the woman stands pondering, she defines herself as a "concerned environmentalist." But the next person might define herself as an environmental scoffer by chucking the wad of gum into the "no conscience" bin or the "climate change denier/ polluter" bin. This cartoon both mocks environmentalists and honors the definitional difficulties of defining and sorting different kinds of waste.

Case 2: Is a Frozen Embryo a Person or Property?

An infertile couple conceived several embryos in a test tube and then froze the fertilized embryos for future use. During the couple's divorce, they disagreed about the disposition of the embryos. The woman wanted to use the frozen embryos to try to get pregnant, and the man wanted to destroy them. When the courts were asked to decide what should be done with the embryos, several questions of definition arose: Should the frozen embryos be categorized as "persons," thus becoming analogous to children in custody disputes? Or should they be divided up as "property," with the man getting half and the woman getting the other half? Or should a new legal category be created for them that regards them as more than property but less than actual persons? The judge decided that frozen embryos "are not, strictly speaking, either 'persons' or 'property,' but occupy an interim category that entitles them to special respect because of their potential for human life."*

What Is at Stake in an Argument about Definition and Resemblance?

12.1 **Explain what is at stake in arguments about definition and resemblance.**

Definition and resemblance arguments occur whenever a community disagrees about the category a particular person, thing, act, or phenomenon should be placed in or identified with. Here are some examples:

Issues Involving Categories

Question	Does this specific phenomenon . . .	. . . belong to (or is it similar to) this category?
Is atmospheric carbon dioxide a pollutant?	Atmospheric carbon dioxide	Pollutant
For purposes of our state's tax on candy, is a cough drop "candy" or an "over-the-counter drug"?	Cough drop	Candy (or over-the-counter drug)
Is women's obsession with thinness today similar in effect to women's footbinding in ancient China?	Women's obsession with thinness	Footbinding in ancient China

* See Vincent F. Stempel, "Procreative Rights in Assisted Reproductive Technology: Why the Angst?" *Albany Law Review* 62 (1999), 1187.

Much is at stake when we place things into categories because the category that something belongs to can have real consequences. Naming the category that something belongs to makes an implicit mini-argument.

Consequences Resulting from Categorical Claims

To appreciate the consequences of categorical claims, consider the competing categories proposed for whales in the international controversy over commercial whaling. What category does a whale belong to? Some arguers might say that "whales are sacred animals," implying that their intelligence, beauty, grace, and power mean they should never be killed. Others might argue that "whales are a renewable food resource" like tuna, crabs, cattle, and chickens. This category implies that we can harvest whales for food the same way we harvest tuna for tuna fish sandwiches or cows for beef. Still others might argue that "whales are an endangered species"—a category that argues for the preservation of whale stocks but not necessarily for a ban on controlled hunting of individual whales. Each of these whaling arguments places whales in a separate, different category that implicitly urges the reader to adopt that category's perspective on whaling.

Significant consequences can also result from resemblance claims. Consider the way that media analysts tried to make sense of the September 11, 2001, terrorist attacks on the World Trade Center and the Pentagon by comparing them to different kinds of previous events. Some commentators said, "The September 11 attacks are like Timothy McVeigh's bombing of the Alfred P. Murrah Federal Building in Oklahoma City in 1995"—an argument that framed the terrorists as criminals who must be brought to justice. Others said, "The September 11 attacks are like the 1941 Japanese attack on Pearl Harbor"—an argument suggesting that the United States should declare war on some yet-to-be-defined enemy. Still others said, "The September 11 attacks are like an occasionally disastrous earthquake or an epidemic," arguing that terrorists will exist as long as the right conditions breed them and that it is useless to fight them using the strategies of conventional war. Under this analogy, the "war on terror" is a metaphorical war like the "war on poverty" or the "war against cancer." Clearly, each of these resemblance claims had high-stakes consequences. In 2001, the Pearl Harbor claim prevailed, and the United States went to war, first in Afghanistan and then in Iraq. Many critics of these wars continue to say that war is an inappropriate strategy for fighting the "disease of terrorism."

The Rule of Justice: Things in the Same Category Should Be Treated the Same Way

As you can see, the category we place something into—either directly through definition or indirectly through comparison—can have significant implications for people's actions or beliefs. To ensure fairness, philosophers refer to the *rule of justice*, which states that "beings in the same essential category should be treated in the same way." For example, the problem of how the courts should treat the users or sellers of marijuana depends on the category marijuana belongs to. Marijuana might be placed in the same category as tobacco and alcohol, in which case the possession and sale of marijuana would be legal but subject to regulation and taxes. Or marijuana could be placed in the same category as meth, cocaine, and heroin; in this case, it would be an illegal drug subject to criminal prosecution. Some states have placed marijuana in the same category as penicillin and insulin, making it a legal drug so long as it is obtained from a licensed dispensary with a doctor's prescription. Many states are not happy with any of these categories and are trying to define marijuana in some fourth way. To take another example, suppose your professor says that absence from an exam can be excused for emergencies only. How would you define "emergency"? Clearly, if you broke your leg on the morning of an exam, you would be excused. But is attending your grandmother's funeral or your best friend's wedding an "emergency"? How about missing an exam because your car wouldn't start? Although your interests might be best served by a broad definition of emergency, your professor might prefer a narrow definition, which would permit fewer exceptions.

The rule of justice becomes especially hard to apply when we consider contested cases marked by growth or slow change through time. At what point does a child become an adult? When does a binge drinker become an alcoholic, an Internet poker player a compulsive gambler, or a fetus a human person? In most category debates, an argument, not a quick trip to the dictionary, is required to settle the matter.

For Writing and Discussion

Applying the Rule of Justice

Suppose your landlord decides to institute a "no pets" rule. The rule of justice requires that all pets have to go—not just your neighbor's barking dog, but also Mrs. Brown's cat, the kids' hamster downstairs, and your own pet tarantula. That is, all these animals have to go, unless you can argue that some of them are not "pets" for purposes of the landlord's "no pets" rule.

1. Working in small groups or as a class, define pets by establishing the criteria an animal would have to meet to be included in the category "pets." Consider your landlord's "no pets" rule as the cultural context for your definition.
2. Based on your criteria, which of the following animals is definitely a pet that would have to be removed from the apartment? Based on your criteria, which animals could you exclude from the "no pets" rule? How would you make your argument to your landlord?
   - a German shepherd
   - a small housecat
   - a tiny, well-trained lapdog
   - a gerbil in a cage
   - a canary
   - a tank of tropical fish
   - a tarantula

Types of Categorical Arguments

12.2 Explain four types of categorical arguments

Categorical arguments assert that a disputed phenomenon is (or is not) either a member of a certain category or is like a certain category. Such arguments can be divided into four kinds:

1. **Simple categorical arguments**, in which there is no dispute about the definition of the category.
2. **Definition arguments**, in which there is a dispute about the boundaries of the category and hence its definition.

3. **Resemblance arguments by analogy**, in which the writer uses metaphor or other figurative language to link the phenomenon to a certain category.

4. **Resemblance arguments by precedent**, in which the arguer claims that one phenomenon or situation is similar to another phenomenon or situation.

Let's look at each in turn.

Simple Categorical Arguments

A categorical argument is "simple" if there is no disagreement about the definition of the category into which a person, event, or phenomenon is placed. For example, if you make the claim that "Joe is bossy," you are placing him in the category of "bossy people." In this case, you assume that you and the audience agree on what "bossy" means. Your dispute is simply whether Joe meets the criteria for "bossy." To support your claim, you would provide examples of his bossiness (his poor listening skills, his shouting at people, his making decisions without asking the committee). Similarly, if you want to make the simple categorical claim that "low-carb diets are dangerous," you would need to provide evidence of this danger (scientific studies, testimony from doctors, anecdotes). The dispute in this case is about low-carb diets, not about the definition of "dangerous." To rebut a simple categorical claim, you would provide counterevidence to show that the person, event, or phenomenon does not meet the criteria for the category.

For Writing and Discussion

Supporting and Rebutting Simple Categorical Claims

Working individually or in small groups, consider how you would support the following simple categorical claims. What examples or other data would convince readers that the specified case fits within the named category? Then discuss ways you might rebut each claim.

1. Bottled water is environmentally unfriendly. [That is, bottled water belongs in the category of "environmentally unfriendly substances."]
2. Macklemore is a pure rapper.
3. Americans today are obsessed with their appearance. [That is, Americans belong in the category of "people obsessed with their appearance."]
4. Competitive cheerleading is physically risky.

Definition Arguments

Simple categorical arguments morph into definition arguments whenever stakeholders disagree about the boundaries of a category. In the previous exercise, suppose that you had said about Macklemore, "Well, that depends on how you define 'pure rapper.'" The need to define the term "pure rapper" adds a new layer of complexity to your arguments about Macklemore. You are disputing not only specifics about Macklemore but also the definition of "pure rapper" itself.

Full-blown definition arguments occur, then, when the disputants don't agree on the definition of the category into which a person, event, or phenomenon is placed. Consider, for example, the environmental controversy over the definition of *wetland*. Section 404 of the federal Clean Water Act provides for federal protection of wetlands, but it leaves the task of defining *wetland* to administrative agencies and the courts. Currently, about 5 percent of the land surface of the contiguous forty-eight states is potentially affected by the wetlands provision, and 75 percent of this land is privately owned. Efforts to define *wetland* have created a battleground between pro-environment and pro-development or property-rights groups. Farmers, homeowners, and developers often want a narrow definition of wetlands so that more property is available for commercial or private use. Environmentalists favor a broad definition in order to protect different habitat types and maintain the environmental safeguards that wetlands provide (including control of water pollution, spawning grounds for aquatic species, and floodwater containment).

The problem is that defining *wetland* is tricky. For example, one federal regulation defines a wetland as any area that has a saturated ground surface for twenty-one consecutive days during the year. But how would you apply this law to a pine flatwood ecosystem that was wet for ten days this year but thirty days last year? And how should the courts react to lawsuits claiming that the regulation itself is either too broad or too narrow? One can see why the wetlands controversy provides hefty incomes for lawyers and congressional lobbyists.

As we will explain in more detail later in this chapter, definition arguments require a *criteria-match structure* in which the arguer must first define the category term by specifying the criteria that must be met for something to be placed in that category. The writer then shows that the disputed person, event, or phenomenon matches those criteria.

Resemblance Argument Using Analogy

Whereas definition arguments claim that a particular phenomenon belongs to a certain category, resemblance arguments simply compare one thing to another. A common kind of resemblance argument uses *analogies*—imaginative comparisons often with subtle persuasive effects. If you don't like your new boss, you can say that she's like a Marine drill sergeant or the cowardly captain of a sinking ship. Each of these analogies suggests a different category in which to place your boss, clarifying the nature of your dislike while conveying an emotional charge. The arguer's intention is to transfer the audience's understanding of (or feelings about) the second thing back to the first. The risk of resemblance arguments is that the differences between the two things being compared are often so significant that the argument collapses under close examination.

Sometimes, as in the "My boss is like a Marine drill sergeant" example, arguers use short, undeveloped analogies for quick rhetorical effect. At other times, arguers develop extended analogies that carry a substantial portion of the argument. As an example of an extended analogy, consider the following excerpt from a professor's argument opposing a proposal to require a writing proficiency exam for graduation. In the following portion of his argument, the professor compares development of writing skills to the development of physical fitness.

> A writing proficiency exam gives the wrong symbolic messages about writing. It suggests that writing is simply a skill, rather than an active way of thinking and learning. It suggests that once a student demonstrates proficiency, then he or she doesn't need to do any more writing.
>
> Imagine two universities concerned with the physical fitness of their students. One university requires a junior-level physical-fitness exam in which students must run a mile in less than 10 minutes, a fitness level it considers minimally competent. Students at this university see the physical-fitness exam as a one-time hurdle. As many as 70 percent of them can pass the exam with no

practice; another 10–20 percent need a few months' training; and a few hopeless couch potatoes must go through exhaustive remediation. After passing the exam, any student can settle back into a routine of TV and potato chips having been certified as "physically fit."

The second university, however, believing in true physical fitness for its students, is not interested in minimal competency. Consequently, it creates programs in which its students must take a one-credit physical-fitness course each term for the entire four years of the undergraduate curriculum. There is little doubt which university will have the more physically fit students. At the second university, fitness becomes a way of life, with everyone developing his or her full potential. Similarly, if we want to improve our students' writing abilities, we should require writing in every course throughout the curriculum.

Thus analogies have the power to get an audience's attention like virtually no other persuasive strategy. But seldom are they sufficient in themselves to provide full understanding. At some point, with every analogy, you need to ask yourself, "How far can I legitimately go with this? At what point are the similarities between the two things I am comparing going to be overwhelmed by their dissimilarities?" Analogies are useful attention-getting devices, but they can conceal and distort as well as clarify.

For Writing and Discussion

Developing Analogies

The following exercise will help you clarify how analogies function in the context of arguments. Working individually or in small groups, think of two analogies for each of the following topics. One analogy should urge readers toward a positive view of the topic; the other should urge a negative view. Write each of your analogies in the following one-sentence format:

_____ is like _____: A, B, C . . . (in which the first term is the contested topic being discussed; the second term is the analogy; and A, B, and C are the points of comparison).

Example

- **Topic:** Cramming for an exam
- **Negative analogy:** Cramming for an exam is like pumping iron for ten hours straight to prepare for a weight-lifting contest: exhausting and counterproductive.
- **Positive analogy:** Cramming for an exam is like carbohydrate loading before a big race: It gives your brain a full supply of facts and concepts, all fresh in your mind.
- **Topics:**
    1. Checking social media constantly
    2. Building a wall to secure U.S. borders
    3. Using steroids to increase athletic performance
    4. Paying college athletes
    5. Eating at fast-food restaurants

Resemblance Arguments Using Precedent

Another kind of resemblance argument uses precedent for its persuasive force. An argument by precedent tries to show that a current situation is like a past situation and that therefore a similar action or decision should be taken or reached. You can refute a precedence argument by showing that the present situation differs substantially from the past situation.

Precedence arguments are very common. For example, during the debate about healthcare reform in the first year of Barack Obama's presidency, supporters of a single-payer, "Medicare-for-all" system pointed to Canada as a successful precedent. According to supporters, a single-payer system was successful in Canada; it would therefore also be successful in the United States. But opponents also used the Canadian precedent to attack a single-payer system. They pointed to problems in the Canadian system as a reason to reject a Medicare-for-all system in the United States.

For Writing and Discussion

Using Claims of Precedent

Consider the following claims of precedent, and evaluate how effective you think each precedent might be in establishing the claim. How would you develop the argument? How would you cast doubt on it?

1. To increase alumni giving to our university, we should put more funding into our football program. When University X went to postseason bowls for three years in a row, alumni donations to building programs and academics increased by 30 percent. We can expect the same increases here.
2. Postwar democracy can be created successfully in Afghanistan because it was created successfully in Germany and Japan following World War II.
3. Euthanasia laws work successfully in the Netherlands. Therefore they will work successfully in the United States.

Examining Visual Arguments

Claim about Category (Definition)

This cartoon, by political cartoonist Randy Bish of the *Pittsburgh Tribune Review,* creates a visual pun that makes a categorical argument against heroin. How does Bish's rendering of the letter "r" make a categorical claim? What is that claim? How effective do you find this cartoon in highlighting the seductive danger of heroin?

The Criteria-Match Structure of Definition Arguments

12.3 Explain the criteria-match structure of categorical arguments based on definition.

Of the four types of categorical arguments explained in the previous section, definition arguments require the fullest range of argumentative skills. For the rest of this chapter, we'll explain more fully the argumentative moves required to write your own definition argument.

Overview of Criteria-Match Structure

Definition arguments usually have a two-part structure: (1) a definition part that tries to establish the boundaries of the category and (2) a match part that argues whether a given case meets that definition. To describe this structure, we use the term *criteria-match*. Here are two examples:

> **Definition issue:** In a divorce proceeding, is a frozen embryo a "person" rather than "property"?
>
> **Criteria part:** What criteria must "a person" meet?
>
> **Match part:** Does a frozen embryo meet these criteria?
>
> **Definition issue:** Is this thirty-acre parcel of land near Swan Lake a "wetland"?
>
> **Criteria part:** What criteria must a wetland meet?
>
> **Match part:** Does this parcel of land meet these criteria?

To show how a definition issue can be developed into a claim with supporting reasons, let's look more closely at a third example:

> **Definition issue:** For purposes of my feeling good about buying my next pair of running shoes, is the Hercules Shoe Company a socially responsible company?
>
> **Criteria part:** What criteria must a company meet to be deemed "socially responsible"?
>
> **Match part:** Does the Hercules Shoe Company meet these criteria?

Let's suppose you work for a consumer information group that wishes to encourage patronage of socially responsible companies and the boycott of socially irresponsible companies. Your group's first task is to define *socially responsible company*. After much discussion and research, your group establishes three criteria that a company must meet to be considered socially responsible:

> *Your definition:* A company is socially responsible if it (1) avoids polluting the environment, (2) sells goods or services that contribute to the community's well-being, and (3) treats its workers justly.

The criteria section of your argument would explain and illustrate these criteria.

The match part of the argument would then try to persuade readers that a specific company does or does not meet the criteria. A typical thesis statement might be as follows:

> *Your thesis statement:* Although the Hercules Shoe Company is nonpolluting and provides a socially useful product, it is not a socially responsible company because it treats workers unjustly.

Toulmin Framework for a Definition Argument

Here is how the core of the preceding Hercules definition argument could be displayed in Toulmin terms. Note how the reason and grounds constitute the match argument while the warrant and backing constitute the criterion argument.

Toulmin Analysis of the Hercules Shoe Company Argument

ENTHYMEME

CLAIM The Hercules Shoe Company is not a socially responsible company

REASON because it treats workers unjustly.

GROUNDS

Evidence of unjust treatment:

• Evidence that the company manufactures its shoes in East Asian sweatshops

• Evidence of the inhumane conditions in these shops

• Evidence of hardships imposed on displaced American workers

CONDITIONS OF REBUTTAL

Attacking reasons and grounds

• Possible countervidence that the shops maintain humane working conditions

• Possible questioning of statistical data about hardships on displaced workers

WARRANT

Socially responsible companies treat workers justly.

BACKING

• Arguments showing that just treatment of workers is right in principle and also benefits society

• Arguments that capitalism helps society as a whole only if workers achieve a reasonable standard of living, have time for leisure, and are not exploited

CONDITIONS OF REBUTTAL

Attacking warrant and backing

Justice needs to be considered from an emerging nation's standpoint:

• The wages paid to workers are low by American standards but are above average by East Asian standards.

• Displacement of American workers is part of the necessary adjustment of adapting to a global economy and does not mean that a company is unjust.

As this Toulmin schema illustrates, the warrant and backing constitute the criteria section of the argument by stating and defending "just treatment of workers" as a criterion for a socially responsible company. The reason and grounds constitute the match section of the argument by arguing that the Hercules Shoe Company does not treat its workers justly. How much emphasis you need to place on justifying each criterion and supporting each match depends on your audience's initial beliefs. The conditions of rebuttal help you imagine alternative views and see places where opposing views need to be acknowledged and rebutted.

For Writing and Discussion

Identifying Criteria and Match Issues

Consider the following definition claims. Working individually or in small groups, identify the criteria issue and the match issue for each of the following claims.

> **Definition issue:** A Honda assembled in Ohio is (is not) an American-made car.
> **Criteria part:** What criteria must an "American-made car" meet?
> **Match part:** Does a Honda assembled in Ohio meet these criteria?
> **Claims:**

1. American Sign Language is (is not) a "foreign language" for purposes of a college graduation requirement.
2. The violence in *Grand Theft Auto* is (is not) constitutionally protected free speech.
3. Bungee jumping from a crane is (is not) a "carnival amusement ride" subject to state safety inspections.
4. For purposes of a state sales tax on "candy," a Twinkie is (is not) candy.
5. A skilled video game player is (is not) a true athlete.

Creating Criteria Using Aristotelian Definition

When creating criteria for a category, you can often follow the pattern of *Aristotelian definition*. The Aristotelian definitional strategy, regularly used in dictionaries, defines a term by placing it within the next larger class or category and then showing the specific attributes that distinguish the term from other terms within the same category. For example, according to a legal dictionary, *robbery* is "the felonious taking of property" (next larger category) that differs from other acts of theft because it seizes property "through violence or intimidation." Legal dictionaries often provide specific examples to show the boundaries of the term. Here is one example:

> There is no robbery unless force or fear is used to overcome resistance. Thus, surreptitiously picking a man's pocket or snatching something from him without resistance on his part is *larceny*, but not robbery.

Many states specify degrees of robbery with increasingly heavy penalties. For example, *armed robbery* involves the use of a weapon to threaten the victim. In all cases, *robbery* is distinguished from the lesser crime of *larceny,* in which no force or intimidation is involved.

As you can see, an Aristotelian definition of a term identifies specific attributes or criteria that enable you to distinguish it from other members of the next larger class. We created an Aristotelian definition in our example about socially responsible companies. A socially responsible company, we said, is any company (next larger class) that meets three criteria: (1) it doesn't pollute the environment; (2) it creates goods or services that promote the community's well-being; and (3) it treats its workers justly.

Creating Criteria Using an Operational Definition

In some rhetorical situations, particularly those arising in the physical and social sciences, writers need precise *operational definitions* that can be measured empirically and are not subject to problems of context and conflicting values and beliefs. A social scientist studying the effects of television on aggression in children needs a precise, measurable definition of *aggression.* Typically, the scientist might measure "aggression" by counting the number of blows a child gives to an inflatable bobo doll over a fifteen-minute period when other play options are available. In our wetlands example, a federal authority created an operational definition of *wetland:* a wetland is a parcel of land that has a saturated ground surface for twenty-one consecutive days during the year.

Such operational definitions are useful because they are precisely measurable, but they are also limited because they omit criteria that may be unmeasurable but important. Thus, we might ask whether it is adequate to define an *honors student* as someone with a 3.8 GPA or higher or a *successful sex-education program* as one that results in a 25 percent reduction in teenage pregnancies. What important aspects of an honors student or a successful sex-education program are not considered in these operational definitions?

Conducting the Match Part of a Definition Argument

In conducting a match argument, you need to supply examples and other evidence showing that your contested case does (does not) meet the criteria you established in your definition. In essence, you support the match part of your argument in much the same way you would support a simple categorical claim.

For example, if you were developing the argument that the Hercules Shoe Company is not socially responsible because it treats its workers unjustly, your match section would provide evidence of this injustice. You might supply data about the percentage of shoes produced in East Asia, about the low wages paid to these workers, and about the working conditions in these factories. You might also describe the suffering of displaced American workers when Hercules closed its American factories and moved operations to Asia, where the labor is non-union and cheap. The match section should also summarize and respond to opposing views.

Idea-Generating Strategies for Creating Your Own Criteria-Match Argument

12.4 **Use criteria-match reasoning to generate ideas for your own definition argument.**

In constructing criteria to define your contested term, you can either research how others have defined your term or make your own definitions. If you use the first strategy, you turn to standard or specialized dictionaries, judicial opinions, or expert testimony to establish a definition based on the authority of others. The second strategy is to use your own critical thinking to make your own definition, thereby defining the contested term yourself. This section explains these approaches in more detail.

Strategy 1: Research How Others Have Defined the Term

When you take this approach, you search for authoritative definitions acceptable to your audience yet favorable to your case. When the state of Washington tried to initiate a new sales tax on candy, lawyers and legislators wrestled with a definition. They finally created the following statute, which is available to the public on a government website:

What Is the Definition of Candy?

"Candy" is a preparation of sugar, honey, or other natural or artificial sweeteners combined with chocolate, fruits, nuts, or other ingredients or flavorings in the form of bars, drops, or pieces. Candy does not require refrigeration, and does not include flour as an ingredient.

> "Natural or artificial sweeteners" include, but are not limited to, high fructose corn syrup, dextrose, invert sugar, sucrose, fructose, sucralose, saccharin, aspartame, stevia, fruit juice concentrates, molasses, evaporated cane juice, and rice syrup.
> "Flour" includes any flour made from a grain, such as wheat flour, rice flour, and corn flour.
> Items that require "refrigeration," either before or after opening, are not candy. For example, popsicles, ice cream bars, and fruits in sweetened syrups are not candy.

This definition made it easy for state officials to exclude from the "candy tax" any snack food that contained flour. Thus Twinkies, Fruit Loops cereal, and chocolate-covered pretzels were exempt from the tax. But considerable debate occurred over cough drops and halvah (a traditional dessert in India and Mediterranean countries). The state decided to exclude cough drops if the package contained a "drug facts" panel and a list of active ingredients. (Such cough drops were then classified as "over-the-counter drugs.") Halvah made with nut-butter was taxed as candy but not halvah made with flour.

Turning to established definitions is thus a first step for many definition arguments. Common sources of these definitions are specialized dictionaries, such as *Black's Law Dictionary*, which form a standard part of the reference holdings of any library. Other sources of specialized definitions are state and federal appellate court decisions, legislative and administrative statutes, and scholarly articles examining a given definition conflict. Lawyers use this research strategy exhaustively in preparing court briefs. They begin by looking at the actual text of laws as passed by legislatures or written by administrative authorities. Then they look at all the court cases in which the laws have been tested and examine the ways courts have refined legal definitions and applied them to specific cases. Using these refined definitions, lawyers then apply them to their own case at hand.

If your research uncovers definitions that seem ambiguous or otherwise unfavorable to your case, you can sometimes appeal to the "original intentions" of those who defined the term. For example, if a scientist is dissatisfied with definitions of *wetlands* based on consecutive days of saturated ground surface, she might proceed as follows: "The original intention of Congress in passing the Clean Water Act was to preserve the environment." What Congress intended, she could then claim, was to prevent development of those wetland areas that provide crucial habitat for wildlife or that inhibit water pollution. She could then propose an alternative definition based on criteria other than consecutive days of ground saturation.

Strategy 2: Create Your Own Extended Definition*

Often, however, you need to create your own definition of the contested term. An effective strategy is to establish initial criteria for your contested term by thinking of hypothetical cases that obviously fit the category you are trying to define and then altering one or more variables until the hypothetical case obviously doesn't fit the category. You can then test and refine your criteria by applying them to borderline cases. For example, suppose you work at a homeless shelter where you overhear your clients discuss an incident that strikes you as potential "police brutality." You wonder whether you should write to your local paper to bring attention to the incident.

---

* The defining strategies and collaborative exercises in this section are based on the work of George Hillocks and his research associates at the University of Chicago. See George Hillocks Jr., Elizabeth A. Kahn, and Larry R. Johannessen, "Teaching Defining Strategies as a Mode of Inquiry: Some Effects on Student Writing," *Research in the Teaching of English* 17 (October 1983), 275–84. See also Larry R. Johannessen, Elizabeth A. Kahn, and Carolyn Calhoun Walter, *Designing and Sequencing Prewriting Activities* (Urbana, IL: NCTE, 1982).

A Possible Case of Police Brutality

Two police officers confront an inebriated homeless man who is shouting obscenities on a street corner. The officers tell the man to quiet down and move on, but he keeps shouting obscenities. When the officers attempt to put the man into the police car, he resists and takes a wild swing at one of the officers. As eyewitnesses later testified, this officer shouted obscenities back at the drunk man, pinned his arms behind his back in order to handcuff him, and lifted him forcefully by the arms. The man screamed in pain and was later discovered to have a dislocated shoulder. Is this officer guilty of police brutality?

To your way of thinking, this officer seems guilty: An inebriated man is too uncoordinated to be a threat in a fight, and two police officers ought to be able to arrest him without dislocating his shoulder. But a friend argues that because the man took a swing at the officer, the police were justified in using force. The dislocated shoulder was simply an accidental result of using justified force.

To make your case, you need to develop a definition of "police brutality." You can begin by creating a hypothetical case that is obviously an instance of police brutality:

A Clear Case of Police Brutality

A police officer confronts a drunk man shouting obscenities and begins hitting him in the face with his police baton. *[This is an obvious incidence of police brutality because the officer intentionally tries to hurt the drunk man without justification; hitting him with the baton is not necessary for making an arrest or getting the man into the police car.]*

You could then vary the hypothetical case until it is clearly *not* an instance of police brutality.

Cases That Are Clearly Not Police Brutality

Case 1:

The police officer handcuffs the drunk man, who, in being helped into the police car, accidentally slips on the curb and dislocates his arm while falling. *[Here the injury occurs accidentally; the police officer does not act intentionally and is not negligent.]*

Case 2:

The police officer confronts an armed robber fleeing from a scene and tackles him from behind, wrestling the gun away from him. In this struggle, the officer pins the robber's arm behind his back with such force that the robber's shoulder is dislocated. *[Here aggressive use of force is justified because the robber was armed, dangerous, and resisting arrest.]*

Using these hypothetical cases, you decide that the defining criteria for police brutality are (1) *intention* and (2) use of *excessive force*—that is, force beyond what was required by the immediate situation. After more contemplation, you are convinced that the officer was guilty of police brutality and have a clearer idea of how to make your argument. Here is how you might write the "match" part of your argument:

Match Argument Using Your Definition

If we define police brutality as the *intentional* use of *excessive* force, then the police officer is guilty. His action was intentional because he was purposefully responding to the homeless man's drunken swing and was angry enough to be shouting obscenities back at the drunk (according to eyewitnesses). Second, he used excessive force in applying the handcuffs. A drunk man taking a wild swing hardly poses a serious danger to two police officers. Putting handcuffs on the drunk may have been justified, but lifting the man's arm violently enough to dislocate a shoulder indicates excessive force. The officer lifted the man's arms violently not because he needed to but because he was angry, and acting out of anger is no justification for that violence. In fact, we can charge police officers with police brutality precisely to protect us from being victims of police anger. It is the job of the court system to punish us, not the police's job. Because this officer acted intentionally and applied excessive force out of anger, he should be charged with police brutality.

The strategy we have demonstrated—developing criteria by imagining hypothetical cases that clearly do and do not belong to the contested category—gives you a systematic procedure for developing your own definition for your argument.

For Writing and Discussion

Developing a Definition

Individual task:

1. Suppose you want to define the concept of courage. In each of the following cases, decide whether the person in question is acting courageously or not. In each instance explain your reasoning.
   a. A neighbor rushes into a burning house to rescue a child from certain death and emerges, coughing and choking, with the child in his arms. Is the neighbor courageous?
   b. A firefighter rushes into a burning house to rescue a child from certain death and emerges with the child in her arms. The firefighter is wearing protective clothing and a gas mask. When a newspaper reporter calls her courageous, she says, "Hey, this is my job." Is the firefighter courageous?
   c. A teenager rushes into a burning house to recover a memento given to him by his girlfriend, the first love of his life. Is the teenager courageous?
   d. A parent rushes into a burning house to save a trapped child. The fire marshal tells the parent to wait because there is no chance that the child can be reached from the first floor. The fire marshal wants to try cutting a hole in the roof to reach the child. The parent rushes into the house anyway and is burned to death. Was the parent courageous?
2. Now formulate your own definition of a "courageous act." Use the following format: "An act would be considered courageous if it meets the following criteria: [you specify]."
3. Finally, apply your definition to the following case: An extreme sport enthusiast sets a record for a hang-gliding descent from a certain state's highest cliff. Is this record-setting descent a courageous act? Write a paragraph in which you argue that the descent is or is not courageous.

Group task:

Share the results from the individual task on courage. Then make up your own series of controversial cases, like those given previously for "courage," for one or more of the following concepts:

a. cruelty to animals
b. child abuse
c. true athlete
d. sexual harassment
e. free speech protected by the First Amendment

Finally, using the strategy of making up hypothetical cases that do and do not belong to each category, construct a definition of your chosen concept.

Writing Assignment: A Definition Argument

12.5 Write your own definition argument.

The assignment for this chapter focuses on definition disputes about categories. Write an essay in which you argue that a borderline or contested case fits (or does not fit) within a given category. In the opening of your essay, introduce the borderline case you will examine and pose your definition question. In the first part of your argument, define the boundaries of your category (criteria) by reporting a definition used by others or by developing your own extended definition. In the second part of your argument (the match), show how your borderline case meets (or doesn't meet) your definition criteria.

Exploring Ideas

Ideally, in writing this argument you will join an ongoing conversation about a definition issue that interests you. What cultural and social issues that concern you involve disputed definitions? In the public arena, you are likely to find numerous examples simply by looking through news stories—for example, the disputes about the definition of "torture" in interrogating terrorist suspects or about "freedom of religion" in debates about religious organizations having to pay for contraception in employees' health insurance. Often you can frame your own definition issues even if they aren't currently in the news. Is using TiVo to avoid TV commercials a form of theft? Is flag burning protected free speech? Is solitary confinement "cruel and unusual punishment"? Is Walmart a socially responsible company? Are voter ID laws racist?

If you have trouble discovering a local or national issue that interests you, you can create fascinating definition controversies among your classmates by asking whether certain borderline cases are "true" or "real" examples of some category: Are highly skilled video game players (race car drivers, synchronized swimmers, marbles players) true athletes? Is a gourmet chef (skilled furniture maker, tagger) a true artist? Is a chiropractor (acupuncturist, naturopathic physician) a "real doctor"? Working as a class or in small groups inside or outside class, create an argumentative discussion on one or more of these issues. Listen to the various voices in the controversy, and then write out your own argument.

You can also stimulate definition controversies by brainstorming borderline cases for such terms as *courage* (Is mountain climbing an act of courage?), *cruelty to animals* (Are rodeos [zoos, catch-and-release trout fishing, use of animals for medical research] guilty of cruelty to animals?), or *war crime* (Was the U.S. firebombing of Tokyo in World War II a war crime?).

As you explore your definition issue, try to determine how others have defined your category. If no stable definition emerges from your search, create your own definition by deciding what criteria must be met for a contested case to fit within your category. Try using the strategy for creating criteria that we discussed earlier in this chapter with reference to police brutality. Once you have determined your criteria, freewrite for five or ten minutes, exploring whether your contested case meets each of the criteria.

Identifying Your Audience and Determining What's at Stake

Before drafting your argument, identify your targeted audience and determine what's at stake. Consider your responses to the following questions:

- What audience are you targeting? What background do they need to understand your issue? How much do they already care about it?
- Before they read your argument, what stance on your issue do you imagine them holding? What change do you want to bring about in their views?
- What will they find new or surprising about your argument?
- What objections might they raise? What counterarguments or alternative points of view will you need to address?
- Why does your argument matter? Who might be threatened or made uncomfortable by your views? What is at stake?

Organizing a Definition Argument

As you compose a first draft of your essay, you may find it helpful to understand typical structures for definition arguments. There are two basic approaches, as shown in Figures 12.1 and 12.2. You can either discuss the criteria and the match separately or interweave the discussion.

Questioning and Critiquing a Definition Argument

A powerful way to stimulate global revision of a draft is to role-play a skeptical audience. The following questions will help you strengthen your own argument or rebut the definition arguments of others. In critiquing a definition argument, you need to appreciate its criteria-match structure because you can question the criteria argument, the match argument, or both.

Figure 12.1 Definition argument: Organization Plan 1

Introduce the issue and state your claim.	• Engage reader's interest in your definition issue and show why it is controversial or problematic. • Show what's at stake. • Provide background information needed by your audience. • State your claim.
Present your criteria.	• State and develop criterion 1. • State and develop criterion 2. • Continue with the rest of your criteria. • Anticipate and respond to possible objections to the criteria.
Present your match argument.	• Consider restating your claim for clarity. • Argue that your case meets (does not meet) criterion 1. • Argue that your case meets (does not meet) criterion 2. • Continue with the rest of your match argument. • Anticipate and respond to possible objections to the match argument.
Conclude.	• Perhaps sum up your argument. • Help reader return to the "big picture" of what's at stake. • End with something memorable.

Questioning Your Criteria

- Could a skeptic claim that your criteria are not the right ones? Could he or she offer different criteria or point out missing criteria?
- Could a skeptic point out possible bad consequences of accepting your criteria?
- Could a skeptic cite unusual circumstances that weaken your criteria?
- Could a skeptic point out bias or slant in your definition?

Questioning Your Match

- Could a skeptic argue that your examples or data don't meet the STAR criteria (see Chapter 4) for evidence?
- Could a skeptic point out counterexamples or alternative data that cast doubt on your argument?
- Could a skeptic reframe the way you have viewed your borderline case?

Figure 12.2 Definition argument: Organization Plan 2

Introduce the issue and state your claim.	• Engage reader's interest in your definition issue and show why it is problematic or controversial. • Show what's at stake. • Provide background information needed by your audience. • State your claim.
Present series of criterion-match arguments.	• State and develop criterion 1 and argue that your case meets (does not meet) the criterion. • State and develop criterion 2 and argue that your case meets (does not meet) the criterion. • Continue with the rest of your criterion-match arguments.
Respond to possible objections to your argument.	• Anticipate and summarize possible objections. • Respond to the objections through rebuttal or concession.
Conclude.	• Perhaps sum up your argument. • Help reader return to the "big picture" of what's at stake. • End with something memorable.

Reading

This reading, by student Alex Mullen, was written for the definition assignment in Learning Objective 12.5. Alex's argument was stimulated by class discussions of property ownership in digital environments.

Student Essay

A Pirate But Not a Thief: What Does "Stealing" Mean in a Digital Environment?

Alex Mullen

I am a pirate. In the eyes of the law, I could face serious punishment in fines, up to thousands of dollars, or jail time for my crime. Legally, it matters very little that my crime is one perpetrated by millions of people every year (you yourself may be guilty of it) or that there are far worse offenders out there. But before we get out the noose and head for the yardarm, I think I ought to describe my crime. In my History of Film class we were asked to watch Jean Renoir's *La Grande Illusion*. Now, if you've spent any time searching for 1930s foreign films you will undoubtedly know what a pain it is to find them, and of the twenty or so films we watched for my class a grand total of three were available on streaming sites such as Netflix, Hulu, and YouTube. While there were several copies of this particular film at my university library, all had been checked out. I planned to make a journey to the fabled Scarecrow Video (one of the largest rental libraries in the United States), but time was running low at this point. Finally, I broke down and used a person-to-person torrent site to download the film illegally. In the end all the trouble was worthwhile, as *La Grande Illusion* remains one of the greatest films I have ever seen. After watching it several times and writing a brief paper, I deleted the film from my computer. Although I feel that my action was justifiable, many people think what I did was no better than shoplifting and that I am guilty of theft. As a film lover and aspiring filmmaker, I am conflicted on the issue of online piracy. Nevertheless, I contend that what I did wasn't stealing because I deprived no one of either property or profit.

Let's take a step back from online piracy and focus simply on what stealing is in its most basic form. In my mind, stealing is the unlawful taking of another's property or profits without permission. It is the underlying assumption about what makes stealing wrong that needs to be considered. In the case of property, stealing is wrong not because the thief has the property but because the original owner has been deprived of it. The owner's loss causes the wrong, not the thief's gain. To give an example in very simple terms, if you have a phone case and I make a copy of that case (as is quite possible with a 3D printer), you still possess the original case, so no harm has been done to you, the owner. However, suppose that you made your living by selling these phone cases. If I made exact duplicates with my 3-D printer and then sold these cases to others, then you could be deprived of profits that you might otherwise have received. Again, the wrong comes from the creator's loss and not the thief's gain.

Now let's focus on my particular example of online piracy. While I concede that piracy has the distinct potential to be stealing, I reject the accusation that all piracy is stealing. Based on the first part of my definition of stealing, my downloading *La Grande Illusion* deprived no consumer or creator of his or her copy of the film. This is why accusations that compare online piracy to shoplifting are false. In the case of shoplifting, the owner/creator has one fewer piece of merchandise to make a profit on; with online piracy, such loss does not occur because the original copy still exists.

However, the second part of my definition, which focuses on profits, still remains to be examined. Perhaps by downloading the film I have deprived the creators/owners of profits they would normally receive. Let me begin by saying that I never intended to purchase *La Grande Illusion*. While intention does not often register in legal matters, it does have a bearing on the type and degree of wrongdoing. Film-industry lawyers often argue that every time a film is pirated, the rightful owner is deprived of money because the pirate would have otherwise purchased the film. This claim, however, is fallacious because there is no way to show that these

(continued)

potential consumers would have purchased the film (I certainly wouldn't have). So while we may agree that some of these people would have purchased the film, it would be inaccurate to claim that in all cases piracy directly deprives creators of profit. I argue that what I did in the case of *La Grande Illusion* was more like borrowing than theft. Borrowing a film from a library (or renting it from a video store) has the same basic effect on the owner/creator as online piracy. That is, a library or video store purchases a copy and then loans it or rents it to others. Thus, many persons may not purchase a copy from the owner/creator because they can use this single public or commercial copy. Yet we do not consider borrowing or renting stealing even though it can have the same economic ramification as piracy. To go a step further, any time I borrow a film from a friend I cause the same outcome found so reprehensible in online piracy. In my case, instead of borrowing *La Grande Illusion* from an institution or business, I borrowed it from another individual via the Internet.

5   There is, of course, the counterargument that I could have rented the film from Scarecrow and thus stole profit from this film-rental store much loved by film buffs. While it is true that I did not benefit Scarecrow with my patronage (a fact that I partially regret because I do try to support Scarecrow as often as possible), it would be inaccurate to say that I stole from Scarecrow. I am under no obligation to supply them with profits. When I pay money to a rental organization, I am not paying for the film; I am paying for the service of being able to use their copy of the film for 24 hours. Had I purchased the film directly from the filmmaker, I would do the same harm to Scarecrow. Thus my not utilizing Scarecrow to obtain *La Grande Illusion* is not theft.

While I understand why the film industry (and also the music industry) views downloading from file-sharing torrent sites as piracy, their motives focus on preserving profits and blur the distinctions among buying, renting, and borrowing. If I owned a DVD version of a movie and loaned it to a friend, no one would object. But if I make the same movie available to a friend via a torrent or file-sharing site, I become a pirate subject to huge fines. The intention is the same; only the format changes. The problem stems from the hazy concept of "ownership" in a digital environment where physical copies are replaced by digital copies. Certainly, we pay to possess digital copies of films, music, and video games, but is this really the same as physical ownership? After all, I can lend, rent, or even sell a physical DVD, but such actions are impossible with digital copies without committing piracy. Our consumption of media is evolving rapidly, and while undoubtedly there will always be those who exploit these changes for personal gain, I feel we need to realize that our understanding of ownership, stealing, and illegal use must evolve along with these changes.

Chapter 13
Causal Arguments

Learning Objectives

In this chapter you will learn to:

13.1 Explain and illustrate kinds of causal arguments.

13.2 Explain how different causal mechanisms function in cause/consequence arguments.

13.3 Understand key causal terms and avoid inductive fallacies in causal arguments.

13.4 Write your own cause or consequence argument.

We encounter causal issues all the time. What has caused the declining birth rate among teens in the United States? Why has kombucha become a popular drink among millennials? Why has there been a marked decline in the number of teenagers getting a driver's licence? Why are white teenage girls seven times as likely to smoke as African American teenage girls? Why do couples who live together before marriage have a higher divorce rate than those who don't? Why did fidget spinners become a fad? In addition to asking causal questions like these, we pose consequence questions as well: What might be the consequences of installing stricter proof-of-citizenship requirements for voting? What might be the social and economic consequences of establishing public preschool programs? What have been the consequences of the smart phone on the social life of pre-teens and teens? Often arguments about causes and consequences have important stakes because they shape our view of reality and influence government policies and individual decisions. This chapter explains how to wrestle responsibly with cause/consequence issues to produce effective causal arguments.

Case 1: What Causes Global Warming?

One of the early clues linking global warming to atmospheric carbon dioxide (CO_2) came from side-by-side comparisons of graphs plotting atmospheric carbon dioxide and global temperatures over time. These graphs show that increases in global temperature parallel increases in the percentage of carbon dioxide in the atmosphere. However, the graphs show only a correlation, or association, between increased carbon dioxide and higher average temperature. To argue that an increase in CO_2 could cause global warming, scientists needed to explain the links in a causal chain. They did so by comparing the earth to a greenhouse. Carbon dioxide, like glass in a greenhouse, lets some of the earth's heat radiate into space but also reflects some of the heat back to the earth. The higher the concentration of carbon dioxide, the more heat is reflected back to the earth.

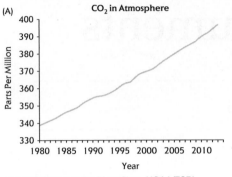

(A) CO$_2$ in Atmosphere

SOURCE: Data from Dr. Pieter Tans, NOAA/ESRL

(B) Mean Global Temperature

SOURCE: Data from NASA Goddard Institute for Space Studies Surface Temperature Analysis

Case 2: What Has Caused the Change in the Rate of Teen Pregnancies in the United State in the Last Five Years?

Although the United States still has the highest rate of teen pregnancies among developed countries, studies show a decline in teen pregnancies since the early 1990s. What has caused this decline? Some economists point to the recession of 2007–2009 as a major cause, claiming that as the job market tightened, teens became afraid of not being able to get jobs when encumbered with babies. Other sources emphasize the role of parents in cautioning teens about irresponsible choices concerning sexual behavior and reproduction. A quite different explanation comes from a recent study by the National Bureau of Economic Research analyzing the impact of media images on viewers. This study has found a correlation between the decline in teen pregnancies and the watching of the MTV docudrama *16 and Pregnant* (which premiered in 2009) and its spinoff *Teen Moms*. While the Parents Television Council and other critics argue that these shows sensationalize and glamorize the lives of the teen moms, researchers, using Nielsen ratings and geographic data on viewership and data from Google Trends and Twitter, found that watching these shows "led to more searches and tweets regarding birth control and abortion, and ultimately led to a 5.7 percent reduction in teen births in the eighteen months" after *16 and Pregnant* first aired.[*] This study broadens social thinking on the use of reality TV and social media in promoting safe sex, as well as its potential value in addressing other social and health causes.

An Overview of Causal Arguments

13.1 Explain and illustrate kinds of causal arguments.

Typically, causal arguments try to show how one event brings about another. When causal investigation focuses on material objects—for example, one billiard ball striking another—the notion of causality appears fairly straightforward. But when humans become the focus of a causal argument, the nature of causality becomes more vexing. If we say that something happened to "cause" a person to act in a certain way, what do we mean? Do we mean that she was "forced" to act in a certain way, thereby negating her free will (as in, an undiagnosed brain tumor caused

---

[*] Melissa S. Kearney and Phillip B. Levine. "Media Influences on Social Outcomes: The Impact of MTV's *16 and Pregnant* on Teen Childbearing," NBER Working Paper No. 19795, National Bureau of Economic Research, January 2014.

her to act erratically), or do we mean more simply that she was "motivated" to act in a certain way (as in, her anger at her parents caused her to act erratically)? When we argue about causality in human beings, we must guard against confusing these two senses of "cause" or assuming that human behavior can be predicted or controlled in the same way that nonhuman behavior can. A rock dropped from a roof will always fall at thirty-two feet per second squared, and a rat zapped with electricity for turning left in a maze will always stop turning left. But if we raise interest rates, will consumers save more money? If so, how much money will they save? This is the sort of question that can be debated endlessly.

Kinds of Causal Arguments

Arguments about causality can take a variety of forms. Three typical kinds are speculations about possible causes, arguments for an unexpected or surprising cause, and predictions of consequences.

- **Speculations about possible causes.** Sometimes arguers speculate about possible causes of a phenomenon. For example, whenever a shooter opens fire on innocent bystanders (as in the 2015 mass killing at the Pulse gay nightclub in Orlando, Florida; the 2012 Sandy Hook Elementary School massacre in Connecticut; or the nearly fatal wounding of a Republican legislator practicing for a congressional baseball game in June 2017) social scientists, police investigators, terrorism specialists, and media commentators begin analyzing the causes. One of the most thoroughly studied and heavily debated shooting incidents occurred in 1999 when the nation was shocked by one of the first incidents of mass school shooting—the Columbine High School massacre in Littleton, Colorado, in which two male students opened fire on their classmates, killing thirteen people, wounding twenty-three others, and then shooting themselves. Figure 13.1 illustrates some of the proposed theories for the Columbine shootings. What was at stake was not only our desire to understand the sociocultural sources of school violence but also our desire to institute policies to prevent future school shootings. If a primary cause is

Figure 13.1 Speculation about possible causes: Columbine High School massacre the availability of guns, then we might push for more stringent gun-control laws. But if the primary cause is the disintegration of the traditional family, the shooters' alienation from high-school cliques, or the dangerous side effects of antidepressant medications, then we might seek different solutions.

- **Arguments for an unexpected or surprising cause.** Besides sorting out possible causes of a phenomenon, sometimes arguers try to persuade readers to see the plausibility of an unexpected or surprising cause. This was the strategy used by syndicated columnist John Leo, who wanted readers to consider the role of violent video games as a contributing cause to the Columbine massacre.* After suggesting that the Littleton killings were partly choreographed on video-game models, Leo suggested the causal chain shown in Figure 13.2.

Figure 13.2 Argument for a surprising cause: Role of violent video games in the Columbine massacre

Many youngsters are left alone for long periods of time (because both parents are working).

↓

They play violent video games obsessively.

↓

Their feelings of resentment and powerlessness "pour into the killing games."

↓

The video games break down a natural aversion to killing, analogous to psychological techniques employed by the military.

↓

Realistic touches in modern video games blur the "boundary between fantasy and reality."

↓

Youngsters begin identifying not with conventional heroes but with sociopaths who get their kicks from blowing away ordinary people ("pedestrians, marching bands, an elderly woman with a walker").

↓

Having enjoyed random violence in the video games, vulnerable youngsters act out the same adrenaline rush in real life.

---

* John Leo, "Kill-for-Kicks Video Games Desensitizing Our Children," *Seattle Times*, 27 April 1999, B4.

- **Predictions of consequences.** Another frequently encountered kind of causal argument predicts the consequences of current, planned, or proposed actions or events. Consequence arguments have high stakes because we often judge actions on whether their benefits outweigh their costs. As we will see in Chapter 15, proposal arguments usually require writers to predict the consequences of a proposed action, conduct a cost/benefit analysis, and persuade readers that no unforeseen negative consequences will result. Just as a phenomenon can have multiple causes, it can also have multiple consequences. Figure 13.3 shows the consequence arguments considered by environmentalists who propose eliminating several dams on the Snake River in order to save salmon runs.

Toulmin Framework for a Causal Argument

Because causal arguments can involve lengthy or complex causal chains, they are often harder to summarize in *because* clauses than are other kinds of arguments. Likewise, they are not as likely to yield quick analysis through the Toulmin schema. Nevertheless, a causal argument can usually be stated as a claim with *because* clauses. Typically, a *because* clause pinpoints one or two key elements in the causal chain rather than summarize every link. John Leo's argument linking the Columbine massacre to violent video games could be summarized in the following claim with a *because* clause:

> Violent video games may have been a contributing cause to the Littleton massacre because playing these games can make random, sociopathic violence seem pleasurable.

Figure 13.3 Predictions of consequences: Eliminating dams on the Snake River

Once stated as an enthymeme, the argument can be analyzed using Toulmin's schema. It is easiest to apply Toulmin's schema to causal arguments if you think of the grounds as the observable phenomena at any point in the causal chain and the warrants as the shareable assumptions about causality.

Toulmin Analysis of the Violent Video Games Argument

ENTHYMEME

CLAIM Violent video games may have been a contributing cause to the Columbine school shooting

REASON because playing these games can make random, sociopathic violence seem pleasurable.

→ Qualifiers

GROUNDS

- Evidence that the killers, like many young people, played violent video games

- Evidence that the games are violent

- Evidence that the games involve random, sociopathic violence (not good guys versus bad guys) such as killing ordinary people—marching bands, little old ladies, etc.

- Evidence that young people derive pleasure from these games

CONDITIONS OF REBUTTAL
Attacking the reason and grounds

- Perhaps the killers didn't play violent video games.

- Perhaps the video games are no more violent than traditional kids' games such as cops and robbers.

- Perhaps the video games do not feature sociopathic killing.

WARRANT

If young people derive pleasure from random, sociopathic killing in video games, they can transfer this pleasure to real life, thus leading to the Columbine shooting.

BACKING

- Testimony from psychologists

- Evidence that violent video games desensitize people to violence

- Analogy to military training in which video games are used to "make killing a reflex action"

- Evidence that the distinction between fantasy and reality becomes especially blurred for unstable young people

CONDITIONS OF REBUTTAL
Attacking the warrant and backing

- Perhaps kids are fully capable of distinguishing fantasy from reality.

- Perhaps the games are just fun with no transference to real life.

- Perhaps the games are substantially different from military training games.

For Writing and Discussion

Developing Causal Chains

Individual task:

1. Create a causal chain to show how the item on the left could lead to the item on the right.

   a. Invention of the automobile — Changes in sexual mores

   b. Increased dependence on smartphones — New cultural trend toward "bailing" (abrupt canceling of social engagements)

   c. Growth of social media as a source of news — The increasing polarization of politics in the United States

   d. Millennials' desire for an urban lifestyle — Redesign of cities

   e. Development of way to prevent rejections in transplant operations — Liberalization of euthanasia laws

2. For each of your causal chains, compose a claim with an attached *because* clause summarizing one or two key links in the causal chain—for example, "Millennials' desire for an urban lifestyle is spurring the redesign of cities because Millennials' car- and house-free habits are prompting developers to build new high-density urban communities that offer easy access to work and pleasure."

Group task:

Share your causal claim and *because* clause links with the other members of your class.

Two Methods for Arguing That One Event Causes Another

13.2 Explain how different causal mechanisms function in cause/consequence arguments.

One of the first things you need to do when preparing a causal argument is to note exactly what sort of causal relationship you are dealing with: a onetime phenomenon, a recurring phenomenon, or a puzzling trend. Here are some examples.

Kind of Phenomenon	Examples
Onetime phenomenon	• Volvo's 2017 decision to stop building gasoline-powered cars and move entirely to electric or hybrid vehicles • The election of Donald Trump as president of the United States • The 2017 collision of the *USS Fitzgerald* (a guided-missile destroyer) with a Philippine-flagged merchant vessel near Yokosuka, Japan
Recurring phenomenon	• Failure of teenagers to practice safe sex • Homelessness • Recidivism (tendency of former prisoners to return to crime after release from prison)
Puzzling trend	• Increase in the number of events counted as Olympic sports • Increase in opioid addiction (prescribed pain killer) in rural America • Declining populations of both bats and honeybees

With recurring phenomena or with trends, one has the luxury of being able to study multiple cases, often over time. You can interview people, make repeated observations, or study the conditions in which the puzzling phenomenon occurs. But with a onetime occurrence, one's approach is more like that of a detective than a scientist. Because one can't repeat the event with different variables, one must rely only on the immediate evidence at hand, which can quickly disappear. Having briefly stated these words of caution, let's turn now to two main ways that you can argue that one event causes another.

First Method: Explain the Causal Mechanism Directly

The most convincing kind of causal argument identifies every link in the causal chain, showing how an initiating cause leads step by step to an observed effect. A causes B, which causes C, which causes D. In some cases, all you have to do is fill in the missing links. In other cases—when your assumptions about how one step leads to the next may seem questionable to your audience—you have to argue for the causal connection with more vigor.

A careful spelling out of each step in the causal chain is the technique used by science writer Robert S. Devine in the following passage from his article "The Trouble with Dams." Although the benefits of dams are widely understood (they produce pollution-free electricity while providing flood control, irrigation, barge transportation, and recreational boating), the negative effects are less commonly known and understood. In this article, Devine tries to persuade readers that dams have serious negative consequences. In the following passage, he explains how dams reduce salmon flows by slowing the migration of smolts (newly hatched, young salmon) to the sea.

Causal Argument Describing a Causal Chain

Such transformations lie at the heart of the ongoing environmental harm done by dams. Rivers are rivers because they flow, and the nature of their flows defines much of their character. When dams alter flows, they alter the essence of rivers.

Consider the erstwhile river behind Lower Granite (a dam on Idaho's Snake River). Although I was there in the springtime, when I looked at the water it was moving too slowly to merit the word "flow"—and Lower Granite Lake isn't even one of the region's enormous storage reservoirs, which bring currents to a virtual halt. In the past, spring snowmelt sent powerful currents down the Snake during April and May. Nowadays hydropower operators of the Columbia and Snake systems store the runoff behind the dams and release it during the winter, when demand—and the price—for electricity rises. Over the ages, however, many populations of salmon have adapted to the spring surge. The smolts used the strong flows to migrate, drifting downstream with the current. During the journey smolts' bodies undergo physiological changes that require them to reach salt water quickly. Before dams backed up the Snake, smolts coming down from Idaho got to the sea in six to twenty days; now it takes from sixty to ninety days, and few of the young salmon reach salt water in time. The emasculated current is the single largest reason that the number of wild adult salmon migrating up the Snake each year has crashed from predevelopment runs of 100,000–200,000 to what was projected to be 150–750 this year.*

---

* Robert S. Devine, "The Trouble with Dams," *Atlantic* (August 1995), 64–75. The example quotation is from page 70.

Smolts use the river flow to reach the sea.

Dams restrict the flow of the river.

A trip that took 6 to 20 days before development now takes 60 to 90 days.

Migrating smolts undergo physiological changes that demand quick access to salt water.

Lengthened migration time kills the smolts.

This tightly constructed passage connects various causal chains to explain the decline of salmon runs.

Second Method: Infer Causal Links Using Inductive Reasoning

If we can't explain a causal link directly, we often employ a reasoning strategy called *induction*. Through induction we infer a general conclusion based on a limited number of specific cases. For example, if on several occasions you got a headache after drinking red wine but not after drinking white wine, you would be likely to conclude inductively that red wine causes you to get headaches, although you can't explain directly how it does so. However, because there are almost always numerous variables involved, inductive reasoning leads to only probable truths, not certain truths.

THREE WAYS OF THINKING INDUCTIVELY   When your brain thinks inductively, it sorts through data looking for patterns of similarity and difference. In this section we explain three ways of thinking inductively: looking for a common element, looking for a single difference, and looking for correlations.

1. **Look for a common element.** One kind of inductive thinking sends you on a search for a common element that can explain recurrences of the same phenomenon. For example, psychologists attempting to understand the causes of anorexia have discovered that many anorexics (but not all) come from perfectionist, highly work-oriented homes that emphasize duty and responsibility. This common element is thus a suspected causal factor leading to anorexia.

2. **Look for a single difference.** Another approach is to look for a single difference that may explain the appearance of a new phenomenon. When infant death rates in the state of Washington shot up in July and August 1986, one event making these two months different stood out: increased radioactive fallout over Washington from the April Chernobyl nuclear meltdown in Ukraine. This single difference led some researchers to suspect radiation as a possible cause of the increase in infant deaths.

3. **Look for correlations.** Still another method of induction is correlation, which means that two events or phenomena tend to occur together but doesn't imply that one causes the other. For example, there is a correlation between nearsightedness and both intelligencesand academic achievement. (That is, in a given sample of nearsighted people and people with normal eyesight, the nearsighted group will have a somewhat higher average IQ score as well as higher academic rankings.) But the direction of causality isn't clear. It could be that high intelligence causes people to read more, thus ruining their eyes (high intelligence causes nearsightedness). Or it could be that nearsightedness causes people to read more, thus raising their academic achievement level and their IQ scores (nearsightedness causes high intelligence). Or it could be that some unknown phenomenon, perhaps a gene, is related to both nearsightedness and intelligence. So keep in mind that correlation is not causation—it simply suggests possible causation.

For Writing and Discussion

Developing Plausible Causal Chains Based on Correlations

Working individually or in small groups, develop plausible causal chains that may explain the relationship between the following pairs of phenomena:

a. A person who registers a low stress level on an electrochemical stress meter   does daily meditation

b. A binge drinker at college parties   has increased risk of becoming a perpetrator or victim of sexual violence

c. A person who grew up in a house with two or more bathrooms   is likely to have higher SAT scores than a person who grew up in a one-bathroom home

Examining Visual Arguments

A Causal Claim

This billboard is part of a Texas campaign to fight sex trafficking. How do both the text and image in this billboard suggest links in a causal chain? Although this ad oversimplifies the complex issue of human trafficking, and some would say it represents only one view of sex workers, how do the words and the choice of images combine to make powerful appeals to both *logos* and *pathos*?

Key Terms and Inductive Fallacies in Causal Arguments

13.3 **Understand key causal terms and avoid inductive fallacies in causal arguments.**

Because causal arguments are often easier to conduct if writer and reader share a few specialized terms and concepts, this section explains key terms in causal reasoning and offers ways to avoid inductive fallacies.

A Glossary of Key Terms

- **The problem of oversimplified cause.** One of the great temptations is to look for *the* cause of something, as if a phenomenon has only one cause rather than multiple causes. For example, in recent years the number of persons in the United States sending out Christmas cards has declined substantially. Many commentators attribute the decline to the increasing use of Facebook, which keeps old friends in touch year-round, eliminating the need for holiday "family letters." But there may be other causes also, such as a decline in the number of nuclear families, fewer networks of long-term friends, or generational shifts away from older traditions. When you make a causal argument, be especially careful how you use words such as *all, most, some, the,* or *in part.* For example, to say that *all* the decline in Christmas cards is caused by Facebook is to make a universal statement about Facebook as *the* cause. An argument will be stronger and more accurate if the arguer makes a less sweeping statement: *Some* of the cause for the decline in Christmas cards can be attributed to Facebook. Arguers sometimes deliberately mix up these quantifiers to misrepresent and dismiss opposing views.

- **Immediate and remote causes.** Every causal chain extends backward indefinitely into the past. An *immediate cause* is the closest in time to the event being examined. Consider the causes for the release of nuclear contaminants around the Fukushima nuclear power plant following the 2011 earthquake off the coast of Japan. The immediate cause was loss of power to the water pumps that cooled the reactor's fuel rods, causing the rods to overheat and partially melt. A slightly less immediate cause (several days earlier) was the earthquake-produced tsunami that had swept away the diesel fuel tanks needed to run the backup generators. These immediate causes can be contrasted with a *remote cause*—in this case, a late-1960s design decision that used backup diesel generators to power the water pumps in case of an electrical power loss to the reactor facility. Still more remote causes were the economic and regulatory systems in the late 1960s that led to this particular design.

- **Precipitating and contributing causes.** These terms are similar to immediate and remote causes but don't designate a temporal link going into the past. Rather, they refer to a main cause emerging out of a background of subsidiary causes. For example, if a husband and wife decide to separate, the *precipitating cause* may be a stormy fight over money, after which one of the partners (or both) says, "I've had enough." In contrast, *contributing causes* would be all the background factors that are dooming the marriage: preoccupation with their careers, disagreement about priorities, in-law problems. Note that contributing causes and the precipitating cause all coexist at the same time.

- **Constraints.** Sometimes an effect occurs because some stabilizing factor—a *constraint*—is removed. In other words, the presence of a constraint may keep a certain effect from occurring. For example, in the marriage we have been discussing, the presence of children in the home may be a constraint against divorce. As soon as the children graduate from high school and leave home, the marriage may well dissolve.

- **Necessary and sufficient causes.** A *necessary cause* is one that has to be present for a given effect to occur. For example, fertility drugs are necessary to cause the conception of septuplets. Every couple who has septuplets must have used fertility drugs. In contrast, a *sufficient cause* is one that always produces or guarantees a given effect. Smoking more than a pack of cigarettes per day is sufficient to raise the cost of one's life insurance policy. This statement means that if you are a smoker, no matter how healthy you appear to be, life insurance companies will always place you in a higher risk bracket and charge you a higher premium. In some cases, a single cause can be both necessary and sufficient. For example, lack of ascorbic acid (Vitamin C) is both a necessary and a sufficient cause of scurvy. (Think of those old-time sailors who didn't eat fruit for months.) It is a necessary cause because you can't get scurvy any other way except through absence of ascorbic acid; it is a sufficient cause because the absence of ascorbic acid always causes scurvy.

AVOIDING COMMON INDUCTIVE FALLACIES THAT CAN LEAD TO WRONG CONCLUSIONS   Largely because of its power, informal induction can often lead to wrong conclusions. You should be aware of two common fallacies of inductive reasoning that can tempt you into erroneous assumptions about causality. (Both fallacies are treated more fully in Appendix 1.)

- *Post hoc* **fallacy:** The *post hoc, ergo propter hoc* fallacy ("after this, therefore because of this") mistakes sequence for cause. Just because event A regularly precedes event B doesn't mean that event A causes event B. The same reasoning that tells us that flipping a switch causes the light to go on can make us believe that low levels of radioactive fallout from the Chernobyl nuclear disaster caused a sudden rise in infant death rates in the state of Washington. The nuclear disaster clearly preceded the rise in death rates. But did it clearly *cause* it? Our point is that precedence alone is not proof of causality and that we are guilty of the *post hoc* fallacy whenever we are swayed to believe that one thing causes another just because it comes first.

- **Hasty generalization:** The *hasty generalization* fallacy occurs when you make a generalization based on too few cases or too little consideration of alternative explanations: You flip the switch, but the light bulb doesn't go on. You conclude—too hastily—that the light bulb has burned out. (Perhaps the power has gone off or the switch is broken.) How many trials does it take before you can make a justified generalization rather than a hasty generalization? It is difficult to say for sure.

Both the *post hoc* fallacy and the hasty generalization fallacy remind us that induction requires a leap from individual cases to a general principle and that it is always possible to leap too soon.

For Writing and Discussion
Brainstorming Causes and Constraints

The terms in the preceding glossary can be effective brainstorming tools for thinking of possible causes of an event. For the following events, try to think of as many causes as possible by brainstorming possible *immediate causes, remote causes, precipitating causes, contributing causes,* and *constraints.*

1. Why you decided to attend your present college
2. Why women's fashion and beauty magazines are the most frequently purchased magazines in college bookstores
3. Why large supermarket chains are selling more organic food

---

Writing Assignment: A Causal Argument

13.4 Write your own cause or consequence argument.

Choose an issue about the causes or consequences of a trend, event, or other phenomenon. Write an argument that persuades an audience to accept your explanation of the causes or consequences of your chosen phenomenon. Within your essay you should examine alternative hypotheses or opposing views and explain your reasons for rejecting them. You can imagine your issue either as a puzzle or as a disagreement. If a puzzle, your task will be to create a convincing case for an audience that doesn't have an answer to your causal question already in mind. If a disagreement, your task will be more overtly persuasive because your goal will be to change your audience's views.

Exploring Ideas

Arguments about causes and consequences abound in public, professional, and personal life, so you shouldn't have difficulty finding a causal issue worth investigating and arguing.

Responding to his experiences as a junior-high math tutor, student writer Jesse Goncalves investigated the causes of math anxiety. He argued that math anxiety is primarily a learned behavior passed onto children from math-anxious parents and instructors (see the Readings at the end of this chapter). Student writer Carlos Macias, puzzled by the ease with which college students are issued credit cards, wrote a researched argument disentangling the factors leading young people to bury themselves in debt (see the Readings at the end of this chapter). Other students have focused on causal issues such as these: Why do kids join gangs? What are the consequences of mandatory drug testing (written by a student who has to take amphetamines for narcolepsy)? Why has the age of first marriage steadily increased since 1970?

If you have trouble finding a causal issue to write about, you can often create provocative controversies among your classmates through the following strategies:

- **Make a list of unusual likes and dislikes.** Think about unusual things that people like or dislike. You could summarize the conventional explanations that people give for an unusual pleasure or aversion and then argue for a surprising or unexpected cause. What attracts people to extreme sports? How do you explain the popularity of the paleo diet or of *Game of Thrones* or *The Walking Dead*?

- **Make a list of puzzling events or trends.** Another strategy is to make a list of puzzling phenomena and then try to explain their causes. Start with onetime events (a curriculum change at your school, the sudden popularity of a new app). Then list puzzling recurring events (failure of intelligent teenagers to practice safe sex). Finally, list some recent trends (growth of naturopathic medicine, increased interest in tattoos and piercing). Engage classmates in discussions of one or more of the items on your list. Look for places of disagreement as entry points into the conversation.

- **Explore contested or puzzling causes or consequences from your experience.** What causal issues or surprising consequences emerge from your participation in a group, club, sports team, internship, or job? Based on your experience, does having an internship during the academic year lead to a higher GPA or a lower GPA (or neither)? Based on your interviews with persons who have worked in assisted-living businesses, does animal therapy decrease depression in elderly residents? Based on your own experiences, what causes and consequences that others in this community might care about have you been inspired to explore?

- **Brainstorm consequences of a recent or proposed action.** Arguments about consequences are among the most interesting and important of causal disputes. If you can argue for an unanticipated consequence of a real or proposed action, whether good or bad, you can contribute importantly to the conversation. What might be the consequences, for example, of placing "green taxes" on coal-produced electricity; of legalizing marijuana; of overturning *Roe v. Wade* (which legalized abortion); or of requiring national public service for all young adults?

Identifying Your Audience and Determining What's at Stake

Before drafting your argument, identify your targeted audience and determine what's at stake. Consider your responses to the following questions:

- What audience are you targeting? What background do they need to understand your issue? How much do they already care about it?
- Before they read your argument, what stance on your issue do you imagine them holding? What change do you want to bring about in their views?
- What will they find new or surprising about your argument?
- What objections might they raise? What counterarguments or alternative points of view will you need to address?
- Why does your argument matter? Who might be threatened or made uncomfortable by your views? What is at stake?

Organizing a Causal Argument

At the outset, it is useful to know some of the standard ways that a causal argument can be organized. Later, you may decide on a different organizational pattern, but the standard ways shown in Figures 13.4, 13.5, and 13.6 will help you get started.

Figures 13.5 and 13.6 are similar in that they examine numerous possible causes or consequences. Figure 13.5, however, tries to establish the relative

Figure 13.4 Argument explaining links in a causal chain

Introduce the issue and state your claim.
- Engage reader's interest in your causal issue and show why it is controversial or problematic.
- Show what's at stake.
- State your claim.

Explain the links in the chain going from cause to effect.
- Explain the links and their connections in order.
- Anticipate and respond to possible objections if needed.

Conclude.
- Perhaps sum up your argument.
- Return to the "big picture" of what's at stake.
- End with something memorable.

Figure 13.5 Argument proposing multiple causes or consequences of a phenomenon

Introduce the issue and state your claim.	• Engage reader's interest in your causal issue and show why it is problematic or controversial. • Show what's at stake. • State your claim.
Propose relative contributions of different causes of a phenomenon or relative importance of different consequences.	• Describe the first possible cause or consequence and explain your reasoning. • Continue with the rest of your causes or consequences. • Arrange causes or consequences in increasing order of importance, significance, or surprise.
Respond to possible objections to your argument (if needed).	• Anticipate and summarize possible objections. • Respond through rebuttal or concession.
Conclude.	• Perhaps sum up your argument. • Return to the "big picture" of what's at stake. • End with something memorable.

importance of each cause or consequence, whereas Figure 13.6 aims at rejecting the causes or consequences normally assumed by the audience and argues for an unexpected, surprising cause or consequence. Figure 13.6 can also be used when your purpose is to change your audience's mind about a cause or consequence.

Questioning and Critiquing a Causal Argument

Knowing how to question and critique a causal argument will help you anticipate opposing views in order to strengthen your own. It will also help you rebut another person's causal argument. Here are some useful questions to ask:

- When you explain the links in a causal chain, can a skeptic point out weaknesses in any of the links?
- If you speculate about the causes of a phenomenon, could a skeptic argue for different causes or arrange your causes in a different order of importance?
- If you argue for a surprising cause or a surprising consequence of a phenomenon, could a skeptic point out alternative explanations that would undercut your argument?

Figure 13.6 Argument proposing a surprising cause or consequence

Introduce the issue and state your claim.	• Engage reader's interest in your causal issue and show why it is problematic or controversial. • Show what's at stake. • State your claim.
Reject commonly assumed causes or consequences.	• Describe the first commonly assumed cause or consequence and show why you don't think the explanation is adequate. • Continue with the rest of your commonly assumed causes or consequences.
Argue for your surprising cause or consequence.	• Describe your surprising cause or consequence. • Explain your causal reasoning. • Anticipate and respond to possible objections if needed.
Conclude.	• Perhaps sum up your argument. • Return to the "big picture" of what's at stake. • End with something memorable.

- If your argument depends on inferences from data, could a skeptic question the way the data were gathered or interpreted? Could a skeptic claim that the data aren't relevant (for example, research done with lab animals might not apply to humans)?
- If your causal argument depends on a correlation between one phenomenon and another, could a skeptic argue that the direction of causality should be reversed or that an unidentified, third phenomenon is the real cause?

Readings

The following reading, by student writer Jesse Goncalves, was written in response to the assignment in this chapter. He became interested in the causes of math anxiety when he worked as a math tutor in a junior high school. Jesse's argument illustrates the format and documentation system for a paper following the guidelines of the American Psychological Association (APA). For further discussion of the APA documentation system, see Appendix 2.

What Causes Math Anxiety?

Jess Goncalves

October 18, 2018

What Causes Math Anxiety?

Why are so many people afraid of math? As an applied mathematics major, I did not realize the extent to which math can become inaccessible to those who fear it until I began working in a middle-school math classroom. Math anxiety is defined as "feelings of fear, apprehension, or dread that many people experience when they are in situations that require solving math problems" (Casad, Hale, & Wachs, 2015). After I learned about math anxiety, I quickly came to recognize the anxiety in many of my students, several of my college peers, and occasionally myself. Indeed, nearly half of all children in the United States develop moderate to severe math anxiety, a condition that often remains with them for the rest of their lives (Boaler, 2016). A great deal of research has been conducted on the causes of math anxiety over the past 50 years, and a wide variety of factors have been implicated. Contrary to the prevailing view that math anxiety is directly caused by a combination of genetics, institutional policies, and cultural forces, I argue that math anxiety may be best understood as a learned behavior that is passed on to children from math-anxious parents and teachers, leading to an intergenerational cycle of math anxiety.

Harkening back to the age-old question of nature versus nurture, many scholars have proposed and researched a connection between genetics and math anxiety, and some studies indicate that nature is indeed a strong predictor of a child's level of anxiety. A team of psychology researchers headed by Dr. Zhe Wang found that "[g]enetic factors accounted for roughly 40% of the variation in mathematical anxiety" when they studied 514 pairs of 12-year-old twins (2014). Dr. Wang and her co-authors argue that many of the same genetic factors that make people more likely to develop other anxieties also put them at a higher risk of developing math anxiety. They also note that biological factors such as dyscalculia, better known as mathematical dyslexia, are linked to poor math performance (Wang et al., 2014). Citing studies that implicate poor performance as both a cause and consequence of math anxiety, Dr. Wang contends that being genetically predisposed to struggle in math constitutes a predisposition towards math anxiety. Despite these findings, Dr. Wang does not side strongly with nature in the debate; her team discovered that "environmental factors independent of both general anxiety and math problem solving accounted for ... 53% of the total variance" in math anxiety (2014). What, then, are the factors that assume 53% responsibility for the epidemic of math anxiety?

Education policy is one environmental influence often cited as a cause of math anxiety. For example, Dr. Jo Boaler, a professor of mathematics education at Stanford University, condemns the frequency of timed testing as a major cause of math anxiety. She argues that "timed testing ... transforms children's brains, leading to an inevitable path of math anxiety and low math achievement" (2016). Timed testing is a policy problem due to mandated standardized testing. Moreover, as Dr. Boaler says, "some of the wording in the Common Core State Standards may point to an increased use of timed tests" (2016). Therefore, according to Dr. Boaler, education policy contributes substantially to the epidemic of math anxiety. Beyond policy, many cultural influences have also been accused of inducing math anxiety.

Perhaps the most often blamed and highly researched cultural cause of math anxiety is the unfounded stereotype that males are better at math than females. As Dr. Bettina Casad, a professor of psychology at University of Missouri–St. Louis, and her collaborators assert, "[C]ultural biases about the superiority of boys and men in math permeate our social consciousness" (2015). In a study of the interplay between these biases and math anxiety, Casad found that the "endorsement of math-gender stereotypes may be an antecedent for developing math anxiety for both boys and girls" (2015). Therefore, males and females alike who believe in men's mathematical superiority are at greater risk of developing math anxiety. Because "girls and women are more negatively impacted by cultural biases," a higher number of females suffer from math anxiety (Casad, Hale, & Wachs, 2015). However, the degree to which children are exposed to and influenced by math-gender stereotypes is primarily predicated on their parents and teachers.

While genetics, policy, and culture are all contributing causes of math anxiety, I argue that they do not contribute as significantly or directly as math-anxious parents and teachers. The instructors that shape children's relationships to math are foremost among the "environmental factors" responsible for math anxiety (Wang et

WHAT CAUSES MATH ANXIETY?   4

al., 2014). Teachers also play a major role in determining the influence of education policies on children, as they are charged with the implementation of policy in their classrooms. Similarly, the extent to which math-gender stereotypes impact children depends in large part on their parents' and teachers' endorsement or rejection of those stereotypes. Thus, parents and teachers are the most immediate and significant causes of math anxiety, as they are the primary vehicles through which policy and culture exert influence.

When they frequently help with homework, math-anxious parents can instill math anxiety in their children by modeling negative attitudes towards math and promoting math-gender stereotypes. Parental homework help is normally correlated with improvement in students' performance; however, a team led by psychology researcher Dr. Erin Maloney found that when parents with math anxiety frequently helped with homework, their children's performance and level of math anxiety were negatively affected (2015). The correlation between parents' and children's math anxiety was present only when parents helped with homework, another indication that the anxiety is transmitted primarily through socialization rather than genetics. Maloney argues that math-anxious parents can cause their children to develop math anxiety because they "tend to believe that math is not useful and have low math self-efficacy and low motivation to succeed in math," so communicating their beliefs is "demotivating" to their children (2015). She also suggests that parents who are themselves afraid of failure in math "may be more likely to express negativity when their child is struggling, which in turn could cause their children to also learn to fear failing in mathematics and to avoid engaging in challenging situations" (Maloney et al., 2015). A separate study headed by Dr. Bettina Casad and colleagues supported Maloney's discovery that math-anxious parents often instill math anxiety in their children. Their results showed that "parents' anxiety plays a role in children's math anxiety, and the variables interact to predict several math education outcomes including math self-efficacy, math GPA, math behavioral intentions, math attitudes, and math devaluing" (2015). Casad also noted that math-anxious mothers are particularly prone to share their anxiety with their daughters, which she postulated is a result of these mothers endorsing math-gender stereotypes. Accordingly, Dr. Elizabeth Gunderson, a professor of psychology at Temple University, and her collaborators found that "parents' gender stereotypes bias their beliefs about their own child's math ability, and these beliefs affect children's own self-perceptions about math" (2012). So, while the endorsement of math-gender stereotypes can cause females and males alike to develop math anxiety, children generally learn to believe these stereotypes from math-anxious parents who have themselves internalized the beliefs. In this way, through negative attitudes and biases, math anxiety is passed from one generation of parents to the next in a never-ending cycle. Unfortunately, children who do not receive homework help or who internalize stereotypes from a math-anxious parent, are still at risk of learning math anxiety from a teacher who suffers from the condition.

Perhaps even more influential than parents in the perpetuation of math anxiety are the many math-anxious elementary school teachers. An estimated 60% of elementary school teachers report having moderate to high levels of math anxiety (Bekdemir, 2010), which has been shown to affect instructional practices and classroom dynamics to the point where students perform worse and are at an increased risk of developing math anxiety themselves. Dr. Mehmet Bekdemir, an education researcher, speculates that math-anxious teachers gravitate towards elementary school to avoid teaching middle- or high-school math, however points out that elementary school is the time when children are most prone to developing math anxiety (2010). Dr. Kristin Hadley and Dr. Jim Dorward, both professors of teacher education, found that "teachers who were anxious about teaching mathematics tended to teach in a more traditional manner" (2011), meaning they adopted a conventional, by-the-book pedagogical style and declined to try more innovative strategies. This suggests that math-anxious teachers may be more likely to follow policies that increase students' math anxiety by encouraging traditional practices like frequent timed testing. They also may reject innovative new policies meant to reduce students' anxiety, such as accommodating different learning styles. As a result, the effect of education policy on children's math anxiety is mediated by teachers' levels of math anxiety. Teachers with math anxiety are also more likely to endorse and perpetuate

WHAT CAUSES MATH ANXIETY? 6

math-gender stereotypes, and for their students, this translates directly to increased math anxiety (Casad, Hale, & Wachs, 2015). For instance, Dr. Elizabeth Gunderson found that in classrooms where teachers had high math anxiety, girls often came to endorse the stereotype that boys are better at math (2012). Therefore, through their instructional practices and biases, teachers with math anxiety put their students, some of whom will become the next generation of teachers, at an increased risk of developing math anxiety themselves. Luckily, individual parents and teachers can work to overcome math anxiety and thereby begin to break the cycle.

Because cultural forces and policy decisions work primarily through math-anxious parents and teachers to cause math anxiety in children, with genetics playing a subordinate role, addressing math anxiety in adults could greatly reduce the rate of math anxiety in future generations. Policy changes and cultural shifts are necessary to end the epidemic, but those transitions need to begin at the kitchen table and in front of the classroom, where parents and teachers must confront their own anxieties and math gender biases. I will certainly apply the lessons of this research to improve my own practice as a mentor, and perhaps one day as a teacher, to ensure that I do not perpetuate the cycle of math anxiety.

References

Bekdemir, M. (2010). The pre-service teachers' mathematics anxiety related to depth of negative experiences in mathematics classroom while they were students. *Educational Studies in Mathematics*, 75(3), 311–328.

Boaler, J. (2016). Timed tests and the development of math anxiety. *Education Week*. Retrieved from http://www.edweek.org/ew/articles/2012/07/03/36boaler.h31.html

Casad, B., Hale, P., & Wachs, F. (2015). Parent-child math anxiety and math-gender stereotypes predict adolescents' math education outcomes. *Frontiers in Psychology*, 6, 1597.

Gunderson, E. A., Ramirez, G., Levine, S. C., & Beilock, S. (2012). The role of parents and teachers in the development of gender-related math attitudes. *Sex Roles*, 66, 153-166.

WHAT CAUSES MATH ANXIETY?   7

Hadley, K., & Dorward, J. (2011). The relationship among elementary teachers' mathematics anxiety, mathematics instructional practices, and student mathematics achievement. *Journal of Curriculum and Instruction*, 5(2), 27–44.

Maloney, E., Ramirez, G., Gunderson, E., Levine, S., & Beilock, S. (2015). Intergenerational effects of parents' math anxiety on children's math achievement and anxiety. *Psychological Science*, 26(9), 1480-1488.

Wang, Z., Hart, S. A., Kovas, Y., Lukowski, S., Soden, B., Thompson, L. A., … & Petrill, S. A. (2014). Who is afraid of math? Two sources of genetic variance for mathematical anxiety. *Journal of Child Psychology and Psychiatry*, 55, 1056–1064.

Chapter 14

Evaluation and Ethical Arguments

Learning Objectives

In this chapter you will learn to:

14.1 Explain and illustrate the difference between categorical and ethical evaluation arguments.

14.2 Conduct a categorical evaluation argument using a criteria-match strategy.

14.3 Conduct an ethical evaluation argument using principles or consequences.

14.4 Be mindful of common problems encountered in evaluation arguments.

14.5 Write your own categorical or ethical evaluation argument.

In our roles as citizens and professionals, we are continually expected to make evaluations and to persuade others to accept them. In this chapter, you will learn to conduct two kinds of evaluation arguments: categorical and ethical. Both have clarifying power to help us make difficult choices about good or bad, right or wrong.

Case 1: How Should We Evaluate the Film District 9?

In the film *District 9* (2009), directed by South African Neill Blomkamp and produced by Peter Jackson, a spaceship has stalled out over Johannesburg, South Africa, where it has hovered for several decades. Its starving alien passengers, derogatorily called "The Prawns" for their appearance, have been placed in what has become a crowded, militarized prison ghetto called District 9. As the film begins, South Africans have grown disgusted with and intolerantly fearful of the growing alien population, while corporate powers seek these aliens' technologically advanced bio-weapons. As this poster suggests—based on its "No Humans Allowed" sign, its ominous "You are not welcome here" slogan, and its barbed wire perimeter—the film includes graphic echoes of the racism of apartheid and disturbing depictions of xenophobia, abusive corporate powers, and mistreatment of refugees (the aliens). Nominated for numerous awards, *District 9* sparked heated evaluation arguments about whether it is a good film or a flawed film. Part of the debate focuses on what evaluative criteria to use—a decision that depends on the category into which the film should be placed. Should it be evaluated as a science-fiction film, as a corporate espionage thriller, or as a commentary on global social justice? Some critics, for example, have argued that *District 9* is not a great science-fiction film, but they have argued that it *is* a deeply provocative and moving commentary on social justice.

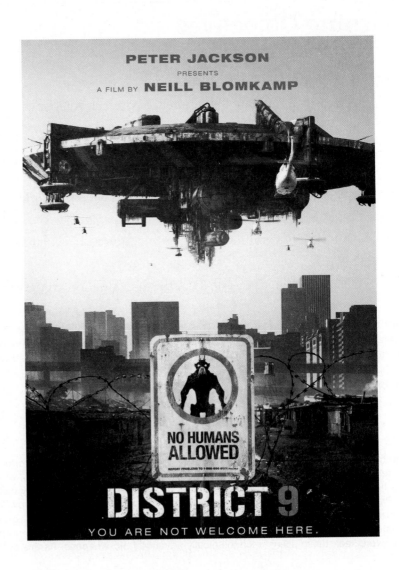

Case 2: What Is a "Good Organ" for a Transplant? How Can an Ill Person Ethically Find an Organ Donor?

In the United States, some 117,000 sick people are waiting for an organ transplant. Some of these people have been waiting as long as six years, and some will die before they can find a donor. The problem of organ shortages raises two kinds of evaluation issues. First, doctors are reevaluating the criteria by which they judge a "good" organ—that is, a good lung, kidney, or liver suitable for transplanting. Formerly, people who were elderly or obese or who had engaged in risky behaviors or experienced heart failure or other medical conditions were not considered sources of good organs. Now doctors are reconsidering these sources as well as exploring the use of organs from pigs. Second, the shortage of organs for donation has raised numerous ethical issues: Is it ethical for people to bypass the national waiting list for organs by advertising on billboards and websites in search of a volunteer donor? Is it morally right for people to sell their organs? Is it right for patients and families to buy organs or in any way remunerate living organ donors? Some states are passing laws that allow some financial compensation to living organ donors.

An Overview of Categorical and Ethical Evaluation Arguments

14.1 **Explain and illustrate the difference between categorical and ethical evaluation arguments.**

In this chapter we explain strategies for conducting two different kinds of evaluation arguments. First, we examine categorical evaluations of the kind "Is this thing a good member of its class?"* (For example: Is Ramon a good leader?) In such an evaluation, the writer determines the extent to which a given something possesses the qualities or standards of its category or class. What are the traits of good leaders? Does Ramon possess these traits? Second, we examine ethical arguments of the kind "Is this action right (wrong)?" (For example: Was it right or wrong to drop atomic bombs on Hiroshima and Nagasaki in World War II?) In these arguments, the writer evaluates a given act from the perspective of some system of morality or ethics.

To see the difference between the two kinds of evaluations, consider the case of terrorists. From a nonethical standpoint, you could make a categorical evaluation by saying that certain people are "good terrorists" in that they fully realize the purpose of the class "terrorist": They cause great anguish and damage with a minimum of resources, and they bring much attention to their cause. In other words, they are good at what they do—terrorism. However, if we want to condemn terrorism on ethical grounds, we have to construct an ethical argument that terrorism is wrong. The ethical question is not whether a person fulfills the purposes of the class "terrorist," but rather whether it is wrong for such a class to exist. In the rest of this chapter, we explain categorical evaluations and ethical evaluations in more detail.

---

*In addition to the term *good*, a number of other evaluative terms involve the same kind of thinking: *effective, successful, workable, excellent, valuable*, and so forth.

Constructing a Categorical Evaluation Argument

14.2 Conduct a categorical evaluation argument using a criteria-match strategy.

A categorical evaluation uses a criteria-match structure similar to the structure we examined in definition arguments (see Chapter 12).

Criteria-Match Structure of Categorical Evaluations

A typical claim-with-reasons frame for an evaluation argument has the following criteria-match structure:

> This thing/phenomenon is/is not a good member of its class because it meets (fails to meet) criteria A, B, and C.
>
> *Claim:* This thing/phenomenon is (is not) a good member of its class.
> *Criteria:* The criteria for being a good member of this class are A, B, and C.
> *Match:* The thing/phenomenon meets (fails to meet) criteria A, B, and C.

The main conceptual difference between an evaluation argument and a definition argument is the nature of the contested category. In a definition argument, one argues whether a particular thing belongs within a certain category. (Is this swampy area a *wetland*?) In an evaluation argument, we know what category something belongs to. For example, we know that this 2014 Nissan Leaf is a *used car*. For an evaluation argument, the question is whether this 2014 Nissan Leaf a *good used car*. Or, to place the question within a rhetorical context: Is this 2014 Nissan Leaf a *good used car for me to buy for commuting back and forth to campus*?

To illustrate the criteria-match structure of an evaluation argument, let's ask whether hydraulic fracturing (commonly called *fracking*) is a good means for extracting natural gas from shale formations. Supporters of fracking might say "yes," because fracking meets three major criteria:

- It is technologically efficient at extracting huge supplies of otherwise untappable natural gas.
- It is cost-effective.
- It is environmentally safe.

Opponents might make two counterarguments: First, they might claim that fracking is not environmentally safe. (Safety is a crucial criterion. Opponents argue that fracking doesn't meet this criterion.) Second, they might argue that fracking, by producing lots of relatively cheap natural gas, removes the urgency from efforts to convert the country to sources of renewable energy, such as the sun and the wind. Thus, fracking might be cost-effective (criterion 2) in the short run but disastrous in the long run. The following figure provides a Toulmin analysis of how proponents of fracking might develop their third reason: "Fracking is environmentally safe."

TOULMIN ANALYSIS OF THE FRACKING ARGUMENT SUPPORTING ENVIRONMENTAL SAFETY

ENTHYMEME

CLAIM Fracking is a good method for extracting natural gas from shale formations

REASON because it is environmentally safe.

GROUNDS

- Descriptions of safety measures employed by industry
- Descriptions of local, state, and federal regulations aimed at insuring safety
- Summaries of peer-reviewed studies and government studies showing the safety of fracking
- Refutation of anecdotal scare stories told by environmentalists

CONDITIONS OF REBUTTAL

Attacking the reason and grounds

Arguments that fracking is not environmentally safe

- Studies pointing to possible dangers such as contamination of aquifers, earthquakes, flaring of methane, and so forth
- Arguments that local, state, and federal regulations are too loose and unenforced
- Statistics about environmental costs in doing the fracking (huge amounts of required water, recovering contaminated water, use of carbon fuels to run the machinery, and so forth)

WARRANT

Environmental safety is an important criterion for evaluating a method of drilling for natural gas

BACKING

Arguments that safety must be a prime consideration of any business plan. One major accident could undermine public support of fracking. [Backing tries to counter the arguments of environmentalists that business interests put profit ahead of safety.]

CONDITIONS OF REBUTTAL

Attacking the warrant and backing

- Environmentalists will endorse the warrant, but may say that even if fracking is safe, it undermines the urgency of finding alternative energy sources.
- Business interests might want to loosen an insistence on absolute safety by acknowledging that some accidents are inevitable.

Developing Your Criteria

To help you develop your criteria, we suggest a three-step thinking process:

1. Place the thing you are evaluating in the smallest relevant category so that you don't compare apples to oranges.
2. Develop criteria for your evaluation based on the purpose or function of this category.
3. Determine the relative weight of your criteria.

Let's look at each of these steps in turn.

STEP 1: PLACE THE THING YOU ARE EVALUATING IN THE SMALLEST RELEVANT CATEGORY   Placing your contested thing in the smallest relevant category is a crucial first step. Suppose, for example, that you want one of your professors to write you a letter of recommendation for a summer job. The professor will need to know what kind of summer job you are applying for. Are you applying to become a camp counselor, a law-office intern, a retail sales clerk, or a tour guide at a wild animal park? Each of these jobs has different criteria for excellence.

To take a different example, suppose that you want to evaluate e-mail as a medium of correspondence. To create a stable context for your evaluation, you need to place e-mail in its smallest relevant category. You may choose to evaluate e-mail as a medium for business communication (by contrasting e-mail with direct personal contact, phone conversations, or postal mail), as a medium for staying in touch with high-school friends (in contrast, say, to text messaging, Facebook or Instagram), or as a medium for carrying on a long-distance romance (in contrast, say, to old-fashioned love letters). Again, criteria will vary across these different categories.

By placing your contested thing in the smallest relevant class, you avoid the apples-and-oranges problem. That is, to give a fair evaluation of a perfectly good apple, you need to judge it under the class "apple" and not under the next larger class, "fruit," or a neighboring class such as "orange." To be even more precise, you may wish to evaluate your apple in the class "eating apple" as opposed to "pie apple" because the latter class is supposed to be tarter and the former class juicier and sweeter.

STEP 2: DEVELOP CRITERIA FOR YOUR EVALUATION BASED ON THE PURPOSE OR FUNCTIONS OF THIS CATEGORY   Suppose that the summer job you are applying for is tour guide at a wild animal park. The functions of a tour guide are to drive the tour buses, make people feel welcome, give them interesting information about the wild animals in the park, and make their visit pleasant. Criteria for a good tour guide would thus include reliability and responsibility, a friendly demeanor, good speaking skills, and knowledge of the kinds of animals in the wild animal park. In our e-mail example, suppose that you want to evaluate e-mail as a medium for business communication. The purpose of this class of communication is to provide a quick and reliable means of communication that increases efficiency, minimizes misunderstandings, and protects the confidentiality of internal communications. Based on these purposes, you might establish the following criteria:

> A good medium for business communication:
> - Is easy to use, quick, and reliable
> - Increases employee efficiency
> - Prevents misunderstandings
> - Maintains confidentiality where needed

STEP 3: DETERMINE THE RELATIVE WEIGHT OF YOUR CRITERIA   In some evaluations, all the criteria are equally important. However, sometimes a phenomenon to be evaluated is strong in one criterion but weak in another. This situation forces the evaluator to decide which criterion takes precedence. For example, the supervisor interviewing candidates for tour guide at the wild animal park may find one candidate who is very knowledgeable about the wildlife but doesn't have good speaking skills. The supervisor would need to decide which of these two criteria gets more weight.

Making Your Match Argument

Once you've established and weighed your criteria, you'll need to use examples and other evidence to show that the thing being evaluated meets or does not meet the criteria. For example, your professor could argue that you would be a good wildlife park tour guide because you have strong interpersonal skills (based on your work on a college orientation committee), that you have good speaking skills (based on a speech you gave in the professor's class), and that you have quite a bit of knowledge about animals and ecology (based on your major in environmental science).

In our e-mail example, you might establish the following working thesis:

> Despite its being easy to learn, quick, and reliable, e-mail is often not an effective medium for business communication because it reduces worker efficiency, leads to frequent misunderstandings, and often lacks confidentiality.

You could develop your last three points as follows:

- *E-mail reduces worker efficiency.* Although much important work can be done efficiently on e-mail, workers have to spend inordinate time separating important e-mail from noise (workplace announcements, annoying "reply all" strings, forwarded jokes, and so forth). You can use personal anecdotes and research data to show how employees must sort through volumes of e-mail daily to sort out what messages need immediate attention. Managing e-mail eats into worker time (one research article says that the average worker devotes ten minutes of every working hour to reading and responding to e-mail).

- *E-mail leads to misunderstandings.* Because an e-mail message is often composed rapidly without revision, e-mail can cause people to state ideas imprecisely, to write something they would never say face to face, or to convey an unintended tone. You could give a personal example of a high-consequence misunderstanding caused by e-mail.

- *E-mail often lacks confidentiality.* You could provide anecdotal or research evidence of cases in which a person clicked on the "reply to all" button rather than the "reply" button, sending a message intended for one person to a whole group of people. Also, people sometimes forward e-mails without the sender's permission. Finally, e-mail messages are archived forever, so messages that you thought were deleted may show up years later in a lawsuit.

As these examples illustrate, the key to a successful match argument is to use sufficient examples and other evidence to show how your contested phenomenon meets or does not meet each of your criteria.

Examining Visual Arguments

An Evaluation Claim

For many people, the polar bear has become the iconic image of the environmental repercussions of global warming. This photograph of a "polar bear" marching in a small-town parade creates a visual argument against climate change. This parade entry was sponsored by the Backbone Campaign, an environmental group that specializes in "artful activism," using visually arresting and often humorous costumes, papier mâché puppets, and other forms of art to advocate for progressive environmental policy. How effective is this visual argument as a small-town parade entry? Imagine that you are on a committee brainstorming for an "artful entry" into the small-town parade. What argument would you make in favor of a polar bear theme? How effective is this two-person polar bear costume?

For Writing and Discussion

Developing Criteria and Match Arguments

The following small-group exercise can be accomplished in one or two class hours. It gives you a good model of the process you can go through in order to write your own categorical evaluation.

1. Choose a specific controversial person, thing, or event to evaluate. To help you think of ideas, try brainstorming controversial members of the following categories: *people* (athletes, political leaders, musicians); *technology* (new car features, phone apps); *media* (a social network, a TV program, a radio station); *government and world affairs* (an economic policy, a Supreme Court decision); *the arts* (a film,

a book); *your college or university* (food service, an administrative policy); *the world of work* (a job, a company operation, a dress policy); or any other categories of your choice.

2. Place your controversial person or thing within the smallest relevant class, thus providing a rhetorical context for your argument and showing what is at stake. Do you want to evaluate Harvey's Hamburger Haven in the broad category of *restaurants,* in the narrow category of *hamburger joints,* or in a different narrow category such as *late-night study places?*

3. Make a list of the purpose or function of that class, and then list the criteria that a good member of that class would need to have in order to accomplish its purpose or function. (What is the purpose or function of a hamburger joint versus a late-night study place? What criteria for excellence can you derive from these purposes or functions?

4. If necessary, rank your criteria from most to least important. (For a late-night study place, what is most important: good ambience, Wi-Fi availability, good coffee, or convenient location?)

5. Provide examples and other evidence to show how your contested something matches or does not match each of your criteria. (As a late-night study place, Carol's Coffee Closet beats out Harvey's Hamburger Haven. Although Harvey's Hamburger Haven has the most convenient location, Carol's Coffee Closet has Wi-Fi, an ambience conducive to studying, and excellent coffee.)

Constructing an Ethical Evaluation Argument

14.3 Conduct an ethical evaluation argument using principles or consequences.

A second kind of evaluation argument focuses on moral or ethical issues, which can often merge or overlap with categorical evaluations. For example, many apparently straightforward categorical evaluations can turn out to have an ethical dimension. Consider again the criteria for buying a car. Most people would base their evaluations on cost, safety, comfort, and so forth. But some people may feel morally obligated to buy the most fuel-efficient car, to buy an American car, or not to buy a car from a manufacturer whose labor policies they find morally repugnant. Depending on how large a role ethical considerations play in the evaluation, we may choose to call this an ethical argument based on moral considerations rather than a categorical evaluation based on the purposes of a class or category.

When we are faced with an ethical issue, we must move from arguments of good or bad to arguments of right or wrong. The terms *right* and *wrong* are clearly different from the terms *good* and *bad* when the latter terms mean, simply, "effective" (meets purposes of class, as in "This is a good laptop") or "ineffective" (fails to meet purposes of class, as in "This is a bad cookbook"). But *right* and *wrong* often also differ from what seems to be a moral use of the terms *good* and *bad.* We may say, for example, that sunshine is good because it brings pleasure and that cancer is bad because it brings pain and death, but that is not quite the same thing as saying that sunshine is "right" and cancer is "wrong." It is the problem of "right" and "wrong" that ethical arguments confront.

There are many schools of ethical thought—too many to cover in this brief overview—so we'll limit ourselves to two major systems: arguments from consequences and arguments from principles.

Consequences as the Base of Ethics

Perhaps the best-known example of evaluating acts according to their ethical consequences is *utilitarianism*, a down-to-earth philosophy that grew out of nineteenth-century British philosophers' concern to demystify ethics and make it work in the practical world. Jeremy Bentham, the originator of utilitarianism, developed the goal of the greatest good for the greatest number, or "greatest happiness," by which he meant the most pleasure for the least pain. John Stuart Mill, another British philosopher, built on Bentham's utilitarianism by using predicted consequences to determine the morality of a proposed action.

Mill's consequentialist approach allows you to readily assess a wide range of acts. You can apply the principle of *utility*—which says that an action is morally right if it produces a greater net value (benefits minus costs) than any available alternative action—to virtually any situation, and it will help you reach a decision. Obviously, however, it's not always easy to make the calculations called for by this approach because, like any prediction of the future, an estimate of consequences is conjectural. In particular, it's often very hard to assess the long-term consequences of any action. Too often, utilitarianism seduces us into a short-term analysis of a moral problem simply because long-term consequences are difficult to predict.

Principles as the Base of Ethics

Any ethical system based on principles will ultimately rest on moral tenets that we are duty bound to uphold, no matter what the consequences. (See our discussion of "sacred values" in Chapters 1 and 2.) Sometimes the moral tenets come from religious faith—for example, the Ten Commandments. At other times, however, the principles are derived from philosophical reasoning, as in the case of German philosopher Immanuel Kant. Kant held that no one should ever use another person as a means to his own ends and that everyone should always act as if his acts are the basis of universal law. In other words, Kant held that we are duty bound to respect other people's sanctity and to act in the same way that we would want all other people to act. The great advantage of such a system is its clarity and precision. We are never overwhelmed by a multiplicity of contradictory and difficult-to-quantify consequences; we simply make sure we are following (or not violating) the principles of our ethical system and proceed accordingly.

Example Ethical Arguments Examining Capital Punishment

To show you how to conduct an ethical argument, let's now apply these two strategies to the example of capital punishment. In general, you can conduct an ethical evaluation by using the frame for either a principles-based argument or a consequences-based argument or a combination of both.

- *Principles-Based Frame:* An act is right (wrong) because it follows (violates) principles A, B, and C.
- *Consequences-Based Frame:* An act is right (wrong) because it will lead to consequences A, B, and C, which are good (bad).

A principles-based argument looks at capital punishment through the lens of one or more guiding principles. Kant's principle that we are duty bound not to violate the sanctity of other human lives could lead to arguments opposing capital punishment. One might argue as follows:

> *Principles-based argument opposing capital punishment:* The death penalty is wrong because it violates the principle of the sanctity of human life.

You could support this principle either by summarizing Kant's argument that one should not violate the selfhood of another person or by pointing to certain religious systems such as Judeo-Christian ethics, where one is told "Vengeance is mine, says the Lord" and "Thou shalt not kill." To develop this argument further, you might examine two exceptions in which principles-based ethicists may allow killing—self-defense and war—and show how capital punishment does not fall into either category.

Principles-based arguments can also be developed to support capital punishment. You may be surprised to learn that Kant himself—despite his arguments for the sanctity of life—supported capital punishment. To make such an argument, Kant evoked a different principle about the suitability of the punishment to the crime:

> There is no sameness of kind between death and remaining alive even under the most miserable conditions, and consequently there is no equality between the crime and the retribution unless the criminal is judicially condemned and put to death.

Stated as an enthymeme, Kant's argument is as follows:

> *Principles-based argument supporting capital punishment:* Capital punishment is right because it follows the principle that punishments should be proportionate to the crime.

In developing this argument, Kant's burden would be to show why the principle of proportionate retribution outweighs the principle of the supreme worth of the individual. Our point is that a principles-based argument can be made both for and against capital punishment. The arguer's duty is to make clear what principle is being evoked and then to show why this principle is more important than opposing principles.

Unlike a principles-based argument, which appeals to certain guiding maxims or rules, a consequences-based argument looks at the consequences of a decision and measures the positive benefits against the negative costs. Here is the frame that an arguer might use to oppose capital punishment on the basis of negative consequences:

> *Consequences-based argument opposing capital punishment:* Capital punishment is wrong because it leads to the following negative consequences:
>
> - The possibility of executing an innocent person
> - The possibility that a murderer who may repent and be redeemed is denied that chance
> - The excessive legal and political costs of trials and appeals
> - The unfair distribution of executions so that one's chances of being put to death are much greater if one is a minority or is poor

To develop this argument, the reader would need to provide facts, statistics, and other evidence to support each of the stated reasons.

A different arguer might use a consequences-based approach to support capital punishment:

> *Consequences-based argument supporting capital punishment:* Capital punishment is right because it leads to the following positive consequences:
>
> - It may deter violent crime and decrease the murder rate.
> - It saves the cost of lifelong imprisonment.
> - It stops criminals who are menaces to society from committing more murders.
> - It helps grieving families reach closure and sends a message to victims' families that society recognizes their pain.

It should be evident, then, that adopting an ethical system doesn't lead to automatic answers to one's ethical dilemmas. A system offers a way of proceeding—a way of conducting an argument—but it doesn't relieve you of personal responsibility for thinking through your values and taking a stand. When you face an ethical dilemma, we encourage you to consider both the relevant principles and the possible consequences the dilemma entails. In many arguments, you can use both principles-based and consequences-based reasoning as long as irreconcilable contradictions don't present themselves.

For Writing and Discussion

Developing an Ethical Argument

Individual task:

Develop a frame for an ethical argument (based on principles, consequences, or both) for or against any two of the following actions. Use the previous examples on capital punishment as a model.

1. Eating meat
2. Using public transportation instead of owning a car
3. Legalizing assisted suicide for the terminally ill
4. Selling human organs
5. Allowing concealed weapons on college campuses

Group task:

Share your arguments with classmates.

Common Problems in Making Evaluation Arguments

14.4 To be mindful of common problems encountered in evaluation arguments.

When conducting evaluation arguments (whether categorical or ethical), writers can bump up against recurring problems that are unique to evaluation. In some cases, these problems complicate the establishment of criteria; in other cases, they complicate the match argument. Let's look briefly at some of these common problems.

- *The problem of standards—what is commonplace versus what is ideal:* In various forms, we experience the dilemma of the commonplace versus the ideal all the time. Is it fair to get a ticket for going seventy miles per hour on a sixty-five-mile-per-hour freeway when most of the drivers go seventy miles per hour or faster? (Does what is *commonplace*—going seventy—override what is *ideal*—obeying the law?) Is it better for high schools to pass out free contraceptives to students because students are having sex anyway (what's *commonplace*), or is it better not to pass them out in order to support abstinence (what's *ideal*)?

- *The problem of mitigating circumstances:* This problem occurs when an arguer claims that unusual circumstances should alter our usual standards of judgment. Ordinarily, it is fair for a teacher to reduce a grade if you turn in a paper late. But what if you were up all night taking care of a crying baby? Does that count as a *mitigating circumstance* to waive the ordinary criterion? When you argue for mitigating circumstances, you will likely assume an especially heavy burden of proof. People assume the rightness of usual standards of judgment unless there are compelling arguments for abnormal circumstances.

- *The problem of choosing between two goods or two bads:* Often an evaluation issue forces us between a rock and a hard place. Should we cut pay or eliminate jobs? Put our parents in a nursing home or let them stay at home, where they have become a danger to themselves? In such cases, one has to weigh conflicting criteria, knowing that the choices are too much alike—either both bad or both good.

- *The problem of seductive empirical measures:* The need to make high-stakes evaluations has led many people to seek quantifiable criteria that can be weighed mathematically. Thus we use grade point averages to select scholarship winners, student evaluation scores to decide merit pay for teachers, and judges' combined scores to evaluate figure skaters. In some cases, empirical measures can be quite acceptable, but they are often dangerous because they discount important non-quantifiable traits. The problem with empirical measures is that they seduce us into believing that complex judgments can be made mathematically, thus rescuing us from the messiness of alternative points of view and conflicting criteria.

- *The problem of cost:* A final problem in evaluation arguments is cost. Something may be the best possible member of its class, but if it costs too much, we have to go for second or third best. We can avoid this problem somewhat by placing items into different classes on the basis of cost. For example, a Mercedes will exceed a Kia on almost any criterion of quality, but if we can't afford more than a Kia, the comparison is pointless. It is better to compare a Mercedes to a Lexus and a Kia to an equivalent Ford. Whether costs are expressed in dollars, personal discomfort, moral repugnance, or some other terms, our final evaluation of an item must take cost into account.

Writing Assignment: An Evaluation or Ethical Argument

14.5 To write your own categorical or ethical evaluation argument.

Write an argument in which you try to change your readers' minds about the value, worth, or ethics of something. Choose a phenomenon to be evaluated that is controversial so that your readers are likely at first to disagree with your evaluation or at least to be surprised by it. Somewhere in your essay you should summarize alternative views and either refute them or concede to them (see Chapter 6).

Exploring Ideas

Evaluation issues are all around us. Think of disagreements about the value of a person, thing, action, or phenomenon within the various communities to which you belong—your dorm, home, or apartment community; your school community, including clubs or organizations; your academic community, including classes you are currently taking; your work community; and your city, state, national, and world communities. Once you have settled on a controversial thing to be evaluated, place it in its smallest relevant category, determine the purposes of that category, and develop your criteria. If you are making an ethical evaluation, consider your argument from the perspective of both principles and consequences.

Identifying Your Audience and Determining What's at Stake

Before drafting your argument, identify your targeted audience and determine what's at stake. Consider your responses to the following questions:

- What audience are you targeting? What background do they need to understand your issue? How much do they already care about it?
- Before they read your evaluation argument, what stance on your issue do you imagine them holding? What change do you want to bring about in their view?
- What will they find new or surprising about your argument?
- What objections might they raise? What counterarguments or alternative points of view will you need to address?
- Why does your evaluation matter? Who might be threatened or made uncomfortable by your views? What is at stake?

Organizing an Evaluation Argument

As you write a draft, you may find useful the prototypical structures for evaluation arguments shown in Figures 14.1 and 14.2. Of course, you can always alter these plans if another structure better fits your material.

Questioning and Critiquing a Categorical Evaluation Argument

Here is a list of questions you can use to critique a categorical evaluation argument:

- *Will a skeptic accept my criteria?* Many evaluative arguments are weak because the writers have simply assumed that readers will accept their criteria. Whenever your audience's acceptance of your criteria is in doubt, you will need to argue for your criteria explicitly.

Figure 14.1 Organization plan 1: Criteria and match in separate sections

Introduce the issue and state your claim.

- Engage reader's interest in your evaluation issue and show why it is controversial or problematic.
- Show what's at stake.
- Provide background information needed by your audience.
- State your claim.

Present your criteria.

- State and develop criterion 1.
- State and develop criterion 2.
- Continue with the rest of your criteria.
- Anticipate and respond to possible objections to the criteria.

Present your match argument.

- Consider restating your claim for clarity.
- Argue that your case meets (does not meet) criterion 1.
- Argue that your case meets (does not meet) criterion 2.
- Continue with the rest of your match argument.
- Anticipate and respond to possible objections to the match argument.

Conclude.

- Perhaps sum up your argument.
- Help reader return to the "big picture" of what's at stake.
- End with something memorable.

- *Will a skeptic accept my general weighting of criteria?* Another vulnerable spot in an evaluation argument is the relative weight of the criteria. How much anyone weights a given criterion is usually a function of his or her own interests relative to your contested something. You should always ask whether some particular group might have good reasons for weighting the criteria differently.

- *Will a skeptic accept my criteria but reject my match argument?* The other major way of testing an evaluation argument is to anticipate how readers may object to your stated reasons and grounds. Will readers challenge you by showing that you have cherry-picked your examples and evidence? Will they provide counterexamples and counterevidence?

Figure 14.2 Organization plan 2: Criteria and match interwoven

Introduce the issue and state your claim.	• Engage reader's interest in your evaluation issue and show why it is controversial or problematic. • Show what's at stake. • Provide background information needed by your audience. • State your claim.
Present series of criterion-match arguments.	• State and develop criterion 1 and argue that your case meets (does not meet) the criterion. • State and develop criterion 2 and argue that your case meets (does not meet) the criterion. • Continue with the rest of your criterion-match arguments.
Respond to possible objections to your argument.	• Anticipate and summarize possible objections. • Respond to the objections through rebuttal or concession.
Conclude.	• Perhaps sum up your argument. • Help reader return to the "big picture" of what's at stake. • End with something memorable.

Critiquing an Ethical Argument

Ethical arguments can be critiqued through appeals to consequences or principles. If an argument appeals primarily to principles, it can be vulnerable to a simple cost analysis. What are the costs of adhering to this principle? There will undoubtedly be some, or else there would be no real argument. If the argument is based strictly on consequences, we should ask whether it violates any rules or principles, particularly such commandments as the Golden Rule—"Do unto others as you would have others do unto you"—which most members of our audience adhere to. By failing to mention these alternative ways of thinking about ethical issues, we undercut not only our argument but our credibility as well.

Readings

Our first reading, by student writer Lorena Mendoza-Flores, critiques her former high school for the way it marginalizes Hispanic students. Lorena, a physics major in college, has changed the name of her high school and chosen not to reveal her home state.

Student Essay

Silenced and Invisible:
Problems of Hispanic Students at Valley High School

Lorena Mendoza-Flores

Every year, thousands of Mexican families come to the United States in order to escape economic hardships in Mexico and hope for better schools for their children. While many American schools try to accommodate immigrant non-native speakers, many immigrant families, according to case-study interviews, have increasingly negative perceptions of these attempts (Roessingh). There are action plans to bridge the gap between disadvantaged and advantaged students, yet Hispanic ESL (English as a Second Language) youth continue to perform considerably below that of other students (Good et al.). These problems pose the question: What is wrong with the way our schools treat Hispanic immigrants? Perhaps we could gain some understanding if we looked at a specific school—my own Valley High School in an agricultural region of [name of state]. Valley High School is a perfect example of a school with a growing Hispanic population, well-intentioned teachers, and hopes for Latino students' success that simply fall through. The failures at my school include inadequate ESL training for teachers, inadequate counseling for immigrant students, poor multicultural training for all teachers, and failure to value Hispanic identity and provide support for families.

Despite the fact that the Valley School District has 52 percent Hispanic students, a large percentage of whom have Spanish as their first language and parents who speak only Spanish, the staff at Valley High School is overwhelmingly white, with only one Hispanic teacher and only three or four teachers who speak Spanish. Even with a large number of ESL students, Valley High School has not hired teachers who are adequately trained in ESL. There is only one ESL teacher, who is responsible for all the ESL students. These students are assigned to regular classes and then go to the ESL classrooms for what is supposed to be extra support. When I've gone into the ESL classroom, I've found students surfing random sites online and the teacher, also the yearbook advisor, working on pages for the annual. Because I was senior editor of the yearbook, he was very open to talking to me about his students, always complaining that they didn't work hard enough even though I could see they weren't being given meaningful work. I was frustrated because it was obvious that the ESL classroom did not engage either the students or the teacher. The students' language progress remained stagnant, while the expectations of standardized testing became increasingly more demanding, dooming ESL students to failure.

Another problem is inadequate counseling for Hispanic students and inadequate methods of assessing their progress so they can be placed in the right classes. When immigrant students need help, teachers often recruit other students to address their needs. As a student mentor, I was called upon a few times to speak with students about their performance in class. In one particular situation, the math teacher called me in to talk to a student who had decided to drop out. The teacher was visibly concerned for the

(continued)

student's welfare but didn't have any means for understanding or addressing the student's issues. The student told me that he did not feel like he belonged at school. The lack of adequate counseling sent the message that immigrant students were not worth fighting for to stay in our school.

Additionally, when students enter the school, their skills in other coursework are not taken into consideration. All ESL students are placed in the basic math and English courses, and while they might move down, sometimes as far as being placed in special education classes, they're never moved up. A student's aptitude in math or science may never get recognized in the four years that he or she is in high school because the ESL students move as a single group and take just about all coursework together. Their status as ESL students becomes the sole determinant of their identity as a student within the school system, and they are not given the same considerations and levels of attention required to grow and develop academically. Personally, I have fallen victim to our school's overlooking of student progress. When I entered the Valley School District in 8th grade, I had already taken several years of algebra and tested far above other students in my grade. At my previous school in another district, I had surpassed the school's highest level of math. In fact, my 5th–7th grade math instructor had to find advanced online material for me so that I could keep progressing. Entering the Valley School District, however, I regressed two years. Even though I communicated to both my math teacher and the counselor that I was being placed too low and that the nearby high school had several higher-level courses, I was kept in the same class. The next year, I was shocked to see that two 8th grade white students were in my 9th grade geometry class; the system had catered to them while it had denied to me an acknowledgement of the same earned achievement. I felt dismissed because I was Hispanic.

5   A third problem is that outside of the ESL classroom, in the regular classroom settings, teachers are often untrained in how to create safe multicultural dialogue. One time in sociology my teacher asked the class why the Hispanic students were performing so much worse than white students. I tried to explain that our support was inadequate. I stated that since most Hispanic students came from immigrant backgrounds, our parents weren't able to help us maneuver through the school system. In doing our homework, we had no one to turn to, and if the instructions were unclear, we did not have access to a resource such as an English-speaking parent, something that many white students and faculty never even thought about when considering this gap in performance. When I started talking about these things, white students around the room started becoming upset. They argued that they were hard workers and didn't have their parents do their homework for them. Obviously, my point was not to dismiss their efforts but to emphasize that these are two different worlds we're living in. Coming from an immigrant background, I and my fellow Hispanic students undoubtedly had more obstacles to overcome every step of the way. What was most troubling about this situation was that at no point did my sociology teacher step up and defend the validity of my arguments. Teachers need to know how to facilitate these multicultural clashes by helping make injustices more visible rather than marginalizing someone for bringing up uncomfortable issues.

Finally, Valley High School does little to honor cultural identity or reach out to immigrant families. My senior year I was president of the International

Club (the only club at our school that had lots of immigrant student participation). Without my consent, or that of the members, my advisor began a transition to convert the International Club into the InterAct club affiliated with the community's Rotaract Club (part of Rotary). While this new connection with the Rotary would provide more funding, the only club that was primarily made up of Hispanic members was now being taken over by one sponsored by an all-white organization. In this transition, our advisor had pre-elected leaders (also all white) to move it forward. By the time I graduated, the transition was well underway. In fact, on Cinco de Mayo, International Club's major event every year, our club members realized that our advisor didn't think this event was worth our time. As the only Mexican teacher, this advisor did not even advocate for the desires of our community. Ultimately, she turned her back on the members, and the following year InterAct became a primarily white club, just like every other club at school.

The loss of a club supporting Hispanic students is matched by failure to create a welcoming environment for Hispanic parents and families. When immigrant parents come to the school, they have to wait around until they can find a translator if they want to speak to a teacher or administrator. Usually this interpreter is another student, creating awkward moments for parents who don't want to discuss their children's problems in front of another student. The school occasionally does try to reach out to Hispanic parents by holding Hispanic Nights where all the events are held in Spanish. However, all the other school events are held only in English. Considering that the school population is more than half Hispanic, the absence of any interpreters makes it clear the school thinks of itself as white. In addition, there are no translators at larger school events such as academic award nights or sporting banquets. As a result, immigrant parents and families feel isolated from the school and unwelcomed.

Debate remains over the exact or best procedures for helping immigrant ESL students successfully integrate into schools, but what is not debated is that these students deserve equal opportunities to learn and grow. Just as any other students, immigrant students should meet the demanding academic standards needed for higher education, but first they must have adequate support. It is essential that schools support educational reforms that address the problem areas apparent at Valley High School. Particularly, schools need to hire qualified ESL instructors, provide adequate counseling for immigrant students, enable teachers to develop multicultural sensitivity and skills at handling ethnic conflict, and provide outreach to immigrant families while valuing their culture.

Works Cited

Good, Mary Ellen, et al. "Latino English Language Learners: Bridging Achievement and Cultural Gaps Between Schools and Families." *Journal of Latinos & Education*, vol. 9, no. 4, 2010, pp. 321–39.

Roessingh, Hetty. "The Teacher Is the Key: Building Trust in ESL High School Programs." *Canadian Modern Language Review*, vol. 62, no. 4, 2006, pp. 563–90.

Our final reading, by Judith Daar and Erez Aloni, addresses ethical issues emerging from recent research on therapeutic cloning at the Oregon Health and Sciences University. It appeared as an op-ed piece in the *Los Angeles Times*. Judith Daar, a professor of both law and medicine, is a member of the Ethics Committee of the American Society for Reproductive Medicine. Her co-author Erez Aloni is a professor at Whittier Law School.

Three Genetic Parents—For One Healthy Baby

JUDITH DAAR AND EREZ ALONI

Since January, a new California law allows for a child to have more than two legal parents. But children are still limited to two genetic parents. That could change soon, if the Food and Drug Administration approves human clinical trials for a technique known as mitochondrial replacement, which would enable a child to inherit DNA from three parents.

News of the pending application has caused a kind of panic not seen since Dolly the sheep was cloned, raising the possibility of a single genetic parent. But far from being the end of the human race as we know it, the technique might be a way to prevent hundreds of mitochondrial-linked diseases, which affect about one in 5,000 people.

The idea of multi-person reproductive collaborations is not new. Over the last several decades we have acclimated to various forms of assisted reproductive technologies. Indeed, in the U.S. about 75,000 infants are born each year to parents who enlist the aid of egg donors, sperm donors, or gestational carriers. These methods, however, still involve the "traditional" merger of DNA from one male and one female.

Mitochondrial replacement would alter this two-genetic-parent model by introducing a third set of DNA into the procreative process. The technique would enable women who carry harmful mutations in their mitochondria to have a child without those harmful mutations. As with all human reproduction, the child would carry a combination of genes from one male and one female. However, in this technique, the nucleus of the mother's egg would be injected into a "third parent's" nucleus-free egg containing healthy mitochondrial DNA. As a result, the child would inherit the characteristics of the original male and female but have healthy mitochondria from a third person.

5   Experiments employing the technique conducted on monkeys resulted in healthy offspring that did not carry the harmful mutation. Now, a team at Oregon Health and Sciences University is seeking approval from the FDA to begin human clinical trials.

It seems likely that, if it is proved safe and effective, mitochondrial replacement will eventually join the panoply of techniques facilitating the birth of healthy children through assisted conception. But it should be no surprise that the new technology is causing a furor.

The introduction of assisted reproductive technologies has followed a predictable pattern: initial panic followed by widespread condemnation, followed by gradual acceptance as a technique becomes more widespread. In the 1950s, when reports of pregnancies using donor sperm first appeared in medical journals, lawmakers declared the process "mechanical adultery" and sought its criminalization. Early reports of success with in vitro fertilization in the 1970s provoked editorials that decried the process as totally immoral. In the 1990s, the introduction of pre-implantation diagnosis of genetic diseases provoked allegations of a war on disabled individuals.

Today, detractors remain, but the methods have been embraced as the standard of care in reproductive medicine. Once a technique proves safe and effective, its ability to assist in the birth of healthy children generally paves the way for public approval.

For some, the introduction of a third genetic parent is alarming because the novel genetic configuration could be embedded in the child's DNA in perpetuity, with unknown implications for future generations. But the panic also rests in part on simple discomfort with upending the notion of genetic parenthood involving just two people.

A similar anxiety seized the public this year after California authorized judges 10 to recognize more than two people as a child's lawful parents. The law grew out of a horrendous situation in which the court's inability to recognize a third parent diverted a young child into foster care. Though it's hardly on par with the scientific breakthrough represented by mitochondrial replacement, the so-called three-parent law stirred deep fears about the durability of traditional family life in the modern era.

But the fears about three-parent possibilities—both genetic and legal—are likely to subside as people realize that they are aimed at one goal: the well-being of children. The California law orders judges to recognize three parents when not doing so "would otherwise be detrimental to the child." And mitochondrial replacement will be employed to avoid transmission of a heritable disease. If the "power of three" has the ability to improve a child's well-being, isn't that something worth embracing?

Chapter 15
Proposal Arguments

Learning Objectives

In this chapter you will learn to:

15.1 Explain the special features and concerns of proposal arguments.

15.2 Use a problem-solution-justification structure to develop proposal arguments.

15.3 Use heuristic strategies to develop supporting reasons for your proposal argument.

15.4 Use words and images to create an advocacy poster or advertisement.

15.5 Write your own proposal argument.

Proposal arguments are essential for the workings of a free and open society. A proposal argument motivates its audience to recognize a problem and then proposes a solution to the problem. When effective, proposal arguments call an audience to action. Whether you are writing a grant proposal to seek funding for a research project, a practical proposal for remedying a problem at your workplace, or a policy proposal to address a national issue, proposal arguments are among the most important kinds of writing you will ever be called upon to produce.

Case 1: Should the Supreme Court Overturn Roe v. Wade?

Among the most heated debates in the United States is whether the due process and privacy protections of the Fourteenth Amendment can be extended to a woman's right to an abortion. The right-to-life movement has intensified its efforts to restrict access to abortions at the state level and to overturn *Roe v. Wade* in the U.S. Supreme Court. Meanwhile, pro-choice advocates such as Planned Parenthood have vigorously defended a woman's right to an abortion. Both sides make effective use of visual arguments. Right-to-life groups frequently use posters showing ultrasound images of unborn babies (often not using the word "fetus"). The poster in Figure 15.1, sponsored by Planned Parenthood, features a starkly black question mark that on second look is seen to be made from a coat hanger. It makes an

Figure 15.1 Planned Parenthood poster

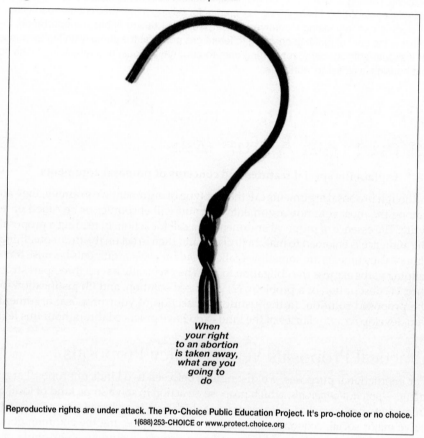

*When
your right
to an abortion
is taken away,
what are you
going to
do*

Reproductive rights are under attack. The Pro-Choice Public Education Project. It's pro-choice or no choice.
1(688)253-CHOICE or www.protect.choice.org

implied proposal claim ("Abortion should remain legal") and supports it with a consequence argument: If abortions are outlawed, women will have abortions anyway—using coat hangers instead of medically safe procedures. The image of the coat hanger (reminiscent of horror stories about abortions prior to *Roe v. Wade)* appeals simultaneously to *logos* and *pathos.*

Case 2: How Should the United States Reduce the Carbon Footprint of Automobiles?

The concern for climate change—combined with the high price of gasoline—has increased the popularity of small, energy-efficient cars. Much debated among policy makers is the role that federal or state governments should play in further promoting a green transportation system. Some argue that the government should stay out of free markets, letting buyers decide for themselves what kinds of cars they want to buy. Others argue that free markets do not currently make gasoline consumers pay for the "externalities" (societal costs) of gasoline consumption—particularly the cost to the environment of emitting more carbon into the atmosphere. Concerned citizens have proposed dozens of ideas for reducing the carbon footprint of cars and trucks. Among the proposals are the following: placing a "green tax" on gasoline; requiring auto manufacturers to increase the fuel efficiency of their fleets; giving tax credits for buying a fuel-efficient car, particularly an electric car; increasing incentives for carpooling or taking public transportation; increasing the cost of parking; charging different gas prices at the pump (with higher prices for less fuel-efficient cars); retrofitting cars to burn natural gas; and rebuilding cities so that housing is closer to worksites.

The Special Features and Concerns of Proposal Arguments

15.1 Explain the special features and concerns of proposal arguments.

Although proposal arguments are the last type of argument we examine, they are among the most common arguments that you will encounter or be called on to write. The essence of proposal arguments is a call for action. In reading a proposal, the audience is enjoined to make a decision and then to act on it—to *do* something. Proposal arguments are sometimes called *should or ought* arguments because those helping verbs express the obligation to act. They typically have a three-part structure: (1) description of a problem, (2) proposed solution, and (3) justification for the proposed solution. In the justification section of your proposal argument, you develop *because* clauses of the kinds you have practiced throughout this text.

Practical Proposals Versus Policy Proposals

For instructional purposes, we distinguish between two kinds of proposal arguments—*practical proposals*, which propose an action to solve some kind of local or immediate problem, and *policy proposals*, which propose a broad plan of action to solve major social, economic, or political problems affecting the common good. A student's proposal to build bike paths on campus would be an example of a practical proposal. In contrast, an argument that the United States should abolish the income tax would be a policy proposal.

The primary difference is the narrowness versus breadth of the concern. Practical proposals are narrow, local, and concrete; they focus on the nuts and bolts of getting something done in the here and now. They are often concerned with the exact size of a piece of steel, the precise duties of a new person to be hired, or a close estimate of the cost of paint or computers to be purchased. Policy proposals, in contrast, are concerned with the broad outline and shape of a course of action, often on a regional, national, or even international issue. What government should do about overcrowding of prisons would be a problem addressed by policy proposals. How to improve the security alarm system for the county jail would be addressed by a practical proposal.

Learning to write both kinds of proposals is valuable. Researching and writing a policy proposal is an excellent way to practice the responsibilities of citizenship, which require the ability to understand complex issues and to weigh positive and negative consequences of policy choices. In your professional life, writing practical proposals may well be among your most important duties on the job. Effective proposal writing is the lifeblood of many companies and constitutes one of the most powerful ways you can identify and help solve problems.

Toulmin Framework for a Proposal Argument

The Toulmin schema is particularly useful for proposal arguments because it helps you support your proposal with reasons linked to your audience's beliefs, assumptions, and values. Suppose that your university is debating whether to banish fraternities and sororities. Suppose further that you are in favor of banishing the Greek system. One of your arguments is that eliminating the Greek system will improve your university's academic reputation. The following chart shows how you might use the Toulmin schema to make this line of reasoning as persuasive as possible.

Toulmin Analysis of the Greek System Argument

ENTHYMEME

CLAIM Our university should eliminate the Greek system

REASON because doing so will improve our university's academic reputation.

GROUNDS

Evidence that eliminating the Greek system will improve our academic reputation:

- Excessive party atmosphere of some Greek houses emphasizes social life rather than studying—we are known as a party school.

- Last year the average GPA of students in fraternities and sororities was lower than the GPA of non-Greek students.

- New pledges have so many house duties and initiation rites that their studies suffer.

- Many new students think about rush more than about the academic life.

CONDITIONS OF REBUTTAL

Attacking the reason and grounds

- Many of the best students are Greeks. Last year's highest-GPA award went to a sorority woman, and several other Greeks won prestigious graduate school scholarships.

- Statistics on grades are misleading. Many houses had a much higher average GPA than the university average. Total GPA was brought down by a few rowdy houses.

- Many other high-prestige universities have Greek systems.

- There are ways to tone down the party atmosphere on campus without abolishing the Greek system.

- Greeks contribute significantly to the community through service projects.

WARRANT

It is good for our university to achieve a better academic reputation.

BACKING

- The school would attract more serious students, leading to increased prestige.

- Campus would be more academically focused and attract better faculty.

- Losing the "party-school" reputation would put us in better light for taxpayers and legislators.

- Students would graduate with more skills and knowledge.

CONDITIONS OF REBUTTAL

Attacking the warrant and backing

- No one will argue that it is not good to have a strong academic reputation.

- However, skeptics may say that eliminating sororities and fraternities won't improve the university's academic reputation but will hurt its social life and its wide range of living options.

Special Concerns for Proposal Arguments

In their call for action, proposal arguments entail certain emphases and audience concerns that you don't generally face with other kinds of arguments. Let's look briefly at some of these special concerns.

- *The need for presence.* To persuade people to *act* on your proposal, particularly if the personal or financial cost of acting is high, you must give your argument presence as well as intellectual force. By *presence* we mean an argument's ability to grip your readers' hearts and imaginations as well as their intellects. You can give presence to an argument through appeals to *pathos,* such as effective use of details, provocative statistics, dialogue, illustrative narratives, and compelling examples that show the reader the seriousness of the problem you are addressing or the consequences of not acting on your proposal.

- *The need to overcome people's natural conservatism.* Another difficulty with proposals is the innate conservatism of all human beings, whatever their political persuasion, as suggested by the popular adage "If it ain't broke, don't fix it." The difficulty of proving that something needs fixing is compounded by the fact that frequently the status quo appears to be working. So, when writing a proposal, sometimes you can't argue that what we have is bad, but only that what we could have would be better. Often, then, a proposal argument will be based not on present evils but on the evils of lost potential. And getting an audience to accept lost potential may be difficult indeed, given the inherently abstract nature of potentiality.

- *The difficulty of predicting future consequences.* Most proposal makers will be forced to predict consequences of their proposed action. As the "law of unintended consequences" suggests, few major decisions lead neatly to their anticipated results without surprises along the way. So when we claim that our proposal will lead to good consequences, we can expect our audience to be skeptical.

- *The problem of evaluating consequences.* A final problem for proposal writers is the difficulty of evaluating consequences. In government and industry, managers often use a *cost-benefit analysis* to reduce all consequences to a single-scale comparison, usually money. Although this scale may work well in some circumstances, it can lead to grotesquely inappropriate conclusions in other situations. Just how does one balance the environmental benefits of a green tax on gasoline against the suffering of drivers who can't afford to get to work? Also, a benefit for one group often entails a cost for others. For example, a higher minimum wage will benefit low-wage workers at a cost to consumers, who must pay higher prices, or to other low-wage workers who get laid off.

These, then, are some of the general difficulties facing someone who sets out to write a proposal argument. Although these difficulties may seem daunting, the rest of this chapter offers strategies to help you overcome them and produce a successful proposal.

Examining Visual Arguments

A Proposal Claim

This photo of a dead baby albatross on a Pacific island near an albatross nesting ground resembles the photos taken by environmental photographer Chris Jordan in his well-known 2009 exhibit entitled *Midway: Message from the Gyre*. The purpose of that exhibit was to draw attention to the effects of the increasing amount of ocean garbage on albatrosses, which mistake the garbage for food. How could this photo be used to generate concern and activism regarding this environmental problem? The colorful, plastic-filled carcass of the baby albatross creates a complex appeal to *pathos* in the way that it illustrates the problem. What verbal text would you use to interpret the photo's message and call people to action?

Developing a Proposal Argument

15.2 Use a problem-solution-justification structure to develop proposal arguments.

Writers of proposal arguments must focus on three main phases or stages of the argument: showing that a problem exists, explaining the proposed solution, and offering a justification.

Convincing Your Readers That a Problem Exists

There is one argumentative strategy generic to all proposal arguments: calling your reader's attention to a problem. In some situations, your intended audience may already be aware of the problem and may have even asked for solutions. In such cases, you do not need to develop the problem extensively or motivate your audience to solve it. But in most situations, awakening your readers to the existence of a problem—a problem they may not have recognized before—is your first important challenge. You must give your problem presence through anecdotes, telling statistics, or other means that show readers how the problem affects people or otherwise has important stakes. Your goal is to gain your readers' intellectual assent to the depth, range, and potential seriousness of the problem and thereby motivate them to want to solve it.

Typically, the arguer develops the problem in one of two places: either (1) in the introduction prior to the presentation of the arguer's proposed solution or (2) in the body of the paper as the first main reason justifying the proposed solution. In the second instance the writer's first *because* clause has the following structure: "We should do this action *because* it addresses a serious problem."

Here is how one student writer gave presence to a proposal, addressed to the chair of the mathematics department at her school, calling for redesign of the first-year calculus curriculum in order to slow its pace. She wants the chair to see the problem from her perspective.

Example Passage Giving Presence to a Problem

I want to become a high-school math teacher. For me, the problem with introductory calculus is not its difficulty but its pace. My own experience in the Calculus 134 and 135 sequence last year showed me that it was not the learning of calculus that was difficult for me. I was able to catch on to the new concepts. My problem was that it went too fast. Just as I was assimilating new concepts and feeling the need to reinforce them, the class was on to a new topic before I had full mastery of the old concept.... Part of the reason for the fast pace is that calculus is a feeder course for computer science and engineering. If prospective engineering students can't learn calculus rapidly, they drop out of the program. The high dropout rate benefits the Engineering School because it uses the math course to weed out an overabundance of engineering majors. Thus the pace of the calculus course is geared to the needs of the engineering curriculum, not to the needs of someone like me, who wants to be a high-school mathematics teacher and who believes that my own difficulties with math—combined with my love for it—might make me an excellent math teacher.

By describing the fast pace of the math curriculum from the perspective of a future math teacher rather than an engineering student, this writer brings visibility to a problem. What before didn't look like a problem (it is good to weed out weak engineering majors) suddenly became a problem (it is bad to weed out future math teachers). Establishing herself as a serious student genuinely interested in learning calculus, she gave presence to the problem by calling attention to it in a new way.

Explaining the Proposed Solution: Showing the Specifics of Your Proposal

Having decided that there is a problem to be solved, you should lay out your thesis, which is a proposal for solving the problem. Your goal now is to stress the feasibility of your solution, including costs. The art of proposal making is the art of the possible. Certainly, not all proposals require elaborate descriptions of the implementation process. For example, if you are proposing that a local PTA chapter buy new tumbling mats for the junior-high gym classes, the procedures for buying the mats will probably be irrelevant. But in many arguments, the specifics of your proposal—the actual step-by-step methods of implementing it—may be instrumental in winning your audience's support.

You will also need to show how your proposal will solve the problem either partially or wholly. Sometimes you may first need to convince your reader that the problem is solvable and not something intractably rooted in "the way things are," such as earthquakes or jealousy. In other words, expect that some members of your audience will be skeptical about the ability of any proposal to solve the problem you are addressing. You may need, therefore, to "listen" to this point of view in your refutation section and to argue that your problem is at least partially solvable.

To persuade your audience that your proposal can work, you can follow any one of several approaches. A typical approach is to use a causal argument to show that your solution is feasible. Another approach is to use a resemblance argument to show how similar proposals have been successful elsewhere. Or, if similar things have failed in the past, you try to show how the present situation is different.

Offering a Justification: Convincing Your Readers That the Benefits of Your Proposal Outweigh the Costs

The justification phase of a proposal argument will need extensive development in some arguments and minimal development in others, again depending on your particular problem and the rhetorical context of your proposal. If your audience already acknowledges the seriousness of the problem you are addressing and has simply been waiting for the right solution to come along, then your argument will be successful, provided you can convince your audience that your solution will work and that it won't cost too much. Such arguments depend on the clarity of your proposal and the feasibility of its implementation.

But what if the costs are high? What if your readers don't think the problem is serious? What if they don't appreciate the benefits of solving the problem or the bad consequences of not solving it? In such cases you have to develop persuasive reasons for enacting your proposal. You may also have to determine who has the power to act on your proposal and apply arguments directly to that person's or agency's immediate interests. You need to know to whom or to what your power source is beholden or responsive. You must also know what values your power source holds that can be appealed to. In short, you're looking for the best pressure points.

Using Heuristic Strategies to Develop Supporting Reasons for Your Proposal

15.3 Use heuristic strategies to develop supporting reasons for your proposal argument.

To help you find supporting reasons for your proposal—the pressure points that will move your audience—we offer two heuristic strategies. (A *heuristic* is an exploratory problem-solving technique or invention aid that helps you generate ideas.) We call these heuristics the *claim types strategy* and the *stock issues strategy*.

The Claim Types Strategy

In Chapter 11 we explained how evaluation and proposal claims often use claims about category, cause, or resemblance for their supporting reasons. This fact leads to a powerful idea-generating strategy based on arguments from category (particularly from a category of actions that adhere to a certain principle), on arguments from consequences, or on arguments from resemblance. Table 15.1 illustrates this claim types strategy.

Before we give you some simple strategies for using this approach, let's illustrate it with another example.

Example

The United States should levy a "carbon tax" on carbon-based fuels

- because such a tax accords with the free-market principle that the price of a good should reflect the full cost of production (category/principle).
- because such a tax will accelerate the transition to cleaner fuels and thus help reduce global warming (cause/consequence).
- because this approach is similar to the market-based tax on sulfur emissions that helped solve the problem of acid rain (resemblance).

Note how each of these supporting reasons appeals to the value system of different kinds of voters. The writer argues that a carbon tax belongs to the category of things that use free market principles (particularly valued by conservative, pro-business voters); that it will lead to the good consequence of reducing global warming (valued particularly by environmentalists and others worried about climate change); and that it is similar to something that has already proved successful (the market-based approach to fighting acid rain, which has been applauded by both liberals and conservatives). The claim types strategy for generating ideas is easy to apply in practice. Table 15.2 shows you how.

Table 15.1 Explanation of Claim Types Strategy for Supporting a Proposal Claim

Claim Type	Generic Template	Example from Biotechnology Issue
Argument from principle or category	We should do this action • because doing so adheres to this good principle [or] • because this action belongs to this good category	We should support genetically modified foods • because doing so values scientific reason over emotion [or] • because genetically modified foods are safe [belong to the category of safe things]
Argument from consequences	• because this action will lead to these good consequences	• because biotech crops can reduce world hunger • because biotech crops can improve the environment by reducing use of pesticides
Argument from resemblance	• because this action has been done successfully elsewhere [or] • because this action is like this other good action	• because genetic modification is like natural crossbreeding that has been accelerated [or] • because genetic modification of food is like scientific advancements in medicine

Table 15.2 Suggestions for Applying the Claim Types Strategy to Your Proposal

Claim Type	Your Goal	Thinking Strategy
Argument from principle or category	Show how your proposed action follows a principle valued by your audience or belongs to a category valued by your audience.	Think of how your proposed action adheres to an audience-valued rule or principle or belongs to an audience-valued category (for example, "doing this action is kind, just, constitutional, appropriately restrained, safe, efficient, and so forth").
Argument from consequences	Show how your proposed action will lead to consequences valued by your audience.	Brainstorm consequences of your proposal and identify those that the audience will agree are good.
Argument from resemblance	Show how your proposed action has been done successfully elsewhere or is like another action valued by your audience.	Find analogies that compare your proposed action to something the audience already values or find previous places or times that your proposed action (or something similar to it) has been done successfully.

For Writing and Discussion

Generating Ideas Using the Claim Types Strategy

Individual task:

Use the strategies of principle/category, consequence, and resemblance to create *because* clauses that support each of the following claims. Try to have at least one *because* clause for each of the claim types, but generate as many reasons as possible. Don't worry about whether any individual reason exactly fits the category. The purpose is to stimulate thinking, not fill in the slots.

Example

Congress should not pass gun-control laws (proposal claim)

- because the Second Amendment guarantees the right to own guns (principle or category).
- because owning a gun allows citizens to protect themselves, their homes, and their loved ones from intruders (consequence).
- because laws to ban guns will be as ineffective as laws to ban alcohol during Prohibition (resemblance).

Claims:

1. For graduation, colleges should require one course with an integrated community service component.
2. Restaurants should be required to post calorie counts and other ingredient information for all menu items.
3. Division-1 college athletes should receive salaries.

Group task:

Share your efforts with classmates. Then, working in small groups or as a class, repeat the exercise, taking the opposite position on each issue.

The Stock Issues Strategy

Another effective heuristic for a proposal argument is to ask yourself a series of questions based on the stock issues strategy. For example, suppose you wanted to develop the following argument: "To solve the problem of students who won't take risks with their writing, the faculty should adopt a pass/fail method of grading in all writing courses." The stock issues strategy invites the writer to consider "stock" ways (that is, common, usual, frequently repeated ways) that such arguments can be conducted.

Stock issue 1: *Is there really a problem here that needs to be solved?* Is it really true that a large number of student writers won't take risks in their writing? Is this problem more serious than other writing problems, such as undeveloped ideas, lack of organization, and poor sentence structure? This stock issue invites the writer to convince her audience that a true problem exists. Conversely, an opponent of the proposal may argue that a true problem does not exist.

Stock issue 2: *Will the proposed solution really solve this problem?* Is it true that a pass/fail grading system will cause students to take more risks with their writing? Will more interesting, surprising, and creative essays result from pass/fail grading? Or will students simply put less effort into their writing? This stock issue prompts a supporter to demonstrate that the proposal will solve the problem; it also prompts the opponent to show that the proposal won't work.

Stock issue 3: *Can the problem be solved more simply, without disturbing the status quo?* An opponent of the proposal may agree that a problem exists and that the proposed solution might solve it. However, the opponent may say, "Are there not less radical ways to solve this problem? If we want more creative and risk-taking student essays, can't we just change our grading criteria so that we reward risky papers and penalize conventional ones?" This stock issue prompts supporters to show that *only* the proposed solution will solve the problem and that no minor tinkering with the status quo will be adequate. Conversely, opponents will argue that the problem can be solved without acting on the proposal.

Stock issue 4: *Is the proposed solution really practical? Does it stand a chance of actually being enacted?* Here an opponent to the proposal may agree that the proposal would work but contends that it involves pie-in-the-sky idealism. Nobody will vote to change the existing system so radically; therefore, it is a waste of our time to debate it. Following this prompt, supporters would have to argue that pass/fail grading is workable and that enough faculty members are in favor of it that the proposal is worth debating. Opponents may argue that the faculty is so traditional that pass/fail has no chance of being accepted, despite its merits.

Stock issue 5: *What will be the unforeseen positive and negative consequences of the proposal?* Suppose we do adopt a pass/fail system. What positive or negative consequences may occur that are different from our initial predictions? Using this prompt, an opponent may argue that pass/fail grading will reduce the effort put forth by students and that the long-range effect will be writing of even lower quality than we have now. Supporters would try to find positive consequences—perhaps a new love of writing for its own sake rather than for the sake of a grade.

For Writing and Discussion

Brainstorming Ideas for a Proposal

The following collaborative exercise takes you through the process of creating a proposal argument.

1. In small groups, identify and list several major problems facing students in your college or university.
2. Decide among yourselves which are the most important of these problems and rank them in order of importance.
3. Take your group's number-one problem and explore answers to the following questions. Group recorders should be prepared to present their group's answers to the class.
    a. Why is the problem a problem?
    b. For whom is the problem a problem?
    c. How will these people suffer if the problem is not solved? (Give specific examples.)
    d. Who has the power to solve the problem?
    e. Why hasn't the problem been solved up to this point?
    f. How can the problem be solved? (That is, create a proposal.)
    g. What are the probable benefits of acting on your proposal?
    h. What costs are associated with your proposal?
    i. Who will bear those costs?
    j. Why should this proposal be enacted?
    k. Why is it better than alternative proposals?
4. As a group, draft an outline for a proposal argument in which you
    a. describe the problem and its significance.
    b. propose your solution to the problem.
    c. justify your proposal by showing how the benefits of adopting that proposal outweigh the costs.
5. Recorders for each group should write their group's outline on the board and be prepared to explain it to the class.

Proposal Arguments as Advocacy Posters or Advertisements

15.4 Use words and images to create an advocacy poster or advertisement.

A frequently encountered kind of proposal argument is the one-page newspaper or magazine advertisement often purchased by advocacy groups to promote a cause. Such arguments also appear as web pages or as posters or fliers. These condensed advocacy arguments are marked by their bold, abbreviated, tightly planned format. The creators of these arguments know they must work fast to capture our attention, give presence to a problem, advocate a solution, and enlist our support. Advocacy advertisements frequently use photographs, images, or icons that appeal to a reader's emotions and imagination. In addition to images, they often use different type sizes and styles. Large-type text in these documents frequently takes the form of slogans or condensed thesis statements written in an arresting style.

To outline and justify their solutions, creators of advocacy ads often put main supporting reasons in bulleted lists and sometimes enclose carefully selected facts and quotations in boxed sidebars. To add an authoritative *ethos,* the arguments often include fine-print footnotes and bibliographies. (For more detailed discussion of how advocacy posters and advertisements use images and arrange text for rhetorical effect, see Chapter 9 on visual argument.)

Another prominent feature of these condensed, highly visual arguments is their appeal to the audience through a direct call for a course of action: for example, go to an advocacy website to find more information on how to support the cause; send an e-mail to a decision maker or political representative; vote for or against the proposition or the candidate; or donate money to a cause.

Figure 15.2 shows an example of a student-produced advocacy poster. Here, environmental studies student Janie Bube urges residents of her city to build rain gardens to help solve the problem of excess stormwater. At the top of this poster, Janie gives the problem presence by using a flood photo she took during her internship fieldwork. She then offers her proposed solution, made visually appealing by another of her own photos—a neighborhood rain garden. She offers three reasons to justify the creation of rain gardens, asserting why and how rain gardens work. The final lines of the poster send readers to a website for more information. The rhetorical effect of the text, image, and layout is to attract readers' attention, remind them of the problem, and push them toward adopting her proposed solution.

Writing Assignment: A Proposal Argument

15.5 Write your own proposal argument.

Option 1: A Practical Proposal Addressing a Local Problem Write a practical proposal offering a solution to a local problem. Your proposal should have three main sections: (1) description of the problem, (2) proposed solution, and (3) justification. Proposals are usually accompanied by a *letter of transmittal*—a one-page business letter that introduces the proposal to its intended audience and provides some needed background about the writer. Document design is important in practical proposals, which are aimed at busy people who have to make many decisions under time constraints. An effective design helps establish the writer's *ethos* as a quality-oriented professional and helps make the reading of the proposal as easy as possible. For a student example of a practical proposal, see Megan Johnson's argument at the end of this chapter.

Option 2: A Policy Proposal as a Guest Editorial Write a two- to three-page policy proposal suitable for publication as a feature editorial in a college or city newspaper, on an appropriate website, or in a publication associated with a particular group, such as a church newsletter or employee bulletin. The voice and style of your argument should be aimed at readers of your chosen publication or website. Your editorial should have the following features:

1. The identification of a problem (Persuade your audience that this is a genuine problem that needs solving; give it presence.)
2. A proposal for action that will help alleviate the problem
3. A justification of your solution (the reasons why your audience should accept your proposal and act on it)

Option 3: A Researched Argument Proposing Public Policy Write an eight- to twelve-page proposal argument as a formal research paper, using researched data for development and support. In business and professional life, this kind of research proposal is often called a *white paper*, which recommends a course of action internally within an organization or externally to a client or stakeholder. An example of a researched policy proposal is student writer Ivan Snook's "Flirting with Disaster: An Argument against Integrating Women into the Combat Arms" at the end of this chapter.

Option 4: Multimedia Project: A One-Page Advocacy Poster or Advertise-ment Using the strategies of visual argument discussed in Chapter 9 and earlier in this chapter, create a one-page advocacy advertisement urging action on a public issue. Your advertisement should be designed for publication in a newspaper or website or for distribution as a poster or flier. For an example of a student-produced advocacy poster, see Janie Bube's poster in Figure 15.2.

Option 5: Multimedia Project: A Proposal Speech with Visual Aids Deliver a proposal argument as a prepared but extemporaneous speech of approximately five to eight minutes, supported with visual aids created on presentation software such as PowerPoint or Prezi. Your speech should present a problem, propose a solution, and justify the solution with reasons and evidence. Use visual aids to give presence to the problem and to enhance appeals to *logos*, *ethos*, and *pathos*.

Figure 15.2 Student advocacy poster

Is Stormwater Turning Your Street Into a Lake?

Installing green stormwater infrastructure technologies like rain gardens will address this problem.

Install a rain garden to:

- Slow, retain, and absorb runoff
- Replicate the functioning of a forest in cleaning pollutants from the water
- Add natural beauty

For further information contact RainWise through Seattle Public Utilities at rainwise@seattle.gov

Good aids use visual strategies to create encapsulated visual arguments; they are not simply bullet point outlines of your speech. Sandy Wainscott's speech outline and selected PowerPoint slides (at the end of this chapter) illustrate this genre.

Exploring Ideas

Because *should or ought* issues are among the most common sources of arguments, you may already have ideas for proposal issues. To think of ideas for practical proposals, try making an idea map of local problems you would like to see solved. For initial spokes, try trigger words such as the following:

- Problems at my university (dorms, parking, registration system, financial aid, campus appearance, clubs, curriculum, intramural program, athletic teams)
- Problems in my city or town (dangerous intersections, ugly areas, inadequate lighting, parks, police policy, public transportation, schools)
- Problems at my place of work (office design, flow of customer traffic, merchandise display, company policies)
- Problems related to my future career, hobbies, recreational time, life as a consumer, life as a homeowner

If you can offer a solution to the problem you identify, you may make a valuable contribution to some phase of public life.

To find a topic for policy proposals, stay in touch with the news, which will keep you aware of current debates on regional and national issues. Also, visit the websites of your congressional representatives to see what issues they are currently investigating and debating. You might think of your policy proposal as a white paper for one of your legislators.

Once you have decided on a proposal issue, we recommend you explore it by trying one or more of the following activities:

- Explore ideas by using the claim types strategy.
- Explore ideas by using the stock issues strategy.
- Explore ideas using the eleven questions (3a–3k) in the For Writing and Discussion exercise, "Brainstorming Ideas for a Proposal."

Identifying Your Audience and Determining What's at Stake

Before drafting your argument, identify your targeted audience and determine what's at stake. Consider your responses to the following questions:

- What audience are you targeting? What background do they need to understand your problem? How much do they already care about it? How could you motivate them to care?
- After they read your argument, what stance do you imagine them holding? What change do you want to bring about in their view or their behavior?
- What will they find uncomfortable or threatening about your proposal? Particularly, what costs will they incur by acting on your proposal?
- What objections might they raise? What counterarguments or alternative solutions will you need to address?
- Why does your proposal matter? What is at stake?

Figure 15.3 Organization plan for a proposal argument

Introduce and develop the problem.	• Engage readers' interest in your problem. • Provide background, including previous attempts to solve the problem. • Give the problem "presence" by showing who is affected and what is at stake. • Argue that the problem is solvable (optional).
Present your proposed solution to the problem.	• First, state your proposal concisely to serve as your thesis statement or claim. • Then, explain the specifics of your proposal.
Justify your proposed solution through a series of supporting reasons.	• Restate your claim and forecast your supporting reasons. • Present and develop reason 1. • Present and develop reason 2. • Present and develop additional reasons.
Respond to objections or to alternative proposals.	• Anticipate and summarize possible objections or alternative ways to solve the problem. • Respond appropriately through rebuttal or concession.
Conclude.	• Sum up your argument and help readers return to the "big picture" of what's at stake. • Call readers to action. • End with something memorable.

Organizing a Proposal Argument

When you write your draft, you may find it helpful to have at hand an organization plan for a proposal argument. The plan in Figure 15.3 shows a typical structure for a proposal argument. In some cases, you may want to summarize and rebut opposing views before you present the justification for your own proposal.

Designing a One-Page Advocacy Poster or Advertisement

As an alternative to a traditional written argument, your instructor may ask you to create a one-page advocacy advertisement. The first stage of your invention process should be the same as that for a longer proposal argument. Choose a controversial public issue that needs immediate attention or a neglected issue about which you want to arouse public passion. As with a longer proposal argument, consider your audience in order to identify the values and beliefs on which you will base your appeal.

When you construct your argument, the limited space available demands efficiency in your choice of words and in your use of document design. Your goal is to have a memorable impact on your reader in order to promote the action you advocate. The following questions may help you design and revise your advocacy ad:

1. How could photos or other graphic elements establish and give presence to the problem?

2. How can type size, type style, and layout be used to present the core of your proposal, including the justifying reasons, in the most powerful way for the intended audience?

3. Can any part of this argument be presented as a memorable slogan or catchphrase? What key phrases could highlight the parts or the main points of this argument?

4. How can document design clarify the course of action and the direct demand on the audience this argument is proposing?

5. How can use of color enhance the overall impact of your advocacy argument? (Note: One-page advertisements are expensive to reproduce in color, but you might make effective use of color if your advocacy ad were to appear as a poster or web page.)

Designing PowerPoint Slides or Other Visual Aids for a Speech

In designing visual aids, your goal is to increase the persuasive effect of your speech rather than to demonstrate your technical wizardry. A common mistake with PowerPoint presentations is to get enamored with the program's bells and whistles. If you find yourself thinking about special effects (animations, fade-outs, flashing letters) rather than about "at a glance" visual appeals to *logos or pathos*, you may be on the wrong track. Another common mistake is to use slides simply to project a bullet-point outline of your speech. Our best advice in designing slides is thus to "think visual argument."

In terms of visual argument, effective presentation slides can usually be placed in three design categories:

- Slides using images (photographs, drawings) to enhance *pathos* or to create a snapshot that visually clarifies a concept (*logos*)

- Slides using graphs or other visual displays of numbers to make numeric arguments

- Slides using bulleted (all-text) subpoints for evidence

All the strategies for visual arguments discussed in Chapter 9 and in this chapter under the heading "Proposal Arguments as Advocacy Posters or Advertisements" apply equally to presentation slides.

In most cases, the title of the slide should put into words the slide's *take-away point*. That is, the title should provide a verbal summary of the slide's visual argument. Most rhetoricians suggest that the title of a slide be a short sentence that makes a point rather than just a topic phrase.

Topic as Title (Weak)	Point as Title (Strong)
Coal and the Environment	Burning Coal Produces Dangerous Greenhouse Gases
The Effect of Money on Happiness	More Money Doesn't Mean More Happiness

Student writer Sandy Wainscott follows these principles in her speech and accompanying PowerPoint slides, shown in the reading at the end of this chapter.

Questioning and Critiquing a Proposal Argument

As we've suggested, proposal arguments need to overcome people's innate conservatism, the difficulty of anticipating all the consequences of a proposal, and so forth. What questions, then, can we ask about proposal arguments to help us anticipate these problems?

- *Will a skeptic deny that my problem is really a problem?* Be prepared for skeptics who aren't bothered by your problem, who see your problem as limited to a small group of people, or who think you are exaggerating.

- *Will a skeptic doubt the effectiveness of my solution?* A skeptic might agree that your problem is indeed important and worth solving but might not be convinced that your solution will work. For these skeptics, you'll need to provide evidence that your solution is feasible and workable. Also be prepared for skeptics who focus on the potential negative or unintended consequences of your proposed solution.

- *Will a skeptic think my proposal costs too much?* The most commonly asked question of any proposal is simply, "Do the benefits of enacting the proposal outweigh the costs?" Be wary of the (understandable) tendency to underestimate the costs and exaggerate the benefits of a proposal. Honesty will enhance your *ethos.*

- *Will a skeptic suggest counterproposals?* Once you've convinced readers that a problem exists, they are likely to suggest solutions different from yours. It makes sense to anticipate alternative solutions and to work out ways to argue why your solution is better. And who knows? You may end up liking the counterproposal better and changing your mind about what to propose!

Readings

Our first reading, by student writer Ivan Snook, is a researched public policy proposal written in response to the option 3 assignment in Learning Objective 15.5. Snook's argument is based both on library and Internet research and on personal experience (he is a returning veteran who served as a Marine infantry soldier in Iraq). The kairotic moment for this paper (written in March 2014) was a January 2014 decision by the Obama administration to allow women to serve in the combat arms—a policy decision to which Snook objects. Snook's paper is formatted as a formal research paper using the documentation style of the Modern Language Association (MLA). This format is explained in Appendix 2.

Ivan Snook

Dr. Johnson

Argumentative Writing

March 31, 2014

Flirting with Disaster: An Argument against Integrating
Women into the Combat Arms

In 2005 I was a rifleman for the elite 1st Reconnaissance Battalion in Iraq. My deployment was not all bad. When we returned to Camp Fallujah to repair our humvee we ate great chow, enjoyed good entertainment, and drank contraband vodka. I never had a girlfriend, though. I was too busy working in my all-male infantry unit. At the time I wished we had a few girls in the unit. What can I say? I wanted female companionship like the guys in noncombat jobs had. But I realized that women could never serve in the infantry because of the negative impact of boyfriend/girlfriend dramatics on unit morale, cohesiveness, and ultimately combat effectiveness.

However, America's civilian leadership recently moved towards integrating women into frontline combat arms units such as infantry, tanks, and artillery. In January 2014, Secretary of Defense Leon Panetta lifted the Pentagon's policy on all-male combat arms occupations. "The department's goal...is to ensure that the mission is met with the best qualified and most capable people, regardless of gender," he said. "I'm not talking about reducing the qualifications for the job—if they can meet the qualifications for the job, then they should have a right to serve" (qtd. in Michaels and Vanden Brook). President Obama expanded upon Panetta's sentiment by saying, "Every American can be proud *that our military will grow even stronger*, with our mothers, wives, sisters, and daughters playing a greater role in protecting this country we love" (qtd. in Michaels and Vanden Brook, emphasis mine.)

If this policy change will indeed strengthen our military, every American should support it. However, no one has specified how integrating women into the combat arms will strengthen our military. I wholeheartedly agree with integrationists who claim that women can meet the rigorous physical and mental requirements for frontline combat. Any CrossFit has at least half a dozen women more physically and mentally fit than some of my Marine brothers in arms. If those were the sole criteria by which we evaluate infantrymen, I would endorse integration. But, how an individual soldier affects the combat unit as a whole must be considered. The great military theorist Carl von Clausewitz coined the term "friction" to represent the "[c]ountless minor incidents . . . [that] combine to lower the general level of performance [of the military machine]." He continues, "We should bear in mind that none of its components is of one piece: each part is composed of individuals, every one of whom retains his potential of friction." Therefore, we must not judge individual soldiers only by their individual physical capabilities, but also by their impact on the unit as a whole.

Introducing women to previously all-male combat units means introducing the friction of romantic relationships. Petty jealousies and other dramatic relational issues combine to lower the general level of performance. In 1997, the nonprofit global policy think tank RAND Corporation studied how romantic relationships affect coed military units. The study reported that such relationships "sexualize" the work environment, making it "difficult for colleagues to regard one another as just coworkers. Thus, the cohesion of the unit is negatively affected" (Harrell and Miller 81). One respondent complained, "The [cafeteria] . . . at night looks more like a singles club or promenade deck than a cafeteria [for a military unit]." Another said, "I get tired of seeing a junior enlisted female and her boyfriend [at the cafeteria]. . . . This place is like high school all over again. Everyone is dating others. To me this is not the military. We are here to do a job not meet our spouse. Guys seem more worried about getting a girl than doing their job" (Harrell and Miller 81-82).

Integrationists claim the military's high level of discipline coupled with strict rules against fraternization will prevent romantic relationships. However, those strict rules have always been in place and have never worked. During the Gulf War, 5 percent of deployed women were sent home early due to pregnancy. The Navy sends home on average 10 percent of deployed female sailors for the same reason.

The USS *Theodore Roosevelt*, one of America's largest aircraft carriers, lost 45 of its 300 female sailors to pregnancy leave and became one of the many U.S. Navy ships to earn the nickname "The Love Boat" (Browne 246). My point is not about morality. These statistics demonstrate that despite strict rules against fraternization, 18-to-25-year-olds succumb to their natural urges. What else should one expect when young adults are locked away on ship or deployed to Afghanistan for months at a time? It is analogous to locking the doors on a coed college dormitory for a year and making rules against sex. It is preposterous to expect 18-to-25-year-olds to work, live, and relax together in such close proximity and expect no romantic relationships to sprout.

These problems are more than just trifling lovers' quarrels. They affect a serious decline in performance and can lead to a total breakdown of command structure. In 2005, Brian Kates of the *New York Daily News* visited Camp Bucca, a military prison in Southern Iraq, which he described as a drunken "out-of-control frat party." "In front of a cheering male audience, two young women wearing only bras and panties threw themselves into a mud-filled plastic kiddie pool and rolled around in a wild wrestling match." Sergeant Emil Ganim, who refereed the match, said other non-commissioned officers "had been lending out their rooms for soldiers to have sex." These were not just young privates, either. A witness told investigators that a drunken first sergeant and master sergeant, two high-ranking non-commissioned officers, were in attendance (Kates). Although Camp Bucca was far away from any actual fighting, it is safe to assume similar sexual antics and command-structure breakdowns will occur in coed frontline combat units, whose members confront their own mortality on a daily basis.

Still, Camp Bucca is not the worst-case scenario. The military is currently battling an epidemic of rape and sexual assault. A study conducted by the Department of Veterans' Affairs reported that one-third of female veterans say they were victims of rape or attempted rape. A third of those claim they were raped multiple times, and 14 percent claim they were gang raped (Browne). Introducing females to frontline combat units will only exacerbate the problem. Dr. David Grossman, one of the world's foremost experts on human aggression and the psychology of combat, has explained how combat stress affects the human sex drive. He analogizes the human body's ability to cope with stress to a bathtub: It can hold only so much water before overflowing. When our body overflows with stress, the midbrain releases hormones causing a fight-or-flight response, often followed by a dramatic change in hunger and sex drive. Grossman writes, "Some people lose their appetite for food in response to stress, but many have an enhanced craving to eat. In the same way, some individuals can lose their sex drive in response to great stress, but other people experience a tremendous sex drive, especially after a combat situation in which they were triumphant" (275). Frontline combat is fueled by stress hormones, and the potential for a woman to be sexually assaulted is very high. An inter-unit sexual assault costs the unit two soldiers: the victim is typically transferred to a new unit, the assaulter is sent to prison. Replacing two comrades integrated in a tight-knit unit with two new recruits is a difficult blow to a unit's esprit de corps and trust members have in one another. Thus, to put at risk a female soldier's sexual well-being is to also put at risk her unit's combat ability.

Rather than respond to the physiological realities of preparing for and engaging in combat, integrationists such as CNN's Maren Leed deflect to a false analogy connecting integration of women to past arguments against integrating minorities and homosexuals. Regarding minorities, race is a social construct, not a biological difference. Whereas the military somewhat successfully trained its men to not act on racial prejudices, it is improbable that 18-to-25-year-old men can be trained not to be sexually attracted to women. Regarding homosexuals, one homosexual has little effect on a group of heterosexuals, but one female can have a significant impact on a large group of heterosexual men driven by stress hormones.

Another integrationist argument is that changes in modern warfare already put women in combat. They say modern warfare is "asymmetric" and attacks can come from anywhere. It is true that women have served in combat in Afghanistan and Iraq, but integrationists erroneously believe the nature of warfare has evolved beyond traditional frontlines. Every American military engagement since World War II has been a limited war, but that does not mean all future wars will be. The wars our military must prepare to fight are global conflicts where combat troops face well-armed and well-trained enemies on traditional frontlines.

Perhaps the most important argument made by integrationists, and one to which I am sympathetic, concerns fairness and equity. It is extremely difficult to be promoted to general without infantry training. Some may say the Army should change its promotion policy, but this would harm overall morale. Frontline troops more enthusiastically follow leaders who are sharing, or have at one time shared, the toils and dangers of war. Thus, high-ranking female officers hit a glass ceiling because no such experience is available to them. However, there is an alternative to break through this glass ceiling without making all combat units coed. The U.S. Army National Guard consists of every imaginable combat-arms occupation. If these occupations were opened to aspiring female soldiers, those women would have access to the necessary experience for advancement to the military's upper echelon and have the option of transferring from the National Guard to active duty. General John Vessey began his illustrious career in the National Guard infantry and was later selected as Chairman of the Joint Chiefs of Staff. This compromise would give women the opportunity to get infantry training while still protecting our active-duty frontline infantry units from the unnecessary friction caused by romantic relationships.

Although some outsiders call terms like friction, morale, and unit cohesion mere buzzwords, to the Marines they mean life or death. Coed infantry is a parlous experiment with too much at stake. The restriction against women joining the infantry must be reinstated before the policy becomes entrenched and the negative side effects of romantic relationships deteriorate our fighting ability. I fully support gender equality, and I am proud of the brave women in the Marines, Army, Navy, and Air Force who have sacrificed so much defending this country I love. But when one considers the ultimate mission of the military, which is to win wars, we must not risk losing the cohesion of combat units when there is no exigent reason to do so except for the sake of expanding military career opportunities for women.

Snook 6

Works Cited

Browne, Kingsley. *Co-Ed Combat: The New Evidence That Women Shouldn't Fight the Nation's Wars*. Sentinel, 2007.

Clausewitz, Carl von. *On War.* Translated by Michael Howard and Peter Paret, Princeton UP, 1984.

Grossman, David. *On Combat: The Psychology and Physiology of Deadly Conflict in War and in Peace*. 3rd ed., Warrior Science, 2008.

Harrell, Margaret C., and Laura L. Miller. "New Opportunities for Military Women: Effects Upon Readiness, Cohesion, and Morale." *RAND Corporation*, 1 Jan. 1997, www.rand.org/pubs/ monograph_reports/MR896.html.

Kates, Brian. "Out of Control at Camp Crazy! Female Soldiers Dress Down & Get Dirty for Mud Romps." *New York Daily News*, 6 Feb. 2005, www.nydailynews.com/archives/news/control-camp-crazy-female-soldiers-dress-dirty-mud-romps-g-s-wild-article-1.590262.

Leed, Maren. "Will Infantry Men Accept Women as Peers?" *CNN*, 26 Jan. 2013, www.cnn.com/2013/01/25/opinion/ leed-women-in-infantry.

Michaels, Jim, and Tom Vanden Brook. "Women, Men Must Meet Same Combat Standards in Military." *USA Today*, 25 Jan. 2013, www.usatoday.com/story/news/world/2013/01/24/ women-in-combat-briefing/1861887.

Our second reading, by student Sandy Wainscott, illustrates option 5 in Learning Objective 15.5. It is a proposal speech supported by visual aids. We have reproduced Sandy's outline for her speech, along with her scripts for the introduction and conclusion. (Although she delivered the body of the speech extemporaneously from her outline, she scripted the introduction and conclusion to reduce nervousness.) We have also reproduced four of her ten PowerPoint slides in Figure 15.4. She used these four slides to introduce each of the four main points shown on the outline. Note how she has constructed her slides as visual arguments supporting a main point (stated in the slide title).

Student Essay

Why McDonald's Should Sell Meat and Veggie Pies: A Proposal to End Subsidies for Cheap Meat

Sandy Wainscott

Script for Introduction: McDonald's hamburgers are popular because they're satisfying and pretty darn cheap. But I will argue that the hamburger is cheap because the American taxpayer subsidizes the cost of meat. Uncle Sam pays agribusiness to grow feed corn while not requiring agribusiness to pay the full cost for water or for cleaning up the environmental damage caused by cattle production. If meat producers had to recover the true cost of their product, the cost of meat would be substantially higher, but there would be offsetting benefits: a healthier environment, happier lives for cows and chickens, and healthier diets for all of us.

Figure 15.4 Sandy's PowerPoint slides used to introduce main points

1. Meat is relatively cheap partly because taxpayers help feed the cows.
   a. U.S. taxpayers give farmers money to grow feed corn, which is fed to cows.
   b. U.S. taxpayers provide farmers with cheap water.

2. Cheap meat threatens health.
   a. Factory-style farms significantly reduce effectiveness of antibiotics.
   b. Antibiotic-resistant pathogens are potentially huge killers.
   c. Factory farms are likely sources of new swine and bird flus.
   d. Meat-related food poisoning harms millions of people per year and causes thousands of deaths.

3. Cheap meat hurts the environment.
   a. Factory farms create 130 times more sewage than humans.
   b. Animal farming contributes more to global warming than all forms of human transportation combined.
   c. Farming uses much of the world's land and water.

4. Cheap meat requires cruelty to animals.
   a. Ninety-eight percent of egg-laying hens in the United States spend their entire lives in stacked cubicle cages with 9-inch sides.
   b. Cruel conditions also exist for pigs and cows.

Script for Conclusion: If we stop providing taxpayer subsidies to farmers and require farmers to pay for the pollution they cause, the cost of meat would be much higher—but with great benefits to our health and to our environment. A restaurant like McDonald's would likely adjust its menus. McDonald's would move the burger off its 99-cent menu and replace it with something like a meat pie, a similarly warm, quick, and satisfying choice, but with a lower proportion of meat than a burger. In a fair market, we should have to pay more for a hamburger than for a meat pie or a stir fry. But we would have the benefit of a healthier Earth.

APPENDIX 1
Informal Fallacies

In this appendix, we look at ways of assessing the legitimacy of an argument within a real-world context of probabilities rather than within a mathematical world of certainty. Whereas formal logic is a kind of mathematics, the informal fallacies addressed in this appendix are embedded in everyday arguments, sometimes making fallacious reasoning seem deceptively persuasive, especially to unwary audiences. Fallacies of *pathos* rest on flaws in the way an argument appeals to the audience's emotions and values. Fallacies of *ethos* rest on flaws in the way the argument appeals to the character of opponents or of sources and witnesses within an argument. Fallacies of *logos* rest on flaws in the relationship among statements in an argument.

Fallacies of *Pathos*

Argument to the People (Appealing to Stirring Symbols)

This is perhaps the most generic example of a *pathos* fallacy. Arguments to the people appeal to the fundamental beliefs, biases, and prejudices of the audience in order to sway opinion through a feeling of solidarity among those of the group. Thus a "Support Our Troops" bumper sticker, often including the American flag, creates an initial feeling of solidarity among almost all citizens of goodwill. But the car owner may have the deeper intention of actually meaning "support our president" or "support the war in _____." The stirring symbol of the flag and the desire shared by most people to support our troops is used fallaciously to urge support of a particular political act. Arguments to the people often use visual rhetoric, as in the soaring eagle used in Walmart corporate ads or images of happy families in marketing advertisements.

Appeal to Ignorance

This fallacy persuades an audience to accept as true a claim that hasn't been proved false or vice versa. "Jones must have used steroids to get those bulging biceps because he can't prove that he hasn't used steroids." Appeals to ignorance are particularly common in the murky field of pseudoscience. "UFOs (ghosts, abominable snowmen) do exist because science hasn't proved that they don't exist." Sometimes, however, it is hard to draw a line between a fallacious appeal to ignorance and a legitimate appeal to precaution: "Genetically modified organisms may be dangerous to our health because science hasn't proved that they are safe."

Appeal to Popularity—Bandwagon

To board the bandwagon means (to use a more contemporary metaphor) to board the bus or train of what's popular. Appeals to popularity are fallacious because the popularity of something is irrelevant to its actual merits. "Living together before marriage is the right thing to do because most couples are now doing it." Bandwagon appeals are common in advertising where the claim that a product is popular substitutes for evidence of the product's excellence. There are times, however, when popularity may indeed be relevant: "Global warming is probably caused by human activity because a preponderance of scientists now hold this position." (Here we assume that scientists haven't simply climbed on a bandwagon themselves, but have formed their opinions based on research data and well-vetted, peer-reviewed papers.)

Appeal to Pity

Here the arguer appeals to the audience's sympathetic feelings in order to support a claim that should be decided on more relevant or objective grounds. "Honorable judge, I should not be fined $200 for speeding because I was distraught from hearing news of my brother's illness and was rushing to see him in the hospital." Here the argument is fallacious because the arguer's reason, while evoking sympathy, is not a relevant justification for speeding (as it might have been, for instance, if the arguer had been rushing an injured person to the emergency room). In many cases, however, an arguer can legitimately appeal to pity, as in the case of fundraising for victims of a tsunami or other disaster.

Red Herring

This fallacy's funny name derives from the practice of using a red herring (a highly odiferous fish) to throw dogs off a scent that they are supposed to be tracking. It refers to the practice of throwing an audience offtrack by raising an unrelated or irrelevant point. "Debating a gas tax increase is valuable, but I really think there should be an extra tax on SUVs." Here the arguer, apparently uncomfortable with the gas tax issue, diverts the conversation to the emotionally charged issue of owning SUVs. A conversant who noted how the argument has gotten offtrack might say, "Stop talking, everyone. The SUV question is a red herring; let's get back to the topic of a gas tax increase."

Fallacies of *Ethos*

Appeal to False Authority

Arguers appeal to false authority when they use famous people (often movie stars or other celebrities) to testify on issues about which these persons have no special competence. "Joe Quarterback says Gooey Oil keeps his old tractor running sharp; therefore, Gooey Oil is a good oil." Real evidence about the quality of Gooey Oil would include technical data about the product rather than testimony from an actor or hired celebrity. However, the distinction between a "false authority" and a legitimate authority can become blurred. For example, in the early years of advertising for drugs that treat erectile dysfunction, Viagra hired former senator and presidential hopeful Bob Dole to help market the drug. (You can see his commercials on YouTube.) As a famous person rather than a doctor, Dole would seem to be a false authority. But Dole was also widely known to have survived prostate cancer, and he may well have used Viagra. To the extent a person is an expert in a field, he or she is no longer a "false authority."

Ad Hominem

Literally, *ad hominem* means "to the person." An *ad hominem* argument is directed at the character of an opponent rather than at the quality of the opponent's reasoning. Ideally, arguments are supposed to be *ad rem* ("to the thing"), that is, addressed to the specifics of the case itself. Thus an *ad rem* critique of a politician would focus on her voting record, the consistency and cogency of her public statements, her responsiveness to constituents, and so forth. An *ad hominem* argument would shift attention from her record to features of her personality, life circumstances, or the company she keeps. "Senator Sweetwater's views on the gas tax should be discounted because her husband works for a huge oil company" or "Senator Sweetwater supports tax cuts for the wealthy because she is very wealthy herself and stands to gain." But not all *ad hominem* arguments are *ad hominem* fallacies. Lawyers, for example, when questioning expert witnesses who give damaging testimony, often make an issue of their honesty, credibility, or personal investment in an outcome.

Poisoning the Well

This fallacy is closely related to *ad hominem*. Arguers poison the well when they discredit an opponent or an opposing view in advance. "Before I yield the floor to the next speaker, I must remind you that those who oppose my plan do not have the best interests of working people in their hearts."

Straw Man

The straw man fallacy occurs when you oversimplify an opponent's argument to make it easier to refute or ridicule. Rather than summarizing an opposing view fairly and completely, you basically make up the argument you wish your opponent had made because it is so much easier to knock over, like knocking over a straw man or scarecrow in a corn field.

Fallacies of *Logos*

Hasty Generalization

This fallacy occurs when someone makes a broad generalization on the basis of too little evidence. Generally, the evidence needed to support a generalization persuasively must meet the STAR criteria (sufficiency, typicality, accuracy, and relevance) discussed in Chapter 4. But what constitutes a sufficient amount of evidence? The generally accepted standards of sufficiency in any given field are difficult to determine. The Food and Drug Administration (FDA), for example, generally proceeds cautiously before certifying a drug as "safe." However, if people are harmed by the side effects of an FDA-approved drug, critics often accuse the FDA of having made a hasty generalization. At the same time, patients eager to have access to a new drug and manufacturers eager to sell a new product may lobby the FDA to quit "dragging its feet" and get the drug to market. Hence, the point at which a hasty generalization passes over into the realm of a prudent generalization is nearly always uncertain and contested.

Part for the Whole

Sometimes called by its Latin name *pars pro toto*, this fallacy is closely related to hasty generalization. In this fallacy, arguers pick out a part of the whole or a sample of the whole (often not a typical or representative part or sample) and then claim that what is true of the part is true for the whole. If, say, individuals wanted to get rid of the National Endowment for the Arts (NEA), they might focus on several controversial programs funded by the NEA and use them as justification for wiping out all NEA programs. The flip side of this fallacy occurs when an arguer picks only the best examples to make a case and conveniently forgets about examples that may weaken the case.

Post Hoc, Ergo Propter Hoc

The Latin name of this fallacy means "after this, therefore because of this." The fallacy occurs when a sequential relationship is mistaken for a causal relationship. For example, you may be guilty of this fallacy if you say, "Cramming for a test really helps because last week I crammed for my psychology test and I got an A on it." When two events occur frequently in conjunction with each other, we've got a good case for a causal relationship. But until we can show how one causes the other and until we have ruled out other causes, we cannot be certain that a causal relationship is occurring. For example, the A on your psych test may have been caused by something other than your cramming. Maybe the exam was easier, or perhaps you were luckier or more mentally alert. It is often difficult to tell when a *post hoc* fallacy occurs. When the New York police department changed its policing tactics in the early 1990s, the crime rate plummeted. But did the new policing tactics cause the drop in the crime rate? Many experts suggested other clauses, including economist Steven Levitt, who attributes the declining crime rate to the legalization of abortion in the 1970s (and hence to a decline in unwanted children who might grow up to be criminals).

Begging the Question—Circular Reasoning

Arguers beg the question when they provide a reason that simply restates the claim in different words. Here is an example: "Abortion is murder because it is the intentional taking of the life of a human being." Because "murder" is defined as "the intentional taking of the life of a human being," the argument is circular. It is tantamount to saying, "Abortion is murder because it is murder." In the abortion debate, the crucial issue is whether a fetus is a "human being" in the legal sense. So in this case the arguer has fallaciously "begged the question" by assuming from the start that the fetus is a legal human being. The argument is similar to saying, "That person is obese because he is too fat."

False Dilemma—Either/Or

This fallacy occurs when an arguer oversimplifies a complex issue so that only two choices appear possible. Often one of the choices is made to seem unacceptable, so the only remaining option is the other choice. "It's my way or the highway" is a typical example of a false dilemma. Here is a more subtle one: "Either we allow embryonic stem cell research, or we condemn people with diabetes, Parkinson's disease, or spinal injuries to a life without a cure." Clearly, there may be other options, including other approaches to curing these diseases. A good extended example of the false dilemma fallacy is found in sociologist Kai Erikson's analysis of President Truman's decision to drop the A-bomb on Hiroshima. His analysis suggests that the Truman administration prematurely reduced numerous options to just two: either drop the bomb on a major city, or sustain unacceptable losses in a land invasion of Japan. Erikson, however, shows there were other alternatives.

Slippery Slope

The slippery slope fallacy is based on the fear that once we put a foot on a slippery slope heading in the wrong direction, we're doomed to slide right out of sight. The controlling metaphor is of a slick mountainside without places to hold on rather than of a staircase with numerous stopping places. Here is an example of a slippery slope: "Once we allow app-based ride services to compete with regular taxi companies, we will destroy the taxi business and the livelihood of immigrant taxi drivers. Soon anyone who wants to pose as a ride service will be able to do so, using uninspected vehicles and untrained drivers, leading to more accidents and crimes against passengers." Slippery slope arguments are frequently encountered when individuals request exceptions to bureaucratic rules: "Look, Blotnik, no one feels worse about your need for open-heart surgery than I do. But I still can't let you turn this paper in late. If I were to let you do it, then I'd have to let everyone turn in papers late." Slippery slope arguments can be very persuasive—and often rightfully so because every slippery slope argument isn't necessarily a slippery slope fallacy. Some slopes really are slippery. The slippery slope becomes a fallacy when we forget that we can often dig a foothold into the slope and stop. For example, we can define procedures for exceptions to rules so that Blotnik can turn in his paper late without allowing everyone to turn in a paper late. Likewise, a state could legalize app-based ride services, but regulate them to prevent a complete slide down the slope.

False Analogy

In Chapter 12 on definition and resemblance arguments, we explained that no analogy is perfect. Any two things being compared are similar in some ways and different in other ways. Whether an analogy is persuasive or false often depends on the audience's initial degree of skepticism. For example, people opposed to gun control may find the following argument persuasive: "Banning guns on the basis that guns accidentally kill people is like banning cars on the basis that cars accidentally kill people." In contrast, supporters of gun control are likely to call this argument a false analogy on the basis of dissimilarities between cars and guns. (For example, they might say that banning cars would be far more disruptive to our society than would be banning guns.) Just when a persuasive analogy turns into a false analogy is difficult to say.

Non Sequitur

The name of this fallacy means "it does not follow." *Non sequitur* is a catchall term for any claim that doesn't follow from its premises or is supported by irrelevant premises. Sometimes the arguer seems to make an inexplicably illogical leap: "Genetically modified foods should be outlawed because they are not natural." (Should anything that is not natural be outlawed? In what way are they not natural?) At other times there may be a gap in the chain of reasons: "Violent video games have some social value because the army uses them for recruiting." (There may be an important idea emerging here, but too many logical steps are missing.) At still other times an arguer may support a claim with irrelevant reasons: "I should not receive a C in this course because I currently have a 3.8 GPA." In effect, almost any fallacy could be called a *non sequitur* because fallacious reasoning always indicates some kind of disconnect between the reasons and the claim.

Loaded Label or Definition

Sometimes arguers try to influence their audience's view of something by creating a loaded label or definition. For example, people who oppose the "estate tax" (which calls to mind rich people with estates) have relabeled it the "death tax" in order to give it a negative connotation without any markers of class or wealth. Or to take another example, proponents of organic foods could create definitions like the following: "Organic foods are safe and healthy foods grown without any pesticides, herbicides, or other unhealthy additives." "Safe" and "healthy" are evaluative terms used fallaciously in what purports to be a definition. The intended implication is that nonorganic foods are not safe and healthy.

APPENDIX 2
A Concise Guide to Evaluating, Using, and Documenting Sources

When you research material for your arguments, you will probably use sources from licensed databases and the World Wide Web as well as from a library's print collection. You must be able to evaluate these sources, use them effectively in your own arguments (avoiding plagiarism), and cite and document them accurately so that readers can retrace your steps. This appendix provides brief instruction for evaluating and using sources and for citing and documenting them using both the MLA (Modern Language Association) and APA (American Psychological Association) systems.

Evaluating Your Sources by Reading Rhetorically

To be an effective researcher, you need to read your sources rhetorically. In this section we show you how to read your sources with your own goals in mind, take purposeful notes, and evaluate sources for reliability, credibility, angle of vision, and degree of advocacy. We also provide some additional advice for evaluating Web sources.

Reading with Your Own Goals in Mind

How you read a source depends to a certain extent on where you are in the research process. Early in the process, when you are in the thesis-seeking, exploratory stage, your goal is to achieve a basic understanding about your research problem. You need to become aware of different points of view, learn what is unknown or controversial about your research question, see what values or assumptions are in conflict, and build up your store of background knowledge.

Given these goals, at the early stages of research you should select overview kinds of sources to get you into the conversation. In some cases, even an encyclopedia or specialized reference work can be a good start for getting general background.

As you get deeper into your research, your questions become more focused, and the sources you read become more specialized. Once you formulate a thesis and plan a structure for your paper, you can determine more clearly the sources you need and read them with purpose and direction.

Reading with Rhetorical Awareness

To read your sources rhetorically, you should keep two basic questions in mind:

1. What was the source author's purpose in writing this piece?
2. What might be my purpose in using this piece?

Table A2.1 sums up the kinds of questions a rhetorical reader typically considers.

Table A2.1 reinforces a point we've made throughout this text: All writing is produced from an angle of vision that privileges some ways of seeing and filters out other ways. You should guard against reading your sources as if they present hard, undisputed facts or universal truths. For example, if one of your sources says that "Saint John's wort [an herb] has been shown to be an effective treatment for depression," some of your readers might accept that statement as fact—but many wouldn't. Skeptical readers would want to know who the author is, where his views have been published, and what he uses for evidence. Let's say the author is someone named Samuel Jones. Skeptical readers would ask whether Jones is relying on published research, and if so, whether the studies have been peer reviewed in reputable, scholarly journals and whether the research has been replicated by other scientists. They would also want to know whether a trade association for herbal supplements sponsored the research and whether Jones has financial connections to companies that produce herbal remedies and supplements. Rather than settling the question about Saint John's wort as a treatment for depression, a quotation from Jones may open up a heated controversy about medical research.

Table A2.1 Questions Asked by Rhetorical Readers

What was the source author's purpose in writing this piece?	What might be my purpose in using this piece in my own argument?
• Who is this author? What are his or her credentials and affiliations? • What audience is this person addressing? • What is the genre of this piece? (If you downloaded the piece from the World Wide Web, did it originally appear in print?) • If this piece appeared in print, what is the reputation and bias of the journal, magazine, or press? Was the piece peer reviewed? • If this piece appeared only on the Web, who or what organization sponsors the website (check the home page)? What is the reputation and bias of the sponsor? • What is the author's thesis or purpose? • How does this author try to change his or her audience's view? • What is this writer's angle of vision or bias? • What is omitted or censored from this text? • How reliable and credible is this author? • What facts, data, and other evidence does this author use, and what are the sources of these data? • What are this author's underlying values, assumptions, and beliefs?	• How has this piece influenced or complicated my own thinking? • How does this piece relate to my research question? • How will my own intended audience react to this author? • How might I use this piece in my own argument? • Is it an opposing view that I might summarize? • Is it an alternative point of view that I might compare to other points of view? • Does it have facts and data that I might use? • Would a summary of all or part of this argument support or oppose one or more of my own points? • Could I use this author for testimony? (If so, how should I indicate this author's credentials?) • If I use this source, will I need to acknowledge the author's bias and angle of vision?

Reading rhetorically is thus a way of thinking critically about your sources. It influences the way you take notes, evaluate sources, and shape your argument.

Taking Purposeful Notes

Many beginning researchers opt not to take notes—a serious mistake, in our view. Instead, they simply photocopy or print articles, perhaps using a highlighter to mark passages. This practice, which experienced researchers almost never use, reduces your ability to engage the ideas in a source and to find your own voice in a conversation. When you begin drafting your paper, you'll have no notes to refer to, no record of your thinking-in-progress. Your only recourse is to revisit all your sources, thumbing through them one at a time—a practice that leads to passive cutting and pasting (and possible plagiarism).

Good note taking includes recording bibliographic information for each source, recording information and ideas from each source, and responding to each source with your own ideas and exploratory writing.

RECORDING BIBLIOGRAPHIC INFORMATION   To take good research notes, begin by making a bibliographic entry for each source, following the documentation format assigned by your instructor. Although you will be tempted to put off doing this mechanical task, there are two reasons to do it immediately:

- Doing it now, while the source is in front of you, will save you time in the long run. Otherwise you'll have to try to retrieve the source, in a late-night panic, just before the paper is due.
- Doing it now will make you look at the source rhetorically. Is this a peer-reviewed journal article? A magazine article? An op-ed piece? A blog? Making the bibliographic entry forces you to identify the source's genre.

RECORDING IDEAS AND INFORMATION AND RESPONDING TO EACH SOURCE   To take good research notes, follow the reading habits of summary and exploration discussed in Chapter 2, weaving back and forth between walking in the shoes of the source author and then standing back to believe and doubt what the source says.

- **Your informational notes on each source:**   Using the skills of summary writing explained in Chapter 8, summarize each source's argument and record useful information. To avoid the risk of plagiarism later, make sure that you put quotation marks around any passages that you copy word for word (be sure to copy *exactly*). When you summarize or paraphrase passages, be sure to put the ideas entirely into your own words.
- **Your own exploratory notes as you think of ideas:**   Write down your own ideas as they occur to you. Record your thinking-in-progress as you mull over and speak back to your sources.

An approach that encourages both modes of writing is to keep a dialectic or double-entry journal. Divide a page in half; enter your informational notes on one side and your exploratory writing on the other. If you use a computer, you can put your informational notes in one font and your own exploratory writing in another.

Taking effective notes is different from the mechanical process of copying out passages or simply listing facts and information. Rather, make your notes purposeful by imagining how you might use a given source in your research paper. Table A2.2 shows the different functions that research sources might play in your argument and highlights appropriate note-taking strategies for each function.

Evaluating Sources

When you read sources for your research project, you need to evaluate them as you go along. As you read each potential source, ask yourself questions about the author's reliability, credibility, angle of vision, and degree of advocacy.

RELIABILITY   "Reliability" refers to the accuracy of factual data in a source. If you check a writer's "facts" against other sources, do you find that the facts are correct? Does the writer distort facts, take them out of context, or otherwise use them unreasonably? In some controversies, key data are highly disputed—for example, the frequency of date rape or the risk factors for many diseases. A reliable writer acknowledges these controversies and doesn't treat disputed data as fact. Furthermore, if you check out the sources used by a reliable writer, they'll reveal accurate and careful research—respected primary sources rather than hearsay or secondhand reports. Journalists of reputable newspapers (not tabloids) pride themselves on meticulously checking out their facts, as do editors of serious popular magazines. Editing is often minimal for Web sources, however, and they can be notoriously unreliable. As you gain knowledge of your research question, you'll develop a good ear for writers who play fast and loose with data.

Table A2.2 Strategies for Taking Notes According to Purpose

Function that Source Might Play in Your Argument	Strategies for Informational Notes	Strategies for Exploratory Notes
Provides background about your problem or issue	• Summarize the information. • Record specific facts and figures useful for background.	• Speculate on how much background your readers will need.
Gives an alternative view that you will mention briefly	• Summarize the source's argument in a couple of sentences; note its bias and perspective. • Identify brief quotations that sum up the source's perspective.	• Jot down ideas on how and why different sources disagree. • Begin making an idea map of alternative views.
Provides an alternative or opposing view that you might summarize fully and respond to	• Summarize the article fully and fairly (see Chapter 8 on summary writing). • Note the kinds of evidence used.	• Speculate about why you disagree with the source and whether you can refute the argument, concede to it, or compromise with it. • Explore what research you'll need to support your own argument.
Provides information or testimony that you might use as evidence	• Record the data or information. • If using authorities for testimony, quote short passages. • Note the credentials of the writer or person quoted.	• Record new ideas as they occur to you. • Continue to think purposefully about additional research you'll need.
Mentions information or testimony that counters your position or raises doubts about your argument	• Note counterevidence. • Note authorities who disagree with you.	• Speculate how you might respond to counterevidence.
Provides a theory or method that influences your approach to the issue	• Note credentials of the author. • Note passages that sparked ideas.	• Freewrite about how the source influences your method or approach.

CREDIBILITY "Credibility" is similar to "reliability" but is based on internal rather than external factors. It refers to the reader's trust in the writer's honesty, goodwill, and trustworthiness and is apparent in the writer's tone, reasonableness, fairness in summarizing opposing views, and respect for different perspectives. Audiences differ in how much credibility they will grant to certain authors. Nevertheless, a writer can achieve a reputation for credibility, even among bitter political opponents, by applying to issues a sense of moral courage, integrity, and consistency of principle.

ANGLE OF VISION AND POLITICAL STANCE By "angle of vision," we mean the way that a piece of writing is shaped by the underlying values, assumptions, and beliefs of its author, resulting in a text that reflects a certain perspective, worldview, or belief system. Of paramount importance are the underlying values or beliefs that the writer assumes his or her readers will share. You can get useful clues about a writer's angle of vision and intended audience by doing some quick research into the politics and reputation of the author on the Internet or by analyzing the genre, market niche, and political reputation of the publication in which the material appears.

DEGREE OF ADVOCACY By "degree of advocacy" we mean the extent to which an author unabashedly takes a persuasive stance on a contested position as opposed to adopting a more neutral, objective, or exploratory stance. For example, publications affiliated with advocacy organizations (the Sierra Club, the National Rifle Association) will have a clear editorial bias. When a writer has an ax to grind, you need to weigh carefully the writer's selection of evidence, interpretation of data, and fairness to opposing views. Although no one can be completely neutral, it is always useful to seek out authors who offer a balanced assessment of the evidence. Evidence from a more detached and neutral writer may be more trusted by your readers than the arguments of a committed advocate. For example, if you want to persuade corporate executives of the dangers of global warming, evidence from scholarly journals may be more persuasive than evidence from an environmentalist website or from a freelance writer for a leftist popular magazine such as *Mother Jones*.

CRITERIA FOR EVALUATING A WEB SOURCE When you evaluate a Web source, we suggest that you ask five different kinds of questions about the site in which the source appeared, as shown in Table A2.3. These questions, developed by scholars and librarians as points to consider when you are evaluating websites, will help you determine the usefulness of a site or source for your own purposes.

As a researcher, the first question you should ask about a potentially useful Web source should be, "Who placed this piece on the Web and why?" You can begin answering this question by analyzing the site's home page, where you will often find navigational buttons linking to "Mission," "About Us," or other identifying information about the site's sponsors. You can also get hints about the site's purpose by asking, "What kind of website is it?" Different kinds of websites have different purposes, often revealed by the domain identifier following the site name: .com or .biz (commercial); .org (nonprofits and advocacy groups); .edu (college or university); .gov (government agency); and .mil (military site).

Table A2.3 Criteria for Evaluating Websites

Criteria	Questions to Ask
1. Authority	• Is the document author or site sponsor clearly identified? • Does the site identify the occupation, position, education, experience, or other credentials of the author? • Does the home page or a clear link from the home page reveal the author's or sponsor's motivation for establishing the site? • Does the site provide contact information for the author or sponsor such as an e-mail or organization address?
2. Objectivity or Clear Disclosure of Advocacy	• Is the site's purpose clear (for example, to inform, entertain, or persuade)? • Is the site explicit about declaring its point of view? • Does the site indicate whether the author is affiliated with a specific organization, institution, or association? • Does the site indicate whether it is directed toward a specific audience?
3. Coverage	• Are the topics covered by the site clear? • Does the site exhibit a suitable depth and comprehensiveness for its purpose? • Is sufficient evidence provided to support the ideas and opinions presented?
4. Accuracy	• Are the sources of information stated? • Do the facts appear to be accurate? • Can you verify this information by comparing this source with other sources in the field?
5. Currency	• Are dates included in the Web site? • Do the dates apply to the material itself, to its placement on the Web, or to the time the site was last revised and updated? • Is the information current, or at least still relevant, for the site's purpose? For your purpose?

Using Sources for Your Own Purposes

To illustrate the purposeful use of sources, we will use the following short argument from the website of the American Council on Science and Health (ACSH)—an organization of doctors and scientists devoted to providing scientific information on health issues and to exposing health fads and myths. Please read the argument carefully in preparation for the discussions that follow.

Is Vegetarianism Healthier Than Nonvegetarianism?

Many people become vegetarians because they believe, in error, that vegetarianism is uniquely conducive to good health. The findings of several large epidemiologic studies indeed suggest that the death and chronic-disease rates of vegetarians—primarily vegetarians who consume dairy products or both dairy products and eggs—are lower than those of meat eaters . . . .

The health of vegetarians may be better than that of nonvegetarians partly because of nondietary factors: Many vegetarians are health-conscious. They exercise regularly, maintain a desirable body weight, and abstain from smoking. Although most epidemiologists have attempted to take such factors into account in their analyses, it is possible that they did not adequately control their studies for nondietary effects.

People who are vegetarians by choice may differ from the general population in other ways relevant to health. For example, in Western countries most vegetarians are more affluent than nonvegetarians and thus have better living conditions and more access to medical care.

An authoritative review of vegetarianism and chronic diseases classified the evidence for various alleged health benefits of vegetarianism:

- The evidence is "strong" that vegetarians have (a) a lower risk of becoming alcoholic, constipated, or obese and (b) a lower risk of developing lung cancer.
- The evidence is "good" that vegetarians have a lower risk of developing adult-onset diabetes mellitus, coronary artery disease, hypertension, and gallstones.
- The evidence is "fair to poor" that vegetarianism decreases risk of breast cancer, colon cancer, diverticular disease, kidney-stone formation, osteoporosis, and tooth decay.

For some of the diseases mentioned above, the practice of vegetarianism itself probably is the main protective factor. For example, the low incidence of constipation among vegetarians is almost certainly due to their high intakes of fiber-rich foods. For other conditions, nondietary factors may be more important than diet. For example, the low incidence of lung cancer among vegetarians is attributable primarily to their extremely low rate of cigarette smoking. Diet is but one of many risk factors for most chronic diseases.

How you might use this article in your own writing would depend on your research question and purpose. To illustrate, we'll show you three different hypothetical examples of writers who have reason to cite this article.

- **Writer 1: A Causal Argument Showing Alternative Approaches to Reducing Risk of Alcoholism.**   Writer 1 argues that vegetarianism may be an effective way to resist alcoholism. She uses just one statement from the ACSH article for her own purpose and then moves on to other sources.

Writer's claim

Another approach to fighting alcoholism is through naturopathy, holistic medicine, and vegetarianism. Vegetarians generally have better health than the rest of the population and particularly have, according to the American Council on Science and Health,

Identification of source

Quotation from ACSH

"a lower risk of becoming alcoholic." This lower risk has been borne out by other studies showing that the benefits of the holistic health movement are particularly strong for persons with addictive tendencies . . . . [goes on to other arguments and sources]

- **Writer 2: A Proposal Argument Advocating Vegetarianism.**   Writer 2 proposes that people become vegetarians. Parts of his argument focus on the environmental costs and ethics of eating meat, but he also devotes one paragraph to the health benefits of vegetarianism. As support for this point he summarizes the ACSH article's material on health benefits.

Not only will a vegetarian diet help stop cruelty to animals, but it is also good for your health. According to the American Council on Science and Health, vegetarians have longer life expectancy than nonvegetarians and suffer from fewer chronic diseases. The Council cites "strong" evidence from the scientific literature showing that vegetarians have reduced risk of lung cancer, obesity, constipation, and alcoholism. The Council also cites "good" evidence that vegetarians have a reduced risk of adult-onset diabetes, high blood pressure, gallstones, and hardening of the arteries. Although the evidence isn't nearly as strong, vegetarianism may also lower the risk of certain cancers, kidney stones, loss of bone density, and tooth decay.

Writer's claim

Identification of source

Summary of ACSH material

- **Writer 3: An Evaluation Argument Looking Skeptically at Vegetarianism.** Here, Writer 3 uses portions of the same article to make an opposite case from that of Writer 2. She focuses on those parts of the article that Writer 2 consciously excluded.

The link between vegetarianism and death rates is a classic instance of correlation rather than causation. While it is true that vegetarians have a longer life expectancy than nonvegetarians and suffer from fewer chronic diseases, the American Council on Science and Health has shown that the causes can mostly be explained by factors other than diet. As the Council suggests, vegetarians are apt to be more health conscious than nonvegetarians and thus get more exercise, stay slender, and avoid smoking. The Council points out that vegetarians also tend to be wealthier than nonvegetarians and see their doctors more regularly. In short, they live longer because they take better care of themselves, not because they avoid meat.

Writer's claim

Identification of source

Paraphrased points from ACSH

Using Summary, Paraphrase, and Quotation

As a research writer, you need to incorporate sources gracefully into your own prose. Depending on your purpose, you might (1) summarize all or part of a source author's argument, (2) paraphrase a relevant portion of a source, or (3) quote small passages from the source directly. To avoid plagiarism, you'll need to reference the source with an in-text citation, put quotation marks around quoted passages, and convert paraphrases and summaries entirely into your own words. Table A2.4 gives you an overview of summary, paraphrase, and quotation as ways of incorporating sources into your own prose.

Table A2.4 Incorporating Sources into Your Own Prose

Strategy	What to Do	When to Use This Strategy
Summarize the source.	Condense a source writer's argument by keeping main ideas and omitting details.	• When the source writer's whole argument is relevant to your purpose • When the source writer presents an alternative or opposing view that you want to push against • When the source writer's argument can be used in support of your own
Paraphrase the source.	Reproduce an idea from a source writer but translate the idea entirely into your own words; a paraphrase should be approximately the same length as the original.	• When you want to incorporate factual information from a source or to use one specific idea from a source • When the source passage is overly complex or technical for your targeted audience • When you want to incorporate a source's point in your own voice without interrupting the flow of your argument
Quote short passages from the source using quotation marks.	Work brief quotations from the source smoothly into the grammar of your own sentences.	• When you need testimony from an authority (state the authority's credentials in an attributive tag) • In summaries, when you want to reproduce a source's voice, particularly if the language is striking or memorable • In lieu of paraphrase when the source language is memorable
Quote long passages from the source using the block method.	Results in a page with noticeably lengthy block quotations	• When you intend to analyze or critique the quotation—the quotation is followed by your detailed analysis of its ideas or rhetorical features • When the flavor and language of testimonial evidence is important

Summarizing

Detailed instructions on how to write a summary of an article and incorporate it into your own prose are provided in Chapter 8. Summaries can be as short as a single sentence or as long as a paragraph. Make the summary as concise as possible so that you don't distract the reader from your own argument. In many cases, writers summarize only parts of a source, depending on what is relevant to their own argument. Writer 3's summary of the article by the American Council on Science and Health is a good example of a partial summary.

Paraphrasing

Unlike a summary, which is a condensation of a source's whole argument, a **paraphrase** translates a short passage from a source's words into the writer's own words. Writers often choose to paraphrase when the details of a source passage are particularly important or when the source is overly technical and needs to be simplified for the intended audience. When you paraphrase, be careful to avoid reproducing the original writer's grammatical structure and syntax. If you mirror the original sentence structure while replacing occasional words with synonyms or small structural changes, you will be doing what composition specialists call **"patchwriting"**—that is, patching some of your language onto someone else's writing.* Patchwriting is a form of academic dishonesty because you aren't fully composing your own sentences and are thus misrepresenting both your own work and that of the source writer. An acceptable paraphrase needs to be entirely in your own words. To understand patchwriting more fully, track the differences between unacceptable patchwriting and acceptable paraphrase in the following examples.

Original

- The evidence is "strong" that vegetarians have (a) a lower risk of becoming alcoholic, constipated, or obese and (b) a lower risk of developing lung cancer.
- The evidence is "good" that vegetarians have a lower risk of developing adult-onset diabetes mellitus, coronary artery disease, hypertension, and gallstones.

Unacceptable Patchwriting

According to the American Council on Science and Health, there is strong evidence that vegetarians have a lower risk of becoming alcoholic, constipated, or obese. The evidence is also strong that they have a lower risk of lung cancer. The evidence is good that vegetarians are less apt to develop adult-onset diabetes, coronary artery disease, hypertension, or gallstones.

Identification of source

Note phrases taken word for word from original.

Acceptable Paraphrase

The Council summarizes "strong" evidence from the scientific literature showing that vegetarians have reduced risk of lung cancer, obesity, constipation, and alcoholism. The council also cites "good" evidence that vegetarians have a reduced risk of adult-onset diabetes, high blood pressure, gallstones, or hardening of the arteries.

Identification of source

Doesn't follow original sentence structure

Quotes "strong" and "good" to indicate distinction made in original

Both the patchwriting example and the acceptable paraphrase reproduce the same ideas as the original in approximately the same number of words. But the writer of the acceptable paraphrase has been more careful to change the sentence structure substantially and not copy exact phrases. In contrast, the patchwritten version contains longer strings of borrowed language without quotation marks.

Quoting

Besides summary and paraphrase, writers often choose to quote directly in order to give the reader the flavor and style of the source author's prose or to make a memorable point in the source author's own voice. Always quote the source

---

* We are indebted to the work of Rebecca Moore Howard and others who have led composition researchers to reexamine the use of sources and plagiarism from a cultural and rhetorical perspective. See especially Rebecca Moore Howard, *Standing in the Shadow of Giants: Plagiarists, Authors, Collaborators* (Stamford, CT: Ablex Pub., 1999).

author's words exactly (unless you indicate changes with ellipses or brackets), and don't misrepresent the author's meaning by taking quotations out of context.

In the following sections, we show you the two main ways to use quotations: quoting a complete sentence from your source versus inserting brief words and phrases from your source into your own sentence. For special cases using quotations (brackets, ellipses, quotations within a quotation, or block quotations), consult a good handbook.

QUOTING A COMPLETE SENTENCE   In some cases, you will want to quote a complete sentence from your source.

Original Passage

Many people become vegetarians because they believe, in error, that vegetarianism is uniquely conducive to good health. [found on page 319 of source]*

Writer's Quotation of This Passage

Quotation introduced with comma.
Quotation is a complete sentence, so it starts with a capital letter.

Attributive tag

Page number from source;
period comes after parentheses.

Final quotation mark goes before parentheses.

According to the American Council on Science and Health, "Many people become vegetarians because they believe, in error, that vegetarianism is uniquely conducive to good health" (319).

QUOTING WORDS AND PHRASES   Instead of quoting a complete sentence, you often want to quote only a few words or phrases from your source and insert them into your own sentence. In these cases, make sure that the grammatical structure of the quotation fits smoothly into the grammar of your own sentence.

Original Passage

The health of vegetarians may be better than that of nonvegetarians partly because of nondietary factors: Many vegetarians are health-conscious. They exercise regularly, maintain a desirable body weight, and abstain from smoking. [found on page 319]

Quoted Phrase Inserted into Writer's Own Sentence

Attributive tag

Quotation marks show where quotation starts and ends.

No comma or capital letter: Punctuation and capitalization determined by grammar of your own sentence.

Period comes after parentheses containing page number.

The American Council on Science and Health argues that the cause of vegetarians' longer life may be "nondietary factors." The Council claims that vegetarians are more "health-conscious" than meat eaters and that they "exercise regularly, maintain a desirable body weight, and abstain from smoking" (319).

---

* The cited page is from this text. When quoting from print sources or other sources with stable page numbers, you indicate the page number as part of your citation. To illustrate how to punctuate page citations, we'll assume throughout this section that you found the American Council on Science and Health article in this textbook rather than on the Web, in which case it would not be possible to cite page numbers.

Creating Attributive Tags to Indicate Use of a Source

Our previous examples use attributive tags to indicate words or ideas taken from a source. *Attributive tags* are phrases such as "according to Hahn . . . " or "Smith and Perosi claim that. . . ." Such phrases indicate that the material immediately following the tag is from the cited source. You can also add to the tag a phrase indicating the source author's credentials, biases, or angle of vision: "Climate scientist James Hansen states that. . . . " Although some disciplines (particularly the social sciences) indicate a source only by citing it in parentheses at the end of the borrowed material, the preferred practice for non-specialized audiences is to use attributive tags.

Less Preferred: Indicating Source through Parenthetical Citation

Vegetarians are apt to be more health-conscious than nonvegetarians (American Council on Science and Health).

More Preferred: Indicating Source through Attributive Tag

According to the American Council on Science and Health, vegetarians are apt to be more health-conscious than nonvegetarians.

Avoiding Plagiarism

Unethical use of sources—called **plagiarism**—is a major concern not only for writing teachers but for teachers in all disciplines. To combat plagiarism, many instructors across the curriculum use plagiarism-detection software like turnitin .com. Their purpose, of course, is to discourage students from cheating. But sometimes students who have no intention of cheating can fall into producing papers that look like cheating. That is, they produce papers that might be accused of plagiarism even though they had no intention of deceiving their readers. Our goal in this section is to explain the concept of plagiarism more fully and to sum up the strategies needed to avoid it.

Why Some Plagiarism May Occur Unwittingly

To understand how unwitting plagiarism might occur, consider Table A2.5, where the middle column—"Misuse of Sources"—shows common mistakes of novice writers. Everyone agrees that the behaviors in the "Fraud" column constitute deliberate cheating and deserve appropriate punishment. Everyone also agrees that good scholarly work meets the criteria in the "Ethical Use of Sources" column. Novice researchers, however, may find themselves unwittingly in the middle column until they learn the academic community's conventions for using research sources.

You might appreciate these conventions more fully if you recognize how they have evolved from Western notions of intellectual property and patent law associated with the rise of modern science in the seventeenth and eighteenth centuries. A person not only could own a house or a horse, but also could own an idea and the words used to express that idea. Laws and professional codes of ethics protect an

Table A2.5 Plagiarism and the Ethical Use of Sources

Plagiarism		Ethical Use of Sources
Fraud	**Misuse of Sources (Common Mistakes Made by New Researchers)**	**Ethical Use of Sources**
The writer	The writer	The writer
• buys a paper online • submits someone else's work as his own • copies chunks of text from sources with obvious intention of not being detected • fabricates data or makes up evidence • intends to deceive	• copies passages directly from a source, references the source with an in-text citation, but fails to use quotation marks or block indentation • in attempting to paraphrase a source, makes some changes, but follows too closely the wording of the original ("patchwriting") • fails to indicate the sources of some ideas or data (often is unsure what needs to be cited or has lost track of sources through poor note taking) • in general, misunderstands the conventions for using sources in academic writing	• writes paper entirely in her own words or uses exact quotations from sources • indicates all quotations with quotation marks or block indentation • •indicates her use of all sources through attribution, in-text citation, and an end-of-paper list of works cited

author's words in the same way they protect song lyrics, drawings, or patents. In the academic world, the conventions protecting a source author's words and ideas are essential if research findings are to win the community's confidence. Effective research can occur only within ethical and responsible research communities, where people respect the words and ideas of those who have gone before them.

Strategies for Avoiding Plagiarism

Table A2.6 will help you review the strategies presented throughout this appendix for using source material ethically and avoiding plagiarism.

Table A2.6 Avoiding Plagiarism or the Appearance of Plagiarism

What to Do	Why to Do It
At the beginning	
Read your college's policy on plagiarism as well as statements made by your teachers in class or noted on course syllabi.	Understanding policies on plagiarism and academic integrity will help you research and write ethically.
Pose a research question rather than a topic area.	Arguing your own thesis gives you a voice, establishes your *ethos,* and urges you to write ethically.
At the note-taking stage	
Create a bibliographic entry for each source.	This action makes it easy to create an end-of-paper bibliography and encourages rhetorical reading.
When you copy a passage into your notes, copy it word for word and enclose it within quotation marks.	It is important to distinguish a source's words from your own words.
When you enter summaries or paraphrases into your notes, avoid patchwriting.	If your notes contain any strings of a source's original wording, you might later assume that these words are your own.
Distinguish your informational notes from your personal exploratory notes.	Keeping these kinds of notes separate will help you identify borrowed ideas when it's time to incorporate the source material into your paper.

What to Do	Why to Do It
When writing your draft	
Except for exact quotations, write the paper entirely in your own words.	This strategy keeps you from patchwriting when you summarize or paraphrase.
Indicate all quotations with quotation marks or block indentation. Use ellipses or brackets to make changes to fit your own grammar.	Be careful to represent the author fairly; don't change meaning by taking quotations out of context.
When you summarize or paraphrase, avoid patchwriting.	Word-for-word strings from a source must either be avoided or placed in quotation marks. Also avoid mirroring the source's grammatical structure.
Never cut and paste a Web passage directly into your draft. Paste it into a separate note file and put quotation marks around it.	Pasted passages are direct invitations to patchwrite.
Inside your text, use attributive tags or parenthetical citations to identify all sources. List all sources alphabetically in a concluding Works Cited or References list.	This strategy makes it easy for readers to know when you are using a source and where to find it.
Cite with attributive tags or parenthetical citations all quotations, paraphrases, summaries, and any other references to specific sources.	These are the most common in-text citations in a research paper.
Use in-text citations to indicate sources for all visuals and media such as graphs, maps, photographs, films, videos, broadcasts, and recordings.	The rules for citing words and ideas apply equally to visuals and media cited in your paper.
Use in-text citations for all ideas and facts that are not common knowledge.	Although you don't need to cite widely accepted and noncontroversial facts and information, it is better to cite them if you are unsure.

For Writing and Discussion

Avoiding Plagiarism

Reread the original article from the American Council on Science and Health (earlier in this appendix) and Writer 3's use of this source in her paragraph about how nondietary habits may explain why vegetarians are healthier than nonvegetarians. Then read the paragraph below by Writer 4, who makes the same argument as Writer 3 but crosses the line from ethical to nonethical use of sources. Why might Writer 4 be accused of plagiarism?

Writer 4's Argument (Example of Plagiarism)

According to the American Council on Science and Health, the health of vegetarians may be better than that of nonvegetarians partly because of nondietary factors. People who eat only vegetables tend to be very conscious of their health. They exercise regularly, avoid getting fat, and don't smoke. Scientists who examined the data may not have adequately controlled for these nondietary effects. Also in Western countries most vegetarians are more affluent than nonvegetarians and thus have better living conditions and more access to medical care.

Working in small groups or as a whole class, respond to the following questions.

1. How does this passage cross the line into plagiarism?
2. The writer of this passage might say, "How can this be plagiarism? I cited my source." How would you explain the problem to this writer?
3. Psychologically or cognitively, what may have caused Writer 4 to misuse the source? How might this writer's note-taking process or composing process have differed from that of Writer 3? In other words, what happened to get this writer into trouble?

Citing Sources in Your Text in MLA Style

When academic writers cite sources, they use the conventions appropriate to their discipline. In this section, we will explain briefly the MLA style used in the humanities. (We explain the APA system used in the social sciences later in this appendix.) Our discussion of MLA style and our citation examples are based on the eighth edition of the *MLA Handbook* (2016).

In the MLA system of in-text citation, you place the author's last name and the page number of the cited source in parentheses, usually at the end of the material you wish to cite. (If the author's name is mentioned in a preceding attributive tag, such as "according to Karnow" or "Karnow says," only the page number is placed in parentheses.) In the following examples, note that the citation precedes the period. If you are citing a quotation, the parenthetical citation follows the quotation mark but precedes the final period.

> The Spanish tried to reduce the status of Filipina women who had been able to do business, get divorced, and sometimes become village chiefs (Karnow 41).

> According to Karnow, the Spanish tried to reduce the status of Filipina women who had been able to do business, get divorced, and sometimes become village chiefs (41).

> "And, to this day," Karnow continues, "women play a decisive role in Filipino families" (41).

A reader who wishes to look up the source will find the bibliographic information in the Works Cited section by looking for the entry under "Karnow." If more than one work by Karnow was used in the paper, the writer would also include an abbreviated title of the book or article following Karnow's name in the in-text citation.

> (Karnow, *In Our Image* 41)

When citing sources and page numbers, you should know about two special cases:

CITING FROM AN INDIRECT SOURCE   Occasionally you may wish to use a quotation that you have seen cited in one of your sources. You read Jones, who has a nice quotation from Smith, and you want to use Smith's quotation. To do so, quote Smith, but then cite Jones in your text preceded by the terms "qtd in." List only Jones in your Works Cited.

> According to the ex-mayor of Gotham City, Rupert Smith, "the rate of crime was at an all-time low" during his term of office (qtd. in Jones 25).

CITING A WORK WITHOUT PAGE NUMBERS   If the work you are citing in your paper has no page numbers but does have numbered paragraphs, use *par.* or *pars.* and give the number of the paragraph(s): (Helvarg, par. 10). If the source has neither page nor paragraph numbers, as is typical of many Web sources in HTML format, do not give any numbers in the in-text citation but cite the source in its entirety. (Do not use the page numbers from an HTML printout because they will not be consistent from printer to printer.)

Documenting Sources in a "Works Cited" List (MLA)

In the MLA system, you place a complete bibliography, titled "Works Cited," at the end of the paper. The list includes all the sources that you mention in your paper. However, it does not include works you read but did not use. Entries in the Works Cited follow these general guidelines:

- Entries are arranged alphabetically by author, or by title if there is no author.
- If there is more than one entry by the same author, the second and subsequent entries begin with three hyphens followed by a period and the title.

> Smith, Roberta. *Body Image in Non-Western Cultures.* London: Bonanza, 1999.
> —. *Body Image in Western Cultures, 1750-Present.* London: Bonanza, 1995.
> —. "Eating Disorders Reconsidered." *Journal of Appetite Studies,* vol. 45, no. 3, 1999, pp. 295–300.

For an example of how to format a "Works Cited" page in MLA style, see the last page of Ivan Snook's researched argument at the end of Chapter 15.

Table A2.7 provides MLA models for the most common kinds of citations. This table will help you distinguish the forest from the trees when you try to cite sources. All the major categories of sources are displayed in this table.

Student Example of an MLA-Style Research Paper

For an illustration of a student research paper written and formatted in MLA style, see Ivan Snook's researched policy proposal at the end of Chapter 15.

Citing Sources in Your Text in APA Style

Our discussion of APA style is based on the *Publication Manual of the American Psychological Association,* 6th ed. (2010).

To cite sources in the body of your paper in the APA system, you include the year of the source and you place a "p." or "pp." before the page number(s). The author's last name, date, and page numbers are separated by commas. When the author is mentioned in an attributive tag, place only the date and page number in parentheses, usually directly after the author's name.

> The Spanish tried to reduce the status of Filipina women who had been able to do business, get divorced, and sometimes become village chiefs (Karnow, 1989, p. 41).

> According to Karnow (1989, p. 41), the Spanish tried to reduce the status of Filipina women who had been able to do business, get divorced, and sometimes become village chiefs.

Table A2.7   Quick Reference Guide for MLA Citations

Kind of Source	Basic Citation Model
Print Sources	
Article in scholarly journal	Pollay, Richard W., et al.* "Separate, but Not Equal: Racial Segmentation in Cigarette Advertising." *Journal of Advertising*, vol. 21, no. 1, 1992, pp. 45-57.
Article in print magazine or newspaper	Beam, Alex. "The Mad Poets Society." *The Atlantic*, July–Aug. 2001, pp. 96–103.
	Lemonick, Michael D. "Teens Before Their Time." *Time*, 30 Oct. 2000, pp. 66–74.
	Liptak, Adam. "In Abortion Rulings, Idea of Marriage Is Pivotal." *The New York Times*, 2 Nov. 2005, p. A1.
Book	Tannen, Deborah. *The Argument Culture: Moving From Debate to Dialogue.* Random House, 1998.
Article in anthology with an editor	Shamoon, Linda. "International E-mail Debate." *Electronic Communication Across the Curriculum*, edited by Donna Reiss, Dickie Self, and Art Young, NCTE, 1998, pp. 151-61.
Sources That You Have Downloaded from an Academic Database	
Article downloaded from database	Matsuba, M. Kyle. "Searching for Self and Relationships Online." *CyberPsychology and Behavior*, vol. 9, no. 3, 2006, pp. 275-84. *Academic Search Complete*, doi:10.1089/cpb.2006.9.275.**
Other Internet and Web Sources	
Home page (use for citing an entire website)	*NRA Programs*. National Rifle Association, home.nra.org/nra-programs. Accessed 15 Apr. 2016.
Document within a website	Rosenman, Mark. "A Call for National Service." *The Chronicle of Philanthropy*, vol. 20, no. 1, 18 Oct. 2007, philanthropy.com/article/A-Call-for-National-Service/165721.
Article from scholarly Web journal (retrieved from a database)	Welch, John R., and Ramon Riley. "Reclaiming Land and Spirit in the Western Apache Homeland." *American Indian Quarterly*, vol. 25, no. 4, 2001, pp. 5-14. *JSTOR*, www.jstor.org/stable/1185999?seq=1#.
News article found on the Web	Brennan, Charlie. "Boulder Scientists over the Moon at Chance to Work on Lunar Dust." *Daily Camera Boulder News*, 3 Oct. 2015, www.dailycamera.com/news/boulder/ci_28913824/boulder-scientists-over-moon-at-chance-work-lunar.
Blog posting	Wright, Jeremy. "*MySpace* Is the New Blogosphere." *Ensight.org*, 21 Feb. 2006, www.ensight.org/archives/2006/02/21/myspaceis-the-new-blogosphere.
Miscellaneous Sources	
Interview	Van der Peet, Rob. Personal interview, 24 June 2009.
Lecture, address, or speech	Sharples, Mike. "Authors of the Future." Conference of European Teachers of Academic Writing, 20 June 2001, University of Groningen, Groningen, Netherlands.

*For two authors, give both authors' names in this format: "Smith, John, and Frank Peters." For three or more authors, give only the first author's name, followed by *et al.*

**If a DOI (digital object identifier) is not available, give the URL. If no publication date is provided for the source, end your entry with the date on which you accessed the source.

If your readers wish to follow up on this source, they will look for "Karnow" in the References section at the end of the essay. If Karnow had more than one entry in the References section, they would look for the 1989 source. If Karnow had published more than one work in 1989, you would add a lowercase "a" to the date of the first one and a lowercase "b" to the date of the second one. Your in-text parenthetical citation would then be either (Karnow, 1989a) or (Karnow, 1989b).

When you quote or use data from an indirect source, in your parenthetical citation use "as cited in" rather than the MLA's "qtd in."

According to the ex-mayor of Gotham City, Rupert Smith, "the rate of crime was at an all-time low" during his term of office (as cited in Jones, 1995, p. 25).

Documenting Sources in a "References" List (APA)

The APA system includes a complete bibliography, called "References," at the end of the paper. Entries are listed alphabetically, with a hanging indentation. If you list more than one item for an author, repeat the author's name each time and arrange the items in chronological order beginning with the earliest. If two works appeared in the same year, arrange them alphabetically, adding an "a" and a "b" after the year for purposes of in-text citation. Here is a hypothetical illustration:

> Smith, R. (1995). *Body image in Western cultures, 1750–present.* London, England: Bonanza Press.
> Smith, R. (1999a). *Body image in non-Western cultures.* London, England: Bonanza Press.
> Smith, R. (1999b). Eating disorders reconsidered. *Journal of Appetite Studies, 45,* 295–300.

Table A2.8 provides examples in APA style for the most common kinds of citations to be placed in a "References" list at the end of the paper.

Table A2.8 Quick Reference Guide for APA Citations

Kind of Source	Basic Citation Model
Print Sources	
Article in scholarly journal	Pollay, R. W., Lee, J. S., & Carter-Whitney, D. (1992). Separate, but not equal: Racial segmentation in cigarette advertising. *Journal of Advertising, 21*(1), 45-57.
Article in magazine or newspaper	Beam, A. (2001, July–August). The mad poets society. *Atlantic Monthly, 288,* 96-103.
	Lemonick, M. D. (2000, October 30). Teens before their time. *Time, 156,* 66-74.
	Cauvin, H. E. (2001, July 18). Political climate complicates food shortage in Zimbabwe. *The New York Times,* p. A13.
Book	Tannen, D. (1998). *The argument culture: Moving from debate to dialogue.* New York, NY: Random House.
Article in anthology with an editor	Shamoon, L. (1998). International e-mail debate. In D. Reiss, D. Self, & A. Young (Eds.), *Electronic communication across the curriculum* (pp. 151-161). Urbana, IL: National Council of Teachers of English.
Sources That You Have Downloaded from a Database	
Article with DOI	Adelt, U. (2008). Trying to find an identity: Eric Clapton's changing conception of "blackness." *Popular Music & Society, 31,* 433–452. doi: 10.1080/03007760802052809
Article without DOI—use periodical's home page	Beckham II, J. M. (2008). Placing *Touch of evil, The border,* and *Traffic* in the American imagination. *Journal of Popular Film & Television, 33*(3), 130-141. Retrieved from http://www.heldref.org/pubs/jpft/about.html
Other Internet and Web Sources	
Document within a website	Marks, J. Overview: Letter from the president. Retrieved 2004, June 25 from the Search for Common Ground website: http://www.sfcg.org/sfcg/sfcg_overview.html
Article from scholarly Web journal	Welch, J. R., & Riley, R. (2001). Reclaiming land and spirit in the western Apache homeland. *American Indian Quarterly, 25,* 5–14. Retrieved from http://muse.jhu.edu/journals/american_indian_quarterly

(Continued)

Table A2.8 Continued

Kind of Source	Basic Citation Model
News article downloaded from Web	Thevenot, B. (2004, July 31). Once in a blue moon. *Times Picayune* [New Orleans]. Retrieved from http://www.nola.com/t-p
Blog posting	Wright, J. (2006, Feb. 21). *MySpace* is the new blogosphere. [Web log post]. Retrieved from http://www.ensight.org/archives
	Miscellaneous Sources
Interview, personal communication	R. Van der Peet (personal communication, June 24, 2009) stated that . . . [In-text citation only; not included in References]
Lecture, address, or speech	According to Mike Sharples (lecture given at the Conference of European Teachers of Academic Writing, Groningen, June 20, 2001), authors . . . [in-text citation only; not included in references]

Student Example of an APA-Style Research Paper

An example of a paper in APA style is Jess Goncalves' researched argument at the end of Chapter 13.

Credits

Text Credits

Chapter 1   Page 4 © June Johnson.

Chapter 3   Page 39 Reprinted by permission from Carmen Tieu.

Chapter 4   Page 49 Surowiecki, James. "The Pay Is Too Damn Low" The New Yorker. Used with permission from Chris Calhoun Agency.

Chapter 5   Page 66 Chief Seattle's Letter or Speech to the President (1852)

Chapter 6   Page 77 Reprinted by permission from Trudie Makens; p. 83 Reprinted by permission from Lauren Shinozuka; p. 79 Oh, How I Will Miss the Plastic Bag; Alexander Chancellor. The Spectator, Oct. 10, 2015; Retrieved from https://spectator.com.au/2015/10/oh-how-i-will-miss-the-plastic-bag/;

Chapter 7   Page 95 Lopez, Kathryn Jean, "Egg Heads" 1998 National Review, Inc., Reprinted by permission; p. 103 From The Boston Globe, April 11, © 2008. Boston Globe Media Partners. All rights reserved. Used by permission and protected by the Copyright Laws of the United States. The printing, copying, redistribution, or retransmission of this Content without express written permission is prohibited.

Chapter 8   Page 113 Schmitt, John, and Janelle Jones, 2012 "Low-Wage Workers Are Older and Better Educated than Ever." Washington, DC: Center for Economic and Policy Research; p. 113 Reprinted by permission from Trudie Makens; p. 124 Reprinted by permission from Trudie Makens; p. 115 Reprinted by permission from Trudie Makens; p. 116 Surowiecki, James. "The Pay Is Too Damn Low" The New Yorker. Used with permission from Chris Calhoun Agency; p. 120 Reprinted by permission from Trudie Makens; p. 120 Reprinted by permission from Trudie Makens; p. 121 Reprinted by permission from Trudie Makens; p. 123 Michael Saltsman (2013), "To Help the Poor, Move Beyond 'Minimum' Gestures" Huffington Post. Used with permission; p. 127 Reprinted by permission from Trudie Makens.

Chapter 9   Page 160 Based on U.S. Census Bureau, 2010; p. 157 Source: U.S. Energy Information Administration. Data accessed from: https://www.eia.gov/totalenergy/data/monthly/#consumption; p. 157 Source: Data from United States Energy Information Administration; p. 158 Source: Based on United States Energy Information Administration; p. 158 Source: Data from United States Energy Information Administration; p. 160 Source: Data from United States Energy Information Administration; p. 160 Source: Data from United States Energy Information Administration.

Chapter 10   Page 171 Reproduced with permission from Colleen Fontana; p. 177 Reprinted by permission from Monica Allen.

Chapter 11   Page 189 Hutchinson, Alex, "Your Daily Multivitamin May Be Hurting You - The debate is on: just useless, or truly dangerous?". Used with permission from Outside Magazine.

Chapter 12   Page 210 Reprinted by permission from Alex Mullen.

Chapter 13   Page 220 Robert S. Devine, "The Trouble with Dams," Atlantic (August 1995), 64–75; p.214 Data from Dr. Pieter Tans, NOAA/ESRL; p. 214 Data from NASA Goddard Institute for Space Studies Surface Temperature Analysis; p. 230 What Causes Math Anxiety? By Jess Goncalves. Used with permission.

Chapter 14   Page 253 Reprinted by permission from Lorena Mendoza-Flores; p. 256 Daar, Judith and Erez Aloni, "Three Genetic Parents—For One Healthy Baby" LA Times. Used with permission.

Chapter 15   Page 276 Reprinted by permission from Ivan Snook;

Photo Credits

Chapter 1   Page 1 Blickwinkel/Alamy Stock Photo.

Chapter 5   Page 65 Bullit Marquez/AP Images.

Chapter 7   Page 95 Jim West/Alamy Stock Photo.

Chapter 8   Page 122 © Employment Policies Institute EPI.

Chapter 9   Page 133 Peter Byrne/AP Images; p. 141 The Advertising Council; p. 149 TxtResponsibly.org; p. 150 Milt Priggee/Cagle Cartoons, Inc.; p. 137 The Advertising Council; p. 135 Alex Milan Tracy/Anadolu Agency/Getty Images; p. 139 Kris Saknussemm; p. 144 Source: June Johnson Bube; p. 145 June Johnson Bube; p. 145 June Johnson Bube; p. 145 June Johnson; p. 145 June Johnson; p. 145 Source: June Johnson Bube; p. 145 June Johnson Bube; p. 147 June Johnson Bube.

Chapter 10   Page 167 Felipe Chacon/EFE/Newscom.

Chapter 11   Page 181 Kathy deWitt/Alamy Stock Photo.

Chapter 12   Page 198 Randy Bish/Cagle Cartoons, Inc; p. 192 Tinass Groove used with the permission of Rina Piccolo, King Features Syndicate and the Cartoonist Group. All rights reserved.

Chapter 13   Page 222 Free the Captives.

Chapter 14   Page 238 Neill Blomkamp Film Company Sony Pictures/AF archive/Alamy Stock Photo; p. 244 John Bean.

Chapter 15   Page 259 Devito/Verdi, Sal Devito, Executive Creative Director; p. 263 FLPA/Alamy Stock Photo; p. 271 Jane E Bube; p. 282 Peter Essick/Aurora Photos/Alamy Stock Photo; p. 282 Simon Belcher/Alamy Stock Photo.